W9-AVL-950

SEVEN
FIRES

SEVEN FIRES

THE URBAN INFERNOS
THAT RESHAPED AMERICA

Peter Charles Hoffer

PublicAffairs
New York

973
H698

Copyright © 2006 by Peter Charles Hoffer.

Published in the United States by PublicAffairs™,
a member of the Perseus Books Group.

All rights reserved.
Printed in the United States of America.

No part of this book may be reproduced in any manner whatsoever without written
permission except in the case of brief quotations embodied in critical articles and
reviews. For information, address PublicAffairs, 250 West 57th Street, Suite 1321,
New York, NY 10107. PublicAffairs books are available at special discounts for bulk
purchases in the U.S. by corporations, institutions, and other organizations. For more
information, please contact the Special Markets Department at the Perseus Books
Group, 11 Cambridge Center, Cambridge, MA 02142, call (617) 252-5298, or email
special.markets@perseusbooks.com.

Book design by Jane Raese
Text set in 11.5-point New Caledonia

Library of Congress Cataloging-in-Publication Data
Hoffer, Peter Charles, 1944–
Seven fires : the urban infernos that reshaped America / by Peter Charles Hoffer.—
1st ed.
cm.
Includes bibliographical references and index.
ISBN-13: 978-1-58648-355-5
ISBN-10: 1-58648-355-2
1. United States—History—Anecdotes. 2. Fires—United States—History—
Anecdotes. 3. Cities and towns—United States—History—Anecdotes.
4. United States—History, Local—Anecdotes. I. Title.
E179.H79 2006
973—dc22
2005055345

FIRST EDITION

10 9 8 7 6 5 4 3 2 1

CONTENTS

v

PREFACE

Seven Fires is a book about fire and cities. I grew up after World War II in a part of Brooklyn called East New York. The neighborhood was a monotonous landscape of brick two- and three-story walk-ups, mom-and-pop stores, and a scattering of schools, warehouses, and garages. Our apartment on Hegeman Avenue was small and dark, the single stairway narrow, and the interior building materials as far from flameproof as one could get. At P.S. 165, a block away, FDNY (Fire Department of New York) posters warned about misusing matches, but that did not stop many of our parents from smoking. We had fire drills in school, but otherwise I cannot recall anyone talking about fire prevention or fire safety.

Except when a fire truck passed. For us, these trucks and engines (who knew the difference between the ladder truck and the fire engine then?) were friendly monsters. Fiery red, they seemed to push all the traffic out of their way. The flashing lights, the sirens, and most of all, the turnout equipment of the firemen made them seem larger than life. We all wanted to "grow up to be firemen." On the block, one of our neighbors was a fireman. His face was chiseled out of stone, his smile lit up a room, and you could hear him coughing two houses away.

I never tried out for the fire service. I doubt I could have passed the exhausting physical part of the exam. I tried a sample written exam not long ago—I'm not sure I would have done so well on it either. Getting into the fire academy was never easy. Most firefighters in the city were second or third generation. When we moved from densely populated Brooklyn to a suburban single home in eastern Queens, I could still hear the engines and trucks on their way to fires, but we had no fires in our neighborhood. My father, who owned a small business, knew the men at the nearby firehouse, and once I went to visit, but college, graduate school, a family of my own, and the nomadic life of an academic took me far from New York City. I was still a New Yorker at heart, though, and whenever I saw a fire company engine or rescue squad truck go by, I remembered those intrepid giants I saw on Hegeman Avenue.

On the morning of September 11, 2001, standing in a University of Georgia lounge, I watched television coverage of the emergency at the World Trade Center (WTC). I had dismissed my American history survey class, but many of them followed me in search of a television set. We stood, sat, swayed, and stared.

I was thinking: How are the firemen going to get up all those steps? I knew that the elevator in a building fire is a no-go unless the firefighters can stop it safely below the blaze. Were they able to use the nearly 100 elevators in the towers? Surely the explosion and the fireball had damaged some of the elevators. The firefighters would take to the stairs, but seventy or eighty floors up? How could they get there in time to put out the fire and save the office workers? Where was the water supply? Of course there were standpipes on every floor, but how was the water pumped over 1,000 feet straight up? Still, I knew the men would succeed. This was the FDNY, and no one was better at rescuing victims or putting out fires.

I still have bad dreams about those buildings coming down. The first collapsed less than an hour after it was struck. The second pancaked an hour and forty minutes from the time the plane hit. They each took less than ten seconds to fall to the ground. The debris pile smoldered for months. Under it, nearly 3,000 people died, 343 of them firefighters and officers.

This book is dedicated to all of those who died at the WTC that day. But I hope that it has another message—a message of hope—about cities and their resilience during and after catastrophic fires. It is about the people who fight those fires and their courage, as well as unscrupulous land developers, indifferent landlords, and visionary planners. It is about rich people who want everything back the way it was and poor people who hope everything will be different next time. It focuses on seven American cities and seven fire departments but applies to every city and every fire department in our land. It begins with old cities that are very different from today's and methods of fighting fire that have changed tremendously over the years, and ends with 9/11. For certain things about cities and city life, like those about fire and firefighting, do not change. They are what drew me to the subject in the first place.

I owe readers of this book a word or two about its focus and organization. There are legions of fire buffs in our land. Having donned the turnout gear myself and ridden with the ladder truck on an exercise as a civilian observer, I know what makes the fire buff such an enthusiastic witness to other men's work. The fellowship, the thrill, the foretaste of besting the peril, the knowledge that you will be saving life and property have no equal.

Over a decade ago, I began to think about sensory history, history that takes us back in time to relive an event as contemporaries lived it. Historian John Demos describes it: "[T]he pastness of history briefly dissolves—or, rather, reforms as the succession of present moment it was (and is). The scholar feels that bygone present simultaneously with his own." It is history that engages all the senses by consciously reimagining what it must have been like to be there, then. I realized that no natural or man-made event so overwhelms the senses as fire. We know it by our senses. It cannot be mistaken for any other stimulus, and it changes how our world looks, smells, feels, and sounds. Five years ago, I decided to turn my attention to the sensory impact of fire in the most densely populated of all our human environments—the city.[1]

ACKNOWLEDGMENTS

In the course of researching and writing this book, I have incurred many debts. I am grateful for access to and permission to use collections at the Boston Public Library, the Massachusetts Historical Society, the Old South Meeting House Library and Bookshop, the National Park Service, Boston; the Senator John Heinz Pittsburgh Regional History Center, the Darlington Memorial Library at the University of Pittsburgh, and the Carnegie Library, Pittsburgh; the Chicago Historical Society; the Enoch Pratt Free Library and the Maryland Historical Society, Baltimore; the San Francisco Public Library and the History Room at the Oakland Public Library, Oakland, California; the Detroit Public Library and the Walter P. Reuther Library, Wayne State University, Detroit; the Fire Museum of the City of New York, and the Museum of the City of New York. The libraries of Rutgers University, the University of Pennsylvania, and the University of Georgia provided essential resources and research support.

I am grateful to the Cherry Hill [New Jersey] Fire Department for letting me enroll in the 2005 Civilian Fire Academy, and Captains Jim Bannar and Kevin Kenniff for answering all my questions. The simulations of fire events were especially informative. Sergeant Eric Frey of the Athens, Georgia, Fire Department read the introduction for technical accuracy. Lieutenant Wally Malone (FDNY retired) shared his experiences of the "war years" and former insurance adjuster Michael Calder gave advice on questions of home insurance and the problems of insuring in the East Bay and looked over the Oakland Hills chapters. Dennis Smith, whose firsthand accounts of the FDNY have reminded all of us who did not already know about the everyday heroism of the fire service, was kind enough to read and comment on the 9/11 chapters.

Fellow historians Robert Brugger, Steve Mihm, Ed O'Donnell, William Pencak, Thomas Sugrue, Paul Sutter, and Joel Tarr read particular chapters, and Mark Tebeau and N.E.H. Hull reviewed the entire manuscript. One of the great pleasures of our profession is our willingness to take time from our work to help others. This endeavor is only compensated by an author's expression of gratitude, and the willingness to return the favor if asked. All of these readers' suggestions were most helpful. Any mistakes that remain are my responsibility.

My younger son, Louis Hoffer, traveled with me to some of the fire sites. His unquenchable enthusiasm for cities was an inspiration. His older brother, Williamjames Hoffer, is now a member of the history teaching profession. Our discussions about our common labors are invariably enlightening.

This book would not have been published without the assistance and encouragement of my editor at PublicAffairs, Clive Priddle, and my literary agents, Scott Waxman and Farley Chase. Clive read every word and shaped the whole. Scott and Farley saw the promise of the project from the start. Melissa Raymond managed the project with skill and good humor, and Michele Wynn copyedited it with aplomb and precision. All maps were drawn and/or scanned by Wendy Giminski, and the text was designed by Jane Raese. Permission to reproduce photographs was received from the *New York Times, The Oakland Tribune,* NASA, Korab Photo, the Walter P. Reuther Library at Wayne State University, the Maryland Historical Society, and the Chicago Historical Society.

SEVEN
FIRES

INTRODUCTION

Young Prometheus plotted his revenge in secret. The last of the Titans, sky gods of immense power and cruelty, according to Greek myth he alone was spared when the gods of Olympus claimed the earth, sky, and seas as their dominion. Living among the Olympians, he nursed his hatred. When no one was looking, he stole from the gods the secret of fire and gave it to mere mortals. But mythological figures like Prometheus are not generous by nature and the recipients of his gift would have done well to accept it cautiously.[1]

Instead, unthinkingly, we welcomed fire into our homes and our workplaces. Fire transformed us from bands of opportunistic hunter-gatherers to the dominant species on our planet. Fire brought us metallurgy, the ability to cook and store foods, and to heat ourselves in the winter's cold and light our way in the darkness. Prometheus gained his revenge after all—subordination of fire made us successors to the Olympian gods as masters of earth, sky, and sea.[2]

Would that we had also learned to temper our worship of fire. For what fire could foster, it could destroy utterly. The city, the cradle of our culture, industry, and science, is a testament to the transforming power of fire, and the setting for horrific infernos. One of these was the "Great Fire of London," the beginning of our story.

On early Sunday morning, September 2, 1666, greater London lay in repose. A royal city, resplendent in the spoils of its newfound American empire, London sheltered England's banking, textile, printing, and government offices. Its miles of warehouses, heavy tim-bered guildhalls, shingle-roofed churches, and rows of wooden tene-ments baked in the early morning heat. No one had forgotten the danger of fire in this dry season, but no one noticed that the wind had blown the sparks from a baker's untended oven onto the straw and cinders of the inn next door. Soon the flames escaped the inn and licked eagerly at the wooden structures along the Thames river-side. From there, it rushed into the old city streets faster than a man could run, a 100-foot-high wall of flame melting brick and masonry.

Minister Thomas Vincent watched aghast as the flames swal-lowed his church whole. "Never was there the like" in his life, or his imagination. The mayor arrived, then fled in horror. The king and his brother, with their courtiers, bravely joined the bucket brigades and paid gold and silver coins to volunteer firefighters, but they labored in vain. The king ordered explosives detonated to create fire breaks, but the fire leaped over the blown-down structures. From the sky, born aloft by the fire's own heat, came a downpour of burning cin-ders, the advancing guard of the terrible armies of the conflagration. In three days the blaze reduced the city to a "ruined heap."[3]

The king decreed that the great fire would be the city's last. But his subjects had already voted on the issue with their feet. During the conflagration, they piled their worldly goods on carts and hurried from the city. A frenzy had consumed the people's will, so that "they hardly stirr'd to quench [the fire]. So that there was nothing heard or seene but crying out and lamentation, [and] running about like dis-tracted creatures." While the king listened to plans of all sorts to pre-vent the next fire, merchants, working people, and the pious took ship to flee from the ruins. They traveled across the Atlantic Ocean to join their countrymen settling the New World. To it, they brought Prometheus's gift, smugly confident that they would be safe from its malignity. With space, time, and nature on their side, they would subdue fire, making it bow to human will in "green country towns, which will never be burnt."[4]

A Fire Primer

In our thousands of years of acquaintance with hearth and forge, we have come to know fire intimately. Some of its mysteries still elude us, but we have learned that fire comes in all sizes and shapes. No two fires are the same. Some are no more than a few feet in diameter. You can put them out with a shovelful of dirt. Some raze hundreds of city blocks or thousands of acres of forest and call forth the utmost efforts of thousands of firefighters. Some simply smolder and go out for want of fuel and oxygen. Some rise up 1,000 feet high and hasten over the land at racehorse speeds.

Every fire awakens our senses, and our memory retains the sensations. The smallest fire sends out streams of chemical warning signals. We see a wand of smoke or smell "something burning." The color of smoke reveals the nature of the fuel and the temperature of the fire. A sudden burst of light—"a thousand orange flashbulbs"—is the first (and maybe the only) sign one ever gets of a deadly "flashover." "There are a lot of different smells to smoke." Burned food smells different from burned wiring. Experienced firefighters can say of a fire, "It is burning wood" or "It is burning plaster." A city firefighter with a really good nose can tell you what kind of garbage is burning. Even for those who know fires well, the experience is overwhelming. "Images, sounds, and faces remain in a fireman's consciousness for life."[5]

Indoors, fire dulls your senses. Carbon monoxide released by burning in a closed space causes dizziness and fatal euphoria. In a room, the "wisp of cloying smoke," left to its own devices, darkens the space until you cannot see your hand in front of your face: "It's very scary. You're in there searching without a line [hose] and you have zero visibility . . . A table or chair can become your worst enemy. Your mask gets hooked on it. Maybe all you want to do is back down the hallway, but you get hung up on this table . . . You step into another room and work your way along the walls, always trying to remember that this is your way out when the time comes."[6]

Close to a fully developed fire, the heat is so fierce you feel it sucking the moisture from your pores. Fire singes hair and makes skin crackle and blister. Burned skin turns red and then black. Finally, it melts. The odor of burns is sulfuric; the charred dead smell like overcooked meat and make even a veteran firefighter gag and retch. Smoke, dissolved carbon and other particles, burns the lungs. Firefighters say that they "eat smoke," but this is a figure of speech. They inhale its "abrasive, and gritty and putrid" particulate matter. In the lungs, it tears the tiny alveoli apart. Still, firefighters' lore celebrates the fearless ones who can perform in smoke. One especially famous Philadelphia fire chief was affectionately nicknamed "Leather Lungs" for his ability to eat smoke.[7]

Primitive air packs (known today as SCBA, for self-contained breathing apparatus) and gas masks were introduced after World War I, but many firemen refused to use them because they were bulky, limited visibility, and added weight. The National Fire Protection Association asks departments to require all personnel in a structural or hazardous materials fire to wear the air pack, and the Occupational Safety and Health Administration (OSHA) requires it, but despite the lighter weight and greater ease of donning the modern air packs, some firefighters still regard them as a last resort. It is hard to hear and give orders with the mask on. Firefighters have reported that sometimes "you had to take off the mask and take a blow to be heard."[8]

Writers often portray fire as though it is sentient, knowing what it wants to do. One fire "rocked back and forth like a broadjumper before it started toward the takeoff. Then it jumped." Another fire "drove the crowd ahead of it." Maybe we give fire too much credit and anthropomorphize it—make it human—because we want to understand it better, a kind of magic. We give names to particularly vicious fires, as if by naming we could mitigate the horror they wrecked. The "Triangle Shirtwaist Factory Fire" of 1911 in New York City caused the deaths of 146 young women. Trapped in the upper floors of a burning factory, they leaped to their deaths. The "Mann Gulch Fire" of 1949 incinerated twelve Forest Service "smoke jumpers" unable to outrun a Montana wildfire. The "Happy Land Fire" in the Bronx killed eighty-seven partygoers at an after-hours club. An angry patron set the fire and the victims could not get out. We acknowledge the power of the big conflagration by calling it "great"—the "Great Chicago Fire" of 1871, for example. But fire is neither good nor evil. As historian Simon Winchester has written, "to be evil, you must have intent." Fire lacks this essential human capacity. Still, no one who has gotten close to a serious fire mistakes its will to master its surroundings.[9]

The big fires come back to haunt us. Children who survived the San Francisco fire of 1906 never forgot the experience. Thirteen years later, one wrote, "I can still feel those flames as we rode through the burning district." Other children recalled returning to their burned-out homes "and picking up bright pieces of molten glass." As she fled from the Oakland Hills firestorm of 1991, one home owner remembered that she had "smelled smoke" before she saw or heard anything. Then "darkness fell . . . nothing ahead but black and red, it had no shape." From the distance, others in the East Bay that morning saw a wall of smoke lit up from within, a "black cloud with a pink glow." Those closer to the inferno could "hear the boom, boom, as house after house exploded."[10]

Nothing seems farther away from the immediate human experience of fire than its description as a chemical, physical, and ecological phenomenon. Fire is really nothing more than combustion—the harvesting of the energy in a fuel source through its ignition and burning, a chemical reaction that releases heat and light. (Technically, there's a difference—in combustion the heat actually keeps the process of burning going so long as the oxygen and fuel remain.) Oxygen is midwife to the birth of fire, an essential catalyst, and one part of the "fire triangle." Like fire itself, oxygen is a wonderful servant but a tyrannous master. Oxygen is a chemical poison, responsible for rust, rot, and other forms of decomposition as well as for fire. But like fire, oxygen sustains life, and without it there is no photosynthesis and no respiration. The second part of the "fire triangle" is the fuel. No fuel, no fire. The third is the heat. The triangle itself is the chemical reaction. When a fuel source is raised to its ignition temperature by heating, it combines with oxygen to produce water vapor, carbon dioxide—the soot, or combined with other particles, the smoke from a fire—and energy.[11]

Different fuels have different amounts of energy stored in them. They ignite and sustain combustion at different temperatures. The kindling temperature of paper, for example, is 451° F, a figure made famous by science fiction author Ray Bradbury's deeply disturbing story about a society that burned its books. Wood chips ignite at 300°F, whereas hard brick and mortar can withstand ignition temperatures up to 1000°F, and fire-resistant clays remain unchanged at temperatures in excess of 1500°F. By the same token, the amount of heat released by burning different fuels varies. The "heat yield," or the intensity of the entire fire, is the sum of the heat released by combustion. Among the wood and other plant products most often used in building or found in or near buildings, pine and pine needles and hay give off the most heat, while eucalyptus, often cited as the cause of suburban wildfire activity on the California coast, is one of the lowest on the scale. Oils or resins in wood, chemicals in paper or printing materials, and other components of fuels increase a fire's intensity.

The heat of a fire not only keeps the chemical reaction going, it enables the fire to spread. The fire's heat moves from one location to another through one of three means. The first, conduction, is the direct transfer of heat through a medium—for example, a common wall in a building. The material may be a good conductor of heat, such as dense metals or wood. These absorb heat and pass it along. Less dense materials are poorer conductors. Convection transfers heat through the air. Heated air rises. In very hot fires, the air around the flame becomes superheated and agitated. Such fires create their own windstorms and can carry the heat and the burning debris of a fire for many miles. Heat also moves directly through radiation. Rays of heat can raise the temperature of nearby objects to their ignition point. Hot fires can cause the surfaces (called "exposures") of these objects to burn. That is why firefighters may attack a fire by wetting surfaces of buildings or ground cover that lie in advance of the actual blaze.[12]

Conditions surrounding the fire contribute to its intensity. Cold damp weather and wet ground will inhibit a fire. Because any fire has to change the water in the fuel to water vapor, wet fuel is much harder to ignite and sustain in a fire than dry, warm fuel. These conditions may determine whether a fire smolders, like a peat fire underground, or explodes, like a canopy fire in the treetops. When firefighters pour water on a fire, they are not only cooling its temperature and blocking it from oxygen, they are forcing the burning material to change the water to vapor. That is why firefighters want to vent a fire (giving it an upward escape path) before attacking it with water. Without an upward vent for its heat, the fire would change the water to steam, endangering the firefighters by carrying the heated particles down on them.

The venting of fire employs the same principles of wind and heat that spread street, forest, and prairie fires. Winds supply oxygen to fires. Outdoors, wind spreads fire, carrying it to new sources of fuel. This is also true in a microcosmic way within a building, where the fire will smolder until the opening of a door to a corridor or a stairwell acts like a flue in a chimney. The draft of fresh oxygen can turn the smallest fire into an inferno. A "backdraft" is the fiery explosion of the smoke in a room. As the fire in a room consumes the available oxygen, the heat of the fire diminishes and its color changes from yellow to red. When a new supply of oxygen is added, however, the unburned carbon in the smoke will ignite, turning up the heat of the fire again. In a "flashover," the superheated gases in a room fire "radiate downward," setting objects and structures in the room on fire. In effect, the fire turns up its own thermostat. Flashovers are very rapid sequences, and a firefighter wearing the best personal protective equipment trapped in a room when this happens has about fifteen seconds to get out. If a room or building fire is not vented, it can "roll over" the ceiling and then drop down behind whoever is in the room.[13]

Once combustion has begun, heat travels upward, so that fires create their own winds: the heated gases rising up, creating a vacuum beneath, sucking in more oxygen. This "convection effect" is the great fire's own wind-making machine. In urban firestorms, superheated buildings manufacture updrafts that can carry burning debris and embers miles from the original scene of the blaze. In the worst case on record—actually a surmise, not a record, because no one survived it—a wildfire careened up the walls of Montana's Mann Gulch Canyon at over 120 miles per hour. If they fall on new fuel sources, hot embers start "spot fires." Should the new fires gain intensity, they can trap firefighters between blazes—the nightmare of every firefighter.[14]

High winds contribute to pre-ignition conditions, for they dry out fuel sources. Very often, observers of great fires have noted that the previous days had seen high, dry winds and little rain. Once the fire has started, high winds can increase the duration of the fire as well as spread it, allowing it to consume a larger portion of the available fuels. No fire burns all of the fuel in its path, but a fire with a strong wind, particularly one that shifts direction, can double back on already burned areas and reignite them.

Terrain, landscape, and street design also influence the duration and direction of fire. Open spaces provide natural firebreaks, though spot fires may overleap these breaks and spread the fire beyond them. By contrast, the impact of wind in the city can be mitigated by densely packed fuels, insulation of potentially combustible materials, containment of fires within structures or parts of structures, and various forms of fire prevention. High-fired ceramics, fiberglass, asbestos, concrete, and other insulation have very high ignition temperatures and are the elements of "fireproof" construction. But even steel and stone have their melting points, and no construction is truly fireproof if a fire is hot enough. Leave aside the fireballs that nuclear weapons create and the firestorms that high explosives produce; even the run-of-the-mill urban street fire will always find some weak point in the building—perhaps the windows or the window mullions, perhaps the mortar between the bricks, perhaps the paint, the drywall, or the furnishings. That is the essential fact of all urban fire settings.

Every physical setting either encourages or discourages fire. For example, the city, an array of buildings and streets, simply does not have as much oxygen, nor is its supply of oxygen as evenly distributed over space, as in fields, mountains, and forests. Instead of an open place, the room is the environment in which most urban fires start. Because of the limits of fuel in it and the short supply of oxygen (unless a window or door is open), fire in a room may burn its contents without spreading. The FDNY's first reminder to people who find themselves in a room fire is to close the door as they leave. Open doors or windows may admit enough oxygen for the fire to spread from room to room. Greater danger comes when the room fire is hot enough to become a structural fire—that is, when the walls, supports, floors, ceilings, and other load-bearing members begin to burn.[15]

Fire in a warehouse, a chemical plant, or an oil storage depot more closely resembles a wildfire, because the fuel sources are so volatile and the oxygen supply is much greater than in a room fire. Cites of wood like colonial Boston or antebellum Pittsburgh or much of post–Civil War Chicago, were in effect artificial forests. Ecologist and fire historian Stephen Pyne has called these "rebuilt wildlands," for they are in ecological terms merely forests of a different sort. With wooden shingles or thatch for roofing, soot-filled hearths and chimneys for wood or coal fires, they invited fire. The hay and straw in their barns was highly combustible, and the candles and wick lamps used in night lighting courted accidental fires.[16]

Over the course of our history, we have come to reject the idea that fire is inevitable, attempting first to limit its damage and then to prevent it entirely. Yet one should not assume that this struggle against fire has a uniform upward course and that progress has made America more and more fireproof. As disaster expert Mike Davis reminds us, some urban or suburban localities still seem to invite fire, for example, by placing themselves in the path of a natural fire course. Build a city at the mouth of a canyon in a climate that is dry and windy, and see what happens. Let the residents landscape their dwellings with highly combustible plants or use easily burned materials for their homes, and one should expect periodic devastation by fire. Some of the fires in the Malibu Hills of Southern California are either the result of arson or human error. (Most wildfires today are the result of careless use of matches, cigarettes, or campfires.) But brush accumulation, lighting, and high winds all by themselves will create a deadly fire peril, and placing bigger and more expensive houses in the path of such fires only provides more fuel for them.[17]

Not every fire, even in a setting prone to fires, need become a conflagration. New England has three times as many fires in its forests as California does in its "chaparral" coastal hillsides, but there have been no New England fire disasters to match the burning of Oakland Hills in 1991 or Malibu in 1993. One difference is the degree of dryness of the California coast, but another is what Pyne has called "social restraint." Human conduct or misconduct is the inescapable and unpredictable variable in all fire regimes.[18]

FIREFIGHTERS

Firefighting in our cities has become more and more technologically sophisticated and professional over the course of our history. Today, fire departments are businesses, public agencies, quasi-military outfits, social and cultural bodies, professional groups, and educational organizations, all in one. Departments have experts on acquisition, finance, and public relations, positions that did not exist long ago. Thus, one must resist the temptation of "upstreaming" in talking about firefighting. Upstreaming is applying modern or recent ideas to older events. At the same time, much that we know about firefighting today applies to earlier times.[19]

Techniques of firefighting have changed over the years, but some characteristics of fighting fires remain constant. Teamwork, communication, public support and rapport, and confidence are all essential. Modern fire departments have expanded their mission from fire suppression to fire prevention and community education, rescue, emergency medical response, hazardous materials disposal, civil defense and anti-terror response, and fire code enforcement, but all of these activities were present to some degree in earlier fire events.[20]

The basics of our efforts to suppress fire remain unchanged. Even in the largest and most complicated modern organizational scheme, the firefighter and the company officer are still the keys to the fire service. While three-fourths of our firefighters are part-time or volunteer, all undergo rigorous training and testing. Firefighters and their officers have to be strong of body and heart. In our first fire companies, men pulled the entire apparatus to the fire and worked the primitive pumps by hand. Today they have to be able to wear fireproof (turnout or bunker) gear weighing as much as thirty pounds, haul "radios, light, extra air bottles, forcible entry equipment, ropes, medical kits, or hose packs and appliances" amounting to another fifty pounds, and still be able to hook up and haul hose lines, climb ladders or stairs, and rescue victims. That takes another universal quality and perhaps the most basic and universal quality of all—they have to be willing to face great danger to help people they do not know and save property not their own. Finally, they have to pass written and job performance tests on subjects as disparate as building construction types and knot tying.[21]

Throughout our history, the company has been the functioning unit of the fire service. (More technical details: a "company" refers to firefighters with their apparatus; a "crew" usually means the firefighters are working apart from their engines, trucks, squad vehicles, and the like.) A fully staffed modern fire company has about twenty-five men and four officers, a captain and three lieutenants. Nineteenth-century volunteer companies, by contrast, had hundreds of members. Then, the cost of a steam engine to pump the water ran into hundreds of dollars. Today, a used engine or a ladder truck can start at $350,000, and new ones run even higher.

At first, there were no specific jobs for members of the fire companies. Now, ladder company members find the source of the fire, vent it to reduce smoke inside the structure, search for victims, and "overhaul" the site to make sure that fire is not still hidden in walls, ceilings, or other spaces. Every person on the ladder truck has a particular job and the tools necessary to carry out that function. By contrast, the engine company's duty is to put out the fire. The engine is actually a pump to which a supply line from a water source, most often a hydrant, is attached. From the engine the firefighters run hoses of varying diameters and nozzles. The pumper raises the pressure of the water in the hand or land line. The standard for handheld lines is 50 pounds per square inch (psi) with a smooth bore or solid-stream open nozzle and 100 psi with a variable nozzle or adjustable pattern fog nozzle. (Water pressure in our homes is 2.2 psi.) These lines can

11

deliver up to 300 gallons of water per minute (gpm). More than that and the hose has to be attached or anchored to something or its kick will knock a firefighter on his back.[22]

In theory, the modern fire service is a hierarchical institution, uniformed and disciplined. In fact, just as in earlier times, there is a great deal of equality and mutual respect through the ranks. In the first volunteer companies, men were always on call. Today, city fire-fighters work in shifts. Still, men get to know one another's strengths and weaknesses intimately. Time together in the firehouse cements these personal relationships. Because it is a collective activity, fire-fighting has always had a social aspect. The fire service is a large family, complete with the loyalty, love, competitiveness, and bickering that all families have. Firefighters are as notorious for practical joking, one-upsmanship, and bravado today as they were when our nation was founded. Many come from firefighting families—uncles, fathers, brothers, cousins, in-laws, and friends all are or were fire-fighters. The camaraderie of the firehouse; the conviction that they are performing a heroic task; the pride in doing a job well; the sheer fun of beating one of nature's great forces; the religious faith that motivates firefighters—all these will always attract men and women to serve in city fire departments. And firefighters even have their groupies, fire buffs who visit the firehouses following an elaborate etiquette, listen to the stories, and follow the engines and trucks through the city streets to the fires.[23]

Whether volunteer or professional; wildfire or city fire; accident or arson, the first rule of fighting fire is always the same: Get there as fast as possible. If sufficient fuel and oxygen are at hand, fire doubles its force every thirty seconds. Today, according to the National Fire Academy and the U.S. Fire Administration, the standard is six minutes from report to arrival. Some first-rate departments get there in close to four minutes. The rule is "Go like hell." Drivers have to be careful, however, for not everyone cedes right of way to the apparatus, and the trucks and engines are capable of demolishing vehicles in their path. This was true of the very first horse-drawn fire wagons and remains so today. The arrival of the first responder (or "first due" company) depends on the availability of personnel and machines, and that in turn on staffing and maintenance. The best companies cut time in the firehouse. As Athens, Georgia, ladder company chauffeur Eric Frey, a sergeant with twenty years' experience, relates, "There's no way to make up time on the road. You can make up time in the house, as soon as the call comes in. We run a pretty tight ship, and are usually dressed and out the door in about a minute. Whatever you're doing, you drop it, hit the ground running, kick off your shoes, jump into your boots and pull up your [fire]pants in one motion and get on the truck."[24]

Commanders on the scene will choose between a defensive and an offensive or attack strategy, depending on how long the fire has been burning, the nature and extent of the fire, the structures or ground involved, and other relevant factors. Long-burning fires present immediate dangers of wall, ceiling, or roof collapse fatal to anyone entering the structure. In a defensive mode, the men will stay with the apparatus outside the structure, ventilating it from the outside, and use "master streams" of water that effectively flood the premises as well as hand lines to contain and extinguish the fire.[25]

When commanders believe that the structure may have people inside it, they will opt for an offensive attack. Indeed, in the city, the offensive, interior attack, carrying lines into the building, is the usual first choice. Once in the building, the rules remain simple: Find the fire; get civilians out; bring the hand lines to it; get as close to the fire as possible to "knock it down" with as much water or chemical foam as possible. "'Locate, confine, and extinguish' is the battle cry of most fireground commanders." There is "hot, too hot, far too hot, and too damn hot," but the fire must be extinguished. Before the engine company "takes up" its hoses, truckmen may use their "irons" hooks, axes, and Halligan tools (part crowbar, part hook) to pull down ceilings or tear away walls that may be concealing more of the fire. This is called "overhauling" the fire. Wildfire fighters do the same after a brushfire, to get at any hot spots still burning under the ground. As needed, other companies will be called into the fray. The chief will inspect to make sure that no fire remains, and to find the point of origin of the fire and its cause, if possible. "Firefighting 101" is what Chief Richard Picciotto of the FDNY calls the basics of putting out fire.[26]

These days, new kinds of tower ladders with high-pressure water pumps, better mobile "tool boxes" (rescue trucks), more powerful fire engines, and other improvements in apparatus have increased the efficiency of "defensive" firefighting. Lighter air packs, better fireproof "bunker gear" (personal protection clothing adapted from the Apollo astronaut program) replacing the older rubber "turnout" jackets, and individual communications devices have improved offensive firefighting abilities. Everyone learns rescue techniques. Specially trained squads for handling hazardous materials and difficult rescues are part of every major fire service. Central location and command facilities, the adoption of "incident command" techniques, and computers on board the trucks have brought firefighting into the twenty-first century.

But the improvement in the technical efficiency of firefighting has led to increased rather than decreased risks for individual firefighters. Citing gains in efficiency and decreasing absolute numbers of fires, we underfund our city fire departments. Once five firefighters and one officer staffed a shift of an engine or ladder company. Now the rule is four (and in some departments, three). In the midst of the arson crisis of the early 1970s, New York City was closing firehouses and furloughing nearly 3,000 firefighters. The result was a sharp increase in the number of serious injuries and fatalities from fire. Detroit in the 1990s was sending out pumpers with three men aboard. Penny-pinching is deadly when it comes to fire safety.

So is city politics, when it washes over the fire department. A survey of the Detroit Fire Department in 2000 by two *Detroit News* reporters found faulty and poorly maintained equipment, closed firehouses, inadequate training, and hydrants that had not worked for years. A later study by the *Boston Globe* discovered that many cities, and even more small towns, had response times of over ten minutes to reports of fires. From 1986 to 2000, over 4,000 people died in fires that departments reached after the six-minute standard.[27]

What is more, modern tactics of firefighting increase the risk to the firefighter. In the Great Fire of London, no firefighter died. In the city of New York, over forty died between 1980 and September 1, 2001. In 1970, according to the U.S. Fire Administration statistics, nearly 270 firefighters died in the course of their duties or from job-related incidents. Fully three-fourths of the fatalities were suffered by volunteer firefighters, comparable in numbers to their proportion of the profession. The average age of the victims was over forty years, a reminder of how taxing fighting fires can be. As graduating Oakland firefighters were told at the academy in 1998, "Somebody in your class is going to die . . . from this job."[28]

The reason for continuing mortality is simple. Today firefighters go into the burning premises for victims, carry them to safety if possible, or recover the bodies. The personal protective equipment—leather or fireproof plastic helmet, fireproof coat, gloves, pants, hood, and boots—of a firefighter provides valuable time to escape serious burns but cannot prevent cumulative damage to the body. Chipped vertebrae from falling objects, torn muscles and ligaments, and damage to internal organs ages firefighters before their time. Too often—far too often—the rescues and recoveries are of other firefighters, victims of collapsing walls and floors, flashovers, and backdrafts.

Even absent a catastrophic event, going into a burning building is deadly. Any time a firefighter breathes inside a burning structure without the air pack, he inhales a mix of toxic gases, burning embers, and superheated pollutants. These cause long-term damage to lungs, bronchial tubes, and heart. Dennis Smith, former New York City firefighter and one of the most eloquent observers of the profession, explains the dangers inside a burning structure: "[S]moke and heat make . . . the area surrounding a fire . . . untenable for all but those who have trained themselves . . . the firefighter crawls, nose to the floor, the heat attacking his face and . . . pores." If he has not had time to put on the air pack, "the smoke enters his lungs and works its way through the bloodstream to the brain . . . The body reacts, and viscous black stuff flows from the nose and mouth, mixes with a stream of perspiration . . . there is much coughing and choking, perhaps vomiting" of the poisonous particle cloud of carbon, water vapor, and whatever else was burning. "There is a weakness, a strange sense of semiconsciousness" as blood supply to the extremities is corrupted and the adrenaline runs out.[29]

Our persistent aversion to fire-safe cities further endangers fire-fighters. We avert our eyes when landlords and building superin-tendents flout the fire codes. In 1987, three Detroit firefighters died because a warehouse owner had illegally turned off his sprinkler sys-tem. He wanted to reduce his water bill. Still, his facility was filled with combustible materials, and he expected the fire department to save it. We crowd dozens into apartments meant for couples, allow multiple-use electric lines on outlets meant for a single plug, permit highly toxic and flammable building materials, and ignore shoddy construction shortcuts. In Manhattan's Schomberg Plaza public housing project fire of March 22, 1987, seven residents died because a contractor had cut corners with the garbage chutes. The fire spread because a lit cigarette burning in a chute ignited flammable materi-als within the walls of the building. The sprinkler system for the chute was "clogged with rust and silt." It had never been serviced.[30]

We throw up skyscraping residences and offices whose upper sto-ries are hard for firefighters to reach. The Schomberg was thirty-five stories high. The tower ladders (100 or 120 feet) can go eight or nine stories (assuming that the truck is placed in the most advantageous spot and the ladder held at no more than the safe 70-degree angle), not high enough to fight fires from the outside of a high-rise. The el-evators in a high-rise fire can be deadly unless they are clear of fire, so most of the time it's up the stairs for the firemen. In the event of a retreat, it's down the stairs. The company moves together, at the speed of the slowest man. No one is left behind. High enough, and the legs begin to cramp, followed by severe pain in the lungs, and then the heart starts pounding like a jackhammer.[31]

Firefighters have to face physical and mental challenges and must respond without hesitation to dozens of cues each time they go on a run. Officers and command-level personnel have to make life-and-death decisions at every working fire. Life safety comes first, fol-lowed by protection of property and containment. It sounds scientific, and to some extent "fire science" is just that, but firefight-ing remains as much craft as science, highly dependent on the lead-ership ability of commanders, and the training and personal commitment of the firefighters.[32]

Seven Fires

The great city fire is so overwhelming to those who witness it, it seems isolated in time and space, without precedent or explanation. For many who observed the Great Fire of London, time stopped. Those of us who watched the Twin Towers fall felt the same way. New York City architecture historian Max Page was in New York City on September 11, 2001. He later recalled: "Unimaginable. That is the word people screamed, aloud and in their heads, throughout much of September and October of 2001, and perhaps still do. It is the word survivors and witnesses repeated over and over."[33]

But urban infernos are historical events, like any other. *Seven Fires* examines the relation between fire and city life over the course of 250 years in America. It asks how we as a people and a nation prepare for our city fires, and sometimes negligently increase the risk of them; how we fight them, and sometimes lose; how we are transfixed by the raw spectacle of conflagrations, and yet summon the courage to combat them. It probes how we make sense of urban fires and rebuild after them.

My story begins with a series of critically important urban conflagrations in the eighteenth century and continues to our own day. I have selected seven great urban conflagrations that are typical of the fire regimes of their time and are also critical moments in our urban development. They shaped the larger course of our history. The Boston fire of 1760 was the most destructive of the many colonial city blazes. More important, the resentments it unleashed set the stage for the American Revolution. The Pittsburgh fire of 1845 was no more costly than the conflagrations that ravaged other antebellum cities, but by destroying many of the small factories and craft shops in the old city wards, it opened the way to larger-scale industrial plants. It also presented a case study in the manipulation of historical memory.

The devastation of the Chicago fire of 1871 simultaneously created a uniquely American narrative of recovery from disaster and propelled a political radicalism and class struggle of a sort not seen before in America. Out of its ashes came the modern skyscraper, the White City of the Columbian Exposition, the Haymarket Riots, and the Pullman Strike. The Baltimore fire of 1904 showed how a city's downtown, utterly destroyed, could reinvent itself after a catastrophic fire. The gift of the fire was the identification of the downtown's true needs. Today Baltimore's Inner Harbor is a model for the commercial use of urban space.

By the beginning of the second decade of the twentieth century, older citywide fire regimes had bowed to better fire departments, fireproof insulation, and fire-prevention programs, but new kinds of fires imperiled city dwellers. In the 1960s, widespread outbreaks of arson turned ghetto neighborhoods into war zones. The Detroit fire of 1967, the worst of these arsons, forced politicians to concede what the people of Detroit already knew—racism and racially based deprivation were not changed by the civil rights movement. Forty years after the fire, Detroit is still trying to recover.

A second new kind of danger arose in the "Red Zone" fires such as the Oakland Hills–Berkeley Hills firestorm of 1991. Housing subdivisions placed in the middle of a natural fire course invited ruinous blazes. The Oakland Hills tragedy demolished a landscape of private privilege and imperiled the dream of leisure living in natural settings. Whether it has taught a generation how to plan suburban housing in a hostile environment remains unclear.

The destruction of the Twin Towers of the World Trade Center on 9/11 by fire represents the third of the modern challenges—highrise fires. Little cities in themselves, high-rise buildings are more and more common in our urban environment. Apart from their domestic and global political implications, the fires of 9/11 have prodded a complacent nation to admit to itself that twenty-first-century emergency services, and the urban lifestyles they protected, have to be thoroughly rethought.

The story of fire in American cities reveals a nation and a people at its best and worst. There is courage and foolish pride; optimism and failure; a belief in the power to master nature and a persistent unwillingness to recognize the natural dangers that arrogance cannot overcome; masculine individuality and selfless brotherhood; and charitable impulse and cold-hearted calculation. The story of fire is the story of American cities, and of America itself.

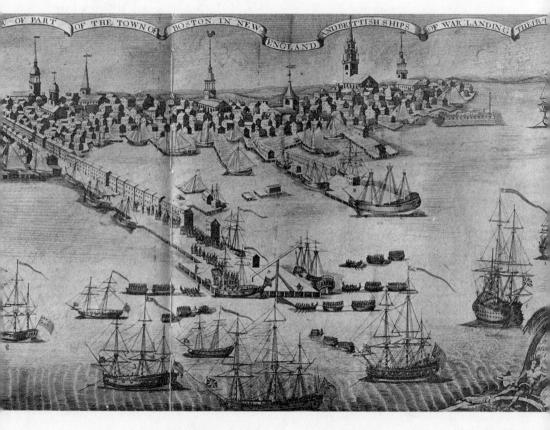

BOSTON, 1760

In the dark days of the French and Indian War, the townspeople of Boston wondered if anyone heard their prayers for victory or saw the signal fires they lit to welcome their warriors home. It had been a long war, another chapter in the endless cycle of raids, sieges, and campaigns between the New Englanders and their hated French-Canadian and Indian enemies dating back a century. In July 1758, the dreaded Papist French bastions at the mouth of the St. Lawrence River finally fell. Boston celebrated with orisons of thanksgiving and a bonfire on the top of Fort Hill. Little Boston, hundreds of whose volunteer soldiers and sailors had died during the conflict and whose treasury had been ransacked to pay for its contributions to the victory, lit fires of joy that night. A year later, when news arrived that the French had surrendered Quebec to the British army, and the prospects for a final victory over the old enemy seemed even brighter, Boston again turned to "'rejoicing fire.'" To this they added many solemnly preached sermons.[1]

Prayer and fire had always been part of the town's history. The devout and pious English immigrants who settled the Shawmut Peninsula in 1630, renaming it after the town in Lincolnshire from which some of them had come, prayed to God that Boston would be "a City on a hill." They prayed too that all its inhabitants would adopt the "model of Christian charity" its leaders espoused. In the first year alone, over 200 settlers, one-half the total, died from cold, deprivation, and despair, but between 1630 and 1640, the survivors were joined by thousands in a "great migration" from England. Their prayers had been answered.[2]

For those who made Boston the capital of the new colony of Massachusetts Bay, there was comfort in knowing that God had chosen them. They were "puritans" (a term of opprobrium hurled at them by their enemies), and they were not easy to live with. They believed that absolute sovereignty belonged to God, not man, and feared the fiery fate that God would rain down upon the wicked. As minister Benjamin Colman sermonized some years later, "the fire of God's wrath" poured out "like a lake of fire" condemning the sinner to "everlasting burning."[3]

For these puritans, the meetinghouse defined the town (it doubled as the town hall), and male membership in the church conferred the right to vote in local and colonial elections. But the meetinghouses themselves hardly inspired the spirit. Called by one wag "the Lord's barn," dreary plain clapboard outside, unadorned and uninsulated within, they were meant not to please the eye but to exalt the words of the sermon and enable the congregants to hear the minister clearly. In a fiery tongue, the ministers harangued the backsliding "sons of death," as Thomas Shepard called his flock, and warned that the Devil had to be driven out of the meetinghouse's shadows and rafters, where he sometimes lurked.[4]

No fires were lit during services. There was no fireplace or oven in the meetinghouse. But without fire, there was no congregation, no town, and no colony. Fire cleared the land for the "commons" on which the meetinghouse sat. Fire enabled the ironmonger to make the nails holding the rude planking together. Mastery of fire enabled the townsfolk to drain marshes, build up the sides of hills, and widen Indian paths into streets. In 1650, Boston boasted over 350 buildings. By the early 1700s, the town covered all seven hills of the Shawmut Peninsula. Growth forced Boston to choose between wood for heating fuel and construction materials, but the puritans found a third answer: cut down forests far from town. The current occupiers of those woodlands—the Narragansetts to the south, the Abenaki to the north, and the Pequots to the west—objected. A series of wars of dispossession and the spread of English diseases to which Indians had no immunities silenced the natives' objections.[5]

Without fire, there was no protection against the arctic winds that whistled down from the Canadian north and the damp mists that crept in from the Atlantic. Climatologists have told us that the northern regions were experiencing a "little ice age" in these years and Boston winters were cold, dark, and long. Families hunkered down in the small, low-ceilinged rooms of houses and shops. Kitchens were gathering places after work, for only the kitchen hearth was warm. Huge woodpiles stood outside every dwelling place. If they wished to go about the house at night, Bostonians lit a lard or whale oil lamp with an open wick. To venture outside, perhaps to visit the outhouse (though at night most people simply filled a night jar), they relied on a handmade, handheld tin or pewter lantern.[6]

In their need for fire, Bostonians created the perfect fire course. Boston's vernacular building was wood frame, clapboard siding, and shingle roofs. Boston's streets were wind tunnels—narrow, winding, and overhung by buildings, "too narrow" and "irregularly disposed" for the liking of Dr. Alexander Hamilton of Annapolis, who visited in 1744. In Boston's "tenements"—apartments that could be rented—poor men and women ignored fire safety. They smoked, lit candles, and left about combustibles including bedding and clothing. Along alleys like Pudding Lane, in the very center of town, rented rooms doubled as piecework shops, and leather, petroleum products, and the raw materials for manufacturing textiles covered their floors.[7]

Workaday Boston was especially vulnerable to fire. Breweries, glassworks, tanneries, forges, candle-makers, dyers, and potters all had to use ovens or open-pit fires. Next to the flames were fuel sources, not only wood or coal to keep the furnace or oven burning but highly inflammable raw materials for manufacturing. Candles, hearth embers, lanterns, and lamps burned hot enough to ignite the fine-textured wood shavings scattered about the warehouses and craft shops. Waiting down the lane or up the hill for wind-blown sparks to arrive were mounds of straw and hay in barns (some converted to temporary residences); gunpowder in armories and forts, and rope, tar, pitch, sails, and turpentine in shipyards. After a 1736 fire, minister Benjamin Colman called the city a "thicket of combustible material."[8]

Even the mansions of the rich and the palaces of the rulers were fire prone. Boston merchant Peter Sargeant's mansion in the center of town that later became the Province House (the governor's home) and the John Foster house (later the home of colonial governor Thomas Hutchinson) were three stories tall and surrounded by gardens. But the building materials the two nabobs adopted—brick, stone, slate, and tile—were not truly fire resistant. The brick came from nearby Medford kilns and was not fired hot enough to withstand a real blaze. The mortar was flammable. The window glass and fittings, along with the doors and lintels, would burst when exposed to heat—letting a fire feast on the rich wooden and fabric interiors. Brick buildings might contain a fire (the walls were less likely to collapse than wooden walls), but all the rich could do as the fire approached was to pay bystanders to put out flying embers, find a carter to carry away the valuables, and hope for the best. Hope was not good fireproofing, however.[9]

Its prayers notwithstanding, Boston seemed built to burn. The year after Governor John Winthrop laid out the town in 1630, two of its houses burned. The owners had insulated the chimneys of their homes with clay, but the soot from hearth fires, itself highly flammable, had built up during the cold first winter, and the chimneys caught fire. Chimneys are designed to draw oxygen over a fire—the open flue at the top of the hearth creates a partial vacuum, sucking in the oxygen as the heated air above the flame rises. The townsmen watched as sparks from the chimney fires rained down on the thatched roofs, and the buildings took only a short time to burn to the ground. Had there been gusty winds, the rest of the settlement might have followed.

In a pattern that would be repeated after each major fire, Boston's town fathers decreed rules and regulations that they and their neighbors then routinely flouted. All new buildings must have shingled roofs and stone or clay inside the chimneys. All householders must have buckets and ladders in good repair. New buildings must be brick with tile roofs. In 1679, command of the bucket brigade was given to the militia muster officers, and in 1712, the term "fire wardens" (the actual term was "fire wards") came into use when the city was divided into wards. And the more comprehensive the regulations, the more flagrant the disobedience to them became.[10]

In 1653, another chimney fire, its embers carried aloft and rained down on the roofs of houses by the wind, nearly consumed the center of the city. Governor Winthrop praised God that the city was not wholly razed and warned that it could not expect Providence to intercede again. An accidental candle fire in 1676 (a tailor's apprentice was the culprit) burned down fifty of the city's structures. A series of suspicious fires in 1679 left the city without 150 of its buildings. It was the worst fire in British-American colonial history to that date, comparable in scale to the impact of the Great Fire of London. The Bostonians blamed the French—the perennial enemy of the New England colonies—and tried a French tavern worker for arson. Three years later, a warehouse fire destroyed thirty-eight buildings.[11]

Boston lived uneasily with the fear of arson—if not the French enemy insinuating himself into the city, then its lowest-status denizens using fire to gain revenge. In 1683, a slave woman was convicted of burning down her master's house; it could have become a conflagration. Boston had hundreds of slaves working in shops and as house servants. Arson was not just a slave crime—the lower orders, the "giddy multitude" and "disgruntled underlings"—practiced it regularly. Thus, Hittee, an Indian girl, was found guilty of burning her master's Boston house in 1712, in an act of revenge. She was hanged.[12]

Everyone in Boston knew about the Great Fire of London and its brief but hellish offshoots in the streets of their colonial city. They prayed for guidance as they lit fires in hearth and forge. But fire was not done with Boston.

"A Torrent of Flame"

The Cornhill" of Boston is aptly named. Like its namesake in London of 1666, it is steep, as tourists walking up today's Washington Street toward the Old South Church will testify. Other hills in Boston were leveled and their soil carted off as landfill in the nineteenth century. But the Cornhill remains as much a breathless climb as it was in colonial days.

Standing at the start of the Freedom Trail across the street from the Old South Church on a cold late winter morning in 2004, it is not hard to imagine the Cornhill district of Boston in the very early morning of March 20, 1760. The winter had been especially cold, and in the drafty, ill-constructed inns, tenements, and shops, people bundled themselves against the chill. Fireplaces had damped down to ash and a few coals. These would be used to restart the fires in the morning. In them housewives and tavern keepers would cook the porridge and bake the bread that was the staff of life for the poor.[13]

A light flared in the windows of the Brazen Head tavern and inn on Pudding Lane. Surely it was too early for widowed Mary Jackson, who ran the inn with her son, to be up and cooking, but the night watchman did not notice the light or thought it a flickering candle. The narrowest street in the city, little more than an alley that connected Water Street and King Street, was not a place where the watch would tarry. Rowdy by day and dangerous by night, the narrow streets of the Ninth Ward were uninviting and the Brazen Head was hardly an upscale accommodation. If the watchmen had known that the Great Fire of London, which originated in a bakery on a Pudding Lane, had been just as easily overlooked as their own, would their curiosity about the light have been piqued?

In the upstairs rooms, soiled and besotted sailors, travelers, and soldiers back from the war shared straw-filled bunks. Guttering candles threw lumpish shadows on the whitewashed walls. The men slept in the depths of drink, indifferent to the dangers of fire though surrounded by piles of combustible materials, including the barrels of ale, cider, and rum they had tapped all evening. As prices of rum and other distilled beverages fell during the eighteenth century and the number of distilleries and breweries mounted, public drunkenness grew to epidemic proportions. Adult per capita consumption of alcohol in the colony exceeded seven gallons per year.

The number of taverns in Boston doubled from 1700 to the middle of the century. Maps show that the Cornhill had more of these than anywhere else in the city. Some were elegant establishments. At its prime location on the Long Wharf, the Crown offered patrons a coffee room and a barroom, and set diners' tables with linen tablecloths and forks. Other taverns were eyesores. Rebecca Fowle's establishment was a notorious haunt for the disorderly poor. The selectmen of the town reluctantly allowed her to keep her license, for without it, she would need poor relief. Widows like Mary Jackson were among the few women in the colony allowed to run their own businesses. Taverns like the Brazen Head had to be licensed. Licensing did not include fire inspections.[14]

Meanwhile, the flickering glow in the Brazen Head's window had revealed itself as a room fire. It spread along the straw on the ground floor and heated the wooden tables and benches enough to ignite them. Dried by days without rain and the continuous blaze in the fireplace, they were ready to burn. The heat from the burning contents of the downstairs rooms and the hot gases the fire released rolled up toward the ceiling and then banked down again along the walls, igniting the plaster and whitewash. Smoke filled the tavern and crept up the stairs. Waking from their drunken slumber, guests threw open the doors and inadvertently welcomed in the superheated smoke.

By 3:00 AM the Brazen Head was fully involved in flames. The cracking of the roof shingles as they succumbed to the fire and the groaning of the timbers as they lost their ability to support the upper floor added bass notes to the high-pitched shouts of the tenants fleeing the dying tavern. The flames shot out of the crumbling roof, sending its burning remnant skyward. The fire had exposed the flimsy construction of the tavern as it reduced the structure to embers and ash. The Brazen Head was doomed. The Cornhill was next.

CORNHILL FIRE STORIES

To understand why the Cornhill burned—why Boston burned—in 1760, one has to understand why it burned so many times before, and why its political and economic leaders allowed it to burn. To be sure, if old Boston was meant to burn, the Cornhill would provide perfect kindling. The John Bonner map of Boston, published in 1722, shows how crowded the housing was in this dilapidated central neighborhood. The intersection of Cornhill and King Streets had the highest density of residential population in the city, only matched by the tenements on Milk Street and Water Street nearby. In the Cornhill, two- and three-story rooming houses sheltered the working poor. Their landlords lived in more comfortable surroundings.[15]

To take one devastating example, a precursor to the 1760 inferno: On the evening of October 2, 1711, a high, dry wind blew through the Cornhill's tenements. Every hearth had a fire going in it that night—except for those renters who could not afford the firewood. The city was attracting more and more immigrants, and they worked long and sometimes carelessly in attic rooms and shanties, the meanest of them fronting on alleys rather than streets. In their drafty quarters the pieceworkers' loose-fitting clothing billowed out toward the flames of the candles by whose light they toiled.

Mary Morse, a Scotswoman, was one of these, renting a single room in a rooming house and eking out a living by picking the loose fibers from old ropes. Tired and malnourished, she either did not see or could not prevent embers from her hearth fire from landing on

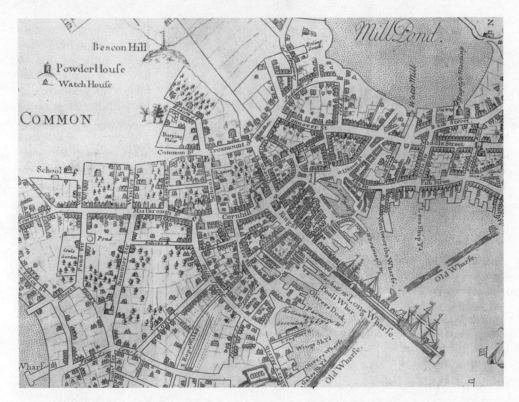

the piles of oakum and setting them afire. Fleeing the blaze, she surely called out, "Fire!"—though little good it would do.[16]

Poor Morse did not have the mandated water bucket at hand. It probably didn't matter. No one was there with her to help fetch water. Certainly, she smelled the fire first, then saw a wisp of smoke that transformed itself, as if by magic, into something darker and evil. The fire must have made itself visible now, flames spreading over the flax, lapping up the clothing and linen, reaching out for her. The room would soon fill with toxic gases and superheated fumes. She panicked, but for this she can be forgiven. Even a little smoke in the eyes is blinding, and in the lungs can be deadly.[17]

The modern mind regards the origin and spread of fire as a natural phenomenon, even when its effects are tragic. Puritans instead located causation in the overlapping realms of divine will and individual morality. For many in Boston that night, the meaning of fire lay not in the accidents inherent in city life but in God's wrath on the sinner poured out in fire.

Leading ministers Increase Mather and his son, Cotton Mather, watched the 1711 fire eat the heart out of Boston, and both preached about the fire the next Sunday. Increase, the dean of the town's ministerial fraternity, had reached his seventy-third year, over fifty of which he had spent in the pulpit. His message was a simple "Jeremiad," using the fire to call a backsliding people to return to the religion of their forefathers. "Many are departed and degenerated from those holy principles which in our first and purest times, New England was distinguished." In the fire, the "hand of heaven" was evident. The wind, "which the Lord holds in his hands," had stopped the progress of the fire just as the wind had spread the fire. Though the Lord's purpose might be "inscrutable" to some, the lesson was plain to him: Fire was the "purgation" of sin. As metal was refined by fire, so was the soul—a "solemn warning" to those untouched by the blaze and a needful reminder to those who had lost everything.[18]

Increase Mather had a special antipathy to fire that combined the supernatural and the moral worlds, for he had seen and heard the effect of the fires that the Indians set during the two horrific years of King Philip's war. The war had destroyed dozens of New England villages, costing thousands of lives. From 1675 though 1676, Indian raids began with the firing of frontier homes to drive the denizens from the cover of their dwellings. In the forty-four raids on colonial towns, Indians had destroyed over 500 houses and 100 barns with fire. At the time, Increase Mather had seen the Indian war as a scourge of the colony's backsliding puritans, a view of events effectively making the Indians into God's tool. But nothing disguised Mather's almost pathological hatred of fire.[19]

Cotton Mather saw fire not as a hellish visitation but as a divine event with natural effects. For him, according to historian Robert Blair St. George, "flames lit the sky with eschatological signs; the burning of houses metaphorically figured the burning of the bodies of the unfaithful." Fires were God's writing on the earth. But Mather was also a naturalist of some ability, and although his credentials as a puritan theologian were above reproach, he advanced one uneasy foot into the modern world. With the learned men of science in Britain, he "equivocated on prodigies, scoffed at magic, fudged on witches, praised reason, hedged on the sufficiency of grace [to save], and . . . sent powerful signals to his [ministerial] brethren about what constituted legitimate areas of religious concern for cultured ministers." In other words, for him "the experience of things [could] confirm one's belief in the truths of the Christian religion."[20]

Mather was fifty-nine years old in 1711 and had spent almost all of those years in Boston. He had preached on the subject of its fires before and did not need divination to explain how fires got started or spread. What he saw and lamented was not so much God's wrath as the fact that "not a little of the wealth of the town is consumed." The night's events themselves had an affecting natural rather than a wrathful divine aspect: "Our eyes, which ought to affect our hearts, have newly been entertained with a very dismal spectacle." True to his calling and its puritan traditions, he insisted that the fire must teach lessons to the haughty, but he rendered these lessons in empirical terms.[21]

Puritans agreed that evil events over which Providence presided taught lessons to both the wicked and the righteous. Judge Samuel Sewall, who lost one of his rental properties in the blaze, condemned Morse for being drunk. Increase Mather thundered from his pulpit that her "wicked" and sinful disregard of others' property was typical of the "poorer and meaner sort of people all over the country" who went "above their quality, above their parentage, and above their estates." Cotton Mather agreed. The material cause of the fire was not a malign providence bent on castigating Boston but the carelessness and "Scottishness" of a woman. She had waited too long and allowed the fire to go too far before she raised the hue and cry.[22]

Making a woman like Morse the scapegoat for the fire had another, sinister side. For some puritans, women were inherently sinful, the spawn of Eve. They brought evil into the world. Women were seductresses and witches. Notably in New England's hundreds of seventeenth-century witchcraft cases, the vast majority of defendants were women, many poor like Morse. Women were common objects of suspicion in outbreaks of disease or social and political dislocation and convenient targets for accusations. Even Cotton Mather, who ought to have known better after urging the judges on in the Salem witchcraft trials of 1692, hinted in 1711 that "this bewitching world is to be burnt in that horrendous conflagration to come" at Judgment Day.[23]

Everything in the path of the fire, from the Cornhill district to Dock Square in the north and the wharves in the south, went up in flame. The fire raged until 2:00 AM, when it ran out of fuel at the water's edge. By then it had consumed over 100 buildings. As many as a dozen people died, most of them young men trying to fight the fire. Two were killed by falling debris, others died trying to rescue the bell from the steeple of the First Church, at the corner of Milk and Cornhill. Still more perished in the explosions of gunpowder that the selectmen ordered to blow up houses in the fire's path. It was a last resort, and as in the Great Fire of London, the firebreak did not work. The gunpowder only blew out the windows of previously untouched houses, allowing the burning embers to enter and set furniture, drapery, and clothing aflame. As quickly as householders dumped their valuables on the street and sought carters with wagons to carry their goods to safety, sneak thieves and toughs ran off with the loot.[24]

LAX BUILDING CODES, INDIFFERENT LANDLORDS, AND GREEDY SPECULATORS

With the lessons of the 1711 fire in front of their eyes, why had the city fathers not taken firm steps to prevent its repetition? They ordained that all new buildings were to be of brick or stone and roofs covered with slate or tile, then looked the other way when there were persistent violations of the ordinance. The selectmen named six leading men to divide the town into fire wards and these men were to supervise organized bands of firefighters, but the position was largely honorific. In 1722, a decade after the regulations were promulgated, 2,000 of the 3,000 structures in the city were still wooden. Building inspection was haphazard—the selectmen responsible under the law turned the job over to eight inspectors, and they dumped it in the lap of chimney sweeps, the least trustworthy of all the craftsmen in the city. The selectmen continued to wail that the city was in danger of catastrophic fire, but they themselves were guilty of not listening.

Why not? The answer is simply that leading puritans were not otherworldly aesthetics. Quite the opposite. They were men of property, commerce, and capital. Increase Mather explained this fire lesson. Those in the North End who had not fled but had stood by their homes, putting out every ember and "defending" their property, had fought off the fire. They were the blessed ones. So, too, Cotton Mather ended his sermon on a practical note. Something had to be done about the thieves who ran off with personal property left on the street.[25]

For all the damage the Great Fire of 1711 caused and the hand-wringing that followed, Boston remained a wooden city because the cost of rebuilding in wood was lower than the cost of fireproofing. Bricks could be had cheaply from the kilns outside of town, but lime for mortar was not so easily found. Masons used stone from quarries south of the city, but it was expensive to haul and skilled stonemasons commanded healthy fees. Stone and brick were thus reserved for refined homes and the newest, most elegant churches. It is no surprise, then, that according to the Bonner Map of 1722, the Cornhill in 1722 looked much as it had before the Great Fire of 1711. It would look the same in 1743 and in 1760.

Indeed, the only obvious difference over time between 1711 and 1760 was the proliferation of churches. Their bells were the city's fire alarms, but even the steeples were not always constructed of brick or stone. The meetinghouse of the First Church was twice destroyed by fire, but in 1712 the congregation erected a third wooden structure right in the center of town. Inside and out, the wood was coated with highly flammable paint. The Old South Meeting House, the largest building in the city (it could hold 5,000 people), was rebuilt in 1729 in the center of the Cornhill. Its walls were brick, but its pews, interior walls, floors, and appurtenances were all wooden. (It still stands, a monument to the first successful effort, in 1876, at historic preservation in the city.) King's Chapel, a wooden structure for Anglican worship built in 1686, was not torn down and replaced by a stone church until 1749. Even when the clapboard meetinghouses were supplanted by brick churches, their steeples, pews, and ornately carved interiors were still wooden. Beautification did not incorporate fire safety.[26]

There was a second reason beyond simple replacement costs that colonial landlords declined to invest in fire safety. The raison d'être of the early modern city was the maximization of private property. Cities in America were giant wealth-making machines, and the most readily available source of that wealth was real estate. Real estate speculation in the city, most often carried on by absentee landlords, used the rent from substandard housing to buy land in undeveloped areas and improve it. To have made tenements conform to municipal ordinances would have required the investment of capital more profitably employed elsewhere—for example, in speculation, manufacturing, commerce, or money lending. Landlords also knew that the cost of renovation is always higher than the cost of rebuilding poor housing stock. The poor renters could not complain; they were happy to gain housing near their place of work—for example, on the docks just down Water Street. Even the less successful businesspeople and master craftsmen who lived and worked in the area had little choice about staying in the ramshackle structures because they had little capital to invest in homes of their own.[27]

Real estate manipulation did not always pay, but a profitable urban real estate market required that the limited stock of housing and extent of land periodically be freed for development. Great fires facilitated speculation in scarce and valuable real estate by clearing away old housing stock, terminating unfavorable rental agreements, ousting deadbeat tenants, and permitting the construction of more profitable structures. So long as the site retained its inherent value, the shanty landlords stood to gain by fire, and Boston remained a premier location for business and residential development.

G. B. Warden, colonial Boston's foremost historian, has collated information on Boston real estate transactions in the eighteenth century that explain the thinking and conduct of the landlords. After the fire of 1711, speculators like Elisha Cooke, Jr., not only rebuilt on the burned land, they used the higher rents to speculate on Maine land and shipbuilding. Efforts by more conservative merchants such as Thomas Hutchinson to curb speculation and impose retail controls failed. Speculators, facing higher taxes as Boston tried to pay its share of the wars against England's colonial enemies, found a hedge in real estate development, as the price of the average house might vary as much as 20 percent per decade. But the land available for residential building was saturated with housing by 1730. Boston housing stock could not expand spatially until the Back Bay, South End, and other areas were created with landfill in the nineteenth century. Indeed, the pressure on available housing increased as the population rose from 10,000 in 1700 to 15,000 by 1760. Poor people needed shelter, and even a fairly prosperous laborer found it hard to afford ownership. For the landlords, rebuilding quickly with wood and renting out rooms was a perfect solution to the problem of scarcity, and for real estate speculators, it resolved the problem of taxation.[28]

The town officials, from the governor down to the justices of the peace and the fire wardens themselves, were among the most active of all the real estate speculators. On average, they conducted slightly fewer than 20 percent of all the property transfers with nearly 30 percent of the value of all transactions from 1730 to 1760. No other group, even the merchants, outdid the officials, except the far more numerous category of "craftsmen."[29]

Moreover, structural properties changed hands frequently—in the 1750s alone there were 1,240 deeds recorded and 580 mortgages taken out, amounting to over 66 percent of the real estate in the city. Buyers and sellers constituted the propertied classes (including 15 percent of the buyers and sellers who were widows). For all of these people, there was no reason to invest scarce capital in improving buildings' fire safety when they might be sold tomorrow.[30]

THE FIRE AND THE FIREMEN

All this explains why the Brazen Head and the rest of Cornhill were still as flame prone in 1760 as they had been in 1711. By now, at 3:00

AM on the morning of March 20, 1760, shaken occupants of the inn had poured into the streets. Fleeing, they had left every door behind them open. Had they not done so, despite all the flammable objects—the bedding, the flax, the straw—the fire would probably have remained in the confines of the building until all the oxygen was exhausted, then decayed and gone out. To spread beyond the rooms, the fire needed a fresh supply of oxygen. By leaving the doors open, the refugees from the Brazen Head allowed more oxygen to reach the hot gases, reigniting the unburned carbon and other fuel in them.[31]

The opened doors were one of a series of dire contingencies. Without the wind, the dry season, and the delay in raising the alarm the fire might have been contained. Every major fire event is the product of overlapping possibilities, human and natural. The "tipping point" that turned a series of little mishaps into a disaster, to borrow a notion from the popular sociologist Malcolm Gladwell, may have been no more than the amount of easily combustible fuel in the tavern, or the drink-induced stupor of the residents, or their delay in recognizing the danger. Indeed, hesitation, particularly the failure to recognize the extent and source of a fire, is the great enemy in containing the fire.[32]

Neighbors awakened by the fleeing patrons' cries of "Fire!" and the first arriving night watchmen realized that the fire was spreading awfully fast. A ragged bucket brigade assembled and stretched itself out to the nearest well. But everyone knew that the surrounding buildings could not be saved by water buckets. The call went out for the volunteer fire companies and their fire engines. They arrived from all corners of the city, the men breathless and sweaty. The bucket brigade now wound its way to the engine instead of the mouth of the blaze. The fire hoses, leather with copper rivets, could throw water to a second story. In displays of manliness and vigor, engine companies competed to see who could work the hand pumps hardest and throw water the farthest.

At the beginning of the eighteenth century, city governments adopted two stopgaps to fight the spread of existing fires. Both steps anticipated the way that Americans would deal with a wide variety of public problems in the coming years. First, Boston sponsored volunteer firefighting "companies" of young men. Voluntary associations would become the heart of much of American charitable and public activity, from temperance societies to consumer protection groups. Second, to enable the fire companies to do their work from the street, Boston adopted a second measure that would become a typical American answer to problems. Boston turned to firefighting machines. An abiding investment of money and faith in machines is still characteristic of American thinking.

The first Boston fire company appeared in 1678, when the city authorized Thomas Atkins to direct twelve men in the use of a newly imported English device called a fire engine. It was little more than a wooden tub with a pump and a hose of a sort already in use in most European cities. London had many of them. By 1760, Boston had nine fire companies of twenty men, each company organized to pull and work engines, now mounted on wheels. The head of the volunteers was called an "engineer" because he was responsible for the care and operation of the fire engine. The men who carried or pulled the engine to the fire and worked it there became an engine company. Other men who specialized in the use of hooks to pull down burning walls and ladders to reach upper floors were part of the company. The companies took the name of their engines or the location where it was housed—for example, the Great Fire Engine, North Copper, Old North Church, Hero, Old Prison, Cumberland, and West. The city paid a bounty of £5 sterling to the first engine company to get to a fire.[33]

From Boston, the idea of volunteer fire companies spread to such other port cities as New York and Philadelphia. Ports were especially vulnerable to fires. Dock men piled combustibles on wharves in great heaps—raw material for textiles, paper, leather, marine goods, and liquor of all types. In 1730, Philadelphia experienced its first great waterfront fire—at Fishbourn's Wharf. Benjamin Franklin, witness as a boy to the 1711 Boston fire, was appalled by his adopted home's inattentiveness to the dangers of fire. He proposed to his small circle of Philadelphia friends in the middle 1730s that it have a "company for the more ready extinguishing of fires, and mutual assistance in removing and securing the goods when in danger." They

chartered the Union Fire Company in 1736. It was to have charge of
a new engine, just imported from England. Another printer, William
Bradford, formed a rival fire company, the Fellowship, in 1738.
(Public service and commercial competition went together then.) A
third company, the Hand-in-Hand, followed in 1742.[34]

Franklin, a practical man and a scientific genius, prepared a report detailing "the different accidents and carelessnesses by which
houses were set on fire, with cautions against them, and means proposed of avoiding them." It was the earliest precursor of the U.S.
Fire Administration/Federal Emergency Management Agency fire
narratives. He published his findings in his own newspaper, the
Pennsylvania Gazette, in 1735 but they would not have been news to
anyone in Boston: Don't carry coals about on the stairs at night; be
careful with embers; don't let flammables get close to the hearth;
clean the chimney.

In 1750, he took the next step in his plan to provide a private alternative to public inaction on fires. He formed a mutual aid society.
Thirty men subscribed to the "articles" of this company, a mutual assistance association whose closed list of members were to come to
one another's aid in case of fire. Although the mutual aid/fire company he envisioned had a plain enough public purpose, one does not
have to read too closely between the lines to see that he was of a
mind with the Boston selectmen. The real danger of fire was not to
the public interest but to private property.[35]

By 1721, the city of Boston owned six fire engines. A decade later,
it had three shops manufacturing engines for other towns. The
Boston fire companies were continually updating the engines, newer
models that could hold more water and throw it farther. In 1736,
James Read, for example, advertised his "large and extraordinarily
good copper fire-engine, newly fixed, that works well, and will be of
excellent use in time of fire, in any populous place." If one wanted to
search out an alternative to Read's machine, one could drop by Row-
land Houghton's place at the north end of the Town House to price a
smaller "hand engine made in the best manner . . . very useful in all
families, convenient for extinguishing fire in chimneys, or in any
room in a house." Richard Newsham, an "engineer," advertised his

English-built "engines for quenching fires" in broadsides—single-page, illustrated flyers. The king had supposedly given these engines his blessing (one was kept at the palace at St. James's and was used to water the garden when not otherwise employed). There were four wheel models and chair models, designed to fit any use.[36]

But the fire companies and the fire engines were never effective fire prevention tools. Nor were the numbers of private societies and associations called "fire-clubs" and "fire societies." They were too limited in membership. What is more, they swung into operation after the fire had started. Under the "rules and orders" of these fire clubs and fire societies, each member was to be "well acquainted with each others houses, shops, and stores," and at the alarm was expected to rush to the nearest member in danger and "remove and secure all his goods and effects" to some "safe place." The articles of these associations fined members who did not have two good buckets, but nothing in the articles bound the members to inspect their own or others' premises for fire risks. Nothing they did made city fires any less inevitable.[37]

A "TORRENT OF FLAME"

The false dawn of March 20, 1760, brought no relief to the people of the Cornhill. In fact, the wind had risen, and the Pudding Lane fire now threatened the entire city. In the preceding months, prophecies of fire-borne disaster regularly issued from the city's pulpits, but these were part of a genre of fire-and-brimstone preaching that had nothing to do with fire safety. The day of judgment was always just around the corner, eager to punish Boston's iniquity. One did not need to be a prophet to worry about more mundane dangers. The city was filled with ammunition for the forthcoming campaign against French Canada. It had been dry and cold, with a brisk wind. On the 17th, a joiner's shop burst into flame, and the wind, "being high, and from the north east," set the West Meeting House roof on fire. In violation of all the ordinances requiring brick and tile, the meetinghouse had been built of clapboard and shingle. "By great exertion" the fire companies extinguished the blaze. The next day, a storehouse on Griffin's Wharf adjoining a warehouse filled with gunpowder caught fire, and the building blew up. Fortunately the tide was in, so there was plenty of water to fight the fire. There was no wind. It was a season of burning, and the Brazen Head fire climaxed a series of escalating calamities.[38]

The Cornhill flames leaped over the narrow streets to involve buildings blocks away from the ruined Brazen Head. Frightened working people spilled from the rental properties with little more than the clothing on their backs as their tenements caught fire. William Cooper, clerk of the selectmen and one of the first on the scene, called the fire "a perfect torrent of flame." Samuel Savage, another bystander, compared the falling ash to a blizzard.[39]

As if motivated by the Devil, the fire licked at the South Meeting House at the top of the Cornhill, but some greater power intervened, the wind shifted, and the fire careened south down Milk Street toward the harbor and Fort Hill, a distance of half a mile. Had the fire not turned in its course, the giant meetinghouse, measuring over forty-five paces by sixty paces, would have succumbed to the flames. Its window frames and doors were wood, as was its steeple—portals for the fire to enter the sanctuary. The window glass would have burst with the heat, inviting the flames into the pews. The roof would then have become a breeding ground for more fire, shooting burning debris into the wind. But the gusts' direction shifted, and herded the fire away from the church.

Wind is the ally of urban fire. It bears the fire on its back and throws its embers into the sky so that the fire can be reborn over and over. On a chilly spring morning take a walk down Milk Street from Washington Street. The upper portion is still winding and narrow, as it was in 1760, and feel the wind in your face. It will take your breath away. Ordinarily, fire prefers to go uphill in the daytime (the sun heats the land and the wind convection carries fire up) and downhill at night "as the land cools and draws the air down." Fire historian John N. Maclean explains that "nighttime winds" are usually "more moderate" downhill, when "temperatures are cooler and the humidity is higher." Thus, a downhill nighttime fire is usually slower moving than an uphill fire and rarely is "a killer." The Great Fire of 1760 was merciful in its human cost for that reason, but wind-driven downhill fires are capricious in their choice of inanimate victims. The burning debris may fly over one building entirely and strike its neighbor.[40]

According to Cooper's firsthand account in the Boston *News-Letter* (reprinted in the Boston *Post-Boy*), "The distressed inhabitants of those buildings wrapped in fire scarcely knew where to take refuge." Sick people were moved from house to house one step ahead of the blaze. One can imagine the scene—the horrible noise of the fire, added to the shrieks and moans of its victims and the shouts of people seeking assistance. City conflagrations howl, moan, shriek, roar, and crack. People crammed streets were already that filled with personal goods, then watched as the flames consumed everything left behind. Through this mass of sleep-tousled and anxious humanity passed carts loaded with more people and more goods, the drivers cursing at bystanders and the bystanders shouting back.[41]

As confusing as the fire must have been at the time, its progress down the slope toward the harbor tracked a kind of "doomsday book" of Boston houses and shops. From the Brazen Head, the flames skipped across the street to Peter Cotter's house, then the wind rose up and carried it up Pudding Lane and down King to Water Street. It did not destroy Andrew Oliver's fine house—evidence of the caprice of downhill-running fire—but ravaged his dock and John Erving's warehouse. It took Hallowell's shipyard, Wendell's Wharf, and all of Quakertown. Two tenements of free Negroes burned, as did the dwellings of John Osbourn, Esq., Andrew Oliver, Jr., and Edward Brattle Oliver. It was a calamity that seemed to select its victims one by one, knowing which to strike and which to pass over.[42]

From on board a ship at anchor in the harbor, the fire must have looked at first like a single lit candle. And then another flame, some distance away, illuminated the sky. Soon the entire shore was alight. Frantic efforts kept the ships at berth from catching fire. Sailors rushed to assist those in the streets. Seaman know the terrors of blazes at sea. The roar of the flames nearly drowned out cries for help. Rushing to help pull down the buildings in the path of the growing conflagration, an observer recalled: "[I]t is almost impossible to conceive of a scene of more horror and distress . . . the sick, the aged, women, and children half naked were seen going they knew not where, and taking refuge in houses which were at a distance from the fire, but from whence they were . . . driven a second and even a third time by the devouring element . . . The terror was increased by the horrid noise of the burning and falling houses. . . ." It was as though the fire were alive and angry.[43]

No one was killed by the fire, but before it ended at the water's edge, ten hours later, it had raged over the twenty acres of the Old South End of the city and had destroyed property worth between £100,000 and £300,000 in colonial currency. (Or very roughly, about $8 million in 2005 dollars. This does not take into account the inflation of housing in modern Boston, where a 2005 house averages nearly $500,000.) Estimates at that time varied according to whether one asked the government or polled the victims.[44]

Governor William Pownall, a canny young English politician who had led the colony for four years, immediately went before the colonial assembly gathered in the State House and expressed his sorrow. He was a very popular figure in the city. There is no doubt that he witnessed at least part of the fire firsthand. His official dwelling was within walking distance. The Boston *News-Letter* account hinted that he joined in the effort to put the fire out. Would not "the presence and the example of the greatest personages among us, who condescended to the most laborious services" have included Pownall? Cooper, a Pownall supporter, had written the account, but it had to be true—everyone must have seen Pownall in the streets, just as the next year, when Faneuil Hall was gutted, Pownall's replacement, Francis Bernard, urged the firefighters on. It was a tradition, after all. In the Great Fire of London, both the king and his brother rushed to the fire scene.[45]

Pownall immediately solicited the country for "briefs" and sent messages to other governors asking them to do the same. The brief was not a lawyer's argument before a court of law, but a description of the fire damage, printed and circulated with an appeal for charitable assistance. It originated in England, where the home secretary sent it to justices of the peace and the archbishop of Canterbury distributed it to parish churches. By the eighteenth century, it was a staple in newspapers, the editors asking their readers for contributions on behalf of victims of fire.

Pownall's appeal estimated the losses and begged that ministers read his brief aloud to their congregations. With this in mind, he began, "[I]t having pleased Almighty God to permit a fire to break out." He was careful not to cast blame for the fire on any one person—a different tack from the Mathers' in 1711. The royal governors of New Hampshire and Maryland publicly repeated Pownall's call for charitable aid. Both Benning Wentworth of New Hampshire and Horatio Sharpe of Maryland were not only acquainted personally with Pownall, they knew as he did how important local support was even for a royal appointee.[46]

John Draper, the editor and publisher (and printer—for these newspapermen were jacks-of-all-trades) of the *News-Letter* was a strong supporter of the royal government and was repaid by the administration with a contract to print all its official documents and with a subvention to underwrite his newspaper. Hence, he published "by authority" and he knew how to polish the apples of the governor's vanity. Draper's press not only printed Pownall's brief, the *News-Letter* commended Pownall for sending out the briefs. Draper further cautioned that "as there was a report spread, that the late fire was owing to carelessness, we do from good authority assert that the report was false . . . by what accident the fire happened is uncertain . . . but not by anyone's neglect." And certainly not by any culpability on Pownall's part. Draper also made clear that he subscribed to the selectmen's view of the real danger of fires. The paper reminded all who had furniture or goods given them for safekeeping to return these to Faneuil Hall, so that they could be returned to their owners.[47]

POWNALL HAD ASKED that all contributions go to the Boston town Overseers of the Poor. To that body also would go the pleas for relief by the victims of the fire. Their plight was heartrending. He knew that Boston's economy was already depressed by six years of war, but they knew the effects of the fire more intimately. They wanted to know who really was to blame.

"Sons of Liberty"

Historians agree that great events have momentous effects. They cause major shifts in attitude and behavior. The Great Fire of Boston belongs in this category. It contributed to the anti-parliamentary protest in Boston, the birthplace of the American Revolution. Boston firefighters would become "sons of liberty," led by fire wardens better known to us as revolutionary politicians. But the path from the fire to the uprising was full of unexpected and unplanned twists and turns, hiding the nature and extent of the causal connections.

The day after the fire, as the people of Boston picked over the wreckage, no one promised a bigger and better city would rise from the ashes. Certainly no one foresaw a republican "new world order" in the debris. The world was a place of toil and trouble, and the fire a just punishment for sin. A chastened Boston would rebuild; it had done so before. Indeed, one of the foremost conservative politicians even saw the irony in the ruin. Lieutenant Governor Thomas Hutchinson, a merchant whose three-story mansion was spared by the flames, dryly commented that the real estate value of the land exceeded the value of the lost buildings on it.[48]

PETITIONS FOR RELIEF

The Great Fire of 1760 struck the city's poor as the closing act in a drama of declining expectations lasting over a decade. For the city's

43

rich, the fire was the opportunity of a lifetime to make a killing in real estate. For imperial authorities an ocean away, the petition for relief from the disaster offered a chance to prove the new sovereign, George III, loved his colonists. For the popular party in the city, the fire opened a door for agitation and ultimately independence.

The fire added to the economic crisis the city faced. Though the density of population in the rental wards had increased, the overall population of the city had declined to 15,000, some 5,000 below its peak in 1750. Young men departed to fight in Canada during the French and Indian War and died there. Much of the taxable wealth of the city went to pay for their arms, food, and transportation. Competition from New York City and Philadelphia, whose growth had gone unimpeded in the war years, reduced the value of Boston's overseas trading. The decline in consumption and production of durable goods hurt the craftsmen and shopkeepers, their clerks and apprentices, and the merchants who imported commodities from abroad. The "rateables"—those who could vote because they held taxable property—declined to a little over one-tenth of the total population, though a man needed only £3 to his name to be registered on the polling lists. Job opportunities in the city evaporated. The result was an increase in the number of workers who were without property themselves and increasingly, without prospects.[49]

When peace came, Boston's economy did not rebound. Instead, serious droughts reduced the yield on surrounding farms, cutting into exports. The departure of the British sailors and soldiers to other parts of the empire cost the city the pounds, shillings, and pence they paid for goods and services. The poor relief rolls shot up as the number of people who could not support themselves jumped 300 percent. The bottom half of the city's population now held less than 10 percent of its property.[50]

The petitions of the fire's victims to the Overseers of the Poor told a graphic story of declining prospects. Not only were the majority of those burned out (214 of 365) reduced to sheer want by the blaze, the petitions reveal the poverty of their lives before the fire. These men and women lost, on average, less than £20 in colony money, showing that they had accumulated little in the way of personal goods. A handful of the claimants did not plead poverty, and the details of their losses demonstrate the growing chasm between rich and poor. Fifty-two individuals reported that they had lost over £300 worth of property.[51]

The record of claims for assistance survives in the town records. It gives the catastrophe a human face. Old and young, poor and rich pled their cases to the Overseers. Aged women who had invested their life savings in rental properties, such as the widow Sarah Ayers, lost their means of self-support. Rebecca Amory's burned house and shop was rented out to a Mr. Graham for £2 4s. per year. The rent was her piteous annuity. Such insurance against misfortune turned out to be no assurance at all. Martha Bentley's Blue Anchor Inn was gone. Women in Massachusetts were restricted in the occupations they could pursue and the property they could hold in their own name. Their legal identity merged with their husbands', and he controlled the family wealth. But owning and running an inn or tavern was a common exception to the rule. Bentley had found a little niche in the law in which a woman could be a proprietor of a business and the master of her own fate—until the fire intervened.[52]

Other elderly petitioners such as Francis Ackley could not read and write (he signed with "his mark"), nor did they own real estate. He worked as a carriage maker and had lost his tools—the only means of his support. Mary Appelton made "her mark" under the list of personal items she had lost—including clothing for her three children, one iron pot, four chairs, a teapot, a looking glass, and "2 brass candlesticks." It was a lifetime's accumulation of treasured small things of little market value, but essential to daily existence. The lot of them was valued at £28. Mary Barnes had even less to her name— four children's shirts, a pair of sheets, two shifts of her own, and a feather pillow. All told, a life worth only £3. Mary Hawk, a widow, and her daughter, Mary Bardin, "with four small children saved nothing but what was on their backs." What they lost to the flames was valued at £17.

On the other end of the economic scale, the merchant John Allen claimed the loss of "one large warehouse at Oliver's dock newly repaired with a new shed" worth £400. The warehouse was filled with furniture, foodstuffs, and kitchenware, along with "2 guns and accoutrements" and "2 swords." His three tenement houses were lost as well, costing him £240. Opportunistic landlords like Josiah Keen wanted recompense for their property and income, in his case on "a dwelling house containing two tenements lately improved." James Beighton's house was filled with consumer durables of great value and barrels of cider, salt, molasses, and corn, as well as top-quality cane chairs and "one wig almost new." Only gentlemen wore wigs. With the land and the house, it came to £510. James Boies lost "a number of bonds, notes, land receipts, deeds, accounts, and a sett of books of a number of tears trading with other papers," of incalculable value. The Overseers, men of affairs themselves, understood and allowed him £949. For his three horses and their tack, as well as other personal possessions, he was credited with £555. Of course this was all in "old tenor"—the paper money of the colony. In pounds sterling, his loss was much lower. But sterling was hard to find in Boston, and Boies knew that whatever he got from the Overseers was pale compensation for what he had lost.

Petitioners tried to express that loss in descriptive as well as numerical terms. They had lost "2 very good bedsteads"; "2 good hoop petticoats"; and "2 chairs very good." Very good was hard to put in pounds, shillings, and pence, but the victims wanted the Overseers to know how loved the lost articles were. Tools lost might seem interchangeable—for example, a ship joiner's chisels and gouges—but to a craftsman their feel (no mass-produced tools here) was irreplaceable. One gunsmith had lost "22 firearms, 50 swords, 18 bayonets," and his tools. His stock was swollen by the demands of the upcoming campaign in Canada, but now he had nothing to sell. A carpenter's 1,000 feet of boards for fences and 22 cedar posts were valued together at less than £3, but for putting up the fences the two men would have made a month's wages. And who could replace the 62 boxes of lemons "at 54/box" that Michael Cassell had lost?

As one reads through this affecting listing of valuables, one sees how flammable the whole city was. The Calef brothers' "233 sides leather" might have survived the flames, but their sheep wool, deer hides, and cedar wood burned completely. Pompey Blackmon, a free

African-American, lost a feather bed, fifty pounds of pork, his jackets, trousers, and a large Bible to the flames. Other victims' wig boxes, spinning wheels and flax cards, gallons of oil and barrels of beer, stockings, handkerchiefs, and silk ribbons could not have lasted a minute in the inferno.

It would have taken even less time for Sarah and John Cotton's feather bed and damask tablecloth to be reduced to ashes, even though they lived in a brick house. (The house was also a total loss.) So was a "brick house in King street belonging to the heirs of captain Jonathan Phillips." The sum total of a life at sea had gone up in smoke. His heirs, minors, no longer had the advantages he had hoped to confer on them. Thomas Marshall thought that building in brick and roofing with slate would save his dwelling, but he was wrong. He had lost the building and the rents from it.

Jonathan Mason, one of the richest men in the city, had lost more, to be sure, starting with "my house and my store in Cornhill" valued at £1,100. The glassware alone was worth, he claimed, an additional £144. But his losses paled beside Sarah McNeal's, whose millinery shop held over £18,000 worth of fine lace, linen, damask, velvet, silks, finished clothing, and all "sorts of metal, glass, silk, and hair buttons." Fire had melted "three thousand [Spanish] dollars." Everything in the shop was ripe for the flames. She had gone from prosperity to ruin in a single night.

No one in Boston expected to be fully recompensed for loses. Nevertheless, the assembly pledged £3,000 and collections in the churches of the colony added a little over £5,200. Merchants in London donated £3,900. Philadelphia contributed £1,212, Maryland £1,120, and New York another £1,333. Andrew Oliver, perhaps the foremost merchant in the city after John Hancock and a big loser in the fire, reported for the town selectmen that a total of £17,756 colony money had been collected for relief. Because the loss in personal goods as allowed by the Overseers (not claimed by the dispossessed) came to £28,008, and the loss in real estate (according to the tax assessors) was £43,103 colony money, the funds for relief were deemed to "verily fall short" of the need. John Tomlinson and William Bollan, London merchants who represented the colony's interests in Parliament, were to present the petition to the House of Commons, but nothing came of it.[53]

The colonists were thrown back upon their own depleted resources. Had England's king George III, preoccupied with "reform" of his own government and affairs in Europe, taken notice, the entire course of American history would have been different. Boston might not have become the cockpit of resistance to Parliament and the Crown in the coming days.

THE POLITICS OF RECOVERY

In a step toward recovery that presaged the revolutionary committees of the next decade, on April 1, 1760, the colonial assembly created a committee composed of the colonial council (the upper house of the legislature) and the town selectmen. The composition of the committee perfectly illustrates the way that the pre-revolutionary colony saw authority. Patronage, deference, and connections dictated who would serve, and all these sources of power ran from the top down. The council members on the committee were friends of Governor Pownall.

The council, according to the charter that William and Mary granted the colony in 1692, was handpicked by the Crown. On it were men of property and standing loyal to the royal interest. Councillors Thomas Hutchinson and Andrew Oliver were wealthy merchants, allied by marriage and tied to the home country by bonds of political and economic allegiance. Hutchinson's "junto" dominated the membership of the council. For his loyalty, Hutchinson was very soon to become lieutenant governor of the colony when Pownall departed at the end of the month. Andrew Oliver was named secretary of the colony at the same time. Another relative, Peter Oliver, Jr., became chief justice of the superior court of judicature. All but three of the committeemen were justices of the peace as well—following the common pattern of local offices going to prominent men.[54]

The new fire relief and reform committee, so typical of the way things were done in the old political world of deference to one's betters, would be the last gasp of the old system, though no one knew it at the time. The fire of popular politics was already burning through the structure of the old system, hidden in the walls and ceilings of local government. In the meantime, the committee acted like a miniature oligarchy, telling householders and businessmen what they could and could not do.

Often, the committee's decisions made perfect sense. It told Benjamin Howell that he could rebuild his home if he used stone or brick for the walls and tile or slate for the roof. Sampson Salter asked if he could rebuild his brew house where its predecessor had stood, in Liberty Lane. Petition granted, so long as the new structure was brick and its windows, doors, and doorposts were framed by tile or slate. He had claimed a loss of over £1,333 in the fire. William Hall and John Wheelwright gained permission to rebuild in stone and tile, but Joseph Calef's pleas that he be allowed to put up a temporary wooden shed "for a few months" to shelter his "stock of hides, leather, etc." was denied. Timothy Lindall was not permitted to use wood even in the facade of his planned warehouse.[55]

The committee also decided which of the streets affected by the fire were to be widened to create firebreaks and allow firefighters and fleeing residents to pass one another. When Mackerel Lane was chosen for renovation, landowners on it had to be convinced to surrender part of their frontage to the city. To widen Pudding Lane (where the fire began) to twenty-five feet, householders had to make similar concessions. Improvement projects proved troublesome when owners objected. Francis Borland objected that a plan to straighten Leverett's Lane, the most crooked in the city, would bring it "nine feet" onto his private property. Men like Borland pleaded with the committee that its proposal to lay out new streets through old lots "will be very expensive to the town as well as very detrimental to the proprietors."[56]

The March 29, 1760, act of the general court that provided for widening the streets explicitly conferred on the committee the power to take land for new streets by eminent domain. No one was to interfere with the laying out of new streets, and housing built in violation of the brick and tile code would be pulled down as a public

49

nuisance. The stern provisions were a sure sign that objections to reform of the street plan were already mounting. Everyone understood
that legislative attempts to make the city safer after the fires of 1676
and 1711 had been disregarded. But without saying so, Borland's petition argued that private property must still be respected; that government, even when its objective might be the public good, had to
take the property holder's rights into account.[57]

To be sure, Boston needed a comprehensive plan for revamping
the streets, but the committee had neither the expertise nor the will
to plan a new and better city. For example, no one on the subcommittee charged with widening the streets could figure out how to
straighten Leverett's Lane. When various subcommittees commis-
sioned surveys of the street plan in the rest of the burned district,
they were dismayed to find that Leverett's Lane was the least of their
problems. Water Street, for example, varied in width and curved, irregularly, suddenly "contracting" from thirty to seventeen feet wide.
Milk Street, where the treasurer of the colony lived, was twenty-
eight feet wide at its top, narrowed a block away to twenty-two feet,
immediately widened to twenty-seven feet where "young Mr. Oliver"
had his house, then became eighteen feet wide, and so "runs of different widths" to its end. To widen thoroughfares like Leverett or
Milk to a uniform forty feet would require that some houses not destroyed by fire would have to be pulled down. The late Elisha
Cooke's stately house would have to go, and so it did. At least he
could not protest to the committee. Volunteers were solicited to fill
in the resulting hole in the ground and even the cobblestones in the
street. Building owners would have to pay to move the sewer.[58]

The government's action in regard to the fire made clear that the
elite assumed they would determine who could rebuild and where—
continuing the deference politics that had marked the colony from
its inception. People were expected to know who were their betters,
to elect them to office, and to defer to their judgment. But increasingly upset at the ineptitude and irritated by the arbitrariness of the
fire committee, the leaders of the town meeting began to break away
from the pattern of deference. They wanted to manage their own affairs. If it was not a truly democratic body in the modern sense, its

"mobbish spirit" "rankled" Hutchinson and his friends, and they tried, in vain, to get the colonial government to abolish the town meeting and run the city through a closed corporation, much like New York City. (The members of a closed corporation chose their own successors.) The result was a hotly contested town election on May 13, 1760. Neither the elite nor the upstarts came away with a clear victory, but the vitriolic sloganeering surrounding the election made clear that the smoldering ruins of the fire were hot spots of political dissent.[59]

The town meeting took a different approach to fire prevention from the fire committee. The town leaders finally decided to build a safer city. Three days after the fire, on the 23rd, the selectmen ordered the repair of Faneuil Hall, a long-standing project. It was built of brick in 1742, but now the "roof was to be slated, the window frames of stone and the ornaments with as little wooden work as possible." Though the building itself was brick, the fire of 1760 had proved that flames would use the slightest crack in a building's defenses to enter. (In fact, the next year a fire gutted the interior of Faneuil Hall.) Although the selectmen concluded that private citizens would make little use of buckets and ladders, the town would provide "sixty good ladders, to be distributed and deposited at convenient places in the town," and the fire companies were to have three more ladders each for their own use. The town also agreed to contract with a well digger to bore more well holes, so that "in case of fire in that part of the town there may be a constant reservoir of water for the supply of engines." In short, the town leaders were beginning to think in terms of collective public duties rather than private interests. Such an approach had within it the seeds of republicanism—private sacrifice for the public good.[60]

In this spirit, the selectmen expanded the number of fire wards and fire wardens to sixteen, and in the coming years would name to the list such leading merchants as John Rowe and John Hancock as well as veteran city officials, such as clerk William Cooper and tax collector Samuel Adams. Included also were "artisans and shopkeepers"—Stephen Cleverly, a brazier, and Thomas Crafts, a painter. Although most of the wardens were men of property and standing, a small number were not on the tax lists at all. By expanding the number of wards and wardens and opening up the office to men from the artisan class, the town meeting was opening up its self-government to a broader (and as time would prove) more independent-minded class of people. And in a very few years, men such as Sam Adams, Hancock, Cooper, Cleverly, and Crafts would use the office to mobilize the firemen for a different kind of blaze.[61]

SMUGGLERS, OFFICIALS, AND FIRE WARDENS

The beginning of the revolutionary campaign lay in the ashes of the Great Fire. Rowe, one of the richest merchants in the city, had on March 24, 1760, written to a friend, "Such devastation in so short a time was hardly ever known. I am a sufferer among the rest." To men like these could be trusted the task of safekeeping of others' valuables left on the streets (the most important duty of fire wards), as well as organizing the fighting of fires. But Rowe did not ask the Overseers for relief, even though he had extensive goods stored in a wharf and in warehouses on the affected docks. Instead, after the fire, Rowe immediately wrote to Peter Hubbert that the fire had not "made me uneasy," a curious response from someone who had just recorded how terrifying the fire was.[62]

Rowe was noted for his even disposition, but personality does not explain his words. Another facet of his life does—that Rowe was a notorious smuggler, bringing in goods from Holland and elsewhere in violation of the Navigation Acts. These were a collection of parliamentary injunctions against trading with nations outside the bounds of the British Empire—particularly with the Dutch and French. If New England wholesalers wanted to sell Dutch and French goods, they had to import them from England—paying English merchants a middleman's cut. Rowe did not ask for relief because he had lost smuggled goods and could not declare them in his petition. Cooper and Hancock, both future patriots in the cause of colonial liberty, were also noteworthy smugglers.[63]

At another twist in the road from the fire to the revolution, one finds a group of lawbreakers arguing the case for American rights. Smugglers like Rowe and Hancock more than anyone else in the colony felt the burdens of parliamentary legislation. One of the most important pieces of criminal law (as far as the imperial government and its handpicked colonial governors were concerned) was enforcement of the Navigation Acts. How to catch the smugglers was the problem.

Smuggling was second nature to many in the English seaports, and against these offenders the Crown employed "writs of assistance." They were search warrants that allowed customs officials to enter the homes and businesses of suspected smugglers. In Massachusetts, the surveyor of customs, who was the supervisor of customs duty collection and chief colonial administrator of the customs service, had a team of searchers to seek out illegal imports, using the writs of assistance. Customs officials had to ask for them from the superior court of judicature—a guarantee that the suspect would have advance knowledge of the officials' planned search.[64]

Once again the fire entered the political controversy. In early March 1760, George Craddock, acting collector at Boston, obtained warrants to search for contraband (smuggled goods from England's wartime enemies). Little tumult followed. Less than a year later, Thomas Lechmere, surveyor of the customs, and Charles Paxton, crier of the superior court and customs searcher for Boston, went back for more warrants. Merchants, among them Hancock and Rowe, replied with a petition to the court arguing that the writs were illegal. No one had objected to Craddock's request; now there was a storm of protest.

What had intervened to change the landscape? The merchants with fire losses (in particular those whose warehouses lay at the foot of Water Street but did not submit a detailed inventory asking for relief) had no doubt hired men to remove the illicit stash from the path of the fire. Lechmere and his searchers, such as Paxton, could see with their own eyes that night, or hear from others who saw, what everyone else had long suspected—some merchants had on hand stocks of goods illegally imported. That is why the Crown's officers asked for new warrants after the fire. From their perspective, the merchants were well aware of the danger this posed to their finances, already imperiled by the war shortages and the depression at home, and they countered by petitioning the court not to grant the new round of warrants. In the economic doldrums of the day, the merchants had no place and no way to dump these goods quickly. There is no direct evidence to support this surmise—no smoking gun. But the smugglers delayed the granting of the writs and then interfered with their execution long enough to unload their smuggled goods.[65]

FIRES OF PROTEST

The niggardly provisions for the poor, the foot-dragging and patronizing charity of the elites, and the indifference of Parliament to the needs of the colony, magnified and focused by the prosecution of the smugglers' cases, linked the fire to the rise of popular opposition to Parliament. The fire demonstrated that when it counted, when the people needed the helping hand of the elites and the British government, those in power had no interest in helping the sufferers. The reverse was true: Their power and wealth came at the expense of the people.

The Reverend Jonathan Mayhew was the first to see in the fire's ruinous course something more than an angry God and a need for more fire engines. Born of a poor missionary family on Martha's Vineyard, deeply moved by the egalitarian implication of the evangelical preaching during the Great Awakening of the 1740s, Mayhew was a modern among the ministers, combining elements of the fervor of the Great Awakening with a modest and liberal view of who might be saved. To this he added a mercurial character and a gift for language that made his sermons and his ministry a lightning rod for controversy. He would soon become the Boston end of a transatlantic correspondence with England's radical political thinkers on what was wrong with the empire.[66]

He preached on the subject of the fire the very next Sunday, as had Cotton and Increase Mather after the Great Fire of 1711, but his sermon was as different as it could be from theirs within the larger common framework of puritan theology. Like Cotton Mather he saw the fire as "a visitation of providence which demands a serious and religious consideration," but unlike the Mathers, who railed against the lower orders who did not know their place, Mayhew thought the fire's lesson was for the "rich and poor together." God might be the "author of the calamity," but God could not do evil. Instead, he read from William Smollett's account of the Great Fire of London and then gave a summary of the Boston fire of 1711. The lesson of history was that fire was a great leveler. It took from the rich their possessions and taught them to share with the poor. Fire was a "public calamity," for all of the city was "one body." Those who were "greedy of gain" should take special heed, for in the wake of the inferno, "we are hereby more particularly reminded of the vanity of worldly riches."[67]

Mayhew's message was political. But the elite moneyed classes who licked their lips waiting to gain from real estate manipulation were not his only target. The burdens that Parliament and Crown had laid upon Boston were breaking its back. "The load of debt and public taxes" that Boston and the entire colony had to bear to support the war in Canada not only impaired relief to the fire victims, it hinted at a far worse fate for the colony. For the "selfish pride and addiction to luxury" that he decried were sins that Hutchinson and his gang of Bostonians shared with their royal friends. Across the ocean, imperial rulers and their minions wallowed in the luxury that Massachusetts's labors had produced. Mayhew's thesis about the danger that corruption posed to liberty echoed that of radical "Commonwealthmen," a band of English writers and thinkers that went back to the first years of the century. In anonymous pamphlets, poems, literary magazines, histories, and sermons, these self-appointed monitors of English liberty had blasted the ministers of the Crown and their cronies. Mayhew was well acquainted with this literature because he received it in the mail.[68]

There was more news coming from the imperial rulers, and it was much disliked in Boston. In 1763, the peace treaty that ended the

French and Indian War brought celebration throughout the British colonies, but young king George III and his new first minister, George Grenville, determined that the colonies should help the home country out of its financial difficulties. The war had nearly bankrupted Britain, and Grenville sought ways to refill the treasury. A lawyer and longtime imperial bureaucrat, pompous and long-winded but incorruptible and persistent, his program gave the popular party a target.[69]

Grenville's Sugar Act of 1764 raised customs duties and sent the imperial navy to colonial waters to interdict smugglers. His Stamp Act, passed in Parliament on March 22, 1765, required that every legal document, newspaper, and license be printed on pre-stamped (embossed) paper. The act was to go into effect on November 1, 1765, but led by such popular politicians as Samuel Adams, the protest against the stamp tax prevented its implementation and brought the firefighters into the center of the political agitation.

Adams was the son of a brewer and had attended Harvard, but classical education did not enhance his business skills and he squandered his inheritance. From 1756 to 1764, he was a tax collector, a close friend of many of the lesser merchants in the town of Boston, a major figure in the Boston town meeting, and a minor player in colonial politics. Only as an agitator did he stand out. Contemporaries described him as austere, rigid, and opinionated, though flexible and prudent when he had to be. He was a master of press releases and public meetings, but he was not above promoting violence. And who better to set fires than firefighters?[70]

SONS OF LIBERTY

Andrew Oliver, named Boston's stamp distributor (he got the job because he was Thomas Hutchinson's brother-in-law), had miraculously escaped loss in the 1760 fire. To convince him to surrender his new post, the Loyal Nine—Samuel Adams and his fellow anti-imperial agitators—turned to Ebenezer Macintosh, the leader of the South End gang and a member of engine No. 9. On the morning of August

14, 1765, Macintosh's crew hanged Oliver in effigy. That evening, Macintosh's men carried the effigy past the government house, inside which Governor Bernard, Lieutenant Governor Hutchinson, and the colonial council cowered, to Oliver's dock in Boston harbor. The mob then tore down a building that Oliver intended to use as a stamp distribution center, marched to Oliver's house and demolished it, then finished their labors by dismantling Hutchinson's mansion. The skills they exhibited were those of able firefighters, who had to pull down buildings quickly to prevent the spread of fires. In one more twist of the fire story, they did to Oliver's and Hutchinson's homes what the Great Fire of 1760 had left undone. Hutchinson fled one step ahead of the mob, and the next day, Oliver quit. That night a triumphant assemblage of firefighters lit a bonfire on Fort Hill. Macintosh was not the only firefighter setting fires that day in Boston. Shubael Hewes was there too, and so, likely, were the other members of engine No. 9. Macintosh may have used the fireman's speaking tube, a kind of "trumpet" to order his men to their places. He had it in hand when the patriots paraded in November.[71]

Mayhew had watched with consternation as the mob pulled down Hutchinson's house and surged through the streets, but he understood the city's fury. He believed that the Stamp Act would enslave Americans, taking away the rights they had as Englishmen and the property they had earned by their own labor. When the act was repealed, he preached a sermon that spoke for all the protesters: "We have seen wide devastations, made by fire" but "never have we known a season of such universal consternation and anxiety among all ranks and ages" as during the Stamp Act. Fire, the real menace of 1760, had become a metaphor for the far more perilous menace of parliamentary exactions and the venality of the corruption of stamp tax collectors.[72]

In the protests, some resistance leaders—including firefighters and fire wardens—inverted the customary function and nomenclature of firefighting to show how seriously they opposed the stamps. Mayhew appropriately called them "incendiaries." The connection between the firemen and the protest against the stamps extended beyond Boston. The stamp resisters in Charlestown, South Carolina, formed a "Fire Company" not to put out blazes, but to burn ships that carried the hated stamps. The Boston "Anti-Stamp Fire Society," re-created in August 1765 (it had been a conventional mutual assistance society), had a similar purpose.

Protesters used real fire to summon their cohorts and cow their enemies. In the New York City riot of November 1, 1765, fire played an essential role. Learning that the hated stamps had arrived at Fort George, protest marchers first lit candles by the hundreds, then, bearing a sea of lights aloft, flowed down Broadway. Another throng, composed mainly of seamen and young men, set off for Bowling Green at the tip of Manhattan island, and there set a bonfire. To the sound of the city's church bells and in the grotesque shadows of the fire, the mob destroyed the property of supporters of the Crown, firebrands with fire brands in their hands.[73]

Although there was little overlap between the 298 men who sought relief from the Overseers of the Poor in 1760 and the 353 "Sons of Liberty" who gathered on August 14, 1769, at the Liberty Tree in Dorchester, outside of Boston, to toast the departure of hated governor Francis Bernard, those who did appear on both lists tell an important story. James Dalton, Thomas Marshall, Jonathan Mason, William Palfrey, Isaac Pierce, David Spear, and Thomas Walley, who made both lists, were substantial real estate owners in 1760, and though William Molyneaux, William Spooner, James Thompson, and Joseph Webb lost no real estate, they claimed £94, £240, £84, and £64 losses in personal property, respectively. It was the householder, the merchant, the professional, the artisan and craftsman, the man with some stake in society who lost out in the fire, who would become a fireman, a fire warden, a Son of Liberty, and a patriot.[74]

Comparing the 61 names of the firefighters in a list of men added to the fire companies from 1764 through 1768 with the attendees at the 1769 Dorchester meeting of the Sons of Liberty reveals that only two, Stephen Greenleaf and John Bryant, can be certainly identified as Sons of Liberty. (To be sure, not every one of Mayhew's "incendiaries" was present at Dorchester that day—Macintosh, for example, was absent.) But firefighters certainly attended the parades celebrating the end of the Stamp Act. Under their watchful eyes, the Sons of

Liberty set up on the Boston commons a four-story pyramid with 280 lamps, surmounted by a fireworks display. The whole structure accidentally caught fire, but the fire did not spread because the fire companies, at the scene to celebrate the repeal, put the fire out. City leaders were aware that the pyrophilic tendencies of the fire companies had to be curbed once the protests were ended. In Boston, the selectmen told the fire wardens and the engine companies to curb all fireworks displays save those the town put on, and to patrol the powder houses and armories on the day that the repeal of the Stamp Act was celebrated.[75]

In the meantime, men like Adams and Hancock were transforming the Boston fire warden's post into a partisan political office, with fire wardens actively organizing the protests. Benjamin Carp, a young historian who has studied these documents, reports that "[a]lmost three-quarters of the forty fire wards who served from 1764 to 1775 were Sons of Liberty . . . along with as many as twenty-nine" members of fire companies. Among the former were Henderson Inches, Samuel Adams, and John Hancock. The fire wardens were the ones who rang the fire bells to summon the people to the scene of what became the Boston Massacre, in March 1770. Fire wardens led in the Boston Tea Party at the end of 1773, "in which at least nine" firemen threw tea into Boston harbor. The committees of correspondence that Samuel Adams formed in 1772 to spread the word of Boston's continuing resistance to Parliament included fire wardens such as William Greenleaf. Others were "members of the fire companies of several wards."[76]

Seen in this light, serving as a fire warden—with its intimate contact with firemen like Macintosh—was a way that partisan leaders who wanted to continue the protests after the repeal could recruit muscular, bold supporters when needed. It was this capacity, built into the role of fire warden, that enabled men like Adams to keep the pot of ferment roiling. The tie was strong in the formation of the town's committee of correspondence, in 1772, and the next year, to oppose the Tea Act, fire wardens like Adams and Hancock had only to reach out to the firemen to transform dockworkers and artisans into Mohawk Indians and lead them to dump the tea into the harbor.[77]

The South Meeting House, spared by the flames in 1760, hosted over 7,000 angry Bostonians on December 16, 1773. They had come to protest the hated Tea Act and to demand that the tea still stored in chests aboard ships berthed at the docks, at the end of Milk Street, be returned to the East India Company's warehouses in England. No help came from Governor Thomas Hutchinson (one of the merchants who had commissions to sell the tea), and at the end of the town meeting, the Sons of Liberty in the back of the church sent up a whoop. Attired in vaguely Indian-like disguises, they rushed down the street to Griffin's Wharf, then onto the ships. Followed by hundreds of their townsmen, they dumped the tea into the harbor. Britain's response was a series of harshly punitive acts, alternatively called the Coercive Acts and the Intolerable Acts by Samuel Adams and John Hancock. It was in response to these that the first Continental Congress gathered. The fiery course of the revolution had thus passed down the same streets as the Great Fire, stoked by Adams, Hancock, and the other fire wardens. No doubt many firefighters from Boston's ten companies were wearing the raiment of Indians that night in December.[78]

Distracted by its political fires, Boston took no decisive steps to make itself fireproof. Indeed, after 1760 the fires kept coming. Any one of them might have grown into a conflagration like that of 1760. That they did not was surely fortunate for the city. Rowe's diary is filled with near misses. On January 18, 1765, for example, "the outhouse of Mr. McNeal the baker" caught fire. It took the companies "about an hour and a half" to "reduce" the blaze. Rowe, eventempered as always, wryly added, "[G]ot myself very wet." The colder the weather, the greater the fire risk, and on the evening of February 2, 1765, with the harbor frozen solid, Rowe rushed to a "fire which proceeded to be the chimney of the Great House at the head of Long Lane . . . The two south end engines were there. Twas a terrible foul chimney." Chimneys were always fouling, particularly during heavy use periods. The ordinances requiring periodic chimney cleaning by the chimney sweeps were commonly ignored—as was just about every other fire prevention regulation.

The fires continued because the city's leaders refused to separate fire-prone business and manufacturing sites from residential ones. On October 16, 1766, Rowe and his wife moved into a new brick mansion on what is now Bedford Street. Barely two months later, "a fire broke out about four o'clock this morning in our lane and burnt Mr. Snow's potash house with the buildings adjoining." Potash is a potassium salt produced by reheating in water and then baking tree ash, and it is used in the making of soap and as a fertilizer. It requires the combination of the refined ashes and rendered animal fat. Both the salts and the fats are highly flammable. So long as residences and potash works were neighbors, no one's house was safe. In January 1766, there was a store fire, followed the next week by more buildings ablaze. On February 3, 1767, one of the city's major bakeshops caught fire. The resulting conflagration consumed twenty-five houses. Had the wind risen, who knows what would have happened? The next month, a warehouse filled with sugar burned to the ground, taking with it a block of buildings.[79]

BECAUSE BOSTON REMAINED FIRE PRONE, the influence of the 1760 blaze on later events faded from public memory. On a blustery Sunday morning not long ago, as I was walking up Washington Street, I saw approaching from the opposite direction a young man in buff knee britches, matching waistcoat, and three corner hat. Obviously an eighteenth-century Boston gentleman in a time warp! We exchanged greetings, business cards, and conversation. It turned out that Gary Gregory had just started a business as a reenactor and tour guide on the Freedom Trail. As we chatted, I concluded that he knew a great deal about the events leading up to the revolution, but oddly and sadly, standing in the very spot where the Great Fire of 1760 began, he admitted that he did not know that there had been a fire in 1760. The Freedom Trail is filled with monuments, plaques, museums, and bookstores catering to the history buff, but like that able young man, the guides, clerks, and even the park rangers had not heard of the fire that started it all.[80]

PITTSBURGH, 1845

The people of Boston feared fire. The founders of Pittsburgh welcomed it. Fire and smoke framed their new city in a grimy halo of industriousness. Across the Monongahela from the city, like Vulcan's forge, Coal Hill burned. For miles around it was "visible by the smoke." The mine beneath the massif had caught fire, "by what means is unknown to any of the present race." But so long as the coal vein fed the ovens and forges of Pittsburgh, no one wrung their hands about the inferno. In 1845, those fires escaped their confines and wrought havoc.[1]

At the end of the American Revolution, the British withdrew their forces from the Ohio Valley. Bostonians cast covetous eyes on the rich lands beyond the Appalachians and sent streams of its young people to settle the West. A former British outpost called Fort Pitt at the confluence of the Monongahela and the Allegheny Rivers, where the Ohio River rose, became the jumping-off place for the wagon trains and the flatboats. By 1845, unmatched if not unrivaled, Pittsburgh was bigger and more wealthy than Boston was in 1760.

How much the scene had changed in a half century! In 1802, a new century for a new nation, visitors to the little town at the forks of the Ohio reveled in its natural charm. French traveler François André Michaux commended "the most pleasing view, produced by the perspective of the river, overshadowed with forests, and especially the Ohio, which flows in a straight line, and, to appearance, loses itself in space."[2]

The swift pace of change as Americans went west was already changing the village into a bustling town. Pittsburgh had become "the key to the western country." One local poet celebrated it as "the western workshop, where useful arts convoke / here chiming hammer and loud puffing steam / the rattling dray and the thundering team . . . are seen and heard throughout the busy place." Though the year-round residents numbered only 2,000 in 1800, ten times as many laid over in the city each year on their way west, and by 1810 nearly 5,000 had decided to stay. By the next decade, population had doubled, and it continued to rise, reaching the mid-20,000 range by 1845.[3]

Beyond "the Point," where the Monongahela and the Allegheny became the Ohio River, migrants could imagine the rich soils of the Ohio Valley. But would-be pioneers needed what the merchants of Pittsburgh sold and its craftsmen made. Into Pittsburgh from Philadelphia on 3,500-pound Conestoga wagons rode the supplies for the migrants. Surrounding farms also offered up their "wheat, flour, corn, beef, apples, and salt" for merchants' storehouses. In the city itself, glassworks and forges produced bottles for the sugar planters of Louisiana, salted pork and butter for the fur traders of the upper Midwest, and packaged coffee, spices, and linens for the westering homesteaders.[4]

The flatboats and barges themselves, framed with western Pennsylvania pine and hardwood, could travel the Ohio to the Mississippi River's terminus at New Orleans in a little over a month. Steamboats would soon make the trip in less than a week, and when steamboats became the rage, Pittsburgh would build more of them than any other river port. Between 1811 and 1836, one historian reports, "252 steamboats were launched at Pittsburgh yards." The rivers and the sandy banks of the city were also cluttered with keelboats, Kentucky arks, ferries, skiffs, and pirogues (giant canoes). Some were large enough to offer cabin service to travelers, whereas others were piled high with furniture and foodstuffs.[5]

Undeterred by such frontier hardships as poor roads and distant communications, merchants and brokers in the city built brick stores, banks, and warehouses with the money the emigrants left behind, bought sugar and cotton on consignment, and arranged for its shipment to the Northeast by sea. The merchants reinvested profits from brokerage commissions and sales into glassworks, iron foundries, shipyards, breweries, and rolling (iron) mills. James O'Hara, a local legend for his military career, established O'Hara Glassworks in the 1790s—the first of many glassworks that would make the city the glass-making capital of the country. An iron foundry appeared in 1804, owned and operated by Joseph McClurg, whose retail outlet was already the largest in the city. The entrepreneurial spirit, exhibiting the speculative passion of the day, was everywhere in these mercantile establishments. Pittsburgh had changed a wilderness into a mart.[6]

By the 1820s, the city had grown from a few thousand to nearly 10,000, and its face was changing apace. George W. Ogden, who toured in 1821, was greeted not by a scene of natural beauty but by "the emporium of almost the whole western world" displayed in the city's shops. "Foreign immigrants" (most of them Irish) provided cheap labor, and "ironmongery" was the rage. So eager were the high and the low born in their "inordinate attachment to money," he feared, that they had created a city of "disagreeable and unfavorable appearance." They seemed to have no inclination to invest in the infrastructure of the city. Its streets were too narrow, its riverbanks were not diked (every freshet resulted in the flooding of the city), and the "complexions of the people are affected" by the effusions of coal fires. As another traveler approaching the city from the north reported, "Pittsburgh was hidden from our view, until we descended through the hills within half a mile of the Allegheny river. Dark dense smoke was rising from many parts, and a hovering cloud of this vapour, obscuring the prospect, rendered it singularly gloomy."[7]

Coal Hill and the smokestacks of the city dictated the weather— dark and gloomy. But soft coal fueled the forges and foundries, the glassworks and the breweries. Soft coal caressed the flames that stoked the city's many small plants, and flame in turn embraced soft coal. Anne Royall, visiting in 1821, thought the sooty pall that crowned the point and pitted the complexions of its residents to be a mark of progress: "[T]he vast black coal wagons; the jolly drivers and work hands, as black as Satan himself; the amazing throng and bustle . . . the volumes of smoke, fires, and thundering steam factories . . . the blood-tinged blaze, intermingled with volumes of smoke, rushing onwards and upwards . . . a foretaste of the Birmingham of America." And of the conflagration to come.[8]

A Dreadful Scene
of Destruction

April 10, 1845, in Pittsburgh dawned chilly, dry, and windy. The winter's grime, a thick layer of coal dust, covered every surface and dirtied everyone's clothing. Washerwomen from the Irish shantytown at the center of the city were out in force, boiling water and scrubbing shirts and pants with lye soap. Underneath the women's heavy iron water pots, fires spewed out sparks. Rising in the shifting wind, they danced like fireflies. Every day, hundreds of these small fires burned in alleys and backyards. April 10 was no different—at first.

A mythology grows up around the origin of urban conflagrations like the Great Fire of Pittsburgh, part conspiracy theory, blaming the "usual suspects," part folk tale, and all of it gaining fanciful detail with each retelling. Novelist Stuart O'Nan explains, "It's rare that people witness the beginning of any fire, even in a crowded place. Accidental fires, by their very nature, are always sudden, unexpected, and catch people unawares . . . and therefore elude detection by the simple mechanism of surprise." In fact, at the time no one noticed the actual beginning of the April 10 fire that would destroy half the city. But even the most horrific of city fires have a moment of inception, and they always start small: no bigger than a man's hand, or a rag, or a carpetbag.[9]

The Great Fire of 1845 started at the back of one of the small rooming houses in the city's South Side in the late morning of April 10. Locals later chalked it up to a careless Irish washerwoman leaving untended her boiling pot of wash water. The embers blew into the open door or window of a shed used as a smokehouse, and ignited shavings there. A century later, the Historical Society of Western Pennsylvania held a contest with a reward for information on the culprit. In the March 31, 1945, issue of the *Pittsburgh Post-Gazette*, William Brophy won the award, claiming that his mother's aunt, Betsy, said her second husband's own mother, a Mrs. Brooks, was the cause. (He passed on the $50 prize.) Wilma Owens added to the story, courtesy of Mrs. Frank East's mother, passed down to Sarah Taylor, and then to Owens. The culprit was an Irish washerwoman, one Ann Brooks, who lived on Wood Street but worked for Colonel Diehl on Ferry Street.[10]

A MORBID FASCINATION WITH FIRE

Who could have foretold, that chilly and windy morning, that a shed fire would rise up into a wall of flame and roar across the southern half of the city? The answer is as stark as it is sad—everyone could see it coming. For the real cause of the catastrophe was not a careless washerwoman or an untended fire under the boiling laundry or the tinder left in a shed. It was the city itself—its morbid fascination with fire; its utter dependence on fire; its arrogant conceit that it could turn fire into an obedient servant.

For Pittsburgh was the "iron city." Iron manufacturing accounted for about one-fourth of the value of the city's industrial output. Returns on investments in iron manufacturing were the best security against "those chimeras and doubtful chances" of speculation in the early national era. By the 1840s, furnaces, mills, and forges in the city numbered over fifty. The iron maker's fire had to burn around the clock and demanded constant attention and fine judgment. And coal. Fortunately, western Pennsylvania was literally "built on coal."

Altogether, the eight foundries in the city in 1826 burned 65,000 bushels of coal each year.[11]

The forge was a miniature factory, generally a stone or brick building, stout and squat. At one end was a white-hot open oven, into which the puddler, or refiner, shoved ingots of pig iron, then, at the right moment, removed them to an anvil. He was the ruler of the mill, with the "roller" as his bailiff. A water- or steam-powered hammer, under the roller's direction, would pound the superheated metal. Over and over the process would be repeated until the impurities were removed from the ore. In 1828, according to James Hall, "the clang of hammers" could be heard in the city's streets at all hours, the sound of the forge men working at their trade. Surrounded by fire.[12]

James Davis was a puddler's boy in Pittsburgh in the middle of the nineteenth century and years later remembered "a constant din by day and night" in the mill, "patches of white heat glare from the opened furnace doors like the teeth of some great dark, dingy devil grinning across the smoky vapors of the pit. Half naked, soot-smeared fellows fight the furnace hearths with hooks, rabbles, and paddles . . . Brilliant blues and rays of green and bronze come from the coruscating metal . . . molten . . . white-hot . . . flaming balls of woolly iron . . . the molten slag runs down red-hot . . . Everywhere are hurrying men, whirring flywheels, moving levers of steam engines and . . . the fiery serpents" of iron soon to become barrel hoops and bridge supports and wagon wheels.[13]

Tanneries and shoemakers, brickyards, potteries, distilleries, and lead factories all contributed ash, flammable dust, and soot to the air, the city's roofs, the streets, and the sidewalks. Flour mills throughout the city were additional sources of fire fuel. Although flour does not burn easily, fine flour dust is highly combustible and entire flour mills and grain elevators have exploded when flour dust ignited. The cotton textile industry, dependent on 500-pound raw cotton bales carried upriver by steamboats, was going full blast by the 1830s. It required steam-driven machinery, and it contributed highly combustible cotton fiber to the atmosphere. The census of 1840 listed five cotton

mills, thirty-two tanneries, seventeen distilleries, seventeen glass factories, thirty-seven flour mills, and eighteen print shops (full of paper
and other flammables) within the city limits.[14]

Fire-breathing, fire-driven Pittsburgh's economy was worth many
millions of dollars by the fourth decade of the new century and over
$25 million by 1860. In 1842, Charles Dickens visited the city on his
tour of America and compared it to Birmingham in England—at
least "[T]hat is what people here say." What he meant was that it "has
a great quantity of smoke hanging over it."[15]

At the beginning of April 1845, with the grime of the winter's coal
and wood fires still coating the surface of buildings, Pittsburgh
looked as if the fire of the heavens had showered its waste products
on the streets. So many of the manufacturing plants in the city had
coal-burning engines, hearths, ovens, or forges that coal dust was
everywhere in the air. As visiting James Hall remarked, the coal was
"very dirty" and its burning "throws up an unusual quantity of cinders and ashes. The latter fill the atmosphere and are continually
falling in showers." The highly flammable coal dust lay on every surface, particularly on rooftops, a kind of reverse flameproofing. It was
just a matter of time until the right conditions came together for any
one of the fires that Pittsburgh stoked to escape into the world.[16]

THE WASHERWOMAN'S FIRE

In the spring of 1845, the contingencies of disaster aligned and produced a holocaust in this city of fire. The winter had been dry. It had
not rained in the city for nearly six weeks. All the reservoirs were low.
Although the city had plans for an extensive water main, pump station, and hydrant program, there were only two water mains with hydrants for the whole of the downtown First Ward—one running
down Third Street, the other on Liberty Avenue. In the hydrants,
water pressure was low. Had there been a fire, the hose-truck men
were supposed to connect a supply line from the hydrant and run it
to the pump. But after an inspection, many of the fire companies'
hoses had been condemned. On top of everything else, the wind,

hurtling out of the west, had been blowing at near gale speeds all week, and the morning of April 10 was no exception.[17]

It was not by accident that an Irish washerwoman kindled a fire that morning. The smoke-filled city was packed with poor Irish laborers and their families drawn to jobs in the mill and forge. By 1834, the new railroad from Philadelphia to Pittsburgh brought thousands of laborers, the vast majority of them Irish. Even before the potato famine set off the 1845–1846 mass migration of poor Irish to the New World, Pittsburgh had welcomed over 5,000 of these men and women. The census of 1840 reported that the iron furnaces had over 1,000 young men working at the fires; the vast majority young, lower-class, and immigrant Irish. And like the poor workers of Boston, Pittsburgh's industrial labor force crowded into rickety wooden tenements in the flatlands of the city. And like the poor women of Boston, Irish women took whatever job they could to help support their families. Tired from child care, cold and sick from damp and drafty rooms, unbalanced diets, and a long cold winter, having to deal with the female necessities in a city that did not have indoor plumbing, an Irish washerwoman might be excused if she left a pot of water boiling over an open fire.[18]

There were many such open fires all over the city that noontime. For the canal workers had arrived. They were finishing the giant ditch connecting Pittsburgh to eastern Pennsylvania. When the canal reached the city, in the spring of 1845, over 900 canal workers found temporary lodgings in a shantytown between Penn and Liberty Avenues. More fuel for fires. Any one of them could have set off a catastrophe.[19]

James Davis recalled that his mother did not want the family to move to Pittsburgh because "in those days, the air was black with soot and the crowded quarters where the workers lived offered no room for gardens" or sunlight. Like Boston, shops and plants were next door to houses. Almost all the housing stock of the poor was cheap milled frame and clapboard, the same stock as in Boston.[20]

And everything—the pace of the work, the proliferation of furnaces and fire-driven engines, the omnipresence of fuel, the gimcrack housing stock—added to the danger that an accidental fire would spread throughout the city. Not only were the poor laborers' hastily constructed frame buildings firetraps themselves, they abutted or faced brick and stone buildings on every downtown street. A contemporary sketch of Seventh Street, in 1836, showed rough plank-sided shops abutting two- and three-story brick homes. Pine-slat stables filled with hay stood next to three-story brick office buildings. The wharves on the Monongahela included framed as well as brick warehouses. The brick courthouse was surrounded by the wooden-roofed and wooden-awninged kiosks of the marketplace. The bridge across the Monongahela was wooden, and a June 1827 regulation for its use barred anyone from carrying a torchlight, candle, or lighted cigar over the span on penalty of a $5 fine. Even the brick mansions of the well-to-do, sometimes fenced and gardened off from the street, faced "low and plain" frame dwellings, inns, and manufacturing establishments.

Public buildings billed as "fireproof" were not. The stone, iron, and wood "fireproofs" of the 1840s were little more than "a woodpile enclosed in noncombustible walls." The inspiring and grand Third Presbyterian Church, erected in 1833, had brick walls, but it would burn to the ground because its cornices and window frames were wooden. The stone-faceted Bank of Pittsburgh claimed to be fireproof, but its zinc roof and framed wooden doors and windows would soon turn traitor to the trustees' fireproof promise. The new and elegant Monongahela House, a six-story brick structure, had a vulnerable zinc roof and wooden doors and window frames. It would be reduced to a mass of charred brick less than ten years after its construction.[21]

Pittsburgh could have burned to the ground on a number of occasions. One Southern visitor was astounded by the number of fire alarms, "amid a scene of confusion: another fire! Bells ringing, people hallowing, engines rattling." An entire row of brick homes was destroyed by a fire in 1809. Three years later, another fire wiped out a commercial block. Fortunately, the wind was quiet and the fire did not spread. In 1823, the buildings on the busy corner of Liberty and Market Streets took fire. The damage was reckoned at $100,000—$2.23 million in modern terms. In 1832, the Breed and Brewer Cotton Works went up in flames too fast for anyone to save it. The city fathers did not ignore the danger. In 1816, the mayor was instructed to give a bonus of $10 to the first fire engine company that arrived at any blaze. Anyone whose chimney caught fire because it had not been swept in over a month had to ante up a $3 fine. Stovepipes that stuck out into the street or "past the four corners" of a house would cost the owner $5. False fire alarms were punishable with a fine of $4, as was setting off fireworks or lighting a bonfire. But the arrival of a citywide fire was just a matter of time.[22]

Running with the Machine

A little after noon, on the 10th of April, the wooden shed in back of Ferry and Second started to smoke. The church bells rang, sounding the fire alarm, and a crowd began to gather. The bells and the cry of "Fire!" brought the first firemen to the scene. The companies ran to their firehouses to haul out their engines and ladder carts. With quick action, they hoped, the fire might be contained.[23]

Antebellum firefighting was still the task of volunteer fire companies. The volunteer fire company had evolved little since its colonial origins. Pittsburgh had ten companies by the middle of the century, constantly turning over their membership as they reorganized and recruited. Much like the revolutionary Boston fire companies, Pittsburgh's formed around the engine itself. The men purchased or built a place to store the engine and used the space for social purposes as well. The heart of the company was still the machine. The care and display of the engine became an object of obsessive pride. Some of the engines were locally made, though more were purchased elsewhere.[24]

Men of position and means joined artisans and mechanics in the earliest companies. When the Eagle Company formed, Alexander McClurg was one of its charter members. The Eagle Company's applicants for membership had to be approved by a unanimous vote of the company. Among the volunteers were a lumber merchant, a chair maker, an attorney, a dry goods retailer, and James R. Butler, a gentleman, soldier, and local notable. The Vigilant, the second company, charged its members $3 to join and required a monthly contribution

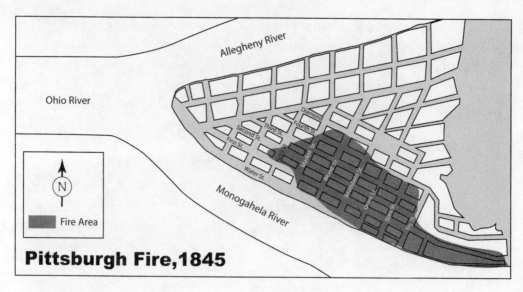

Pittsburgh Fire, 1845

of 12¢. No one in it was going to make a living "running" with the engine to fires. The Neptune Company, a rival, had eighty members, far
more than would ever attend a fire, and doubled as a drinking club
and social association. As in colonial times, officers were elected
based on status and personal reputation rather than expertise. Sons
followed fathers in the companies, as though they were secret societies. Members' duties included watching over the property that fire
victims deposited in the street.

The Niagara and the Hope Companies, organized in the 1830s,
reflected a shift in the demographics of volunteer firefighting. The
number of members was still high (the Hope may have had as many
as 240), but as the middle- and upper-class members began to find
other ways of socializing, younger, less well-to-do individuals joined
the older companies and organized new ones. These latter were not
citywide but neighborhood associations, and their pride lay more in
their masculinity than their gentility.

These companies raced one another to fires, sometimes engaging
in fistfights along the way or pumping their water on one another
rather than on the burning structure. During the early 1840s, a particularly bitter period of fire company contention, a few of the old
companies dissolved and others split into warring factions. In the

meantime, as one veteran recalled, "[I]t was just a lot of young rascals who ran with the machine, fought one another and the other companies, and squirted more water on the spectators for the fun of the thing than on the fire." As the *New York Times* reported of the volunteers who arrived after one fire was extinguished, "[T]he firemen, having nothing else to do, amused themselves with a fight . . . The scrimmage was very lively while it lasted."

Although these companies drank, fought, and played to excess, the work they did was essential and difficult. As David Dana, a Boston volunteer firefighter wrote in 1855, "[T]his large body of useful men are judged harshly and . . . suffer from the wrong-doing and the vice of a few of their numbers." Instead, fair-minded observers should consider the value of the firefighters' labor. "The alarm, the darkness, the bustle, the shriek of terror-stricken women and children, the high wall, the flame-enveloped staircase, the explosion of combustibles, the crazed action of the populous" are "coolly and quickly" surmounted by the "deliberate and efficient action of the fire companies."[25]

The firefighters' nerve was matched against relatively inefficient equipment. Even the newest engines were monsters. Their steam boilers (replacing hand pumps) could throw water 200 feet, but they were too heavy to carry into a building. They were still pulled to the fire by hand from the company's headquarters (horse-pulled engines did not arrive until the 1850s).[26]

The 1840s volunteer fireman represented the ideal of republican masculinity—physically fit, willing to face danger with equanimity, combining individual valor and team spirit. The exertion of pulling the heavy fire engines to the fire as fast as the firemen's legs could go, then heaving at the handles to work the pump tested strength and endurance. Hook and ladder companies exhibited a dexterity and discipline in rescues from ladders or from roofs. Manhood also required daring in the face of danger. The firemen wore a leather helmet and heavy gloves, and some had leather coats and boots, but leather is not fireproof. Sparks burned them, smoke choked them, debris fell on them, and sometimes they died. This, for volunteers, bespeaks volumes about commitment to the civic culture of the early republic. Despite the danger, the ideal fireman had a fighting spirit and, close to falling walls and lashing flames, a calm and almost superhuman will in refusing to give in to the blaze. It was the same ideology that the largely volunteer armies on both sides of the Civil War would embrace, along with the fireman's courage, sense of camaraderie, and belief in the higher good of his actions.[27]

Antebellum writers and artists elevated the volunteer fireman to the highest rank of romantic hero: the man who puts moral duty above personal safety. For example, the immensely popular Currier and Ives lithographs depicting the "Life of Firemen" and "American Fireman" in the 1850s were best-sellers. The depictions of firemen rushing to the blaze and hurling themselves at it was idealized but not fanciful. Nathaniel Currier had seen the ravages of fire firsthand. His lithography shop at 1 Wall Street was at the edge of the burned-over district of lower Manhattan in the New York fire of 1835, and his first big "hit" lithograph was "Ruins of the Merchants' Exchange N.Y. after the Destructive Conflagration of Decbr. 16 & 17, 1835." What's more, he was a volunteer fireman himself. He is the laggard chasing the fire engine in the series' depiction of the Henry Street Fire Company.[28]

There were no call boxes to alert the companies to the existence of a fire. Church bells and cries of "Fire!" were general alarms. Thus, the first responders to a fire were residents of the building, spectators, and passersby. At the corner of Ferry and Second in Pittsburgh that fateful day, bystanders became firefighters until the engines arrived. Robert McKnight, a twenty-five-year-old attorney, was preparing documents in his office at noon when he heard the cries of "Fire!" and the fire bells. Rushing to the scene, he found a shed and a storage facility burning fiercely. With the help of two boys, he tried to put out the sparks as they landed on the street.[29]

Pittsburgh's population, like that of all the new western cities, was younger than in today's metropolises. The census of 1840 counted 10,369 boys and girls under the age of twenty out of a population of 21,115—nearly 50 percent. The city's streets were full of boys carrying goods, running errands, playing hooky, or simply doing nothing. Fire brought them out of their doldrums, and many rushed to aid the firefighters or watch the spectacle.[30]

Youngster William Johnson was there: The bell in the steeple of the Third Presbyterian was ringing the fire signal, the throng in the streets had raised the cry of "Fire! Fire!" and crowds rushed toward Second Street. Dust was flying everywhere as the wind picked up. Although he had jobs to do, he liked to "run with the machine," and he got to the fire just as it had leaped up from the shed to the surrounding houses. Johnson turned on his heel and headed for the Eagle engine barn, on Fourth Street, near Ferry. He had not gone more than a block when the saw a "motley crew" of the company pulling the engine toward him.[31]

Johnson was soon at the pumps, joined by McKnight—volunteers helping the volunteer firemen. Others connected the engine to the hydrant and ran the hose right up to the fire. The engineer attached the long pipe to the pumper and then, suddenly, the pressure failed. "A weak, sickly stream of muddy water" dripped from the nozzle. Freed from the danger of the firefighters' most potent weapon, the fire jumped to the three-story mansion of Colonel William Diehl, kitty-corner to the shed, then up the street to the brick cotton mill of James Woods, then to Johnson's father's home. With neighbors' help, young William tried to save the furniture, but moving it into the street only exposed it to the racing flames. Up to the roof of his employer's bookstore he climbed, where he waited with pails of water, but the fire simply leaped over the roof and licked at the buildings beyond. The frame house at the corner of Fourth and Ross escaped all harm, while those "beyond it, built of brick, were totally destroyed." Writing nearly fifty years later, he remembered as yesterday what he had heard and saw: "The roar of the flames was terrific, and their horrid glare, as they leaped through the dense black clouds of smoke, sweeping earth and sky, was appalling."[32]

THE FIRE HAS ITS WAY

The wind dictated the course of the fire. Second Street, mostly frame structures, went up within an hour and the Woods cotton works across the street was soon consumed as well. The Third Presbyterian

Church on the corner of Third and Ferry was saved when volunteers with axes broke off its burning wooden cornice and hurled it into the flames below. The church's windowless high brick walls acted as a firebreak, preventing the fire from going further west. Had the fire gotten past the church, it might have reached the canal workers' shantytown, and the entire downtown might have been destroyed.

Now the wind veered away from the downtown and blew toward the Monongahela. A wall of flame driven by the wind roared down Fourth, Third, Second, Front, and Water Streets. Some buildings were miraculously spared entirely, as the embers leaped over them. Others, next door and higher, were reduced to rubble. Some were saved by the determined heroism of their employees, for instance, the staff of the *Daily Advertiser*. No one there left an account of what it was like to be inside a building assaulted by fire, but another brave employee in the San Francisco fire of 1851 reported what a similar attack was like: "[T]he deep thunder sound . . . seemed . . . like the voice of hell, howling at our resistance. I placed my hand upon the brick wall that separated my office . . . from the dread fire that surrounded us, and felt the stove-like heat."[33]

The Bank of Pittsburgh proved no match for the fire. Though brick walled, the neoclassical structure (it looked like the Parthenon) had huge windows along its side. When the glass in them burst from the heat of the flames, they ushered fire into the interior. Only the money and papers, locked in a safe by a fleeing banker, survived. Bank safes were supposed to be fireproof, a far more important concern of bankers and their customers than keeping funds secure from robbers. In the same neighborhood, the Monongahela House was built of brick, but its cupola was wood, and when it caught fire, the entire roof burned and collapsed into the floors below. The structure was a total loss, though all the staff and guests escaped unharmed.[34]

The fire companies, out in full force, could do little to stop the progress of the blaze. The fireplug supply of water was too thin to allow the pumpers to gain any foothold against the fire, and the companies' hose was soon burning along with everything else in the path of the flames. The blaze ravaged firehouses while the companies were fighting the blaze. The Vigilant Company's engine house on

Fourth Street collapsed in flame, as did the Duquesne's. The Allegheny Company lost 880 feet of leather hose, the Niagara 300 feet, the Duquesne 1,100 feet (along with its engine), the Neptune 750 feet, the Vigilant 1,100, and the Union 450 feet. Loss of hoses was a black mark on a company, but the damage to an engine was a blow to the company's honor as well. Both hose and engine cost money, and the companies had only a small fraction of hose in good condition after the blaze.[35]

Gawkers filled the streets, got in the firemen's way, and slowed evacuation of the buildings. Some spectators turned looters and made off with interior furnishings that householders left in the street. Owners of small shops and merchant barons alike ran to and fro, mixing with seamstresses and laborers, all unsure what to do next. Eyewitnesses recalled that "the loftiest buildings melting before the ocean of flame." Along the river, grocery warehouses like Holmes's were gutted. Holmes was the biggest sugar and coffee wholesaler in the city, and passersby attempted to save what they could, but the flames were too close and too hot. The warehouse owners and workers piled their wares outside the buildings along the banks of the river, trying to load them onto whatever floated and thus to safety, but even the boats moored along the water caught fire from the flying sparks. City river fires could be devastating, as fires in New York City and St. Louis proved, and the Pittsburgh conflagration had now arrived at the riverside. The steamboats cut their mooring lines and fled to the middle of the Monongahela, while smaller boats strained to navigate down river to safety.

By the afternoon's close, over 1,200 buildings lay in ruins, but the fire's appetite remained unsated. Josiah King's store, "although covered with iron roof, door columns and shutters" that were supposed to be "fire proof," lasted no more than a few minutes. He got out one cartload of tea, as well as "all our books, accounts, and valuable papers." Indeed, for many businessmen, the most important objects in their possession were their ledger and account books. Much of the business of the city, particularly trade among businessmen, was not based on cash but on book debt. Ledgers were the only proof of money owed or paid. Almost worse for King and others was the loss of stock. He had on order some "$5000 worth of goods." Where to warehouse the goods and how to retail them remained a problem.

King and others in his situation, trying to rescue what private property they could, faced another obstacle. The streets, narrow and crowded with wheeled traffic on the best of days, were now impassable and the fire moved faster than the merchants could load wagons. When "we supposed the fire was yet two squares distant, we suddenly saw the glass works two squares in the opposite direction in a blaze . . . Meantime, the flames were gorging on all the intermediate space covering the interval."

The only way out for King was over water. "The family was hurried out of their [endangered home], retreating to the boats [in the river] for shelter." King could afford to hire men to help carry family and personal belongings over the Monongahela Bridge. No sooner had the King party crossed than "the bridge was surrounded on three sides by flames and became the focus of a heat so intense that the acres of property brought there from the buildings were consumed." His family had rescued a small fraction of all he had earned over the years, though "our own silverware and jewelry were saved in a trunk by our girl Margurette."[36]

M. R. Delaney, the abolitionist publisher of *The Mystery*, also celebrated a lucky miss. Pittsburgh was a stop on the underground railroad and Delaney an avowed enemy of Southern slavery. "We just escaped the calamity by removing on Saturday before the fire from our former residence in 3rd St. to where we now reside." The fire, "as though impelled by a destroying angel," ravaged buildings so fast that little could be saved from its path. Surely it demonstrated the futility of prizing private property—a message especially important to those whose wickedness led them to deal in human bondsmen, Delaney thought. "Never did any event appear more like Judgement day." Others fleeing were gouged by the carters or lost what they had saved from the fire to thieves. Even ministers were not safe from the harpies. The Reverend George S. Holmes, according to a *Post-Gazette* report, had about "$300 stolen," lifetime savings for a Methodist minister.[37]

The heat of the fire reinforced the high wind, and convection currents lifted the burning debris into the air. The embers came to earth nearly a mile ahead of the flames. Observers could not remember a faster-moving fire. One visitor fleeing the blaze, the lawyer, judge, and travel writer Henry Marie Brackenridge, reported that "the air was filled with flying pieces of wood in a state of combustion, for a piece of shingle as large as my hand, still blazing, fell at my feet . . . I saw such lighted torches falling at once upon a thousand houses, half a mile from what was still regarded as the scene of danger." Brackenridge knew danger firsthand—he had traveled the length and breadth of the country, braved Indian attacks on the Ohio and Mississippi, served as a judge in frontier Florida, and endured a brief, controversial stint in Congress. But home was the Allegheny country, and he ended his storied career with a seat in the state legislature representing the county. When "the best half of the city" burned, he cried.[38]

A Dreadful Scene

By seven in the evening, having reached the water's edge to the south and the hillsides to the east, the fire stopped as if of its own volition. Actually, it had run out of fuel. The burned-over district continued to smolder for days, and the streets themselves were almost too hot to traverse. The cost, when all was tallied, neared $12 million—today the equivalent of $267 million.[39]

Thousands lost their homes, but only two people died as a result of the fire. "The remains of Samuel Kingston, Esq. were found in the cellar of a house on Second Street." He had rushed into the wrong house to save a treasured piano and, confused by the smoke and heat, had not been able to find his way out. In May, the remains of a woman were recovered from a ruined storefront. They were supposed to be all that was left of a Mrs. Malone, trapped in the flames and seeking shelter in the building. Even the hundreds of people staying at the six-story Monongahela House were able to flee the fire. Many simply climbed above the fire into the hills at the eastern edge of the city (now the Hill District).

Simeon Bulford "took his family up to Scot's Hill, now Grant's Hill"—a steep climb today. Fire can climb such banks so long as there is fuel to succor it, but in Pittsburgh the eastern hills were nearly devoid of vegetation and buildings. Two of his children had wandered off in the confusion of the retreat and he feared the worst. As he explored the night streets looking for them, he happened upon a fellow parishioner: "Brother, there are two little strays," his fellow congregant told him, and they had been taken in and put to bed by a neighbor. Bulford rushed to the house, swept up his two little girls in his arms, and carried them back to their mother. It turned out that the older had led her sister, a toddler, to safety.[40]

Why so few fatalities? Like the cities that had gone up in flame before it, Pittsburgh's housing stock was largely two- and three-story wooden homes; its highest buildings were steepled churches and six-story hotels. People could escape from these dwellings far more easily than the inhabitants of today's high-rise apartments and office buildings. What's more, the 1845 conflagration was a daylight fire, and though it was soon racing through the streets, it had begun slowly enough for news of it to spread ahead of the flames. People went outdoors to see it, and on the streets already, they could more easily flee when the flames arrived at their doors. The very fact that they did not feel safe in their homes and fled them had saved their lives—all but the two, at least.[41]

As a matter of fact, the small number of dead was not so unusual. In the Great Fire of London, only a few died; the same was true of a fire that gutted Charlestown, South Carolina, in 1740, and the Great Fire of Boston, in 1760. Even the horrific fire that reduced much of New York City to ruins in 1776 spared its populace. The Wall Street fire in Manhattan in 1835 destroyed as much property as the Pittsburgh fire, but only took two lives. In fact, the most deadly fires in our history are not those that burn out cities but those in densely packed closed-in spaces—particularly hotels, theaters, passenger boats, schools, and night clubs. The Richmond Theater, Richmond, Virginia, 1811: 160 dead; the Lexington Steamboat, Long Island

Sound, 1840: 140 dead; Sultana Steamboat, Mississippi River, off Memphis, 1865: 1,800 dead; Conroy Theater, Brooklyn, New York, 1876: 295 dead. The list goes on and on, well into our own time. In the Hartford, Connecticut, circus fire of 1944, 167 dead. In the Coconut Grove fire, Boston, in 1942, 487 dead. Negligence and indifference was always the cause—too many people, no thought to fire prevention, greed, and sometimes, arson.[42]

But in Pittsburgh, the smell and heat of the fire remained in the inhabitants' memory, and the poor people of the city lived in free-floating anxiety about a recurrence of the conflagration. Small fires kept erupting, reviving the sense of panic. The very sound of the fire bells "frightened the people . . . since the great fire." With good reason. One man whose home escaped the April 10 fire was not so lucky a month later. He later wrote to a friend, "About the first of May one evening at half past 8 o'clock a fire broke out in a hay stable a few houses from where I live . . . the house next to the stable caught in a few moments and was entirely consumed." Four horses were burned to death before anyone could lead them out of their stalls. "The fire proceeded so quick from the fray that nothing got saved except a quilt, a small pillow and 1 or 2 chairs. The fire soon gathered strength amongst the old frames and it went ahead until it burned 45 or 50 houses and God know where it would have stopped had not the fire men commenced to cut down houses before the fire." In all likelihood, the letter recorded a fire that broke out on May 27 in Young's Stable, spread along Washington Street in the heart of the downtown, and cost 200 families their homes. On June 10, another stable fire erupted on Exchange Street, gorged on the Mickeltree distillery, and finished its meal with a block of dwellings before it was quenched.[43]

Pittsburgh's ordinary folk were right to be afraid. On March 26, 1846, a bakery fire razed the entire block from Seventh to Prospect Streets. Two years later, five fires in stables, smokehouses, dwellings, stores, and the McKee and Griswold foundry resulted in losses of over $200,000. In the next eight years, major fires cost property owners almost $350,000, less than the $12 million estimate for the Great Fire, but surely a continuing burden to a city trying to dig itself out from debt and destruction.[44]

Pittsburgh's agony was acute, the worst case of an epidemic of fire sweeping through all antebellum cities. New York City: On December 16, 1835, the city south of Wall Street, where a number of taverns served the office workers and laborers in the area, exploded in flames, and falling debris landed all over the island. Frozen water mains and blustery winds defeated the city's volunteer fire companies as the fire mastered the night. The next day, the state militia guarded the ruins and watched over property left in the streets, including the books and papers of many of the city's leading financial institutions. The severity of the 1835 fire was nearly matched by a series of stable, factory, and apartment house fires in ensuing years. For example, the explosion of a saltpeter factory in 1845 killed dozens of firefighters, flattened forty buildings, and blew out windows miles away.

St. Louis: On May 18, 1849, a fire on the steamer *White Cloud* skipped to four other fully loaded ships moored nearby. The wind blew the sparks from the boat fires to the warehouses on shore, thence to the squares above the levee, and so up Pine, Chestnut, and Market Streets. Main Street was next. Twenty-seven steam boats, sixteen square blocks, and $7.5 million worth of property, along with twenty people, were lost in the fire.

Philadelphia: On July 9, 1850, a warehouse fire on the Delaware River rushed uphill to Second Street and danced along Race Street. Saltpeter works in the path of the fire accommodated it by blowing up and spreading flaming debris in all directions. Because of the falling walls, people could not escape the conflagration. Thirty died in it.

San Francisco: Hastily constructed of wood and canvas after the Gold Rush began, the city nearly burned down three times between 1849 and 1851. Every shanty, warehouse, and store was packed with goods for the miners. So precious was space that merchants used grounded and abandoned ships for storage. Wooden sidewalks and streets connected a rabbit warren of docks and wharves. On May 3, 1851, the most horrific of these infernos began in a paint shop, spread to a furniture store, and reduced the core of the city to ash. Over sixteen square blocks of buildings—mostly frame construction—disappeared in the space of a few hours. Over 2,500 structures vanished, worth an estimated $15 million.[45]

THE WORKING PEOPLE lost the most in these fires—homes, belongings, jobs. They might well have looked with angry eyes at the leaders of commerce and industry who piled flammable goods into flimsy warehouses and plied fire in their ovens and forges. As Pittsburgh's leading divine put it, in 1845, "If there ever was a people since the sect of Parsees, who in this spiritual sense might be called the votaries, worshipers of fire, truly we are the people." It seemed that greed and the opportunity for profit trumped any consistent concern for fire safety.[46]

In the wake of the Pittsburgh fire, the men who brought fire into the early industrial city thus had two tasks—the first, to rebuild their businesses, and the second, to convince their neighbors that the inferno was an opportunity rather than a catastrophe.

"This Gigantic Workshop"

S tunned by their losses and unsure of their future—for other cities had designs upon Pittsburgh's role as gateway to the West—the people of Pittsburgh longed for answers. Why had fire afflicted them? The ministers, as of old, replied that God sent fire to punish sin, but this admonition no longer sufficed for the leaders of the community. Antebellum men of means expected more than traditional jeremiads. The businessmen and industrialists found other rationales much more attractive than confession of sin and contrition.

Pittsburgh would respond to the old dilemma of catastrophic fire in a strikingly modern fashion—the first and in many ways still the most striking example of fabrication of historical memory of fire. If the city's industries required fire—and they did—the owners of the factories needed to reframe the fire story. And as personal recollections of the actual fire, the incapacity of the fire service, and the panic of the people faded, the leading men underwrote a very different account of resilience and progress. The city fathers turned a disaster into a success story.

GOD'S WILL AND THE APPETITES OF INDUSTRY

For Boston's puritans, fire was God's way of punishing an errant people. Pittsburgh ministers were quick to offer this same explanation for the inferno. They feared that many in the city worshiped the machine and the dollar instead of bowing to the absolute power of God. And these were the very sins that the fire punished, according to Reverend E. P. Swift of the city's First Presbyterian Church. Though God's reasons might be "inaccessible to us," the "special acts of Providence," including the losses from fire, were his "instrument of instruction and reproof." God had a quarrel with those in the city who did not practice "strict honesty and manly integrity in all business transactions; moderation in the desires and pursuits of gain."[47]

The core values of Swift's sermon echoed throughout the city's Baptist, Methodist, and Presbyterian halls of worship. Pittsburgh lay inside the edge of the "burned over district," a congeries of villages, cities, and rural areas in the western part of New York state and the adjoining states in the four decades before the Civil War. Out of it came evangelists with fiery messages of onrushing doom and plans for utopian refuges, while within it membership in Methodist, Presbyterian, and Baptist congregations swelled. Calls for moral reform, overstuffed churches, and a multitude of theology schools spread the word, and the movement soon arrived in Pittsburgh. Some historians have attributed the enthusiasm to rapidly changing economic and social conditions, including industrialization, but the preaching was not a form of social and economic leveling. It was not anti-business, assuming instead that business activity was part of God's plan.[48]

The city had in 1828 twelve congregations with nearly half of the residents affiliating in some fashion. In the next three decades, the number of Presbyterian congregations grew from five to forty; the Baptist presence increased even faster, from one to twenty-one, and the Methodists from one to twenty-six churches. St. Paul's was built to service the overflow of Roman Catholics from St. Patrick's. A great revival in enthusiasm came to the city in the 1820s, with the preaching of Presbyterian minister Francis Herron. Admirers said that "[h]is own soul was aflame as he preached to his people." Swift joined Herron in the effort to increase church membership, start more Bible-study classes, and implant in the breasts of the congregants a sense of their own sinfulness. When cholera came to the city and killed their children, and the efforts of the Sanitary Board were not enough to explain or console the living for their losses, one minister told his auditory, the plague was a "chastisement." When only thirty perished, the pious gave thanks and attributed the relatively light judgment on them to their new sense of repentance.[49]

The leaders of the Presbyterian churches decided to establish a Third Presbyterian Church in the heart of the city, at Third and Ferry. Their new church had a seating capacity of 800 on its ground floor and room for another 400 in its galleries. All seats were filled when Herron preached the inaugural sermon on September 21, 1833. They were even more eager in their sense of repentance than their fellows in the other Presbyterian congregations, writing and subscribing to a confession of faith and conduct "denying ungodliness and worldly lusts . . . especially to observe and practice in . . . life and business the principles of temperance." The members swore to bring religion into their homes as well, "giving to your family religious instruction, endeavoring to restrain them from all sin while under your guardianship; neither teaching them nor causing them to be taught any thing prohibited in the catechisms of our church . . . nor permitting them to attend any such places, or scenes of amusement, or parties of pleasure."[50]

For the evangelicals, God's wrath poured down in fire on the sinner, but that was not really the answer to why Pittsburgh burned. How could it be? For despite the fervor of the evangelicals and the passion of the preachers, in 1844, a fire in a cooper's shop spread to a tobacco warehouse, and then across the square to the First Presbyterian Church, gutting it. In 1849, the Third Presbyterian took fire and was destroyed. In the same year, the First Presbyterian of Allegheny burned. In 1851, the Fifth Presbyterian was gutted by fire, followed by the St. Paul's Cathedral, at the corner of Fifth and Grant. The hill that would give refuge to so many in the Great Fire did not stop the fire from devouring the churches, no more than did the piety of the church members or the sermons of the ministers.[51]

For now the ministers had potent rivals for their congregants' minds and hearts, interpreters of events who preferred the material to the sacred. The city's industrial leaders insisted that Pittsburgh rededicate itself to "the general trade and business of this country." As petitioners from the city told the Pennsylvania legislature on April

12, 1845, with a stiff and pro forma bow to the litany of sins and a far more genuine embrace of the secular, a "dispensation of Providence" had ruined their city, the costs of which were "at this moment beyond all computation." Echoing the religious platitudes and welcoming the realistic commercial message of the city delegation, the governor agreed that "this visitation of providence strikes from beneath us all self-dependence," but even more important, "our western empo-rium" had lost "two-thirds of its business capital." Invocations of the divine were no longer sufficient explorations of the meaning of fire. They had best be accompanied by hardheaded business sense.[52]

If the capitalist reading of the events of the 10th had to accommo-date a rival, it was the romantic and sentimental mentality of the ante-bellum era. As contemporary literary critic Frederic Henry Hedge described it, the romantic manner of the epoch demanded "a record of thoughts and feelings rather than of events, a faithful expression of the struggles and vicissitudes. The trials and the triumphs" of individ-uals. It infused domestic settings with sentimentality and warmth, and made women and children virtuous and dear rather than sinful and willful (the puritans' notion). Historian Elizabeth Clark agreed that this romantic way of seeing the world "relied on appeals to emo-tion to evoke pity for the weak and distressed."[53]

Petitioners from the city to the legislators added a sentimental theme to their plea for public aid to Pittsburgh. Surely "every hu-mane and benevolent emotion of the heart of man" interceded for the suffering of the people. Representative Thomas J. Bigham of Al-legheny City, across the river from Pittsburgh, personalized the ro-mantic motif. "These 6,000 of my constituents—whom last Thursday morning found in the enjoyment of all luxuries and comforts of life . . . are now homeless wanderers . . . at firesides I have exchanged the courtesies and received the kindness of social life. These firesides are now a mass of ruins. Those happy family circles are now broken up." But he did not forget the economics of the loss or the cost of recov-ery. "Foster these advantages [of Pittsburgh industry and location]—give encouragement to that industry, and those burning ruins will rise again." His teary depiction deeply moved the assembly; they put aside a bill on the floor supporting the extension of the railroad to his town. His own tears quickly dried when he contemplated the commercial consequences of their decision—it would allow Pittsburgh's rivals, "our more liberal Northern and Southern sister states" to supplant Pittsburgh as a supplier of western markets.[54]

TALLYING THE LOSSES

Following Bigham's example to particularize their woes, victims of the fire pleaded their cases for relief to the city Board of Assessors. J. Heron Foster, clerk of the Board of Assessors, published the confidential hearings almost immediately after they took place. (No expectation of privacy then.) The list is as revealing of who lost what as the surviving appeals to the Boston Overseers of the Poor in 1760, but it differs in scope and demeanor. These entries are not the submissive pleas for assistance of the victim, but a demand for tax relief. The claimants were citizens of a republic rather than subjects of a distant king begging for his charity, and that entitled them to the consideration of their elected officials. Americans' attitudes toward calamity had changed, as had their attitudes toward government.

Both poor and rich were fire victims. The fire-devastated First Ward of Pittsburgh, like the Cornhill district of Boston, was largely working class. But all its denizens' claims were framed in monetary rather than depictive terms. No chairs, bedspreads, or cooking utensils. George Ammon, a tailor, lost $63.00 of property to the fire. Mrs. Adams, a widow, $35.00; George Abbott, a shoemaker, $70.00; and Henry Anderson, a laborer, $200.00. Foster himself (he was a printer by trade) claimed a small loss of $200. Colonel Diehl, in whose yard the fire began, was out $1,600 for two "frame houses." Shop owners predominated among the claimants. George Albree, a shoe dealer, claimed $4,750; John Albree's burned warehouse was worth $3,000, and Mrs. Mary M. Brackenridge lost $600.

Warehoused goods and professional stocks could push the bill much higher. The array of claims demonstrates how varied occupation and commercial enterprise was in the new cities. Pharmacists lost stores of medicines to the tune of $9,000. There were no banks as such in Boston (colonies were not supposed to have them), but The Bank of Pittsburgh was worth $8,000 and the gutted Bank of the United States, housed with the Merchant's Exchange, was valued at $20,000. The average loss of personal property, including habiliments and chattels (buildings and personal goods) in the First Ward was over $2,500, but this figure is misleading because it gives too much weight to the relatively really large losses—those over $5,000. The median loss was about $1,000 ($28,000 in 2005 dollars).

Building in brick did not save the owners from fire damage. That lesson from the Boston fire remained unlearned. Harmar Denny's four brick houses, worth $7,000, were a total loss; James Gray's three brick houses, gone, were worth $4,500. William Holmes, a grocer, watched his two brick warehouses go up in smoke, a loss of $6,000. Indeed, the largest losses were borne by those with brick houses because they were the most valuable kind of structures in the first place. The biggest losers in this category were the manufacturers. Christina Imsen's glassworks were valued at $17,000. James Woods's cotton mill was worth $15,000.

The Second Ward, along the water, was more commercial, but it too contained a mixture of craft, manufacturing, commercial, and retail establishments. The smallest claims came from female servants, averaging $25.00. The median claim was $400. The ward's biggest losers, such as the Lyons Iron Works, were rocked to the tune of $15,000. More devastating to the economy, a burned mill or foundry meant the loss of jobs. There were inns and hotels in the Second Ward as well. James Crossan, owner of the Monongahela House, claimed $35,000 in damages for himself, while his partners added $60,000 to the bill. Western University, the forerunner of the University of Pittsburgh, was consumed in the fires, a loss of $12,000.[55]

INSURING DISASTER

Next to the entry for Western University in the assessors' books was the notation "partially insured." A number of the larger firms in the city had insured their places of business and their goods. At the same time that Pittsburgh's capitalists were creating their fire course, the quickly growing fire insurance industry, led by companies like Aetna of Hartford, Connecticut, were taking over the fire insurance business. In fact, the fire insurance business had grown apace with urban fires, changing itself, like the firefighting companies, as it evolved.

At first, groups of merchants had pooled their resources to provide relief for one or more of their number struck by fire. But by the beginning of the nineteenth century, these mutual-assistance firms were supplanted by better-capitalized insurance companies, with agents in distant cities selling policies. It was their job to calculate risks—the matching of policy to client, and rate to likelihood of hazard. Such calculations were still highly individualistic, however, and based on the agent's personal assessment.[56]

In 1829, Pennsylvania prohibited out of state insurers from doing business in-state, giving state companies a monopoly. Philadelphia firms led the way, but by 1845, Pittsburgh had four of its own: the Allegheny, Pennsylvania, Fireman's, and Pittsburgh companies that all went belly up after the fire. All were limited partnerships, and so depended upon locally raised capital. They were greatly underfunded. The Firemen's had on hand a capital fund of merely $250,000, of which $330,000 was encumbered by outstanding policies. Its insured lost $310,000 in the fire. The Penn had assets of $250,000, had outstanding policies worth $245,000, and faced claims of $226,000 resulting from the fire. Bankruptcy after a major fire was not uncommon. Commercial ventures crashed all the time in the boom-and-bust economy of the antebellum era. But the collapse of the local companies exposed them to lawsuits.[57]

Early-nineteenth-century Americans loved to litigate. They went to court to vindicate personal dignity in slander suits, to protect property in suits over milldams, nuisances, and illegal takings of land, brought suits over personal injuries, and sued one another over contracts. The most common suits involved debt, however, and the number of suits for debts had skyrocketed in the wake of the Panic of 1837. The fire added to this load of suits, in particular by and against insurance companies in the area.[58]

Pittsburgh's insurance companies had anticipated this problem.

Technically, if their policyholders were "clients," then they were owed the face value of their policies and could sue for payment. Evidently, the policyholders thought that was the case. But Pittsburgh companies clung to the system Benjamin Franklin and his fellow Philadelphians had erected. Policyholders were supposedly part owners of the company. Instead of paying the face value of the policy, the companies apportioned the cash on hand among the policyholders according to a fixed percentage. Every holder got the same percentage of the face value, no matter how much the holder had paid in premiums. The legislature, in assenting to this ploy, clearly favored the insurance company over its policyholders.

The state courts, presiding over cases of policyholders' seeking to set off unpaid premiums against insured fire losses, gave the companies another boost. Judges allowed the companies to call in all payments due, even from those policyholders whose insured businesses or homes had been destroyed. In other words, not only were policyholders shorted on their compensation, they still had to make their scheduled premium payments. On top of that, the courts denied that the insurance companies were liable for losses if the damage was not the direct result of the fire (that is, if the fire was not the "proximate cause" of the damages). Finally, the courts allowed the companies to recoup payment of premiums even when the company agent had lied to the policyholder about the company policies.[59]

The courts favored other types of businesses caught short in the fire against the claims of suppliers and laborers. In traditional "equity" jurisprudence, if a worker performed a part of a job, the beneficiary of the performance, for example, a landlord whose shop the worker helped rebuild, had to pay the worker at least some part of what was promised for the job. If a supplier provided lumber, nails, or other goods on a contract with a builder, the supplier was entitled to be paid for "goods delivered." After the fire, courts permitted businesses to defer, reduce, or dispense with these obligations entirely. But when owners sued for back rent for property ruined by the fire, renters had to pay up. In effect, the courts said that capital needed for rebuilding should not be tied up when the property itself was not producing any income.[60]

For those who were not insured (and some who were) and those who could not go to court (or lost their suits), the only succor was "Christian charity." Funds and sympathy poured in from Philadelphia, New York City, and Boston, as well as from smaller communities all over the country, and even from abroad. Charitable subscriptions ranged from thousands of dollars to small private gifts. In fact, charity was a more important part of antebellum culture than it was in the colonial period. The total of gifts to private charities from individual donors zoomed in the first half of the nineteenth century. Overwhelmingly, the motive was religious—Christian benevolence at work—though there were other incentives. Some donors saw their work as an alternative to the much-despised public dole.[61]

Treasurer Foster's record book listed the gifts by origin and amount. The largest portion of the charitable gifts came from other cities. Individuals in Philadelphia gave $38,565; in Boston they came up with $15,000; New York City's givers offered $16,466; Baltimore came in at $10,590, Cincinnati residents contributed $7,218; St. Louis citizens sent $3,711; New Orleans topped that at $7,167; and Louisville, Kentucky, collected $4,739. All together, state totals were: Pennsylvania, $109,899 (including the state's $50,000 relief fund); New York, $23,265; Massachusetts, $16,741; Ohio, $10,810; and Maryland, $11,513. Some of the charity was in kind. The most common and extensive contributions were barrels of flour and other bread grains, bacon, and potatoes, clothing, tools, and other necessities. A few of the offerings were delicacies. J. Sanderson, of the Diamond Market in the city, supplied corned beef; the town of Bridgeport sent "sour crout," and W. B. McClure, a lawyer, provided one barrel of shad.[62]

The legislature voted $50,000 of direct relief for the city's "destitute," but that did not mean the poor. It meant instead those whose losses were not compensated by insurance. True, it was a pittance compared to the $12 million in estimated losses. In addition, the legislature resolved not to collect state and county taxes from the burned-over district for three years, a measure that helped those who paid taxes (that is, landlords or landowners). The state remitted all license fees as well. In sum, the state acted to relieve some of the burdens on business and land development, a step entirely in accord with state bounties to industries, support for canal and railroad projects, and other pro-business activities routine in this age.[63]

REBUILDING THE FIRE COURSE

With all the evidence that the Great Fire had placed before its leaders, surely the city would take steps to prevent another catastrophe, wouldn't it? As the leading student of nineteenth-century public health regulations has written, "[B]y the late nineteenth century, fire regulations became a paradigm for constitutional exertions of state police power." Indeed, the law in some localities encouraged authorities to put public interest in fire safety ahead of the rights of private property owners. Municipalities passed laws that courts upheld permitting the inspection of structures for fire code violations and the tearing down of buildings to create fire breaks without compensation to their owners. Other cities shifted to professional fire departments or invested in such new firefighting technologies as horse-drawn steam engines.[64]

But nothing of the sort happened in Pittsburgh. It was a city dedicated to the fire god, Vulcan. Within three months of the fire, new buildings abounded in spaces not yet cleared of charred walls and flooring. Where milled (wooden) structures had been, wooden structures reappeared. On Front Street, by the river, nine warehouses, a foundry, a steel factory, two shops, a livery stable, and eight homes went up. Dwellings sprouted like weeds on Second, Third, and Fourth Streets, just as close to one another as their burned predecessors. The cross streets were soon filled with residences and shops. Mrs. Phillips rebuilt her house on Ferry Street, of wood, as did G. A. Bayard on Water Street. Indeed, almost all the new construction on Ferry, Water, Smithfield, and Grant was wood.[65]

Comparing the census returns for 1840, before the fire, with those for 1850 shows that the First and Second Wards remained mixed residential and business use, with small factories next to dwelling places, retail shops, and office buildings. A local survey map of 1872 provides more graphic proof of the resistance to change. At the corner of Second and Ferry, where Mrs. Brooks may have allowed the fire under her pot to escape to a nearby shed, Jonathan Wanderlich's house stood next to Colonel William Diehl's. Behind the houses was the Keystone Iron Works, with its furnaces going night and day. Across Second was a row of tenements, and on Ferry Lane, an alley, was the long wall of the Hill, Bole, and Co. Foundry.[66]

The coal dust had returned as well. On April 14, 1855, *Ballou's Pictorial Drawing-Room Companion* published a panorama of Pittsburgh. The city at the point spreads before the viewer, its eighteen major and countless smaller smokestacks belching black soot into the clouds. When Andrew Carnegie's family came to Pittsburgh, in 1848, "the houses were mainly of wood, a few only were of brick, and not one was fire proof." In 1860, after a three-year sojourn in clean and healthy Altoona, he returned to a city where "smoke permeated and penetrated everything. If you placed your hand on the balustrade of the stair it came away black; if you washed face and hands they were as dirty as ever in an hour. The soot gathered in the hair and irritated the skin."[67]

Carnegie did not exaggerate. Fred Schell's ink drawing of the city, in 1875, showed a scene so smoky that only its outlines were visible. In 1883, the city's Board of Trade estimated that 20 percent of the coal used in the factories fell back upon the city in fine particle form. As one observer wrote, "in truth, Pittsburgh is a smoky, dismal city, at her best. At her worst, nothing darker, dingier, or more dispiriting can be imagined." The smoke was still there as the new century opened, though now it was more than an eyesore. Science had at last recognized a killer. In 1909, Robert Woods described the "'pillars of smoke by day, and at night pillars of fire'" that congealed in the lungs, overlay the gardens, and polluted the water of the city.[68]

Behind the absence of change was the determination not to change. The leading men rejected the improvement of the fire services precisely because they called into question the commitment to bigger furnaces and forges. "Progress, indeed, was the order of the day," and progress was measured in ingots and machines. For example, the city in the 1870s celebrated its first power elevator. No one told the folks at Arbuthnot and Shannon that the wooden shaft of that first power elevator was a perfect chimney should a fire start nearby. Fire was an accident that the city could overlook, not a peril the city must avoid. In other words, it was not worth it to make the city more fire resistant.[69]

To understand this perspective, one has to think like the nineteenth-century capitalist. The city's merchants and manufacturers had become accustomed to very close calculations of profit and loss. All profit had to be reinvested in the business or diverted to another speculative venture. Nothing was left for infrastructure, worker safety, or fire prevention. The entrepreneur developed a kind of rough macroeconomics that regarded the urban centers of the country as its leading economic sector, and they did not want to tamper with the variables in their equation.

As contemporary political economist George Tucker wrote, after examining the 1840 census figures, "[T]he proportion between the rural and town population of a country is an important fact in its interior economy and condition. It determines, in a great degree, its capacity of manufactures, the extent of its commerce, and the amount of its wealth." The key, city business leaders agreed with Tucker, was "the growth of cities." As theologian Samuel Miller preached to a gathering in Baltimore in 1820, "'[A] large city . . . forms, as it were, the heart, the most vital portion of the state or country to which it belongs.'" Thus, not only were the Pittsburgh leaders' individual prospects at stake if they spent money on fire prevention that could have gone to expansion of industry, they were confident that the nation needed their growth for its own progress.[70]

But Pittsburgh would never attract new investment capital if it did not rehabilitate its burned-over image. It had to recast the firescape in the public imagination. First, the ruins had to be romanticized. Pittsburgh had prided itself on its wholesome natural surroundings as well as its advantageous geographic position. Now a good portion of that natural setting was a gutted wasteland. The streets could not be traversed. In the heart of the fire's course, the streets could not be distinguished from the housing blocks. A week after the end of the fire, some ruins were still hot and smoking. The city's boosters insisted that the "fiery lights" of the city were not those of uncontrolled conflagration but signals of "this gigantic work-shop" at work—but how to get that message across? Advocates of the machine were already making their case for its place in the nation's artistic repertoire. Factories with fiery effluvia were not a "wound in-flicted on the earth" but the "domain of vulcan." But first, what to do about the ruins?[71]

In 1845, American art was infatuated with the bucolic and the ex-otic. Painters regarded wilderness as a source of energizing inspira-tion, comparable to landscapes of European ruins (preferably with classical columns in the foreground). With whole blocks of the city still smoldering, a local genre painter named William Coventry Wall depicted the burned district as a mystical Gothic ruin. Seen from a distance, the disaster site exhibited a solemn grandeur. The romanti-cized desolation touched the emotions of viewers and gained pity for the wounded city. Wall arranged for the drawings to be lithographed by James Queen. Between the new technique of lithography and the rotary press newspapers, Wall and Queen created a new genre—the instant, mass-produced, on-the-scene disaster picture.[72]

They soon had competition. Nathaniel Currier had his shop turn out another version of the fire. Currier knew that fires made prof-itable lithographs from his experience with the 1835 New York City fire. The Currier version of the Pittsburgh fire was fabricated from newspaper accounts, painted from an aerial vantage point to heighten the drama, and introduced fictional visual elements to add to the terrible destruction. The artist turned the wooded Allegheny hills north of the city into towering mountains, a convention in pas-toral scenes, and the four-story warehouses in the foreground were pure invention, but together they made the fire course far grander and the event especially spectacular.[73]

While the lithographs were circulating and stimulating sympathy, the rebuilders of the city painted their own glorified prospect in word pictures. Alexis de Tocqueville wrote after his visits to America, in 1840, that the Americans seemed driven by a discontent slaked only by the pursuit of greater wealth. Commerce was a national ma-nia, and "the whole population are engaged in productive industry." With this in mind, it is easy to understand Henry Marie Bracken-ridge's assessment that "the part of the city destroyed was the origi-nal town, the greater part of it held by the first settlers and their descendants; the ground of immense value."

Within two months, visitors from Steubenville, Ohio, found that "although in many places the rubbish is not cleared away, yet the suf-ferers are at work repairing their losses, rebuilding their dwellings and already . . . there are four or five hundred buildings up and in progress, some even now filled with merchandize and places of busi-ness." The visitors were impressed. "How wonderful this energy. A new city, with elegant public and private edifice, has arisen from the ashes of the old." The fuel for the energetic rebuilding was the profit motive. The land not only retained its value, that value had increased because owners could charge higher rents to occupiers. "These new buildings are in great demand at high rents."[74]

In fact, realtors were soon hard at work selling both land and the idea of investment in the West. One of them, Ormsby Gregg, tried to sell parcels in Birmingham, directly across the Monongahela from Pittsburgh. It was, to his mind, land ripe for development after the fire. He only mentioned the fire obliquely, for there was no profit in reminding potential buyers of the continuing danger of fire, even if it had not actually crossed the river to the parcels he was hawking. "Valuable real estate for sale," Gregg promised, hoping that "eastern capitalists and manufacturers would weigh the inherent value of the location against its recent travails." The invocation of "location, loca-tion, location" was evidently as potent then as now. After all, the lots possessed "every description of improvement," excepting only an in-dustrial occupant willing to invest. There was a vein of coal under the land, and clay for brick making. Gregg urged that it was an opportu-nity not to be missed, for the city was and would be again the supplier of cotton textiles, woolens, glass, ironware, steel, and just about everything else for western settlers and downriver settlements. Every one of the enterprises required fire, but "every one in every branch of business, those who have lately come here, as well as our other cit-izens, are highly prosperous, so far as our observation extends."[75]

But promotional literature, particularly literature for potential investors after April 10, 1845, had to do more than persuade readers about the economic potential of the Allegheny region. Gregg's offering went beyond mere description of the land and extolling its future prospects. He presented a comprehensive vision of the city and the world, a promotional ideology. Enterprise was a moral imperative and capitalism the moral ideal. "We want the capitalist, the *experienced and successful* manufacturer" [italics in original], for such a man's work habits and drive was a living model to others. "Businessmen have duties that require the attention both of the hands and the head . . . Give them all the facts and arguments and particulars . . . and they possess the judgment and ability to decide the question of themselves." The successful capitalist was rightfully concerned with "the safety of his investment," but intelligent investors could ignore the question of fire safety if they were assured of the safety of their investments. Gregg had shifted the grounds of the offering from the speculative to the certain, the hazardous to the secure.[76]

FORGETTING THE FIRE

As historian David Blight reminds us, collective memories of great events "construct versions of the past and employ them for self-understanding and to win power and place in an ever changing present." Though the event itself, recaptured by historians, may be terrifying, uncontrolled, and uncontrollable by human conduct or will, the memory can be shaped by both act and desire. So the memory of city fire can be made a "sacred . . . heritage . . . in objects and sites." Such collective memory calls forth celebration, particularly on the anniversary of the event. This, in turn, spurs newspaper pieces, parades, talks, and other forms of recast history. The participants in these may engage in conventional historical research, but their purpose is instead to deploy historical artifacts to reinforce a reassuring collective memory: how "we" endured and triumphed over adversity.[77]

That is what collective, constructive, useful memory did for the Great Fire of 1845. Facts were not important; lessons were. In June

1914, a fire that ravaged a city block convinced the *Pittsburgh Gazette Times* to cite the 1845 blaze. The account noted that the fire department had acted swiftly to limit the damage, unlike the volunteer firemen during the Great Fire. The subtext was that Pittsburgh had gotten better at everything, including fighting fires. On the occasion of the fire's 75th anniversary, *Pittsburgh First* editorialized, "A fire today in two large office buildings would probably cause as great damage as the entire destruction of '45." The lesson went on: "[W]ith characteristic pluck and energy the Pittsburghers 75 years ago set up to repair their loss and within a few months they had begun the reconstruction of a larger and better city." Pluck and energy—that was the Pittsburgh way. In the wake of the influenza epidemic of 1919, Pittsburghers needed a precedent for building a better city. The city's remembered response to the 1845 fire provided a perfect example.[78]

As the city's needs changed, so did its opinion leaders' recounting of the fire. In 1921, after the National Board of Fire Underwriters announced that over $350 million was lost to fires in the preceding year, the *Dispatch* announced that the city "could be justly proud of one of the finest body of firemen in the country . . . however Pittsburgh has not been without its great fires." The fire of 1845 served as text for an admonition against carelessness. The Irish washerwoman was back in the news—this time as a object lesson of the ill consequences of neglecting one's duties.[79]

In the dismal days of the Great Depression, the Great Fire took on another aspect for Pittsburgh readers. Editors admonished readers that in the conflagration, "personal feuds and differences were forgotten." The 1845 fire "spurred the city to greater growth." Soon after the debris was cleared, its industrialists and workers were gouging factories and housing tracts out of the surrounding hills and scouring beneath the soil for veins of coal. The lesson was plain—Pittsburghers, hard hit by unemployment and slow business in the 1930s, had to work together and prosperity would return, just as it had after the Great Fire. On the corner of Smithfield at Fourth, a plaque reported "these buildings form the bordering line of the burnt district of April 10, 1845." No one knew who had placed the plaque, but its discovery, at the end of 1936, gave renewed hope that Pittsburgh was a city that could survive anything.[80]

In 1945, as the war in Europe against the Nazis was coming to its close, the city again celebrated its fire with parades and speeches. The focus, according to the *Post-Gazette*, was to be on "the spirits that rebuilt the city rather than on calamity." Not everyone was happy with the planned pageant. The festivities to commemorate the "indomitable spirit" of the city—including the music of Stephen Foster (a resident of the city), exercises, an exhibition, participation by historical societies, and even a talk by "a noted historian of the period"—turned out to be too historical. When the Drama League–appointed director of the pageant, Eleanor Freeland (a high school arts teacher), insisted that the festivities go on as planned, she was ousted. Margaret Townsend Scully, head of the pageant committee, arranged for it to produce Scully's own pageant.

One thousand people came to see the new production at the Soldiers and Sailors Memorial Hall on the 10th of April, 1945. Scully's first-act festivities featured a French dancing master, fourteen women performing a minuet, a crew of Polka dancers, and a choir portrayed rehearsing for a ball on the day of the fire. The second act, which supposedly took place a month after the fire, featured members of the relief committee. There were girls and boys, a fruit vendor, and the "city treasurer," but only one firefighter.

Scully conceded that she had exercised "dramatic license." What she did not say in the playbill was that the entire purpose of the pageant was to celebrate a lost time and place. The fire had become incidental—its anniversary merely the occasion to recall Old Pittsburgh. Indeed, the highlight of the day's activities was genealogical, not pyrotechnic. The *Press* lauded "the descendants of pioneer Pittsburgh families whose early ancestors helped to build the city's great industrial and cultural background" who loaned to the Historical Society relics of the old days. Scully was herself the descendant of General James O'Hara, one of the founders of the city. Other "old family names" abounded in the centennial committee. The Historical Society recognized the "membership list of 'descendants'" formally in the program for its commemorative publication. There were twenty-one

Scullys, three generations of the entire clan. After all, the mayor of Pittsburgh was none other than Cornelius D. Scully.[81]

By the 1950s, the fire had become a curiosity, a quaint and distant reminder of days of old. The papers reported that the 1945 committee to create an "Association of the Descendants of Pittsburghers of 1845" had never gotten off the ground. The remnants of the fire in collective memory amounted to a few cherished incidents recalled and retold from generation to generation. But the fire was still part of the history and folklore of the city. So long as the city's factories belched fire and smoke, the conflagration of 1845 had something to teach Pittsburghers.[82]

BUT WHEN THE CITY no longer clothed itself in soot and smoke, the fire became a disagreeable reminder of a dirtier and more dangerous age. Its memory had to be erased in the same way that the city cleansed itself. In 1963, historian Roy Lubove arrived in Pittsburgh and "encountered a city that seemed more like a scene out of Dickens' Coketown—one that would not have been altogether foreign to Andrew Carnegie or Henry Clay Frick had they returned to earth." The steel mills, "still exploding with a primeval energy . . . the noise and the heat of the mills," recalled the city a hundred years before. A decade later, with the plants and the mines closing, Pittsburgh literally cleaned up its act. The old First and Second Wards had become part of a "golden triangle." The lesson of the fire, if any lesson was recalled, was not how fire was harnessed but how fire could be prevented entirely.[83]

In the revamped First Ward, the dirt embankment along the Monongahela north shore was long gone, and the low-rise brick and stone structures of the post-fire era began to vanish as well. The "Pittsburgh Renaissance" reinvented historical tradition without mention of the fire. The City Center's "renovated" face, to the tune of a half-billion dollars, replaced the fire-scarred factories with gleaming steel and glass banks and research facilities.[84]

Chicago, 1871

T he Great Fire of 1845 is no longer part of Pittsburgh's public face. If not forgotten, it has been laid aside as an anomaly in the upward spiral of the city's progress. By contrast, the Chicago Fire of 1871 is the best-known conflagration in our nation's history. In the years between the two fires, four years of Civil War tutored the nation's appreciation of fire. Photographs of the fire-gutted ruins of Atlanta, Charleston, and Richmond sobered both sides' enthusiasm for their cause. But the graphic depiction of the Chicago fire would dwarf all others. The reason is simple. Chicago was the great metropolis of the Midwest. It did not fold into a crease in the mountains like Pittsburgh, nor cling to the seashore like Boston. Chicago leaped up from the prairies to its west, "a sea of grass as far as the wind might reach," and threw its shadow on Lake Michigan to its east, "moving waters as far as the eye could follow," like a high-masted ship on the sea.[1]

Maybe a city did not belong there, on lowland marshes at the mouth of the Chicago River that the wet season turned to swamp. In its infancy, the city was always "sinking into the eternal mud. The streets were barely higher than the level of the Lake." Sewage dumped into the river sat there, going nowhere but into the ground-water. In 1858, young George M. Pullman convinced the owner of the biggest hotel, the Tremont House, to let him lift the building on jacks eight feet above the street. He did. Later famous for his railroad sleeping cars, he started his fortune with that feat.[2]

Chicago's history was not just filled with such feats—it was a feat in itself. Who could have predicted a great city on its site? To the north stood old forestland of the French "pays d'en haute"—the uplands—a region of narrow footpaths and vast oceanlike lakes. Hunters, fishermen, and warriors knew its bounds without maps; indeed, there were no detailed maps of it until the nineteenth century. Down along the western shores of Lake Michigan the Indians, the French, the British, and finally the Americans coasted. On the swampy shore, where the Chicago River entered the lake, stood a trading post. And that was enough civilization for everyone except the Americans. The Indians insisted that the land was the Great

Spirit's and belonged to no one, but by the 1830s, the American treaties and cannons had driven the Indians across the Mississippi.[3]

The rich soil of the prairie beckoned the farmer, the tradesman, and the speculator from the East. They came like a swarm of bees. The census recorded great vertical leaps in population. Four thousand, four hundred, and seventeen in 1840; 300,000 by 1870, then 1 million by 1900. The immigrants cut the trees down for fuel and building materials, gouged the loamy soil to plant wheat, oats, and corn, and fed their hogs and cattle what they could not ship to market. Though they came from New England and the North of Europe these were not the subsistence farmers of old. They vied to send their grains and livestock to the tables of city folk in the East and Europe on the spiderweb of railroads soon stretching in almost every direction from the city.

It was the surplus—what the farmer had to sell—that made the city go and grow. By the 1850s, the city was shipping out millions of bushels of corn, wheat, and oats, and thousands of pounds of dressed pork and beef. The buyers and sellers formed a Board of Trade, an oligopoly of wholesalers, retailers, commodities speculators, "men of industry," and entrepreneurs.[4]

Speculation in timber, wheat, hogs, and cattle brought sharp-eyed businessmen to the city. They would vie to "corner" markets by engrossing and forestalling—old tricks that English merchants had perfected 300 years before. The newborn Republican Party national convention met in Chicago in 1860, and the Republican state machine put Abraham Lincoln of Illinois at the head of the ticket. Through the streets marched troops of uniformed "Wide Awakes" demanding Free Soil and "Honest Abe." When Lincoln called for troops to put down the confederate rebellion, thousands from Chicago volunteered. By the end of the war, Chicago had contributed eighteen infantry regiments, each of 1,000 men, ten cavalry troops, and ten artillery batteries. One of the artillery formations was raised by the Chicago Board of Trade.

The Civil War further spurred the growth of the city of grains and rail lines, turning a prosperous mart at the mouth of the Chicago

River into the metropolis at the center of the American empire. The salt pork and hardtack the Union Army ate came from Chicago's stockyards and grain elevators. The manufacturers of the city did not neglect the home front: "By the end of the civil war . . . almost everything of considerable size used on the railroads, in farming, or in the construction or furnishing of houses was made in Chicago." Into the city came the wealth of the Midwest for storage or for slaughter. From it went foodstuffs, millwork, furniture, and paper products. By 1870, Chicago was a visible miracle, a world city with a history no more than fifty years old.[5]

And now no one could miss it. As you approached the city, you could see and hear and smell the living giant: "A full hour before the party reached the city they had begun to note the perplexing changes in the atmosphere. It grew darker all the time, and upon the earth the grass seemed to grow less green . . . the colors of things became dingier; the fields were grown parched and yellow, the landscape hideous and bare. And along with the thickening smoke they began to notice another circumstance, a strange pungent odor . . . you could literally taste it, as well as smell it . . . it was an elemental odor, raw and crude; it was rich, almost rancid, sensual, and strong."[6]

From the south, on the rail lines, or over the lake, the city rose up as if instantaneously—mile upon mile of grain elevators and track.

All around, on every side, in every direction the vast machinery . . . clashed and thundered from dawn to dark and from dark till dawn . . . The blackened waters of the river . . . disappeared under fleets of tugs, of lake steamers, of lumber barges . . . of grain boats . . . of coal scows . . . of cumbersome schooners laden with produce . . . of grimy rowboats dodging the prows and paddles of the larger craft, while on all sides, blackening the horizon, red in color and designated by Brobdingnag letters, towered the hump-shouldered grain elevators . . . A system of grey rails beyond words complicated opened out and spread immeasurably. Switches, semaphores and signal towers stood here and there. A dozen trains, freight and passenger, puffed and steamed, waiting the word to depart . . . Another train, reeking with fatigue, the air brakes screaming, arrived and halted, debouching a flood of passengers, business men, bringing trade—a galvanizing elixir—from the very ends and corners of the continent.[7]

It was a city of contrasts the farm boys and girls, the immigrants from Germany and Scandinavia found, "rows of immense houses, barred and grated like jails or fortresses; palaces where lived the mighty ones of Chicago commerce." Some, like the Terrace Row, were made of marble and reflected the sun itself. But around the corner lay streets home to the "ragged newsboy, the rag-pickers, the street vermin . . . a battle field . . . amid which men moved, sooty, grimy, sullen, and sickly." And all of these physical proofs of Chicago's vast wealth and its masses of poor—the lumber in the yards and the wheat in the grain elevators; the miles of wooden side-walks and planked thoroughfares; the endless streets of simple clap-board houses and the avenues of elegant stores and mansions—all of them were flammable.[8]

"We Are in Ruins"

Imagine the perfect conditions for an entire region to explode into catastrophic fire—a textbook conflagration scenario. It must be hot, dry, and windy. So hot that there is no relief by night or day. Even the wind off a great lake does not cool people or animals. Peat fires burn continuously beneath the land and flash fires spring up every day. Dry all summer; followed by a fall drought leaving the land so thirsty that the swamplands along the lake dry up, the creeks vanish, and the rivers become trickles. It must be so windy that the gusts carry smoke from smoldering brushfires hundreds of miles— leaving a miasma so thick that ships on the lake have to use their foghorns to warn one another of their presence. The skies have to be filled with fire, fireballs rising up from the land and meteoroid show- ers pelting the earth with pebble-sized debris. It must be so hot, dry, and windy, so fire prone, that locals complain of sore throats and in- flamed eyes and preachers go about the back roads warning of the end of the world. Then might "drought, the southwest trade-wind . . . and the devil" form a "conspiracy . . . against the young, frail, vain, boastful, foolish, prosperous hopeful" of such a place.[9]

So it was in early fall, 1871, in the upper Midwest. For three months there had been little rain. The timber country of eastern Wisconsin was so dry that fires burned underground and the sky was a perpetual orange. Timber company clear-cutting and farmers burning out the stumps and deep plowing had bared the soil. Huge piles of ashes, wood chips, and sawdust littered the land. The trains that crisscrossed the farmers' fields and the loggers' villages became unwitting arsonists, leaving trails of burning leaves and smoldering woodpiles by the tracks. Greed and haste ceaselessly despoiled the region: "[S]ix days a week cut down the forests; one day a week pray for rain."[10]

The city of Chicago lay at the southern edge of this island of fire. That year in the city, there were nearly 700 fires before the Great Fire, almost one-third more than the following year. Truly, Chicago was acting its part as "nature's metropolis," only this time it would be the place where all the little fires slashing at the land would concentrate their fury.[11]

THE LUMBERYARD FIRE

On the night of October 7th, the Chicago Fire Department (CFD) barely gained control of a multi-building fire at the Lull and Holmes wood-planing mill on Canal Street, between Jackson and Van Buren. Four blocks burned to the ground, including a row of frame houses, a coal yard, a grain elevator, and a lumberyard. Chicago was the lumber capital of the world. The mouth of its river was choked with steamers carrying timber from the northwest. Rail lines, themselves the consumer of forests, carried thousands more tons of great white pine, fir, and yellow pine, as well as hardwoods to the city. On both sides of the river ran miles of timber yards—1.5 billion feet a year—fencing, siding, crossbeams, floorboards, and entire balloon frames for every construction project in the North. The fire had struck at the heart of the "lumber district" and would have been a fatal blow to the city's economy had the fire department not quelled the blaze.[12]

The editors of the *Chicago Daily Tribune* estimated the damage to the sixteen-acre area of lumberyards at $300,000, but later insurance estimates put the cost at over $1 million. The ruined blocks also hosted saloons—the working people ate as well as drank there—and saloon fires were a common occurrence. The site of the fire, the "red flash" district according to the insurance industry, was well away from the densely packed center of the city, but close enough to pose a danger had the wind been up. In any case, Chicago remained a horizontal forest, a waiting feast for a great fire.[13]

The mill firefight had lasted sixteen hours and exhausted an already overstretched force. Tired firefighters had to return to their firehouses to repair broken equipment, take care of the horses and tackle on the fire trucks, and cope with smoke inhalation and other medical problems many of them had sustained. Exhaustion is cumulative, and there had been twenty-eight little fires since the month began, enough to weary the most heroic and fit fireman.[14]

Chicago had switched from a volunteer to a paid municipal firefighting force in 1858, but it was far too small for the growing city. Though later reports would suggest that the firefighters often brawled and were sometimes unfit for service because of drinking, biographies of the captains and battalion chiefs suggest that most of the officers were dedicated to their jobs. They were not political appointees but had come up through the ranks of the firefighters to become officers and commanders.

For example, chief fire marshal (chief of the department) Robert A. Williams was a Canadian who had started as a volunteer fireman in 1849 on engine No. 6 and worked his way up to assistant chief in 1868. Others in the ranks worked their way up from long service on the engine or hook and ladder companies to officer status. For example, George Taylor was a Chicago lad of seventeen when he joined No. 3 engine, in 1864. Too young for the Civil War but not for the dangers of firefighting, he was one of the firemen who worked the mill blaze on October 7. James Enright, who came to the city as a child from Ireland, was a "torch boy" for the Niagara Company in the volunteer days, and in 1858, at the age of seventeen, signed up with the city to serve on No. 2 engine. At the mill fire, he commanded No. 7 engine.[15]

Many of the paid professional members of the city fire service had earlier been members of volunteer companies. The latter had competed with one another as they ran to the fire. The new fire service companies would have to learn to work together to be mutually supportive, coordinating their staging and attack at the fire scene.

There, reliable communication of orders from commanders to fire-fighters and speedy reports of firefighters to their officers would enable the relatively small CFD to manage large fires. The men had as well to accustom themselves to a military-style regimen, with ranks, discipline, and drill. The firefighters remained a brotherhood of manly individualists, but they had to make room for new values of efficiency, bureaucratic control, and the politics of any municipal agency. Formal education in firefighting had to become a mandatory part of training, adding to the older traditions of learning on the job. Promotion would depend upon merit rather than simply longevity. The changeover would take time, and it was still underway in 1871.[16]

The city's board of police and fire commissioners had lobbied since its creation in 1865 for a larger force, as well as for more hydrants, an ordinance restricting the use of mill-framed houses, and the end of tarred roofs—all in vain. The fire code for the city prohibited new frame construction in the "Loop" (the densely populated area framed by the Chicago River and Lake Michigan). Existing wooden structures did not have to be removed, however, nor did the city ordinance bar wood cornices, window frames, and roof joists, despite clear evidence that these could make a "fireproof" building into an inferno. The Water Works (with its wooden mansard-style roof), the elegant new Chicago Historical Society Building, and the *Tribune* headquarters, all supposedly fireproof, were for these reasons actually fire prone. The city had grown so fast and timber was so cheap that much of the building stock (save the mansions, large hotels, department stores, and banks) south of Madison Street in the Loop was wooden.

The city's common council responded to these appeals of its firemen with indifference. It ignored Chief Williams's request for fire boats and larger water mains. He did get an appropriation for another 10,000 feet of fire hose to replace worn hoses—a drop in the bucket in a city that had over sixteen square miles of streets. In 1871, the city still had only seventeen steam engines, "six hose carts, four hooks and ladder companies, and one hose elevator" (an elevated ladder). After a fire the size and difficulty of the mill fire on Saturday, all of the equipment would need inspection and repair. For the exhausted members of the CFD, this meant that Sunday would not be a day of rest.[17]

The equipment was modern—that is to say, it was new. Horse-drawn steam engines were a tremendous improvement on hand pumpers pulled to the fire by firemen on foot. Fire horses were loved, pampered, and essential to the new era of firefighting. Selected for their stamina, intelligence, and reliability, some fire horses became famous in their own right. Firehouses were part barn, and the apparatus and stalls were next to one another—adding a certain odor to firefighting. The smell, the omnipresent horseflies, and the stamping and the neighing of the horses in the stalls below made it difficult for the men in the dormitory above to get a decent night's sleep. Still, when the alarm came in, a good driver could hitch the horses in minutes, and good horses seemed to know when an emergency required their utmost efforts. They served for ten years on average, hauling the engines and trucks to the fire scenes. Racing through the streets in teams of two, three, and four, they were as much a part of the cityscape as the firemen themselves. Everyone in the street stopped what they were doing to watch the driver urging his team to race to the fire. But on Sunday, the horses, like the men, were tired.[18]

Steam engines and mastery of ladder techniques were other revolutionary innovations in the 1850s. Steam engines could throw streams of water to a height of 200 feet at a rate of 600 gallons a minute—if the water supply was adequate. Hoses were mounted on separate horse-drawn carts. By the 1870s, firemen had begun to master ladder techniques. Hook and ladder carts, also called "trucks" because of their wagonlike appearance, carried multiple three- and four-story ladders to fires. The division of labor into hose and ladder companies was another progressive step—for hose men fought the fire while ladder men rescued victims and used tools to pull down burning walls and roofs before they could spread the fire.

A newly installed system of street call boxes that sent electric signals to a central fire station in the city hall (then relayed to the firehouses) was overrated, however, for the fireboxes required keys and these were held by business establishments near the box, by police

officers, and by fire patrol members. Keyless boxes were not introduced until 1878.[19]

The water to fight fires came from the lake through the waterworks along a system of pipes to hydrants. Fighting fire in the city is
all about water pressure and water supply. Enough water under pressure from the hydrants, and the firefighters were confident they
could knock down any fire. Insufficient water supply or pressure,
and the firefighters might as well have stayed home. Suction from
cisterns or other standing water supplies might suffice for a time, but
it could not take the place of water under pressure from the hydrants.[20]

The pumps that drove the water in Chicago's pipes and hydrants
were a marvel of engineering for the time. Set in the 1863 Water
Works in the North Division (north of the Chicago River), the
pumps brought over 7 million gallons of water from the lake through
a pipe over 500 feet long to the water tower, thence through iron
pipes and local reservoirs to the rest of the city.

That fall, a new engine was being installed in the huge main engine room. The 154-foot-high tower of stone, wrought iron, and
brick was deemed fireproof. The building itself, fireproofed by a
slate and tile roof and walls of stone two feet thick, contained offices
and sleeping quarters for the water engineers. Boilers powered by
steam ran the engine on the site. But there were two weak spots in
these buildings. Ventilators in the roof carried off the heat from the
operation—though if these were left open during a fire outside, they
might admit its sparks into the building itself. The interior of the waterworks featured vaulted wooden timbers and, during the reconstruction of the engine that fall, much wooden scaffolding.[21]

If the water supply (unlike Pittsburgh's) was theoretically adequate for the size of the city, the CFD's force was not. On duty were
193 full-time firemen (although firemen are never full-time employees—they almost always have second jobs) and twenty-three headquarters personnel. Up to that fall, the city spent about $366,000 per
year to pay twenty-six companies to cover three city divisions of over
300,000 souls and over 40,000 buildings, some of which were block
sized, six and eight stories high, and filled with flammable goods.

Most of the building stock was one- and two-story wood and shingle firetraps. As one memoir recalled, it seemed "too inconvenient" to object to the construction of wooden shanties next to the bridges over the north and south branches of the river. And who could question the need for the towering grain elevators that were, in effect, giant chimneys, 130 feet high with storage capacity for 1,250,000 bushels of grain; or quarrel about the city's 561 miles of wooden plank roadways and sidewalks when wood was so cheap and the city was expanding so fast? Pine was the material of choice for the sidewalks. As former New York City fire commissioner Thomas Von Essen recently wrote, "[O]nce fire hits a dry pine tree, it's all but over." To top it all off, many of the sidewalks were elevated above the streets, allowing oxygen to flow beneath them—a perfect horizontal chimney to carry fire from street to street.[22]

THE O'LEARYS' BARN

Like Pittsburgh, Chicago neighborhoods featured mixed-use building stock—manufacturing, commercial, and residential structures coexisted in the same districts. There was no zoning that separated manufacturing plants from homes. Structures with different purposes abutted one another. For example, on the near western side of the Chicago River, at DeKoven Street between Clinton and Jefferson, sprawled a warren of houses, taverns, and barns in a largely Irish immigrant ghetto. Next to it lay lumberyards, mills, and coal dumps. Most of the houses in the ghetto had unpainted wooden siding, without insulation, and wooden shingle roofs, much like houses in Boston a hundred years before. The homes stood on wooden foundation platforms, raised above the pounded earth. It was a neighborhood, young Joseph Edgar Chamberlin, then a cub reporter on the *Evening Post*, recounted "that . . . had always been a *terra incognita* to respectable Chicagoans." Its "miserable alleys" masqueraded as streets. "During a residence of three years in the city I had never visited it."[23]

The irony of Chamberlin's snobbish aversion to the neighborhood was that the plain frame houses represented Chicago's own revolutionary innovation in home construction. They were examples of "balloon framing." Wooden construction from medieval times to the early nineteenth century entailed heavy timber beams connected together with fitted mortise-work, the construction proceeding from the bottom up. Every house was different. The new balloon frame— invented in Chicago in the 1840s—was an open latticework of much lighter milled four-by-four and two-by-four boards, assembled at the site like the pieces of a jigsaw puzzle. Over the open frame, the builders nailed sheets of thin wood. The balloon frame house was cheaper, faster to build, and took advantage of the city's many lumberyards. It was also a firetrap.[24]

Two such houses on the north side of the street belonged to Patrick and Catherine O'Leary, Irish immigrants, who had purchased the shotgun plot (narrow but deep) in 1864. A wooden-slat barn in the back contained hay, wood shavings, and other combustibles, along with milk cows. Nothing about the barn's owners differed from the thousands of other working-class people who owned, rented, or visited in the neighborhood. If the fire began in their barn, it might just as easily have started anywhere in the vicinity.[25]

How then did the Sunday evening fire, the Great Fire of 1871 start? Who was responsible? Local lore had Mrs. O'Leary visiting the barn to check on the welfare of her milk cow and leaving a lantern where the cow could kick it over. The story gained credence after the fire—easy to see why, given the attitudes of editors and reporters like Chamberlin toward the shanty Irish. In nineteenth-century America, as today, Americans are fascinated with individual responsibility and blame. A quarter century after the fire, America's greatest legal thinker, Oliver Wendell Holmes, Jr., wrote that the law's chief concern was to punish the negligence of the bad man. This was one occasion where the popular mind agreed with the elite legal profession: If there was a catastrophe, someone or something must be at fault, and that guilty party must be identified even if he or she could escape punishment. The debate over who started the Great Fire continued for years in Chicago, and is still going on.[26]

There is little doubt that the fire began in the O'Leary cow barn on DeKoven, but Richard Bales's exhaustive study of the evidence

Chicago Fire, 1871

from the city's own investigation, as well as other sources at the Chicago Historical Society, has revealed once and for all the real culprits. The O'Learys' later statement that they were at home and in bed, not in the barn milking the cow by the light of a lantern, stands up. Instead, two of their rapscallion neighbors, "Pegleg" Daniel Sullivan, a twenty-six-year-old cart driver, and his buddy Dennis Regan, a laborer who lived down the block, stopped in the barn for a smoke. They accidentally set the hay and wood shavings on the floor afire, failed to put out the quickly spreading flames, then rushed to the O'Leary house to announce that they had "seen" a fire in the barn. When questioned by authorities, the two men forswore themselves, giving explanations for where they were and how they saw the blaze that could not have been true.[27]

The O'Leary barn was little more than a wooden box, with a "shed" or one-piece roof, rather than a tar-and-shingle layered roof. The O'Learys admitted that they had two tons of coal and two tons of hay in it—in effect, it was a giant matchbook. Catherine O'Leary

118

added that Sullivan and Regan came to the door to report the fire to her and her husband, but none of them went to the firehouse six blocks away or tried to use the firebox alarm on the corner. She simply watched, as did her neighbors, as the fire leaped from house to house and block to block, moving northeast.

In their refusal to bring the CFD to their door, the O'Learys and their neighbors demonstrated how insular and isolated their little world was. It was bounded by their own kind ethnically and occupationally, and in it they rented to one another, watched one another's children, and kept their mouths shut when outsiders came around. In any case, why call on the fire department when the O'Leary house was spared? The wind was gusting up from the southwest, a dry hot wind that carried the fire away from the shanties of the West Division. The O'Learys and their neighbors thus became spectators in the Great Fire, just as they were spectators in the rise of the city.[28]

THE GREAT FIRE BEGINS

The CFD did not arrive quickly. No signal was received at the central office until 9:32 PM, an hour after the first tendril of smoke crept out of the barn. Then, the night watchman at an engine house nine blocks away reported the fire, after engines from other houses had already arrived at the scene. Had companies responded when the fire was small, they might have contained it within the barn, or at least prevented its spread. Each minute of time lost gave the fire more time to involve the roof of the barn. When the first engines began pumping, the roof was fully aflame and the wind was carrying the burning wood embers far beyond the initial site of the fire.[29]

The first man to officially inform the fire department of the blaze was William J. Brown, a telegraph operator at the courthouse in the Loop. Brown had received a report from the watchman in the courthouse tower above. That three-story neo-Roman cupola atop the massive four-story courthouse block was the highest perch in the Loop. Brown reported the fire to Mathias Schaefer, the fire warden on duty, who told Brown to strike the first alarm. Brown added others as he watched the fire's glow spreading. Soon the two men were busy trying to put out the little fires that embers had carried to the courthouse roof.[30]

Fire Chief Williams was sleeping fitfully that evening. He had directed his men at the Saturday night mill fire until 2:00 AM Sunday morning. Exhausted, he did not wake until 2:00 PM on the afternoon of the 8th. He said he went to church, then "hitched up my horse" and checked out the engine companies overhauling the last embers of the previous night's blaze. In any fire, there may be isolated hot spots still alight after the fire has been contained. The wind had not died down, and he feared that an ember from the mill might flare up and be carried to another combustible site. Seeing nothing to worry him, he returned home, laid his turnout gear (helmet, rubber jacket-cloak, gloves, and boots) neatly aside, and tried to go back to sleep. Just when he had closed his eyes, his wife awakened him: "'Robert! Fire!'"

Williams recognized the location of the street firebox. Each had its own three-digit code. He raced to the scene. At the edge of the fire, he saw two barns going up in smoke and "a lot of little outhouses and fences and I don't know what . . . a regular nest of fire." Williams knew from experience that his men's ability to control the flames depended on four factors: the length of time the fire had been burning, the combustible materials nearby, the resources he could summon to his side—men, apparatus, and water—to fight the fire, and the wind. He must have realized that the odds of containment were not good. The fire had a good head start on him; he was surrounded by highly flammable wood and wood products; it would take time to bring in enough personnel and equipment; and the wind had picked up.[31]

Like every good fire officer, Williams moved as close to the fire as he could and encouraged his men. "'Hang on to her boys,'" he called out, but he knew "'she was gaining on us.'" He did not say so in his testimony, but he realized that this was a Great Fire and it would brook no master. Firefighting brings order out of chaos, makes wild nature bow to human will, skill, and technology. But there are times when the firefighter knows when he faces a fire that will not bend its neck to the yoke.

So long as there was water with enough pressure coming from the hydrants to the hoses, however, there was hope. Williams ordered a second and third alarm. Engine companies and hose trucks straggled in, the men still bleary from the previous night's battle. The call for "all hands" could have been swifter, but Williams was not in direct communication with the central firehouse. In every investigation of a major fire disaster from that time to our own, investigators have cited difficulties in communication as a major problem.

Drought, wind, and heat had turned the houses, barns, and lumberyards west of the river into tinderboxes. When the radiant heat of the fire reached them, it set them afire. Falling burning debris also carried the fire beyond the fully involved structures and soon whole blocks were burning, a conflagration far greater than Williams's forces could contain. He ordered the American Company, reinforced by the Chicago, to get in front of the fire. The Illinois arrived, and jumped a block beyond the flames, wetting down the buildings in advance of the fire. In the confusion, Williams was running back and forth to command his engine and hose companies by direct verbal means. Because of the smoke, he could not see much beyond the men in front of him. What's more, the smoke was beginning to put those men at risk. More people die in blazes from smoke inhalation than from burns.

No matter how many streams of water the CFD could throw on the existing blaze, the progress of the fire could not be slowed. The heat of the fire had created a convection current, an upward wind swirl that added force to the gusts from the southwest. Combined, they carried the embers of the fire beyond the companies' reach. Firefighters do not want the fire to get behind them, trapping them within a blaze. This is just what was happening in the early hours of the fire in the West Division of the city. The men knew it. "'Robert, we can't stay long here,' one officer told Williams. "'Said I, hang on as long as you can.'" But the companies barely had enough time to unhook the hoses and drive the wagons at full gallop ahead of the onrushing flames.

The engines were so hot from their work that the men could not touch them. Some had to be abandoned. Williams was everywhere, and everywhere in danger, but as long as his men were battling, "'as long as they were in there, I'd take my chances.'" This is the code of the fire department officer—the first man in, the last man out. "'Do the best you can,'" Williams told each new company's officers as they came on the scene. Enright and Taylor and the rest of the veterans had come, but this was something none of them had seen before. At Williams's command, the firemen moved against the blaze like infantry, one block, one hydrant, one company at a time. But the fire raced on like cavalry, jumping over or veering around the firefighters, capturing mills and lumberyards, amassing more ammunition for its assault on the Loop and later the North Division. Sometime before 11:00 PM, Williams heard what he had dreaded. "'Robert, the fire is on the South Side [the Loop],'" another officer reported. "'The Devil it is,'" Williams rejoined. But he had to give this devil his due. The fire had beaten him and his men to the most affluent part of the city.

As the fire progressed, spectators who thought themselves and their homes safe were driven from their refuges and made refugees. David Swing was one of these. He had gone to see the fire, but with a feeling of dread. "The dryness of every roof, the high wind, the exhausted condition of the fire department, combined to make the [red] sky a painful spectacle . . . already in the sky overhead there was a great line of sparks moving slowly toward the northwest. It was a fiery belt, having a breadth of perhaps two hundred feet." He rushed back to his own house and joined with others to put out the burning cinders, but the wall of flame had grown to 400 feet above the ground and "streets arched over with flame." The roar of the flames seemed to quiet the hurrying refugees, moving not in panic but in a determined flow due north, away from the ruin.[32]

THE MOST IMPORTANT NEWSPAPER STORY

Shortly after the first engine arrived on DeKoven, James Sheahan and George Upton of the *Tribune* pulled up, having seen the fire's glow on the horizon. They followed the fire through the night and into the next day. It was for them, and for their readers, the most important newspaper story of the day.

The *Tribune* was one of the five major dailies in the city, and Upton would go on to become a city editor. Still, reporters were something of a novelty in American newspapers. Following the innovation of the penny press in the 1830s, the subscription system (pay in advance) was replaced by paperboys selling cheap copies on the streets. Something had to be done to market more newspapers. Crime reporting, political coverage, and disaster stories filled the bill nicely. City readers could not get enough of them—particularly fires. Sheahan and Upton would not only cover the story for the *Tribune* (even after its new "fireproof" building melted and its presses became molten lumps), they published their eyewitness book on the fire in December 1871.

The first edition of the book, sitting on my desk as I write this, has a graphic depiction of the city hall engulfed in flames, with the caption "City Hall, Chicago, Oct 9th 1871." The image is embossed in gold paint. I imagine it must have been a kind of souvenir. The two reporters had to go to a Philadelphia press because all the printers in the city were burned out. Only one book scooped them—Elias Colbert and Everett Chamberlin's *Chicago and the Great Conflagration* (which came out at the end of October), but it was not a firsthand account. Still, for all the dislocation of the publishing industry in the city, in the fall and winter of 1871–1872, magazines and pamphlets on the fire, followed by other books, "flooded the market."[33]

All the newspaper accounts used the metaphors of war and battle. In the shadow of Civil War newspaper coverage, that choice of literary device may have been inevitable. Of course, the fire could not match the Civil War in importance. But then, unlike the reporters for *Harper's* magazine and the Eastern papers during the war, only a few newsmen from the Midwest had been able to report from the battle sites, and Sheahan, Upton, and Chamberlin were not among them. For the generation of Chicago newshounds who did not cover the war, the fire offered a chance to write about another battle against a wily and implacable enemy. It was their Civil War. That is why the language they used is so filled with military metaphors and similes.[34]

"Proceeding directly to the scene," Sheahan and Upton could see that the fire had already "rushed forward" across several streets going toward the heart of the city. The fire course was wind directed, with advance guards of the fire blown blocks away, to alight on roofs, slide down ventilator shafts, rush through open windows (recall the heat of the day), and otherwise insinuate themselves into the bastions of the city's life. Behind these fiery skirmishers came the main force, a fire fifty feet, then a hundred, then a block, then twenty blocks wide. This invading force threw itself across the Chicago River into the South Division of the city, scattering the engine and hose companies that dared oppose it. As if they could harness the power of the wind itself, the flames gobbled up the lumber and feasted on the coal in the yards along the western side of the river, then fell upon the banks and hotels in the Loop. "Everywhere was a broad sheet of flame leaping, darting, sending forth, as if from some grand pyrotechnic preparation, the most brilliant dazzling meteors of living fire."

So fast did the fire move through the evening, and so dark did it make the horizon, that no one could or did take its picture, though there were certainly newspaper photographers in its path (as were the buildings of the *Tribune*, the *Times* and the other city dailies). "The two main columns sent out detachments which entered every street with the regularity of an advancing army." What the Confederates in their numbers could not accomplish in four years of war, a cow barn fire had achieved in four hours. The fire blew out windows and sucked itself into buildings, entered alleys and "burst through the rear of buildings on either side," spewing up a "writhing, twisting column of fire into the air a hundred feet." The courthouse lit up from within, the cupola crashed through the burning roof, the walls fell in upon themselves, and the symbol of the city's wealth and power became the symbol of its ruin. The opera house, the great hotels, the office blocks—everything in the Loop succumbed. Indeed, the stone and brick and iron did not even put up a fight. Only the *Tribune* building refused to crumble. Its walls charred and cracked, but they did not come down.[35]

The massive hotels in the center of the Loop, those "immense caravansaries" of business people and tourists, were next. The "nine-story Palmer, the seven-story Sherman, with its miles of halls, the Tremont, Briggs, and the rest" all emptied their guests into the streets. Alexander Frear was in the Sherman House and noted that few took more than passing notice of the fire bells until cinders began to fall all around the building like hail in a storm. Mrs. Alfred Hebard and her husband were already asleep in the Palmer House when porters roused everyone with the cry of fire. She rushed down to the lobby, not neglecting to pay her bill, then fled, little realizing that the guest book, her money, and the entire building would soon be consumed. Piles of coal for the boilers of the hotels and the heating systems of the office buildings became sources of fuel. In the alleys behind the hotels, the tumbledown patches of wooden "hovels and sheds" of saloons and brothels acted the part of a fifth column, allowing the fire to regain its strength and spread itself northward.[36]

"Mobs of men and women rushed wildly from street to street, screaming, gesticulating, and shouting . . . the contents of hovels and the contents of aristocratic residences, huddled together in inextricable confusion." Some had waited too long to leave the Loop and huddled along the lakeside. Others crushed together in the long lines trying to get across the river ahead of the fire. The crush to escape over the Randolph Street Bridge killed as many as the flames. Thieves had a field day with property left in the streets. Wagon men charged exorbitant rates to carry away trunks and prized personal goods, when they weren't driving their horses to death. Behind them, the fire was evenhanded in its irreligion: First Methodist, St. Mary's, First and Second Presbyterian, Trinity Episcopal, the Swedenborgian church, and the Jewish synagogue bowed before the flames. The fire spared the graveyards, leaving little islands of refugees hiding from death amid the already dead. Its workers saved the Oriental Flour Mill, on the west side of the river, by using its own hoses to wet it down. The fire retaliated by jumping the northern branch of the river and taking vengeance on the North Division of the city. Indeed, more of the North Division was devoured than in the South and West Divisions combined.[37]

In the North Division, the waterworks had caught flame, and with the demise of its great pumps, the water supply in the hydrants vanished. The firemen were helpless to stem the advance of the flames and joined the lines of humbled men and women trying to find a way out of the city. In the meantime, the closely grouped wooden houses of the near Northside made a meal for the fire, and by early afternoon, it had gorged on the tree-lined streets and frame houses along the lakeside, leaving only ash.

The residents could see the fire advancing by stages, and they retreated by stages, some to the burial grounds by the lake, others north and west. The 75,000 people of the North Division were all displaced, a ragtag, retreating army of men, women, and many children utterly defeated by the conflagration. At the northern edge of the city, the fuel supply for the fire began to give out, and a gentle rain arrived in mid-evening. After midnight, the heavens finally opened, and the rain doused the smoldering ruins.[38]

"We Are in Ruins"

The fire killed more than 200 people, though no one has ever completed an exact count. Surely there were more deaths than we will ever know. It destroyed nearly $200 million worth of real property (the equivalent of $3.23 billion in 2005), left 90,000 people homeless, ate over 1.5 million bushels of wheat and corn and the same portion of cut beef, and burned up 50 million feet of milled timber and 80,000 tons of coal. It left an indelible mark on the psyches of those who felt its fury. Its relentlessness reminded people that they might impose on nature, but they could not resist it when it was aroused.[39]

The human cost was not so easily computed. The trek from familiar scenes and settings imperiled by the advancing fire was harrowing. "Our ride" to safety "was an anxious one," Mary Fales wrote to her mother, "many of the ladies fairly lost their wits . . . many times we were blocked and it seemed as if the fire must reach the bridge before we did." Anna Higginson, wife of a real estate broker, was so agitated at the loss of her sumptuous home on North Dearborn, that "people sometimes check me for being too despondent when I say I shall never have a home again."[40]

Jonas Hutchinson, a lawyer and notary public, was used to being in command of his pen and his wits, but as the fire approached his office on Washington Street, he despaired. He wrote his mother, in New Hampshire, "We are in ruins. All the business portion of the city has fallen a prey to the fiery fiend. Our magnificent streets for acres and acres lined with elegant structures are a heap of sightless rubbish. It cannot be described." But it had to be; human nature dictated that the experience had to be shared. "What a sight: a sea of fire, the heavens all ablaze, the air filled with burning embers . . . thousands upon thousands of people rushing frantically about." The next day, with the fire burning itself out, Hutchinson's pen had grown even hotter: "the city is thronged with desperadoes who are plundering and trying to set new fires. The police are vigilant . . . every block has its patrolmen and instructions are explicit . . . to shoot any man who acts suspicious . . . several were shot and others hung to lamp posts last night under these instructions . . . the roughs are improving the time to sack and pillage . . . the like of this sight since Sodom and Gomorrah has never met human vision."[41]

Actually, Hutchinson in his distant abode was no more a witness to the events of destruction and pillage that he described than to what happened at Sodom, but his vision of a world in ruins, overrun with crime, was widely shared by the propertied classes driven from their mansions. As Judge Lambert Tree recalled, "[J]udges or courts and police officers were there," in the streets, "but they only formed so many units in that stricken assemblage, and their authority that morning was no greater than that of any other man upon the ground." The prisoners in the holding pens at the courthouse had been released—the alternative was a mass auto-da-fé. Nothing was said of rescue operations; no one was going into the rubble to find any survivors. As the *Evening Journal* had reminded its readers, the "great calamity" was not the displaced poor but "hundreds of millions of dollars' worth of property destroyed."[42]

The fire damage was not the only concern of the well-to-do. They feared that the panic-stricken lower classes would unleash chaos. Accounts depicted the poor people caught in the blaze as though they were wild animals. "Seized with wild and causeless panics they surged together backwards and forwards in the narrow streets" like the cattle in the slaughter pens. Such human debris had no moral excuse for its brutish and aimless conduct. "Ill-omened and obscene birds of night were they," who frenzied "themselves with drink" from the burning saloons. "Villainous, haggard with debauch, and pinched with misery," the city poor, the "Negroes with stolid faces, and white men who fatten on the wages of shame . . . moved here and there, stealing, scolding . . ."[43]

Crowd behavior as a disaster unfolds follows an almost incomprehensible pattern. At first, no one takes much notice—look at the fire, the crowd seems to murmur, but it does not react. Camera pictures of the residents of San Francisco, staring down the hill at the fires as they erupt after the earthquake of 1906 had ruptured the gas lines demonstrate this stage of response. No one is going anywhere. The fire will not reach them; it cannot harm them; they are far enough away. Within an hour the fire would kill hundreds on the very streets in the photograph.[44]

As the fire spreads, individuals exhibit the herd instinct. They panic, often overlooking obvious, nearby escape routes in favor of ones they know, even when these are farther away and dangerous to reach. The larger the body of people, the greater the crush upon the available escape routes. More die or are injured by people pressing against them or knocking them down than from the original source of the danger. As the rush to escape grows, the panic accelerates and the crowd becomes a heaving mob. The intervention of authority figures—police or firefighters—can control such a contagion of panic at its early stages. So does practice leaving a danger area, for example, fire drills or prior experience with evacuation. None of the latter were present in the Loop when the fire arrived. The firemen had fled. There was no significant police presence. Elite authority figures were busy hiring wagons to cart themselves and their families away from the danger. It was not moral turpitude that lashed the crowd, but natural human emotions.[45]

With the rain-soaked ruins still smoldering, the businessmen who ran the city tried to reassert control. They had no intention of conceding their authority because they had lost their buildings or their ledger books. The mayor found a job printer with a press in working order and struck off a "Proclamation . . . Public order will be preserved. The police and special police now being appointed will be responsible for the maintenance of the peace, and the protection of property . . . All persons are warned against any act tending to endanger property." Had the proclamation been read to the fire itself, it could not have had less effect. What property? The only pieces of property left in the burned district were the fireproof safes in the rubble of the banks. These could hardly be opened or carried off. In fact, the proclamation, which no one heard and few would have read, was meant to be hortatory: We have not lost command, it said; and property is still our prime concern. At the same time, the Board of Trade took out an advertisement to remind the *Journal's* readers that the directors of the board would be meeting. Business would go on, even if Randolph Street, home to the financiers, could no longer be identified in the rubble.[46]

A day after the fire ended, a delegation from the Board of Trade descended on the home of General Philip Sheridan, hero of the Civil War, conqueror of Robert E. Lee's cavalry, and currently commander of troops, bases, and armories in the Military Division of the Missouri. They wanted him to impose martial law. Sheridan later recalled that he had been reluctant to call out the troops, but the evidence suggests that he was more than willing to be persuaded. As a formality, Sheridan asked the mayor if he wanted him to bivouac his troops in the city to supplement the 300 regular police officers and 500 special officers already ordered to patrol the streets. The latter was a "force of perhaps 450 'merchant police'— the private guards and watchmen employed by railroads, hotels and banks" (today's security personnel) keeping an eye on their employers' assets. Mayor Roswell Mason assented, and Sheridan telegraphed the barracks at St. Louis and elsewhere for 600 soldiers. Sheridan later upped the ante to over 1,000 troops, billeted them in the middle of the city, and had them patrol the streets with fixed bayonets. Although Sheridan reported to the mayor that there was no evidence of "incendiarism," the troops did not depart for three weeks.[47]

The real danger in the immediate aftermath of the fire was not looting but disease. Typhoid fever might appear in the water supply tainted by dead people who harbored the bacteria. Food or drink handled by infected persons also spread the disease. Cholera, another bacterial infection endemic in nineteenth-century cities, thrived in unsanitary water supplies or untended sewage. Garbage left in the streets might breed rats, and fleas on these might become vectors of typhus or, worse, bubonic plague.

Plague and fire fed on one another in European cities. Municipalities and states were beginning to see the relationship between public health and disease, particularly in the cities. The so-called sanitarian profession, originating in New York and Boston, probed the connection between excrement and other human wastes and disease. Faced with the threat of a cholera epidemic, New York City's "newly formed Metropolitan Board of Health had conducted a successful educational campaign and had enforced the clean-up of streets, cisterns, and privies." A privy (or privy vault) was an outhouse; indoor plumbing was a novel luxury.[48]

Chicago, with its vast stockyard area, its slaughterhouses and packing plants, was a magnet for animal-borne pathogens. The relationship between the disposal of animal waste and water supplies had already occurred to the city and state authorities. Although the pens lay to the west of the burned district, many animals died in the burned area, and their carcasses were left to rot in the streets or were pushed into the river. Chicago had already withstood visitations of cholera and other epidemic diseases. As recently as 1866, almost 1,000 people in the city had succumbed to cholera. With the danger of an epidemic in mind, on Monday, October 9, Governor John Palmer called the Illinois legislature into special session and laid before it an invitation to "appropriate such sum, or sums of money, or adopt such other legislative measures as may be thought judicious, necessary, or proper for relief of the people of the city." These included public health funds.[49]

But unlike Pittsburgh, where the memory of the fire continued to frighten the people who witnessed it, the leaders of Chicago immediately transformed its agony into a heroic saga. "The saddest night" in the city's history became its illuminating moment. According to one observer, "The hungry were fed, the shelterless welcomed, the naked clothed, and a general sharing of everything—an equal division—seemed going forward in every part of the saved district" and "many . . . true hearts were strengthened in their attachment to God."[50]

But Mammon had his scribes rewriting the fire story, too. One of these was William Bross. "Bross, his family just burned out of their elegant townhouse on Michigan Avenue, caught a train to New York. His purpose was to reassure the financial markets." He did—a cheerful, boastful figure with the smell of smoke still lingering on his clothing, "advised wealthy businessmen in New York and elsewhere to invest their fortunes and their sons in the unprecedented opportunities in Chicago created by the fire." Bross, a lay Christian exhorter, Democratic politician, newspaper editor, and promoter, included his talk to the New York City "men of capital" in his miscellany, *History of Chicago*. As he recalled, "I was assured that [my efforts] had done much to inspire confidence in the early restoration of the city." Chicago had a fire, but it was different from other urban fires, just as Chicago was different from other cities. It was always in a state of becoming rather than being; it was defined by its dynamism.[51]

The very last words in Sheahan and Upton's book quoted newly elected mayor Joseph Medill:

> In concluding I point with pride and admiration to the gigantic efforts our whole people are putting forth to rise from the ruins and rebuild Chicago . . . habits of industry and self-reliance, personal integrity, business aptitude, mechanical skill, and unconquerable will . . . can speedily re-create more than was swept away. . . . a prosperity greater than ever dreamed of will be achieved in a period so brief, that the rise will astonish mankind even more than the fall, of Chicago.[52]

BUT WHICH CHICAGO REALLY EMERGED from the ashes—the city whose class barriers were leveled by the blaze or the get-rich-quick city, the heroic city, the city of confident men and dutiful women, or a city of even greater and more discordant class divisions and maldistribution of wealth? Would it be a new kind of city, the precursor of urban modernism, the midwife to suburbia, a marvel of technology? Or would it fall prey to corruption, bossism, and class warfare?

"Heroic and Confident Men"

In the months after the fire, the spectacle of Chicago in ruins lent itself to romantic exaggeration and Victorian sentimentality, on the one hand, and the first truly empirical depictions of urban fire and firefighting, on the other. A highly imaginative Currier and Ives lithograph of the fire was a best-seller in part because it depicted the ferocity of the flames (though the artist got the wind direction wrong). John R. Chapin's eyewitness illustration of "The Rush for Life over Randolph Street Bridge," published first in *Harper's* magazine and then copied by the artists in the Currier and Ives stable, is one of the most dramatic recreations of a disaster scene ever depicted. Personal tales of narrow escapes and tragic deaths filled newspaper and magazine pages. Chicago's fire was also the first for which photography was widely available, making its devastation graphically visible to the whole nation. National magazines rushed their photographers onto trains into the city to record the miles of tumbledown brick and stone. Moreover, the pictures' impact lay, in part, in their number—not a few, as in the Pittsburgh disaster, but hundreds, matching the vast scope of the fire.[53]

The recovery of the city from the fire presented a less distinct picture. Given the extent of the devastation, one would have expected a slow and painful rebuilding process. Not so. The "resilience" of the city made the reconstruction of Chicago into both model and myth of American will, know-how, and optimism. At the same time, not everyone experienced the same giddy optimism or profited from the remarkable achievements of the post-fire era. The story that some contemporaries related of the recovery was avowedly "therapeutic," promising not only healing but a salvation of a kind. Others told of lost hopes and destroyed dreams. Indeed, though the speed and supposed completeness of the recovery attached itself so firmly to the fire story as to almost overwhelm the fire itself, many Chicagoans never really recovered from the catastrophe, and many who came to the city after the fire to take part in the rebuilding became victims themselves.[54]

Fire books like Sheahan and Upton's and Colbert and Chamberlin's, professedly dedicated to fact, were in fact cleverly argued propaganda. They did not conclude with the end of the fire's reign, or even with a journey through the ruins in its immediate aftermath, but instead regarded the epic of recovery as the most important part of the story. Detail mattered, of course, but only those details that fit a predetermined conclusion. The ruins were barely cooled when Colbert and Chamberlin asserted that "the flames could not destroy . . . the genius that had built up Chicago . . . The kind of material of which Chicago men were made was well typified by . . . the business portion of the community."[55]

As the relief effort commenced and the work of rebuilding began, the retrofitting of the story kept pace. It featured the image of a phoenix rising from the ashes while they still smoldered. D. C. Houston, an army engineer at the scene, captured the central theme of the tale: "[T]he spirit displayed by the business men of this city in rebuilding is astonishing, and deserving of the highest praise." Chamberlin's narrative celebrated men of action, with "lightning-like energy," undaunted, farseeing "Anglo-Saxon" leaders, and "principal merchants" in the city who reignited its commercial flames. In the Loop, they swept aside "wooden rookeries" [the workers' shantytown] of moral depravity and idleness and threw up "massive edifices" and "first rate stores" of brick and marble. "Oh, it was an enlivening, an inspiring sight, to look out each morning upon a brave wall of solid masonry, which one had not noticed before—to watch . . . the heroic platoons of workingmen building, building, building them still higher . . . to observe the long files of laborers bearing, in the familiar hods upon their shoulders, the magic elements" of the new inner city.[56]

The reference to "Anglo-Saxon" men was not accidental. Men like Chamberlin considered themselves to be the ruling race. As Boston aristocrat Henry Cabot Lodge put it, "The men of each race possess an indestructible stock of ideas, traditions, sentiments, modes of thought, an unconscious inheritance from their ancestors, upon which argument has no effect." The seeds or germs of superior cultures passed through the blood from generation to generation. History was the story of that inheritance, and American history was the tale of the rise of the Anglo-Saxon peoples. It was right and fitting that the Anglo-Saxon peoples of Chicago direct its recovery. African, Celtic, and other lesser races were best suited to dig, load, and carry.[57]

The Anglo-Saxon's resolute masculinity informed the business community's response, as one businessman wrote shortly after the fire. "A grand manliness of feeling" infused even those who had lost all. Baptist minister E. J. Goodspeed later called it "the indomitable pluck which the Chicago men showed, all which no losses could damp and no wretchedness subdue." Pluck meant courage in the face of adversity, a type of character that the best men showed when the chips were down. Chamberlin agreed that the story of Chicago's recovery was one of "heroic and confident men." Their foresight and determination would make the new Chicago better than the old. It was a "Christian spirit" that encompassed "nerve and brain, energy and courage."[58]

At its most euphoric, this was the genre of anti-history, collecting "usable myths" and selectively forgetting the rest. One major magazine story about the fire, in 1880, even reported that no one had died. But in the willful, wishful separation of terrifying fact and materialist aspiration lay another story. For although everyone was a loser in the conflagration, not everyone was a winner in the rebuilding. Indeed, no sooner was the recovery begun than did the social and economic fissures open, which the incredible growth of the city, its Civil War boom, and the opportunities for employment and capital investment before 1871 had concealed.

To find the evidence of the first confident and heroic tale, one need only follow the footsteps of the large retailers looking for floor space inside the Loop and the real estate developers seeking farmland on the edges of the city. One can peer over their shoulders as they create the modern department store, found the Chicago School of high-rise architecture, and plan the suburbs. One could marvel at architect Daniel Burnham's fifteen-story fireproof office blocks and delight in his "White City," the greatest of our theme parks. Or one could travel on the rails from the city to such landscaped havens as Lake Forest and Hyde Park. There one would delight in their studied re-creation of an English country setting, close enough for commuters, but far from the crowd.

After the fire, a group of energetic city retailers determined to enlarge the physical size of their outlets. They joined with real estate developer John Doane to create a new kind of business district. The store owners bought up and combined narrow lots, allowing them greater street frontage and storage space. This private program of urban renewal was denounced by some as a conspiracy, but it remade the operation of retail and wholesale business. Larger stores could display a greater variety of goods and be more attractive places to buy consumer durables and clothing. In short, the Chicago retailers invented shopping.[59]

The foremost of these innovators was Marshall Field. Born in Massachusetts, Field came to Chicago before the Civil War. As a young salesclerk, his strict personal morality, engaging manner with customers, and drive to succeed were typical of the Yankee migrants. He also had Carnegie's indefatigable work ethic and eye for the main chance. Field partnered at the end of the war with Potter Palmer, a successful dry goods store owner, and Levi Leiter, a tough-minded accountant. They soon ran the biggest retail-wholesale outlet in the city.[60]

Palmer, whose ill health led him to sell out to Field and Leiter in 1865, had turned the store into a nice place to visit and shop instead of a warehouse with shelves. He added cosmetic and notion lines to the linens and ready-made clothing, and introduced fashions from all over the world. He sold on credit to trustworthy customers, always paid his own bills on time, and during the war bought up as much shelf stock as he could—realizing that after the war a consumer buying spree would multiply his profits. Palmer used the newspapers as none had before—not just putting in announcements, but advertising sales and new items in attractive ways. Field adopted all of these innovations and added more: He used female sales clerks to sell to women; found a new site for the store that had more space and more light; and introduced an even greater variety of goods and services in the store.

When the Great Fire destroyed the store on Lake Street, Field immediately found undamaged space to reopen. He had Leiter personally visit insurers and collect on the firm's policies. The two men continued to give credit to customers. In 1872, Field opened up on State Street, recognizing its access to customers from the west and north of the city. A fire in 1877 (the elevator shafts were the culprits) destroyed his new store, but bigger and more elegant buildings followed. By the beginning of the 1890s, Marshall Field on the corner of State and Washington, with its thirteen acres of floor space, its eleven electric elevators and myriad of electric lights, was a shopper's palace, the forerunner of the indoor mall and a place to be even if one had no intention of buying anything. Last but not least, he opened branches of the store all over the country.

The first new buildings on the newly combined and renovated inner-city blocks, like Field's store on State, were not fireproof. Instead, in their hurry to rebuild, the merchants resorted to "pasteboard" fakery, with local limestone gussied up as marble and wooden cornices painted to resemble masonry. The fire codes were not just ignored, they were parodied. As A. T. Andreas wrote in 1886, "haste and expediency" seemed to be the rule in the new buildings, rather than sturdiness and safety, much less elegance or novelty. "Plans were not infrequently conceived by builders destitute of scientific knowledge or skill," to which architects, similarly impoverished in knowledge, gave incautious assent. Some of the new buildings were falling down before they were finished.[61]

A new generation of architects who came to maturity during and after the fire would not stand for any of this. Daniel H. Burnham and his partner John Wellborn Root, along with competitors Louis

Sullivan (the designer of the largest of the Marshall Field stores) and others, built skyscrapers designed to resist fire. Root and Burnham formed a partnership shortly before the depression of 1873 hit the city. They saw around them the substandard buildings that hurry had thrown together in the Loop and cringed. Root and Burnham set out to lobby Fields and others, asserting that they deserved something more than boxy gimcrack. A fire in the Loop on July 14, 1874, helped—at least the city fathers agreed to ban wooden awnings, cupolas, and cornices—but the fire-loving mansard roofs were still there, and so was shoddy construction.

Burnham, New York born and sharp in business ways, and Root, something of a dreamer educated in Georgia, England, and New York City, made a superb partnership. Burnham could talk the birds out of the trees. He set up the first modern architectural firm (with staff) and had a competitive vision that stretched far beyond the Loop. Root was a superb architectural draftsman. Together they survived the dark days of the 1870s, and their firm became the leading designer of commercial blocks in the Loop, corporate headquarters all over the country, railroad terminals and stations, and elegant private dwellings.[62]

What made Burnham and Root especially attractive to their clients was their ability to solve problems, not the least of which was the danger of fire. Chicago stood on marshland under which was a pan of clay that could not support heavy buildings. Burnham and Root invented the floating foundation, a slab of concrete within which was laid a latticework of railroad ties and steel beams. Chicago businessmen wanted their offices to reach high into the sky. Earlier masonry and cast iron structures could bear only enough weight to reach eight or nine stories, and their massive interiors used up valuable office space and reduced available light. Burnham and Root introduced the steel frame building, anchored on concrete piers. Not only could it rise twenty stories, the steel framing opened up space and added to window area. Real estate developers and owners did not want their buildings to collapse into burning heaps. Burnham and Root built "fire-proof" structures using insulating hollow ceramic tiles from the Pioneer Fire-Proof Construction Company of

Chicago. They encased every beam and girder, every column and floor, in fireproof tile. Their facades of brick were also fire-hardened clay. They were not the only practitioners of the new engineering and design fashions—Louis Sullivan of Adler and Sullivan, and later Frank Lloyd Wright, among others, all had learned the lesson of the Great Fire well—but Burnham and Root were the pioneers.[63]

Real estate development in the Loop and near Northside was accompanied, and in some sense driven, by the creation of suburbs—what landscape historian Richard Stilgoe has called the urban "borderland." Larger, more fashionable stores drew the well-to-do denizens of the suburbs into the city as older, plainer retail sites might not. But the suburban development had a value in itself, rooted in a combination of sensory appeal, convenience, and an imagined idyllic American past. The suburbs were close enough to the farmland for occupants to smell the grasses and imagine they were in a country setting. Such settings were supposed to be healthy to the body and the mind. Equally important, they were supposed to be safe from fire.[64]

The first great real estate promotion for these near suburbs, Everett Chamberlin's 437-page *Chicago and Its Suburbs* (1874), extolled their picturesque qualities and their convenience. For example, Lake View, just to the north of the city line along the lake, exhibited "the greatest degree of activity in improvements," to which was added its "fine location and natural attractions." To the south of the city, Hyde Park offered "the delights of *rus in urbe*" but also "kept pace in the march of improvements." The same motif—rustic delight combined with such "improvements" as sewers, pure water, gas, and access to mass transit—ran through all of his listings. In keeping with the theme of the cottage in the glade, houses in these suburbs were wood framed. But they did not resemble the shanties in the western district ghetto. Homes were multistory, individually designed by architects, and featured gothic turrets and Victorian spires. Streets wound around large lots, owners were encouraged to plant gardens, and houses were set back from the street. Trees were de rigueur in this landscape, to shade and to preserve privacy. Though only five to ten miles away from the Loop, the suburban developments were also deemed safe from the ills of the city, including fire—though in fact fire was as much a danger in rural and semi-rural settings as in the city.[65]

The back story of the hustlers and dreamers who developed these alternatives to living in the core city is a remarkable one, and as thoroughly modern as the idea of suburbanization itself. As one might expect of Chicago, its first experiments with suburbs were inseparable from the rail lines. The movement to provide rural-like living for Chicago residents predated the fire, but the fire accelerated the movement out of the city by the well-to-do. They relocated into old farming communities, buying fields and turning them into home lots. Real estate speculators acted in concert, creating syndicates (limited partnerships) to pool resources and avert ruinous competition for the most desirable real estate plots. By 1873, they numbered nearly 50,000, according to Chamberlin. Of course, the city had to cooperate—and its business leaders, taking off their developers' hats and putting on their city fathers', generously spent on extending the infrastructure of the city to the suburbs. The city paid for sewage and water lines, "gas hookups, paved roads, street lamps, sidewalks, parks." The aldermen threw in elegantly rural-looking train stations with money that might have been spent updating the ones in the city itself.[66]

Lake Forest was the most "exclusive" of the new suburbs. It began with the Lake Forest Association, a closed syndicate of wealthy city men who introduced the real estate concept of "red lining" to insure that none but families they approved would move to the 1,300-acre area and build there. They hired a St. Louis landscape architect to lay out the town's "winding graveled walks, smooth green lawns, rustic-bridges—spanning ravines . . . summer houses, rustic chairs and couches, and grand old trees," according to one delighted visitor. The town would achieve its greatest fame when the elite of the city, the McCormicks (Cyrus, the mechanical reaper king), the Palmers (he of Palmer House), and the Swifts (the packing house mogul) moved there in the 1890s.[67]

Hyde Park was a close second in its studied elegance. Hyde Park's evolution was directly related to the Great Fire. Immediately after the fire, the summer retreat and residential haven that Paul Cornell had platted in 1853 eight miles from the city—a New England village surrounded by park land at a stop on the Illinois Central— became a refuge for the better-off victims. The 3,644 inhabitants in 1870 (most of whose families were paying taxes of over $5,000 for real estate alone) ballooned to 15,724 by 1880. Soon its home owners were facing some of the same problems as the city faced—impure water, excessive water use, and insufficient sewage disposal.

Cornell, a lawyer, manufacturer, and visionary, introduced "zoning" to preserve the pastoral character of his town. Zoning barred industry within Hyde Park's town limits. But the stockyards that sprawled to the west and the industrial plants that sprung up along the Calumet River to the south brought the sounds and smells of industrial America to the town.[68]

Closer to the city and far less exclusive were its streetcar suburbs. Smaller houses, often built in cookie-cutter fashion with tiny yards, provided housing for the working man and his family within the city limits. Traction companies with horse-drawn trolleys reached these communities before the fire, but after it, Marshall Field and a consortium of investors introduced a trolley car system using traction cables. These were soon augmented by elevated trains and electric trolleys. With tracks crossing streets posing a danger to pedestrians, horses frightened by the trolley cars bolting in all directions, and various companies cutting one another's throats for rights of way, chaos soon reigned.[69]

Enter Charles Tyson Yerkes, a Quaker from Philadelphia. He decided to make himself into the traction tzar. Chicago was familiar with speculators trying to corner markets and secretly pool prices, but Yerkes outdid them all. He had made a fortune in finance and sat on the Board of Trade, when, in 1892, he introduced electric trolleys with power lines above the streets. He rebuilt the cable lines as well, modernizing, systematizing, and along the way monopolizing the city's transit. It was his idea to build elevated rail lines right down the middle of major arteries. He manipulated stock issues, paying high dividends to keep the capital flowing in, meanwhile stashing away as much as he could. He bought the aldermen's votes and tried to purchase a controlling interest in the state legislature as well. But his plot to gain state approval for a monopoly of the city transit system ultimately failed, and he had to sell off his holdings in the trolley and train business to the very men—Field, for one—whose preeminence he had challenged.[70]

While the magnates and the moguls were building, developing, and scheming, the city's poor were suffering. This is the other story of post-fire Chicago. Although distant in time from the most visible and violent signs of class conflict revealed in the Haymarket riot of 1886 and the Pullman strike of 1894, the Great Fire was a "tipping point" in the movement toward class division. The fire was the moment in real time when gradual changes in little things accelerate suddenly and longtime behaviors or patterns shift dramatically.

There were class divisions and maldistribution of wealth in pre-fire Chicago. But the fire and the business-driven recovery tipped the balance between labor and capital, forcing a segment of the laboring population to reassess its position. It was no longer a partner in the progress but merely a producer of wealth for others. The tipping point worked the other way as well. Conservative and business interests were so sensitized by the destruction of private property— their property—by the fire, that they became extraordinarily wary of any discussion of redistribution of wealth. "Newspapers issued a warning: mobs of unemployed workers" left without jobs after the construction boom collapsed, and "thrown together by the crisis, could ignite a conflagration more terrible than that of 1871."[71]

The new class conflict fueled a series of contretemps, to-dos small enough in themselves but ominous in their implication. The first arose over who should be able to obtain relief from the charitable contributions pouring into the city from outside. The second grew out of an effort to fireproof the inner city.

In the Boston fire, there was no test for eligibility for relief. In Pittsburgh, it was a question of documented losses. The managers of the relief program in Chicago added another criterion—moral probity. At first, the relief effort in Chicago bore similarities to other, earlier disasters. Contributions from other cities poured in, supplementing funds provided by the state. Evangelist Henry Ward

Beecher called the outpouring an evidence of "Christian Love" and Baptist city leader E. J. Goodspeed lauded the "boundless charity of the great-hearted American public." The first agency set up to relieve the suffering of victims, the General Relief Committee, was an ad hoc political body.[72]

Then the business of distributing public charity became a business itself. The quasi-private Relief and Aid Society, run by businessmen, stepped in to take over the job. Marshall Field and George Pullman were among its board members. Over $4 million in aid went out to the needy, but not all the needy were deemed deserving. O. C. Gibbs, whom Goodspeed termed a "warm-hearted and large-minded Christian gentleman," administered the society's "general plan." He also laid out its credo: Those who were willing to work were deserving of succor. The unemployed were so "by choice" and should not be aided, though "special relief" was available to those deserving individuals who could not labor. They had to plead their cases and put themselves upon the untrammeled discretion of the society.[73]

The ideology behind the society's fiat combined both pre–Civil War free labor doctrines and much older Elizabethan English ideas about the poor. The former preached that free labor was better than slavery; the latter that there were deserving poor and undeserving poor. Both converged on the ideal that employment was virtuous and unemployment a mark of moral depravity. Aid to the dependent was bad; instead, the able-bodied who sought aid were given a chance to work. As another relief committee spokesman some years later put the theory: "'[T]here is no better way of rehabilitating a man than by allowing him to earn a living salary.'"

In Chicago, if a job did not materialize or the worker did not fit the needs of the employer, the worker could no longer call upon the society for aid. One strike and you were out. "In the end," the leading student of the aid society has written, "working people who had suffered losses were at times doubly victimized by the Society's basic belief in the latent dangers of benevolence." The worker who sought aid was beholden to the benevolence, and the absolutely unrestrained discretion, of the employer. Thus, the relief effort increased the authority of the business community (a perfectly rational out-come, given its board and its administrative methods), while widen-ing the divide between the rich and the poor.[74]

The second to-do revolved around the so-called fireproof move-ment. A coalition of genteel upper-class city men of "genteel reform" inclinations demanded that all new construction in the burned dis-trict be of brick or stone. Originally called reformers or independ-ents, these men wanted fiscal responsibility (hence their suspicion of the politicians on the city council), public investment in education, public health measures, and honesty in government (unlike the Grant administration in Washington, D.C.). They were largely of New England background, had a faith in science (including the idea that city fire could be prevented if the city was fireproofed), and no particular concern about who might be harmed by their efforts.[75]

A month after the fire, the reformers cobbled together a fusion party, ran "fireproof" candidates for the city council and mayoral elec-tions, and promised to make the city safe from fire. They won, though it was a Pyrrhic victory. By the time the election was over, the city had already begun rebuilding cheaply with wood. But the fireproof move-ment revealed a gash in the fabric of society. The lower-class Ger-mans of the near Northside were opposed to the fireproof movement. They saw themselves as "thrifty working people" whose homes were destroyed through no fault of their own, made victim once again by the fireproof ordinance. Their newspapers rushed to express their shared outrage. Germans' "'friendly flower-framed little houses'" would be lost forever in a maze of "'railroad . . . tracks, smoking ma-chine shops, mills, and lumber depots.'" The enemy was the "native-born commercial class" seeking to dispose the hard-working honest poor, grasping at the opportunity to make a profit before the home owners of the burned-over district could rebound. In the end, the fireproof movement died because no one could enforce a hard and fast ban on building with wood. The hardening of the rhetoric never-theless portended the hardening of class lines in years to come. German-speaking radicals would take a leading role in the battle.[76]

There were other signs of sharply diverging class interests in the wake of the fire. The operation of the insurance companies was not as smugly class conscious about qualification for charitable relief, as indifferent to the housing needs of the working classes, nor as crassly commercial as the real estate gobblers, but the insurance industry had the same impact. Since the Pittsburgh fire, some of these companies had grown to a top rank among American corporations and had introduced methods of assessing risk that were based on mapping fire hazards and surveying buildings. The National Board of Fire Underwriters had established standards for rates based on locality, building safety, and firefighting records. Underwriters of insurance became experts on fire prevention, underwriting not only insurance but the belief that the danger of fire could be reduced to the vanishing point.[77]

Chicago policyholders were covered by 201 insurance companies. Unlike Pittsburgh's insurers, these companies were largely out-of-state firms. The property loss was a little over $185 million, and the insurance repayments mounted to a little over $50 million. For the insurers, the first losses were catastrophic because they exceeded available funds to pay policyholders. A well-managed fire insurance company protected itself by collecting enough premiums to cover losses, in effect redistributing the risk of fire losses to its clients. But it was essential to maintain the confidence of both policyholders and investors if the company was to survive. Thus, local agents of distant companies threw up makeshift offices "on the banks of the Chicago River and told crowds of their policy holders 'they [would] pay every dollar of loss.'" When the insurers tried to bilk Cyrus McCormick, the richest man in the city, he hired New York City lawyers to go after their assets elsewhere. Marshall Field collected almost every penny he had insured on his stock and building. But, as the editors of *The Workingman's Advocate* concluded two weeks after the fire had ended, "as might have been expected . . . the laboring classes have been the greatest losers" in the insurance game. "There was a killing off of the weak companies," dozens of smaller insurance companies that had catered to the poorer segments of the community—"married women, infants, insolvents and persons who have gone out of the country." With their smaller rivals out of business, the big companies could concentrate their control of policy issuance, raise rates, and profit. Henceforth, poor people who wanted insurance would have to pay for premiums what the giants in the industry charged. The result was plain to see: Two of the most imposing of the new Loop skyscrapers, the Home Insurance Company Building and the Insurance Exchange Building, catered to the newly concentrated insurance industry.[78]

The fire had yet another disparate impact on rich and poor. It so weakened the economy of the city that it could not withstand another of those sudden panics that had a domino effect on the national economy. The Panic of 1873 was predictable—an adjustment (modern stock market analysts would call it that) to the overheated economy that emerged during the early Reconstruction period. Fueled by the too rapid growth of rail lines and railroad companies (everyone wanted a stop on the rail near their town, when they were not building a town at a new stop), the economy was heading for a fall. That collapse had biblical proportions when it came, and it fell hardest on the poor.

Lucifer, in the form of Jay Cooke (manager of the Union economic miracle during the Civil War), led speculators on a merry chase, junk-bonding enough capital to begin a Northern Pacific rail line to rival the Union Pacific. It was a venture that depended upon getting rights-of-way, laying track, and actually running a rail line. The plan had hardly begun to gather steam when the entire paper pyramid came crashing down, in September 1873. Cooke went bankrupt. So did eighty-nine other railroad companies. Their worthless stock joined bonds on which Reconstruction Southern state governments defaulted. By 1875, nearly 18,000 businesses had failed. The depression continued until 1879. Unemployment rose to 14 percent, much of it in the railroad business. And Chicago was the country's number one railhead.

Chicago's death toll from starvation, remarkable for a city surrounded by the richest farmland in the nation, soared. The unemployed slept in Chicago police stations and unfinished buildings, demanded public assistance (from the fire fund), marched, and rallied. Radical politics and economic necessity merged, as a People's Party representing the Irish and the German workers elected their mayoralty candidate, Harvey Colvin. But Colvin did not fulfill his promise of reform, and worse, the city was still attracting immigrants who would work for less than the laborers already there.[79]

In the meantime, the eyes of the Chicago rail workers focused on their diminishing paychecks. The owners met secretly to set trunk line rates for shipping cargo, and the workers met publicly to protest their loss of jobs and decline in pay. A series of strikes in Pennsylvania had little effect on the largest lines. The brotherhoods of conductors, engineers, and firemen were cowed by threats of scab labor. But the brakemen, doing the most dangerous job and paid the least, determined upon a new tactic. If the railroad owners were acting in national concert, the workers would follow suit with a national trainman's union. And even if the union did not survive very long, the idea behind it—unity in the face of corporate cupidity—did.

In 1877, a round of strikes began against the Baltimore & Ohio at its Baltimore headquarters. By July, they had reached the Chicago rail yards. Soon Market Square and the marshaling yards were battle grounds. U.S. Army and national guard troops, private police, and a few city police fought pitched combats against the trainmen and their supporters. Allan Pinkerton (whose business included breaking up unions with squads of Pinkerton "detectives") joined in the fray. On July 25, the police killed five union men and wounded seven others. When the protesters began to pelt the police with bricks and stones, army units, including a cavalry troop brought into the city from the Indian country, killed another dozen strikers.[80]

The police response to the strikes of 1877 had fueled both an anarchist movement and radical unionism. The former would lead to the Haymarket Riots of 1886, the latter to the Pullman Strike, later a general railroad strike, of 1894. They are signal events in the history of American organized labor. Chicago was not alone in this progression—Pittsburgh had its Homestead Steel strike in 1880, a bloodier event than any that occurred in Chicago. But the Great Fire had given a particular cast to Chicago's labor unrest and class conflict. Because so many of the poor were displaced first by the fire and then by the developers' real estate boom, they had ceased to have much sense of a common enterprise with the business class. Thus, they came to see the union contest for a part of the American dream in far more cynical and cosmic terms than their aggrieved lower-class counterparts in other cities. If one focuses on "the rank and file" of these radicals, one finds that they were the ones left out of the miracle of recovery, a true "working class" that acted "in working class ways."[81]

On May 4, 1886, after police attempted to break up an anarchist street meeting in the Haymarket called to protest the death of three strikers, someone threw a "homemade bomb" into the ranks of the police. (Sources vary on the number of police, from seventy to 150. No one doubts that they were there to disperse the gathering rather than keep order, or that their leader, Captain "Black Jack" Bonfield had developed a reputation as a sadistic as well as a violent man.) The bomb killed one, injured dozens, and led to a wild melee—with people shooting, running, and fighting (though the anarchists did most of the running).

The major newspapers cried havoc—foreign agitators had invaded America's shores and intended to destroy the very fabric of capitalism. The anarchists had become a symbol of the demonic, like the fire itself. Seven of the anarchists were indicted and condemned to death by a jury and judge (an eighth was sentenced to fifteen years at hard labor). Even Clarence Darrow, the great attorney for the unions, and Jane Addams, the urban reformer who had founded the Hull House settlement, were convinced of the anarchists' guilt. Four were hanged, but Illinois governor John Peter Altgeld pardoned three. He paid for his courage—he never held public office again.[82]

At the height of the anarchist fury, the two cities of Chicago that the fire had severed—the imagined and the real, the fabulous and the impoverished—moved even farther apart. Daniel Burnham looked at the violence and dreamed of a city that would rise above the squalor and dirt of the real Chicago. The colors of industrial waste—the ugly browns and grays—would vanish. It was a dream of modernity, a world of gleaming surfaces and purity, in which the masses would delight and the elite take pride.

He got his chance in 1890. When Chicago won the competition to host the Columbian Exposition, a world's fair commemorating Columbus's arrival in American waters 400 years before, the city asked Burnham and Frederick Law Olmstead (designer of New York City's Central Park, among other large-scale projects) to choose a fair site and direct the construction of the exhibit halls. They chose Jackson Park, a marshy expanse south of the city served by the Illinois Central. One modern student of the fair reports "Olmstead's teeth hurt, his ears roared, and he could not sleep," yet he was everywhere giving orders. Burnham, in the meantime, recruited the nation's elite architects to design the pavilions.[83]

To drain the lakefront marshes and provide a focal point for the fair's buildings, the team decided on a basin–central court plan whose structures would be "formal, impressive, and generally of the same stylistic mode." Root, pencil in hand, sketched the designs, and the staff worked out the infrastructure of roads, services, sewage disposal, and schedules. With so little time, Root and Burnham had to delegate the drafting to McKim, Mead and White of New York City and other firms. It was truly a national effort (though some in Chicago grumbled that its architects did not need outside help). As the planning stages gave way to actual construction, excitement in the city grew.[84]

Root passed away during the early stages of construction, leaving Burnham without his longtime partner; and missing Root's perfectionism, Burnham adopted all sorts of shortcuts in construction methods and materials. Still, Burnham had not lost his persuasive touch. He convinced Richard Hunt of New York to design the Administration Building, modeled on the nation's Capitol; warned Henry Ives Cobb to keep his Fisheries Hall simple; worried about the delays in George Post's Manufactures and Liberal Arts Building; and begged Olmstead to return from Boston to direct the landscaping in person. Louis Sullivan, Burnham's competitor for Chicago projects, was the hardest of the team for Burnham to manage. Like Burnham, Sullivan was a visionary, but his dogged artistic preferences for the solidity of the Romanesque did not fit the neoclassical theme that the team elected for the Honor Court's buildings. Even so, Sullivan was Sullivan, and Burnham swallowed hard and allowed Sullivan's Transportation Building, with its striking mélange of colors and shapes, to deviate from the alabaster facades of the other structures.[85]

In two years, the construction team had turned a marshy tidal basin into 1,000 acres of spectacle. The workers performed miracles, unloading the endless lines of boxcars, carving the waterways and paving the roads, laying the electrical and gas lines, carting and framing and nailing and assembling huge structures. The white-faced, classical columned and domed buildings of the Honor Court; the half barrel shaped glass-roofed exhibition halls; the exotic attractions of the mile-long midway; the many canals leading to the sculptured basin; the great novelty of Mr. Ferris's giant wheel, the largest all-steel frame of its kind—all these drew in millions of visitors. Estimates of attendance from the opening in May to the closing in October ranged as high as 27 million, though the real figure may be lower.[86]

The ideal city of Burnham's imagination and his team's hard labor—called the White City for the color of the facades at the Honor Court—had no crime. Its crowds were not militant armies of desperate men but the most "well-behaved" assemblage of citizens that observers had ever seen. It was a city of dreams, of modern machinery and power, with technology serving human happiness.

But just beyond the depot the Illinois Central built to carry visitors to the fair, on the other side of Yerkes's elevated train station, lay another city. In the winter of 1893–1894, the city of Chicago faced the bleakest times anyone had seen since 1873. A national depression that the fair's fantasies could not avert swept through the midlands. The dismal scenes and shattered hopes were the very opposite of the promise of the fair's sponsors: farmers driven from their land by debt, factories shuttered for lack of orders; block after block of vacant stores, emptied as though the retail market had been stricken by a virus. As always, the first to feel the pinch were the least able to survive it. Only the oldest of professions—vice, prostitution, gambling, and theft—thrived in this bleak economic atmosphere. As Mr. Dooley (columnist Finley Peter Dunne's alter ego) put it: "A panic. An' nobody gets any th' best iv it but th' burglars that breaks in and steals." Visitors to the city who ventured beyond the fair were stunned by the open display of want, anger, and immorality.[87]

The city newspapers reported wrenching stories of starvation and frightening tales of poverty-driven crime. In fact, because of the sharp contrast between the White City and its shabby doppelgänger, Chicago's newspapers became the place to go to start a career in journalism. Their names would become familiar in every literate household in the land: the *Daily News*'s Ray Stannard Baker, father of the "muckrakers" school of investigative journalism; Finley Peter Dunne, whose fictional Chicagoan Mr. Dooley spoke for millions of ordinary people not fooled by the politicians or the corporate mandarins; Brand Whitlock, a future best-selling novelist; and Theodore Dreiser. Dreiser was young enough to be impressionable, and thirty years later, he still recalled "those raw neighborhoods . . . small unpainted tumbledown shanties set in grassless can-strewn yards . . . the rancidity of dirt . . . the icy bleakness of poverty," whose wearied denizens "cursed, or raved, or snarled."[88]

Though it was never intended to be permanent, the White City began to take on the character of the other, bleaker Chicago after the exposition closed. Abandoned because the bankrupt city could not keep it open and the Congress, facing the nation's worst depression yet, would not approve further funding, the White City's crumbling Honor Court became a home for vagrants. Early in the morning of July 5, 1894, the Capitol-look-alike administration building burst into flame. The shortcuts in construction, particularly the pasteboard hemp used to strengthen the plaster facades, turned the Honor Court into a perfect fire course. With a ferocity matched only by the Great Fire itself, the White City was reduced to ash within twelve hours. At the center of the exposition grounds, only the bedraggled Statue of Liberty, safe in the midst of Olmstead's lake, survived. Thousands of spectators rushed from their homes and hotels to witness the death of the fairgrounds. Some wept.[89]

OF COURSE, anarchists and agitators were blamed for setting the fire, though it made no sense that they would burn down the only place where the homeless could get out of the wind and weather. It was probably an accident—a fire set to cook or warm the squatters. No sooner was the fire out than Burnham arrived and began planning a permanent renovation of the entire lakeshore. The present

Lakeshore Drive, the amenities and the museums, all began that day. But the irony of the last Great Fire of the nineteenth century, and of the power of Chicago fires to attract and repel, to destroy and rebuild, could not be missed.[90]

BALTIMORE, 1904

In 1903, Chicago came to the Calvert–Baltimore Street corner of downtown Baltimore. Workers completed construction on the newest and tallest of Baltimore's high-rise office buildings, the Continental Trust. Its architect, Daniel Burnham of White City fame, and its subcontractors, the Pioneer Fireproofing Company of Chicago, had used the most modern fire-prevention materials and methods. Burnham himself would later declare that its "supporting columns . . . its joists and beams" could withstand "great temperatures." All the experience of the Chicago fire and Burnham's distinguished career stood behind the safety of the new structure.[1]

When in 1903, J. William Schaefer, a Baltimore photographer and inventor, wanted to test his new stop-action panoramic camera on the skyline of Baltimore, the Continental was his focal point. "Panorams" had been around for over fifty years, and Eastman Kodak of Rochester, New York, had just brought out its newest version. The panorama was already a popular format for group photos and for cityscapes, but Schaefer thought he had a nice twist on the standard model. Climbing Federal Hill in his home city, he aimed across the Inner Harbor at the gentle slope of the downtown business district. As it rose from the wharves and warehouses at the water's edge, it perfectly filled his lens. He hoped to sell a number of prints. After all, at the turn of the century, Baltimore was the sixth-largest city in the country and one of the most economically important. It was the Mecca for a great emigration from all over Europe. Surely other Americans and Europeans would be interested in the skyline.[2]

Schaefer's panorama of the Baltimore skyline was an imposing sight, and his basic idea was right on the money—modern panoramas of the Inner Harbor are seen by millions of Web surfers, travelogue viewers, and tourists—but the city was hardly a tourist attraction then. A closer look at Schaefer's panorama hints at the reason. The bowl-shaped downtown and the waterfront at its feet are a jumble of boxlike structures dropped on the slope as a child might empty a box of Legos. The blocks of buildings are so close together that even the widest streets like Pratt and Lombard are invisible. In the gray tones of the panorama, one can almost see the pollution of the air. From other sources we know that the screech of the electric trolleys pierced ears in the downtown's narrow streets. Another photographer, Ansel Adams, wrote of downtown San Francisco in the same era, describing "a deep and throbbing space-filling rumble of ironclad wagon wheels on cobbled streets . . . deep with the brutality that only a city can offer in fact and spirit."[3]

The panorama view could not convey the city's other noxious qualities. Baltimore smelled dank and rotten because there was no sewer system or sewage treatment. The sidewalk and street-level gutters and storm drains under the streets doubled as sewers, as did the rank Jones Falls Canal and the Inner Harbor itself (locally called the "back basin"). A bill to replace the storm drains with real sewers languished in the labyrinth of the city council and Frederick Law Olmstead, Jr.'s plan to build a system of parks throughout the city was voted down by ratepayers. On February 2, 1904, the city Board of Estimates finally initialed a plan to add greenery, parks, and sewers, as well as new firehouses, paved streets, and improved water pipes, but work would move ahead slowly; it always had, and slowly this time would be too late.[4]

Though its enclaves of wealth featured lovely mansions, Baltimore then hardly resembled the "charm city" it calls itself today. In fact, in the first years of the twentieth century Baltimore exhibited some of the most extreme differences between the rich and the poor of any of the great cities. From the city hall at the center of downtown, one could walk ten blocks north on Charles Street to the lovely Victorian and Greek Revival mansions of Mount Vernon Place, circling the Washington Monument like miniature ocean liners. Or one could go the same ten blocks west, to the Garment District at Howard and Lombard, where 3,000 women sat side by side on endless rows of factory floor benches sewing for twelve hours a day. The city's wealth came from its railroads' proximity to Southern markets, Midwestern suppliers (the rails ran straight to Chicago), and its fine port facilities, but the rail workers and the dockworkers never shared that wealth and on more than one occasion rose in rebellion against the railroad moguls.[5]

Divisions and divisiveness lay deep in the city's heart. It lay precisely on the boundary between the North and the South. As such,

Baltimore had seen the rise and fall of slavery and the passionate animosities of the Civil War. Racism sparked discrimination and violence. It was a city of neighborhoods that did not always welcome
one another's residents, for instance, Oldtown around East Lombard, home to the flood of Jewish immigrants in the 1880s and
1890s, and West Baltimore, grudgingly conceding living space in alley walk-ups to thousands of African-Americans.[6]

Maybe it was the water. The future city was built on the reaches
of the Patapsco River, Algonquian for "backwater." Indians avoided
the marshes, though a clan of particularly fierce bears seemed to
have found the region attractive. The warlike Susquehannocks
(clothing themselves in you-know-what skins in winter) claimed the
area as their own and exacted tribute from nearby villages, but the
Susquehannocks refused to settle the place. Even the intrepid John
Smith, exploring the upper reaches of the Chesapeake Bay from his
base in Jamestown, decided not to tarry there.[7]

Colonial Baltimore rolled out a welcome to Maryland's tobacco
nabobs, and they brought their slaves to town to serve them. Tobacco warehouses, bakeries, and breweries survived the Revolutionary War and the War of 1812. German immigrants arrived to swell
the population. Fells Point harbor was deep enough for oceangoing
ships and their sailors joined the shipwrights, farmers, and townspeople strolling on the wide streets. The major thoroughfares of the
early town averaged seventy-five feet across, and boulevards like
Market were double that width, giving Baltimore an open, country
aspect. Along the streets were shops where locals could buy the
finest leather goods—saddles, buckets, and, providentially, fire
hoses.

For as fast as the colonial town grew, it burned. In 1747, the
council ordered all householders to own ladders and buckets. The
first volunteer fire company appeared in 1763, and in 1769 the company purchased its first engine from a ship captain. In later years, the
city would follow Boston's example and forbid the building of
wooden structures in the harbor area, and like Boston, the residents
paid their fines, built wooden houses and inns, and ignored the purpose behind the ordinance.[8]

In the nineteenth century, Baltimore was known for its rowdy ways. Its firemen in particular were famous for fighting one another more than the city's blazes. In 1842, the "Rules, Resolutions, and Regulations for the Government of Fire Companies" in Baltimore specified that "in all case when a riot or disturbance takes place [among the volunteers] the company with whom it commences shall be responsible." The rules did not change the feisty demeanor of the firefighters. "By the late 1860s, critics of Baltimore's paid [professional] department . . . claimed that the municipal fireman had become as violent as their [volunteer] predecessors." Dueling fire companies were reminded to return the hose of other companies undamaged.[9]

The city's contrary ways were on display during the Civil War. Southern sympathizers rioted when Lincoln called for volunteers at the beginning of the Civil War, and he had to occupy the city with troops to prevent its slaveholders from holding a secession convention. Its railroad workers began the biggest and most violent of the 1877 strikes and brought the great Baltimore & Ohio Railroad to its knees before the state militia arrived to quell the disturbance. Its sweatshop workers formed the United Garment Workers of America in 1896 and began a half century of organized resistance to unfair labor practices.[10]

The face of the nineteenth-century city mirrored its cross-grained character. Architects and their clients loved the eclectic display of all manner of past styles—from neoclassical, Greek Revival, Gothic, Romanesque, and Second Empire to Victorian. But the particular glory of Baltimore's late-nineteenth-century architecture perfectly expressed the soul of the city—the finest banks, office buildings, hotels and department stores featured hard, brittle, and immensely functional cast iron construction. Relatively thin cast iron columns were able to bear great loads vertically, but cast iron beams or trusses lacked tensile strength, and even thick beams could not support more than six- or seven-story buildings. Still, ornate, elegant, and above all quickly cast, they became the standard for the city's most expensive buildings, and Baltimore architects and cast iron foundries gained commissions to build entire blocks in other cities as well.[11]

Cast iron Baltimore was largely lost in the Great Fire, but in a re-markable quirk of fate, the look and feel of its late-nineteenth-century cast iron commercial blocks is preserved on the other side of the country. Seattle's business district was utterly destroyed by fire on June 6, 1889, but a building boom from the fall of 1889 into 1892 re-placed the lost commercial space. The architects integrated cast iron columns, steel girders, sandstone and brick outside walls, and wood and plaster interiors to reconstruct Seattle's downtown. Many of these buildings have been preserved in the Pioneer Square Park Historic District between Cherry and Jackson along First Street. On First—then called Front—at Jackson Street one can still see the external cast iron columns of the refurbished office buildings and storefronts.[12]

For all the variety of the terra-cotta, marble, and sandstone fa-cade and cast iron features of downtown Baltimore, the city in 1904 was not sensually appealing. Instead, it had grown without a plan and with little interest in open space and landscaping. The city beautifi-cation movement had yet to make its weight felt in the jumble of downtown retail businesses, sweatshops, stores, and offices. The gray piers and warehouses along the Inner Harbor seemed to sulk over that harbor's workaday aspect. The massive, squat financial and gov-ernment buildings deadened the eye. The streets running north from the Inner Harbor were now comparatively narrow, often no more than forty to fifty feet wide, and on some the old cobblestone had not been paved. The sidewalks were cluttered with projecting signs, awnings, telephone and power poles, and cellar openings.[13]

The only exception to the routine of neoclassical columns and New Empire facades were the seven brothers in the downtown—high-rise "fireproof" (more or less, as events would soon prove) buildings that were modeled on the Chicago School's design innova-tions. Burnham's Continental, the Union Trust, the Calvert, the Eq-uitable, the *Herald* building, the Chesapeake & Potomac, and the Baltimore & Ohio buildings, all of which utilized steel columns, cast iron fittings, and hollow floor tile. But all had interiors of plaster and lath, wood, and other much more easily consumable materials. What's more, all had elevators with unfireproofed shafts. Giant chim-neys, waiting for ignition.[14]

"Big Fire Here"

Baltimore, Saturday, February 6, 1904, dawned mild, a break in the pattern of snow, cold, wind, and overcast skies. "Nothing wet was falling out of the sky. No snow, no ice, no hail, no rain changing to sleet, no sleet changing to rain." An unlikely Baltimore winter day. The sidewalks were still coated with a thin layer of grimy ice. The day's newspapers reported on a city government mired in controversy over the reform efforts. Stories of wild-eyed Socialists doing battle to the death with obsessed Single-Tax advocates (the idea was to tax the landlords) spiced up the pages of the *Baltimore Herald,* but the real story was the incapacity of government at all levels to solve the problems of the city. Baltimore's editorial writers happily covered politics-as-usual, which meant treating the city fathers like brawling children, but the problems were real enough.[15]

HARD TIMES IN BALTIMORE

On Sunday morning the wind picked up and the sky clouded over, dashing the hope of an early thaw. The city's population needed some promise of relief, for it reeled from the second year of a nation-wide industrial recession. The so-called Panic of 1903 brought a sharp dip in buying and selling. The New York stock market's leaders lost 23 percent of their value. Some called it a rich man's panic because market speculators lost the most. Others blamed it on President Theodore Roosevelt's tough policy on industrial monopolies and abusive business practices—but whatever the panic was, Baltimore was a working-class city, and times of economic hardship hit the workers first.

The desperation of the workers was revealed in exposés like Marie Van Vorst's. Van Vorst was gentle born, but in 1903 she went undercover to write about the plight of the "working girl." Appalled but deeply sympathetic to the "woman at my side" in a shoe factory, "an untidy degraded looking creature . . . her hands [an object of great care among the well-to-do, and a symbol thus of breeding] beggared description; their covering resembling skin not at all, but a dark blue substance, leatherlike, bruised, ingrained, indigo-hued." The shoe dye was an industrial poison, one of the many chemical toxins routinely soaked up at workplace benches.[16]

Had fire struck one of these piecework factories, the consequences would have been catastrophic. The girls were always smoking, the electrical lines were overloaded, and the machines threw off sparks. The "fabrics, the wicker baskets, and the oil-soaked machines" would have set off the long benches; the woodwork would have burned to cinders and the floors weakened and collapsed. Jammed together, the workers would have become a frightened crowd. They would have pressed upon the only open door—the one the shop steward watched like a hawk. (Owners hated fire drills and rarely held them. They kept the workers from their jobs. Sprinkler systems were too expensive.) The exit doors were locked with iron bars, to prevent workers from carrying off the finished work or sneaking away from their benches. The stairways, so narrow that only one person could pass at a time, would have become bottlenecks for the panicked, fleeing workers. The outside fire escapes, if the building had them (and most did not), could not hold the weight of more than one person at a time. To escape the heat, smoke, and flames, some workers would have bolted for the windows and the narrow ledges along the exterior walls. More would have jumped rather than be burned alive. Crowds would have gathered below the upper-story windows, unable to do anything.[17]

But in the winter of 1904, Baltimore working women and men had little choice about where they worked or what particle debris they inhaled or whether fires might kill hundreds of them in the space of an hour. With demand for industrial products down, and thousands of willing immigrant workers coming into the city every year, the unions had little bargaining power. Layoffs meant less money in the worker's pockets, and Baltimore's downtown retailers felt the decline in consumer sales. Like the character Carrie, created by newspaperman-turned-novelist Theodore Dreiser, they wandered through the aisles, longing but unable to buy. "Each separate counter was a showplace. She could not help feeling the claim of each trinket upon her personally, and yet she did not stop. There was nothing there which she could not have used—nothing that she did not long to own . . . and she keenly felt the fact that not any of these things were in the range of her purchase."[18]

The square of the city with Liberty Street on the west and Charles Street on the east was the wholesale drygoods district, home of warehouses and stores filled with winter overstock that few could afford, even at bargain prices. Desperate retailers and wholesalers advertised their wares in all the city's four major daily newspapers and out-of-town buyers rummaged through the stock to pick up bargains. The overstock of spring clothing piled up next to unsold winter garments.

The *Baltimore American* advertisements' hyperbole could not conceal the terrible holiday season's sales. "Clearance, Clearance, Clearance," the advertisements announced—coats, muffs, shoes, men's underwear, women's handbags, bathrobes, dress trimmings, fine ribbons, table linens, silks, leather, and fur all on sale. Hecht Brothers, on Baltimore Street in the heart of the retail district, promised special prices on "Odds and Ends of All Furniture and Floor Coverings." Shoppers were urged to "rummage" through the store and buy on easy credit terms. Carpets, linoleum, cork, and "Japanese mattings" were all "greatly reduced" in price. The Hub announced its own "sale of the leavings," though apparently a good deal was left from the winter stock because "every department supplies its bargain share." The ladies' section of the store begged women to view what remained of "the very best styles" in the world in velvet, silk, and cloth. The retail clothing and furniture stores, along with the shops selling paper goods, tobacco, and books, constituted one great warehouse of flammable materials, though it does not appear that anyone was paying close attention.[19]

The changing layout of the downtown since the colonial period had actually added to the danger of fire. The stores were old, some dating to the period before the Civil War. Many of the storefronts were narrow, no more than forty feet wide—the Lake Street, Chicago, pattern, before the Great Fire. The basic building format, according to the details in the 1902 Sanborn Insurance Company fire map that the Ferris Map draftsmen prepared, was milled (wooden) and brick exteriors, and plaster and milled interiors. On the alleys at the back of the brick structures stood even older wooden frame buildings.[20]

There was no space between the buildings on these commercial blocks, and thus no way for firefighters to see whether a fire inside one building might have spread to its neighbor, or to get their equipment into position to pour water on the roofs of buildings adjacent to one another. The alleys running behind the streets were too narrow for the fire engines to maneuver. Worse, basement airshafts and poorly insulated window mullions were vents for oxygen to reach cellar or basement fires, deadly to firefighters (because they cannot vent the heat and smoke up and out of the cellar). The multitude of electrical lines strung on the poles presented another obstacle to the firefighters, for the electrically charged lines prevented the easy and safe deployment of ladders and endangered the men climbing them to vent fires on upper stories.[21]

THE HURST DRYGOODS STORE FIRE

That Sunday morning, in the basement of the Hurst wholesale drygoods building—an entire block at the corner of Hopkins Place and German Street—an ember glowed. Perhaps a worker had left a cigarette butt, or a passerby dropped a lighted cigarette through a small

Baltimore Fire, 1904

gap in the deadlight. Perhaps a short circuit sparked in the electrical system that powered the lights, newly installed. Such embers will burn themselves out most of the time, when the oxygen around them gives out or they use up the immediately available fuel. Little accidental fires of this type abound in a city.

But the Hurst fire had other ideas, dreams of grandeur that the drowsing city could not know. The ember became a blaze, likely sustained by a draft of air from a door the watchman opened. (Retailers, banks, and office building owners hired night watchmen to deter the thievery that had spread through the city during the panic.) Or the drafty cellar contributed to its own fiery demise. Whatever the cause, the Hurst fire spread until it reached highly flammable packing crates, then rose through the wooden frame of the six-story elevator shaft to the upper floors and set off the alarm box in the building.[22]

The Hurst fire should not have become Baltimore's version of hell. The Boston, Pittsburgh, and Chicago fires were old-fashioned fires—fuel scattered about in a natural fire course of wooden buildings, sidewalks, and hay barns. Such fires were tragic but common in the first 200 years of American cities. By the second half of the nineteenth century, increasing lip service was accorded the concept of fire prevention, but the term was not in wide use yet because those who lived in the city accepted the inevitability of great fires. Not so in 1904.

The twentieth century had ushered in an age of science—scientific management of the workplace according to modern methods, with increased efficiency based on scientific principles. Measurement of risk; reduction of peril; calculation of where and when danger might appear were but the first steps in a program to reduce occupational injuries and increase productivity. It was the age that spawned quantum physics and Einstein's theory of relativity. The American genius for invention, turning science into technology, had borne fruit in the hundreds of patents Thomas Alva Edison gained for his ideas. General Electric and Bell Telephone made this the electric age, and the Baltimore retail stores brought electricity downtown.[23]

The same fascination, amounting to a new faith, applied to management of fire risks. "The fire insurance industry, led by the National Board of Fire Underwriters . . . embraced fire prevention." The enforcement of building codes was only a start, as insurance companies began to see fire damage as "waste," and fire-safe construction as not only possible, but necessary. The insurers realized that new forms of urban energy—gas and electricity—posed new and potent fire risks as well, and traditional methods of reporting fires when they were visible from the street were inadequate.[24]

In downtown Baltimore, all the major commercial structures had some form of alarm system. Some newly built stores and offices even had sprinkler systems. Floors in the Hurst Building had both trouble alarms and thermostatic fire alarms connected to the central firehouse. But the fire had probably been burning for at least twenty minutes when the fire alarm rang at the central fire department office at 10:48 AM. The first horse-drawn engine and firefighters to arrive took only a few minutes—No. 15 engine, No. 2 hook and ladder truck, and the salvage corps.

The latter, an 1865 London fire department innovation, attended all fires in commercial or warehouse premises and immediately attempted to salvage or save goods from destruction—primarily from water damage. Insurers insisted on these salvage crews to reduce the cost of replacement of goods destroyed by the firefighters. At first, the fire department saw the Hurst fire not as a potential citywide catastrophe but as a localized and containable danger to private property—the Hurst store's stock.[25]

On that Sunday morning, the Baltimore Fire Department (BFD) was a confident force. Unlike Chicago's, on paper it was adequate to the task of buildingwide fires. Still, there were only twenty-five engine companies to cover the entire city. Cities never spend enough on firefighting or firefighters. For the entire city there were only 2,703 hydrants, and not enough hydrants in the downtown. Most of these were of an already obsolete "flip lid" type, according to my examination of pictures taken at the time. The top cover of this type of hydrant is removed to expose the hose connection. The thread design on these (hoses are threaded onto the hose connection of the hydrant) were nonstandard and the opening width was not compatible with other nearby fire departments' hose equipment.[26]

The water pressure in the hydrants ranged from forty to fifty pounds per square inch (psi). That was not substandard in any way. Modern pumpers and fire cannons boost water pressure when fighting high-rise fires because that pressure unmagnified will not reach much beyond the fourth floor of a building. The rule of thumb is about an additional ten psi per floor. A six-story building, thus, should be fought with hoses delivering about 100 psi. The problem with higher pressures is that at 100 psi, a handheld fully charged hose, say, of two and one-half inches, is a bucking bronco and will lift a man off his feet if he is not set. You need two firefighters—one to hold and direct the nozzle and set the spray and the other to back him up, holding and pulling the hose. One man—well, he might "sit on the hose," controlling it between his legs if he did not have to shift position.[27]

The supply of water was barely adequate. The modern standard is 1,500 gallons per minute, although some city hydrants deliver only 500 gpm. The city's system of reservoirs, pumps, and pipes was sufficient for a building fire of this scope, but not for a citywide emergency. And not for fire in tall buildings. The water pressure out of the BFD hoses that morning could not reach the upper floors and roofs of commercial buildings like the Hurst. Unable to wet the roofs to prevent their burning, or to put out roof fires by climbing ladders from the outside of the building, the firefighters could not prevent burning roofing from flying into the air or the flames from radiating heat from one building to the next.[28]

So the firemen had to go into the building, find the fire, and put it out. That is what engine No. 15 intended to do. Either mistaking the smoke coming from the upper windows of the Hurst Building for the only source of the fire or because he did not realize that the entire building was already involved, Captain John Kahl of engine No. 15 ordered his men to hammer down a door on the German Street side of the store and enter the building. The idea was to find the source of the fire, ventilate through windows, and use the water in the hoses to drive the fire out of the building. Once inside, the men saw that the smoke was rolling across the first-floor ceiling from the cellar and banking down. The building's wooden elevator shaft was conducting the fire upward.[29]

Apparently, they propped the door open. Many firefighters carry chocks to prop open doors. A hard-and-fast rule of fighting fires in a building is never to lose control of the doors. Knowing when to keep the door shut (to contain the fire) and when to open it for entrance or exit is the mark of a truly experienced officer. But with the door of the Hurst ajar, the heat of the fire, causing the air to rise, created a partial vacuum and drew in air from outside. The backdraft turned the entire building into a furnace.[30]

Now Captain Kahl's company was in imminent danger. It is almost always a fatal mistake to let the fire get between the men and the door, and in the Hurst Building, the smoke was banking down from the ceiling. Soon the unburned carbon particles and gases in it would ignite and the flashover could cook his men. On a frigid 2004 night in the Bronx, New York, six firefighters seeking victims on the fourth floor of an apartment fire could not get back to the only door to the hallway. The only way out was through the fourth-floor windows. Two died and the others were critically injured when they jumped through the window.[31]

Inside the Hurst, the temperature rose to the point, about 1,000°F, when a fire shifts from burning the contents of a room to burning the structure itself. At Kahl's command, the firefighters took up their lines and retreated out of the building. They had followed the second and third commandments of fighting fire in a big building—they stayed together, close enough to hear their officers' commands, and they obeyed their officer. They had charged lines (hoses with water in them), but they rightly guessed that the lines in their hands were insufficient to fight this one from the inside. It was time to take up and haul out.[32]

How did they figure out that it was time to go? Kahl was a veteran, and veteran officers know when they must call off offensive tactics and get out of a building. Firefighters by inclination and training are aggressive. They do not like to retreat. It is common for a probationary firefighter to find himself pushed closer to the fire by more experienced men. But officers need to balance the danger to the firefighters against the desire to do the job. This is called risk management, and today it is a regular part of the National Fire Academy course work. On the job, the decision is as much experience and observation as book learning. It may be "cracks forming in a masonry wall just below the ceiling" at a warehouse fire. "Maybe it's the way the heat is intensifying. Or the way a certain kind of ceiling looks when it's about to crumble . . . the color of a fire signaling that it's just about to roar, plus a sound that might be a crack in the floorboards." Or perhaps it's the heat buildup, "so intense" that somewhere ahead the fire is consuming the building itself. Just as well for Kahl's men that he ordered the retreat, because in the basement a gasoline engine was alight and the vapor above the gasoline drums nearby was heating up.[33]

At 10:53 in the morning, a half hour after the smoke was first seen by passersby in the street and a few minutes after Kahl and his men retired to the street, the basement gasoline engine exploded, and the building itself followed. One wholesale buyer in town looking for spring bargains recalled an "ear splitting roar." A watchman at the bank opposite the Hurst was blown off his feet and showered with fiery debris. A block away, on Baltimore Street, falling masonry knocked a man down. The blast projected heated roof embers and hot gases onto the buildings across narrow Hopkins Place and radiated its heat to every building wall on the block. Hot fires can radiate their heat across city streets, particularly those as narrow as Baltimore's. The facing buildings' cheaply constructed window frames and single-pane glass blew out, letting the superheated gases and lighted debris attack the interiors of the structures. Four of those buildings on the corners of German and Hopkins were immediately invested by flame.[34]

Gasoline engines and stocks of gunpowder in other buildings would soon emulate the Hurst's example, blowing up soon after the fire had breached the interior of the building. Gunpowder explosions were commonplace in the colonial cities, but gasoline-powered internal combustion engines were modern innovations. Though they provided relatively clean and efficient power for the buildings, the fire dangers the gasoline engines of Baltimore posed were poorly understood at the time. Vapor from the gasoline and the fuel itself are especially volatile when heated. Innovation without prior consideration of the consequences is one of the more vexing problems with Americans' love of technological novelty.[35]

"BIG FIRE HERE"

While the Hurst was showering the street with embers, the captain of the salvage corps turned in a second and then a third alarm, calling out additional fire department units. This was no longer a salvage job, he realized. George Horton, chief engineer (the equivalent of the chief of service today) of the BFD and a respected veteran, coordinated the response. When he arrived on the scene, he issued a citywide call for "all hands." He could not have anticipated the scope of the disaster, but he must have known, as Chicago's Chief Williams realized in 1871, that he would need the cooperation of wind and weather to beat this fire. Photographs of Horton show a man at peace with himself, steely eyed with the hint of a smile under his broad, brush mustache. If anyone could handle this emergency, Horton was the man. (The mustache was de rigueur in the days before air packs—it acted like an air filter, keeping falling debris from entering the mouth.)[36]

Horton stationed himself at the corner of German and Liberty, ready to direct a battle against a fire at its nearest point. Like Chief Williams of Chicago, Horton commanded his men from the front. Fire officers had long had this tradition, dating from the time when fire companies were volunteer and manliness meant coming as close to the fire as one could. Sometimes a chief who was exasperated by his men's lack of aggressive tactics would lead the way into a burning building. But a good chief also balanced "judgment against reckless abandon." As city buildings got bigger and higher, the challenge of knowing how and where to attack fires became as much a matter of firefighting science as personal courage and leadership qualities.[37]

Ten minutes later, at 11:10 AM, on his own authority Horton telegraphed the Washington, D.C., department for help. "Big fire here," he pleaded, "must have help." The capital city sent two engine companies on a special train (flatcars for the engines, boxcars for the horses). It raced "on a clear tack with the throttle wide open" the forty miles to Baltimore on the B&O line. D.C.'s department was happy to "lend a helping hand" to Baltimore's.

Its firefighters had the additional incentive of proving their moxie. It must have been an exhilarating trip for the twenty men, wind whipping their faces, riding the open flatcars with their gear to rescue poor Baltimore. And a chance to fight a big fire. Firefighters love the challenge of a fully developed blaze almost as much as they enjoy competition with other companies. D.C. Fire Department officers came as well, to coordinate with their Baltimore opposite numbers. They arrived less than an hour after Horton had asked for assistance, to the cheers of spectators at the B&O station on Light Street. By midafternoon the D.C. firefighters were fully engaged in the battle. Later that afternoon, the feat was repeated, with two more engine companies arriving by 5:00 PM.[38]

The Philadelphia fire chief learned about the Baltimore fire by telegraph and offered his department's aid, but he could not reach any official until nearly 2:00 PM. At first Mayor John McLane declined the offer, but by 5:00 PM. with the fire still out of control, Philadelphia sent four engine companies and 150 policemen to help keep order. This time it was the Pennsylvania Railroad, the B&O's great rival, providing free transportation to the relief companies. It was just as well; the B&O's seven-story Second Empire–style office building, with its ornate mansard roof, would soon be gutted by the flames.[39]

The great metropolis of New York City, comprising the newly consolidated boroughs of Brooklyn, Queens, the Bronx, Staten Island, and Manhattan, had the biggest fire department in the world. It sent the largest contingent of engines, horses, and men to Baltimore. The seven companies mounted trains in New Jersey early on Monday morning, after ferrying the horses, equipment, and men across the Hudson River. As the train progressed toward Baltimore, crowds at every station cheered the firefighters. The battle to save Baltimore had become a crusade.[40]

New York's professional firefighters had faced their own downtown building fire calamity in 1898, when the supposedly fireproof sixteen-story Home Life Insurance Building caught fire. The department tried to fight the blaze offensively, dragging miles of hose up the stairs. When the entire top floor burst into flame, they retreated to the Postal Telegraph Building next door. They hooked up hoses to the standpipes in that building, poured water on the roof of the Home Life, and prevented it from spreading its fiery embers to other buildings along Broadway.[41]

With the now familiar mixture of cockiness and cynicism associated with "the city," the battalion chief in charge of the FDNY in Baltimore later commented, "[I]t is preposterous that a great prosperous city like Baltimore should have only 25 engine companies." Horton and his men already knew that the city's fire department was too small to fight a conflagration without help. The cooperation of the fire departments along the Washington, D.C.–New York City corridor was the first instance of a mutual response strategy. Here it was ad hoc, later it would become standard in every major city, except, ironically, in the City of New York.[42]

In the meantime, the explosion and the fire-driven winds were carrying the pieces of the Hurst roof east down German and Baltimore toward the most expensive real estate in the city. Falling debris knocked down electric lines and poles. Downed power lines are among the worst street-level dangers that firefighters face. They must maneuver their ladders and engines around the lines lest they touch live wires. The fallen lines denied power to the city's trolley cars, stranding riders and placing another obstacle in the firefighters' way. The trolley conductors nevertheless stayed with their cars throughout the crisis, receiving food and drink from grateful riders. But one of the downed lines fell on Horton, and he had to be carried from the fight.[43]

Horton spent the rest of the day in bed at home, his duties assumed by his deputy, District Chief August Emrich. Emrich had never battled anything like this, and his inexperience would tell in the coming hours, though no one doubted his personal courage. It was he, however, who uttered the words that no firefighter wanted to say or hear: "We're in God's hands; the wind is too much for us and there is not enough water in Baltimore to keep those flames from spreading."[44]

Mayor John McLane also rushed from home to command at the scene. According to the *Baltimore American,* he spent much of the day pacing the hose lines just out of reach of the fire, conferring with subordinates, including the police and fire department officials, as he walked. His mistakes were a combination of a youthful desire to play a role in events for which he had no training and a curious combination of hands-on haste and indecisiveness that let others step in and influence him.[45]

Facing the fire, the firefighters must have reckoned its dangers. Twentieth-century firefighters are consummate realists. The romantic dash of the previous century, along with the volunteer companies' exotic uniforms, had gone, replaced by training regimens and regulations, drab dark rubber coats, and heavy protective helmets.

The experienced firefighter knows that when a fire has fully involved a building, the danger to firefighters at the scene increases exponentially. On the street, the officers were constantly assessing risk. Every fire presents a multitude of similar calculations. As dangerous as leading men at a blaze may seem to observers, it is rarely reckless. The officer balances unknown dangers against "doing the job right." By that noontime in Baltimore, building walls and floors were collapsing. Clearly, the building fires were too hot for offensive tactics.[46]

The peril in the street was almost as great. The first two engines called to the scene were almost immediately destroyed by the Hurst's debris. An engineer tending the boiler would have been buried in the masonry had not the fire horse Goliath turned and pulled him and the rig to safety. The new plan was to stay ahead of the fire, creating a fire-free zone. The truck companies deployed to enable ladder men to break windows, and the engine men then poured water into buildings. It was a defensive fight now, and it might have worked if the wind had cooperated.[47]

But even this defensive plan had a basic flaw. It was not the walls of the adjoining buildings that had to be protected, but their roofs. The fire attacked undefended buildings from above, often leaping over the firefighters' lines in the streets to set alight roofs blocks away from the engines. By early afternoon on Sunday, the seven blocks of stores and offices bounded by Lombard, Liberty, Baltimore, and Hopkins were burning. The rear exposure of the Hurst was a "wholesale matting" store; next to it, on South Liberty, stood a "fancy clothing" shop, another dry goods wholesaler; and down Hopkins Place was "retail shoe alley." Small proprietors' narrow and shallow storefronts were all burning fiercely. The office building and bank across German had succumbed as well.[48]

Then the wind freshened and began to drive out of the southwest, carrying the fire from what had been the roof of the Hurst, hundreds of yards away to the north and east. One block north, the Mullins Hotel crumbled in less than half an hour. Again the wind capriciously shifted, this time to the east, and firefighters splayed out along Fayette to the north had to hurry to take up their hoses and hook up lines down Hanover Street. They were not in time. By late afternoon, the fire had crossed Hanover and was pressing down on Charles.

JUST THE THING TO SELL NEWSPAPERS

On the scene, reporters for the *Sun*, *American*, *Herald*, and *News* were collecting human interest anecdotes. They assumed that their buildings, farther down Baltimore, past Calvert, were safe. Their editors had already planned extra editions. In times of crisis, the need for such stories of peril and heroism grows. Hope attaches great value to intimate tales of rescue and relief. There were plenty of both in the early hours of the fire, and episodes multiplied as the fire consumed more of the city. Almost all had a moral—that the city folk had not lost their valor or their humanity. In fact, there were no stories of looting or crime.

Instead, there were the workers at city hall and the courthouse clerks who refused to surrender their marbled buildings or the invaluable legal records to the fire. Chief Judge Henry D. Harlan led the band of amateur firefighters within the courthouse. They saved it. Protected by the firefighters' lines, the newly completed city hall next door only suffered some damage to its cupola. It still stands. Though "gaunt and defeated," the firefighters regrouped over and over again.[49]

But the residents of East Baltimore and Canton fled, "a heart rending picture . . . of pandemonium." Black citizens were especially affrighted, according to reports, seeing the fiery skies as "the day of judgment" at hand. They gathered together and prayed for forgiveness, the objects of pity and scorn by the newsmen for their gullibility. There was precedent for both the blacks' invocation of the Lord and the reporters' contumely. When Charleston, South Carolina, was rocked by earthquake and fire, in 1886, people of color emptied into the streets and there held deeply emotional impromptu prayer meetings. A visiting *Baltimore Sun* correspondent looked on and sneered, "'I find that the demoralization which is abject exists chiefly among the ignorant, of whom the large mass are colored people, who attribute the visitation [of natural disaster] to the wrath of God for the sins of the people and not to the order of nature.'" In fact, people of color were returning to the explanations of destructive fire once given by the foremost educated men of colonial America—the puritan ministers.[50]

A long-running human interest story revolved around Mayor McLane and cartloads of dynamite. Elected as a reform candidate in May 1903, he represented the "patrician" face of Progressive politics. Over the objections of business leaders and building owners whose goodwill he had courted and whose assistance in coming days he would need, McLane agreed to allow professional dynamiters to take down buildings to the east of the fire as a firebreak. It was a last resort, and he resisted it from 3:00 PM, when the dynamite arrived, until 8:00 PM.

The first building selected for demolition was Schwab Brothers' department store on Charles and German. The next was the John Duer and Son Building. Then came the Armstrong Shoe Company. Spectators waited with bated breath. McLane, removing himself to a safe distance, joined them. The hundreds of sticks of dynamite strategically placed went up with a roar, the buildings lit up from within, but they did not come down. In fact, all the dynamite accomplished was to dig a great hole in the basement of the Schwab Building and send thousands of Armstrong's shoes and boots flying into the night sky. The burning footware became part of a vortex of superhot shingles, masonry, cornice pieces, window frames, and bargain-priced clothing scudding about the spectators' heads and falling like ash from a volcano. The dynamite also blew out the windows of nearby buildings not yet involved in the fire and invited it in.[51]

Some merchants refused to flee the firestorm. They continued to dash into their endangered premises to carry off valuable bolts of cloth, rare books, account ledgers, and glassware. Among them, Thomas O'Neill, whose newly constructed department store stood at the corner of Charles and Lexington, was to Baltimore what Marshall Field was to Chicago. He was well known to his customers (whom he greeted at the door) and good to his employees. Together that afternoon, he and his workers rushed to the roof of his building and opened up the two water storage towers. They stuffed water-soaked blankets into all openings on the roof and denied the dynamite crews access to the building, rightly arguing that blowing up another building would only spread the fire. The building's external sprinkler system, another novelty that the Hurst did not have, kept the exterior walls soaked while a fire crew prevented the blaze from entering through the doors. O'Neill's was saved.[52]

But the evening cooling brought no relief to the rest of the downtown. The fire had burned for twelve hours and consumed over thirty acres of Baltimore's prime commercial real estate and everything inside. Those fire hoses not destroyed by fire or crushed by falling walls began to freeze. At German and Calvert, where the "fireproof" Calvert and Equitable buildings stood shoulder to shoulder and the Continental loomed over the scene, the Sunday fire reached its apogee. Later estimates put the temperature of the fire that attacked the three high-rises at 2500°F, hot enough to cause stone to crumble, brick to melt, and steel to soften and lose its strength. (At over 1000°F, steel expands one inch per 100 feet.) Here the firefighters made another stand, hoping that the massive Calvert and Equitable buildings would act as barriers, but they went up like "so much tinder."[53]

The Western Union telegraph crew refused to abandon the Equitable until the last moment. "This building is fireproof, there is no danger of it catching fire," one telegraph operator naively told a reporter before her supervisor ordered her out of the building. She made the common mistake of confusing fireproof structure with fireproof contents. The fire seemed to delight in bursting through the windows and up the elevator shafts of the two giants and turning their elegant interiors into molten wreckage. The atrium-like foyers of the buildings, another design feature favored by the Chicago School, actually created a greater risk of fires spreading. Open spaces inside buildings are a storehouse of oxygen—and the more oxygen a working fire has available, the greater its heat. None of the seven brothers fell. The stone and steel did not die—only the innards did. Watching from without, reporters agreed that the builders' claim of "fireproof" was "a delusion."[54]

175

By late evening, the conflagration had attacked the newspapers' headquarters. The *Sun* building was the first and perhaps the finest of the cast iron blocks in the city. It was reduced to a bare iron framework not unlike a bus stop kiosk (save only the charred symbol of the sun atop its cast iron pole). The *Herald*, on Fayette, was supposed to be fireproof, but its metal shutters buckled and blew out as the fire closed in. The *American* and the *News* staffs watched their buildings, presses, and furniture vanish in the fire. The dailies' destruction became another news item as the editors and their staffs removed themselves to the B&O station on Light Street. With copy and plates in hand, they raced off to Washington, D.C., to put out the Monday edition. The *Washington Post* and the *New York Times* offered their facilities, free of charge, in a rare act of charity between intensely competing outlets, but one of the more admirable traits American businessmen exhibit in times of great calamity. The *Sun* stayed in Washington, D.C., for two months, mixing its coverage of the fire with not-so-subtle blasts at the politicians for letting it happen.[55]

Watching over it all with a sharp pen and an astute eye for his own advancement was the *Herald*'s young city editor, H. L. Mencken. Thirty-seven years later he remembered the day perfectly, or so he claimed. He was sleeping off a Saturday night toot at home when a reporter raced up to the door and gasped that the fire on German Street "looked to be a humdinger, and promised swell pickings for a dull winter Sunday." Dull is the enemy of all newspaper editors, and Mencken hustled to the new *Herald* building to coordinate his thirty reporters. He would not get home again for a week, working "nonstop" for three days, in three cities. He judged the fire "a razzle-dazzle, superb and elegant" event, a regular "circus in forty-rings" as he watched its progress through the city editor's fifth-floor window.

He assumed that the "hundred streams" of water he saw played upon the flames would soon vanquish them, but then the wind came up, and the fire leaped over the department's engines. Now, "we had a story, I am here to tell you." Still more reporters flocked to the building to type up human interest tidbits, interviews, and firsthand reports. The sounds of the typewriters almost drowned out the growing roar of the flames.

By seven that evening, there was no time to write any more, and he and two of his editorial colleagues just managed to flee the six-story office building with the fire coming down Baltimore Street. They had the presence of mind to take with them the page proofs for their coverage of the first day of the fire. They would publish it and the extras on the fire from four different locations, one step ahead of the blaze each time, finally ending up using the facilities of the *Washington Post*.[56]

THE GREATEST STAND IN FIREFIGHTING HISTORY

At the end of the day, the fire had reduced the western half of the downtown to ash and rubble. All battles have postmortems. This battle was not over, but some observers thought the key moment in the first day was the fall of the New Carrollton Hotel, at Light and German. An elegant example of cast iron construction in the city dating from 1871 and host to many political fetes, it was set back from the street and its facade was stone. But its windows and awnings were perfect fuel and its fine woodwork lobby beckoned the fire to the host hotel's last feast. It went up like a candle in late evening, and its burning debris carried the fire to the fireproof Maryland Trust Building on Calvert.

A change in wind direction spared the rest of Fayette but ensured that the fire would redouble in intensity. Sometime after 10:00 PM the wind shifted and came out of the northwest, with blustering gusts in excess of thirty miles an hour. Had this wind brought with it rain or snow, the fire might have quieted, but the angry current only drove the fire southeast, toward the harbor and the pier warehouses loaded with new sources of fuel. The change in wind direction may have saved the courthouse and the city hall, where the fire departments had gathered their forces for an all-out battle, but it doomed everything all the way to the harbor.

The fire did not rest that night. The burning Calvert and Equitable fireproofs were visible fifty miles away, and few in Baltimore slept. The fire raced through the stalls on both sides of the broad Market Space, consuming the Maryland School of Art and Design just north of the market. To the south, on Federal Hill, householders anxiously watched as the flames licked at the piers on the south side of Pratt. The ships in the Inner Harbor had quit their berths, and tugs and fireboats jockeyed for position to throw water on the advancing wall of flame. The Philadelphia firefighters joined the exhausted and thinned Baltimore crews and helped stop the flames from progressing down Light Street, but in the face of gusts of thirty miles an hour, they could not prevent the fire from crossing Pratt and reducing to ash the warehouses along the harbor.[57]

On Monday, the remaining firefighters from Baltimore, reinforced by New York City's engines and by companies from every town and village within 100 miles, faced the fire across the Jones Falls. Little more than a seventy-five-foot-wide open sewer with structures close to both sides of its stone walls, the canal still gave some protection to the massed firefighters and their officers. What's more, they could draw its fetid waters into their engines and shower the water on every structure on the east side of Jones Falls.

The raging combat of the previous day had turned into an engagement of sudden raids, thrust, and reply across the canal. The fire leaped at targets of opportunity in the lumberyards, malt houses, and dwellings on the east side of the falls. Had it established a beachhead on the east side, all of east Baltimore would have shared the fate of downtown. The land slopes upward, and the fire would have rushed up Lombard, Pratt, and Fayette into the residential neighborhoods.

But "the great army" of firefighters at the Jones Falls canal, thirty-seven engines strong, made one of the most remarkable stands in the history of American firefighting. The docks were gone, now smoking ruins. The downtown area was lost. But the line held. It was literally hand-to-hand combat, as the fire set the icehouse and the power plant aflame (the former succumbed, the latter survived), but combined fire departments' forces put out spot fires at the lumberyards. Most important, the wind had quieted. At 5:00 PM Monday, Mayor McLane declared the fire under control. The combined cities' forces had won, and jockeying for the credit began, as though the fight were a sporting event. For example, the *Times* article on the evening of the 9th reported that "there are many here who say that the New Yorkers accomplished the final checking of the flames."[58]

The out-of-town firefighters said their good-byes and took up their equipment. The way home was lined with cheering civilians, but most of the men were too tired to do more than smile. Baltimore's exhausted force still had to overhaul the smoldering ruins, lest the wind pick up and carry burning debris in search of new fuel.

Fortunately, the fires did not take many lives, though firefighters suffered numerous injuries from falling debris and burning surfaces. Over fifty of them were hospitalized in the first hours, the number growing to nearly 200 before the fire was contained. But only four (possibly five) people would die as a result of the blaze, and only one of them directly from burns. After the fire was contained, Private John Undutch and Lieutenant John Richardson, both members of the Maryland militia companies called out to keep order on February 9, died of pneumonia worsened during their tour of duty in the city. Baltimore firefighter Mark Kelly and FDNY lieutenant John McKew succumbed to respiratory illnesses contracted while they fought the fires. The finely ground dust of the charred stone and brick buildings, added to the smoke from the burning paper, textiles, and chemical waste created a deadly airborne paste.[59]

The ruins continued to attract spectators. They gathered at street corners in the burned-over district to gaze at the magnitude of the disaster. At the start of the fire, ten deep, the spectators had pushed against the police lines to get a better view of the Hurst fire. As the blaze burst out of the building onto the streets, the crowd's mood changed from lively anticipation to concerned agitation. The women and children among them left, and the men who remained dodged burning embers. A few store owners and bank managers tried to push through the throngs to get to their places of business. The police let some of them go, but halted others when the danger seemed too close. No longer excited by the prospect of a swift victory, the bystanders milled about asking one another questions to which no one knew answers, a solemn chorus to the thirty hours of tragedy. In a kind of random motion, clumps of gawkers moved from one ruin to the next, remembering what had proudly stood but days before.[60]

THE FIRE IN PICTURES

To the front of the spectators pushed a corps of photographers. Never before had an American fire been so thoroughly documented in photographs. Some students of fire have claimed pride of place for photographers of the San Francisco fire of 1906. Not so—Baltimore was the first. Photographers from the *Sun* and the *American* determined to capture on film the fire's progress. Freelance photographers such as J. William Schaefer saw the commercial opportunities in fire photos. His shots of the rubble and his panoramas were soon available in book form—in fact the *Official Book of Baltimore Fire* (1910) was nothing more than photographs and captions.[61]

The camera corps benefited from the technical improvements to photographic equipment since the Chicago fire. Newspaper photographers were able to use Eastman Kodak's new rolls of film instead of plates. The new film could be loaded in the camera in daylight, making cameras light enough to be carried about easily (an important feature when staying ahead of a fast-moving fire). Moreover, the roll of film permitted multiple exposures in a short time.

A new genre—the disaster postcard—also came out of the Baltimore fire, the brainchild of Henry F. Rinn. Rinn was an amateur photographer but an experienced businessman, and he happened to have his camera and tripod with him when the first alarms sounded. According to Peter Petersen, "Rinn . . . managed to dart along the narrow streets between blazing buildings, evade the fast moving wagons, and somehow avoid police attention." He made contact prints, sent them off to be printed, and was selling postcards of the disaster within two weeks.[62]

The photographs of the fire on February 7 are almost indistinct, so great was the smoke. Most were taken from a block or so ahead of the flames, others from the roofs of buildings not yet engulfed. But the grainy quality of the photos does not detract from their impact.

Imagine an old silent film unreeling in slow motion frame by frame, as the cameraman backs down Baltimore Street, then turns south at Charles. In the foreground, a tangle of hose and squat fire engines, a company of firefighters directing the master stream to the upper stories of buildings already singed by falling embers. The horses have been detached and sent back for more equipment. The street is narrow, itself framed by telephone and power poles, and the somber walls of three- and four-story brick buildings. The windows of buildings already invested with fire are alight, as though the owners had set out torches in celebration of some druid festival. In the background is an ominous darkness spiraling up and out of the frame. Sometimes the darkness is lit by a burst of light. The flames cannot be seen, though if the movie had sound, they could be heard roaring. The cameraman is cold, shivering, but if he advanced a hundred yards toward the fire he could feel the heat begin to dry his skin and burn the hairs on his eyelids and inside his nose. In the next frame, there are fewer engines and less hose—they have been consumed by the blaze—and fewer firefighters; they have retreated once again to prevent the fire from surrounding them. As night comes, the whole downtown seems to vanish in smoke that is lit by the explosions of building after building. Frame after frame, a pictorial record of a city's downtown dying.

Another group of photographers arrived later in the week. They accompanied the fireproof construction experts from Chicago. Through the charred remains of the Continental and the other seven brothers, these photographers, engineers, and sales representatives moved, stopping to document in graphic photography the innards of the high-rises. They not only wanted to understand what had happened, they needed to counter newspaper criticisms of their building methods. They had promised their customers that the buildings would not succumb to flame, and they carped at the snide tone the dailies adopted whenever they wrote "fireproof." As one of the Chicago experts retorted, "Of course window frames and glass and the doors, and the finish, even the floor strips in the concrete, and all the contents of the . . . fireproof buildings was destroyed . . . but, to say that the [fireproof] structures actually burned is, of course, foolish and manifestly incorrect . . . because they are still standing." The fire-proof elements—the steel and tiles—were not even bent out of shape. Only "highly inflammable materials used in [the buildings'] decoration or stored within" burned like charcoal in a furnace.[63]

At the behest of insurers, Thomas Edison dispatched his moviemakers to the scene to record the disaster. Edison's manufac-turing firm was one of the inventors of the motion picture camera. From 1889, when the firm began to develop the camera, using the new emulsion film that Kodak pioneered in 1890, Edison introduced both filming and projection devices. The Edison Company went into the documentary filming business in 1900 and disaster films were immediate successes, along with training movies for police and fire departments, on-the-scene newsreels of the Boer and Spanish American Wars, and reviews of expositions and fairs. In fact, the 1903 Edison film *The Fireman* was the first to use cutting and edit-ing of scenes. In Baltimore, Edison's cameramen panned across the rubble—a stark and disturbing scene of melted stone and brick piles.[64]

The pictures of the aftermath of the fire had a different quality from the previous days' scenes. In one sense, they are even more in-distinct than the fire photos. They depict street after street of rubble, so thickly strewn that even residents of the city could not tell on which street they stood. The jumble of brick, stone, and masonry of the buildings steals their individuality, but the photographic record documents a hard death—the stores and offices consumed from the inside out as though some ferocious cancer ate at their vitals. Here and there like tombstones stand the empty shells of buildings, some-times almost complete, sometimes only a column of bricks still up-right. All that remains of the Hurst Building is part of an outside wall. The hulks of the fireproofs are the most solemn of the down-town sentinels. Their interiors are gutted but their brick facades, held up by the steel columns and tile reinforced floor trusses, re-main, like skeletons.

The still shots and movie reels of the fire feature crowd scenes, the loungers and the gawkers ringed by sober-faced police guarding what remained of the buildings and their contents. Fearing looting, with its own resources insufficient and its men exhausted by long service in the streets, the police board sought the aid of the militia. The Maryland Fourth and Fifth Regiments, later augmented by a troop from Ft. McHenry, arrived while the fire was still hot.

Though Governor Edwin Warfield was their nominal commander, they deployed five hours before he arrived by train from the capital in Annapolis. Warfield, a veteran Democratic politician and banker whose Fidelity and Trust bank building sat on Saratoga and Charles (just out of the range of the fire), spent the rest of the fire watching like a mother hen over the deposits in his bank.[65]

The field commander of the militia, Brigadier General Lawrason Riggs, was more active. Indeed, he took the job of policing the streets so seriously that he became a target for angry newspaper editors and business people. Building owners wanted to get back into the burned district to search for papers, safes, and other valuables, and the reporters wanted to investigate the scene at close hand. The troops had orders otherwise. The *Baltimore Sun* complained of General Riggs's "popinjay attitude" and petitioned Governor Warfield to relieve Riggs of command. Soon Riggs was summoned to explain his high-handed ways, so mighty was the printed page. The guard, at its height 2,000 strong, stayed until the 23rd of February with little to do but pose for photographers.[66]

THERE WAS A LOT of explaining to do, and no shortage of voices vying to do it. With the sounds of dynamite (now used to bring down the fragments of tottering building walls) in the air, and the ruins still smoldering, Baltimoreans looked for culprits. Finger-pointing was inevitable and mistakes were made in the days after the fire, as they had been during its reign. But the mood of the city was, "Let us get to work."[67]

"We'll Win Again"

In part because no one died during the fire, Baltimore's city fathers did not bear the burden of guilt that Chicagoans had to expiate. The response to the fire, thus, did not rehearse the themes of Christian manliness and redemption, nor did ministers play as important a role in divining the meaning of the fire as did secular authorities and the business community. In fact, because the fire was confined to the business district of downtown, the businessmen and their media, including the newspapers, took the lead in responding to the catastrophe. They were as upbeat as the Chicagoans, but the beat had a different rhythm. Chicago had no real rivals; its recovery was in that sense assured. Baltimore was locked in competition with other Northeastern ports and industrial cities. The ballyhoo and boosterism of its spokesmen after the fire had a desperate undertone. But in the years to come, the fire wreckage would become a potent force for change in the Inner Harbor district.

THE PROGRESSIVES AND THE FIRE

Immediately after the blaze, serious questions were raised about Baltimore's economic future. The *Wall Street Journal* demanded that the insurance companies come up with hard figures on the losses and their ability to pay out what they owed. In turn, the National Board of Fire Underwriters, representing the insurers, expressed concern about the city's firefighting defenses. The New York City banks needed reassurance that the deposits in the Baltimore banks were safe. Capitalists must realize, the paper editorialized, that money spent on recovery would otherwise "have been invested in new creative work that would have increased the wealth of the country." The paper's editors were reassured by Mayor McLane's confidence but worried about the overall impact of the fire on money markets. The *Washington Post* was more confident of Baltimore's revival. The insurance loss of local D.C. firms was "not heavy," the paper reassured its readers, and policies were being paid "promptly." In fact, the *Post* concluded, the fire relief and recovery would act as a "stimulant" to the economy.[68]

Two days after the BFD announced the containment of the Great Fire, the *Baltimore Sun*, still without a building of its own, was effusive in its optimism. "To build a new and greater Baltimore, businessmen and financiers will meet today, not appalled by disaster . . . Those in authority are endeavoring in a sane, calm way . . . to raise up a new and greater Baltimore from the ruins of the old." The editor of the Baltimore *American* agreed that "greater Baltimore will rise from the ashes . . . we'll win again," even though the fire had dispossessed him and his paper.

The insurance companies were taking out ads in the *Baltimore Sun* and other dailies to reassure their policyholders where they could be found. The German American Fire Insurance Company, for example, was now "located above Sappington's Drug Store" at the corner of Gay and Lexington, and pledged not only to "meet all its obligations inflicted by the recent conflagration" but to solicit new business. Banks reported that valuables in their charge had been saved and would be available to customers. The Continental Trust vault had survived the roaring furnace above it and was opened without incident on the 10th. The telegraph and telephone companies had already set up temporary quarters and resumed service. In this case, good fortune favored the prepared—the Chesapeake & Potomac Telephone Company had just stored its new switchboard in a Washington, D.C., warehouse when the fire engulfed its Baltimore Street headquarters. The switchboard was rushed to Baltimore and made operational.[69]

No one minimized the losses. As calculated by the insurance companies and later by the Burnt District Commission, the devastation spread over eighty-six city blocks, made unusable 1,526 structures, and put more than 2,400 businesses out of commission. Estimates varied about the loss in dollars, but they range from $100–150 million ($2.16–3.24 billion in 2005 dollars). The newspapers printed long lists of every building and business burned out by the fire. Collecting data was one of the passions of the Progressives, including those around Mayor McLane. The city seemed to embrace numbers with an almost religious fervor. Every report from city hall featured numbers of some kind—as if there were safety, predictability, and control in exactitude.[70]

McLane was a "Progressive" Democrat, and all Progressives loved to gather data. Information impartially amassed and assessed allowed men of goodwill to reform society and politics. So, for example, to end the evil of child labor in the city, it was necessary first to amass figures: numbers of children employed by each industry; numbers of children maimed at each task; numbers of children's lives shortened.

Historians called these days the "Progressive Era" after a political movement that affected presidential elections, state legislative activity, and urban government. In cities such as Cleveland and Toledo, Ohio, in New York City, and in Oakland, California, dedicated men and determined women campaigned for the end of corruption, alcoholism, and poverty. They founded settlement houses to teach the immigrants how to be Americans, introduced the idea of scientific city management, and funded institutes and universities to gather information on poverty and its causes. They demanded that cities clean themselves up literally and figuratively. Social engineering was their credo, a faith that human will and intelligence, combined with enough information, could be parlayed into healthy cities. Baltimore's new charter appeared to end the reign of the bosses, and if the Progressives had made little headway in their efforts to create parks, replace the storm drains with sewers, pave and widen the streets, and improve conditions for working people, it was not for want of trying.[71]

Faced with urban decay and dissolution, Progressives demanded improvements rooted in efficient management. The Progressives saw themselves as exemplary doers, fixers, and innovators. McLane was an upper-middle-class Progressive Democrat who had trained in the classics at Johns Hopkins University, a lawyer with a business family background (as so many of the Progressives were), and he was committed to rational improvement. So were his supporters in and out of the city government. The state government had Progressive legislators as well. But the real models for Progressive action lay a little farther afield.[72]

The leader of the Progressives nationally was the Republican president, Theodore Roosevelt. From the White House he watched the progress of the Baltimore fire, only forty miles away. At the height of the fire, he briefly considered rushing up the rail line to help out the D.C. firefighters. Prudently, he sent D.C. policemen instead. On the 13th, he delegated his daughter, Alice, as his eyes and ears, and sent her to Baltimore with his best wishes and an offer of federal aid, should the city ask.[73]

Both gestures were characteristic of the man. Roosevelt favored a rugged individualistic approach to getting things done, a bully determination to impose his will on recalcitrant nature, political foes, and economic problems. He projected this attitude in his domestic and foreign policy, cajoling the Japanese and Russians into ending their war, regulating food and drug companies, creating a national wilderness, and cutting down the size of monopolistic corporations. Some years later, Roosevelt ran for reelection to the presidency not as a Republican but as a Progressive, and his party platform urged "a strong federal administrative commission of high standing, which shall maintain permanent and active supervision over industrial corporations . . . publicity as to wages, hours and conditions of labor . . . the abolition of the convict labor system . . . the protection of home life against the hazards of sickness, irregular employment and old age"—in short, the modern social safety net. Not everyone appreciated Theodore Roosevelt. H. L. Mencken caricatured Roosevelt's methods: "He didn't believe in democracy; he believed simply in government. His remedy for all the great pangs and longing of existence was not a dispersion of authority but a hard concentration of authority. He was not in favor of unlimited experiment; he was in favor of a rigid control from above, a despotism of inspired prophets and policemen." But McLane, though a Democrat, shared something of the president's instincts, and Roosevelt, for all his masculine enthusiasm for danger, could not have gotten any closer to the flames than McLane throughout the 7th and 8th.[74]

But McLane decided soon after the fire not to ask for federal aid, and he adopted a posture toward the rebuilding effort closer to Progressive Democrat Woodrow Wilson's "new freedom." In 1904 Wilson was still teaching history at Princeton, but the ideas that would coalesce into the new freedom platform of his 1912 presidential campaign were already in place. In 1887, Wilson wrote what was to become a classic piece of American political theory, laying the groundwork for this version of progressive reform. In defense of the ideal of expert administration, Wilson insisted that "[methods of administration] must be adapted, not to a simple and compact, but to a complex and multiform state, and made to fit highly decentralized forms of government. If we would employ it, we must Americanize it, and that not formally, in language merely, but radically, in thought, principle, and aim as well. It must learn our constitutions by heart; must get the bureaucratic fever out of its veins; must inhale much free American air." Such a government was to work differently from Roosevelt's bully nationalism, adopting a more localized and laissez-faire approach, benignly overseeing competitiveness among small producers and providers. Wilson had never lost his identification with "hard working, upwardly striving people from the South and West." His ideal government's role would be to ensure that no one cheated.[75]

McLane, a Democrat and a Southerner at heart like Wilson, borrowed something of his approach to reform. He deferred to the expertise of city planners and accepted the leadership of the business community. At the same time, he did not hesitate to use his office to press the city council and its administrative boards when their opposition to the reform plans stiffened. In effect, McLane and his cohorts adopted an administrative model of reform. In it, government named a committee or created an agency and delegated to it the job at hand.

The progressive agency was always a collective enterprise and often short term. Its members were not experts but represented important groups in the community or were respected figures themselves. They held hearings, organized rallies, planted news stories, solicited the opinion of experts, bargained with existing political institutions, and then effected the proposed plan of action. They were not nonpartisan but bipartisan, for no commission could afford to ignore the deeply held party affiliations of the city councilmen. They co-opted business leaders when they could, and denounced those who did not go along. In short, the rebuilding of Baltimore would become a precedent for twentieth-century American city management.[76]

STREET FIGHTING

On February 12, McLane named a sixty-three-member committee of leading businessmen and professionals, a "Citizen's Emergency Committee," to coordinate the recovery effort. They came from the best families in the city and donated their time. At its head was William Keyser, a sixty-nine-year-old retired manufacturer and railroad mogul, who had a hand in every Progressive reform from the 1890s. He was also McLane's political mentor. Keyser and the subcommittees he formed knew that the greatest problems were restoring power all over the city, clearing the streets and pulling down dangerous structures, and restoring confidence in the commercial sector of the economy. But they had more permanent goals as well.[77]

Business historian Christine Meisner Rosen has followed the ins and outs of the battle within the city government and the commercial community to effectuate these reforms. It is neither a neat nor a pretty story. Every stage of the recovery debates and implementation was marked by petty politics in the two chambers of the city council (one dominated by the Democrats, the other by the Republicans), hurt feelings, competition among different city agencies, nasty newspaper coverage (with some of the papers acting in their own economic interest), bitter lobbying, and angry threats. Nevertheless, the emergency committee did its work with efficiency and expedition.[78]

One cannot say they wanted to modernize the city, for the densely congested mixed-use city was already modern. Instead, they wanted to turn back the clock to a time just before Baltimore went industrial, to create a livable, spacious, gracious downtown. Hidden not very far beneath the tough veneer of the Progressive reformer was a romantic moralist. In the heart of the corrosive hubbub of the city, the reformers sought a physical and psychological space to restore the values of a simpler and more harmonious time. It did not matter that such a time and place may never have existed in American history or that American cities were always building over open spaces. The restful, restorative ideal of green places soothing the hivelike activity of the downtown was their goal. They had seen the White City and understood Frederick Law Olmstead and Daniel Burnham's ideal of the city. They advocated F. L. Olmstead, Jr.'s 1902 plan for a system of parks in Baltimore, including the creation of neighborhood vest-pocket parks, landscaping wooded areas on the outskirts of the city, and laying out scenic roadways in and out of the city. Their vision was far more than just commercial.[79]

Thus, from the first, McLane and his allies saw the fire as an opportunity to accomplish all the repairs of the city's infrastructure that politics and petty interests had delayed or derailed for the past decade. The committee's stated purposes, to improve traffic flow and reduce congestion, should be read in conjunction with the proposals for harbor reform and the creation of parks. A huge area of the city was to be legally condemned, but this was merely to clear legal title to the land for remodeling the city. Condemnation was the first step in taking the land from private owners and turning it to public use.

A municipality is not a state unto itself that can take land or other property (for example, by taxation) from its citizens. It is not "sovereign." Instead, it derives all its powers—to elect and operate a government, to police the streets, to regulate its markets, and run its schools—from the state. Maryland allowed the taking of private property under two distinct doctrines of law. The first was "eminent domain" and the second was the use of "police power" to condemn private property. In the first, the city could take a piece of land for common good only if it paid the owner a fair and just compensation based on the market value of the property. An owner who did not want to part with the property could take the city to court to block the taking or to adjust the compensation. In court, the city bore the burden of proving that the taking had a legitimate public purpose, in other words, that it was for the common good, and that it was offering a fair market price. Owners could use the legal process to delay the city's plans, in effect pressuring it to pay a higher rate of compensation. This was not really a fair use of the courts (they were not set up to help parties bargain with one another, and the threat to sue someone else is itself a form of misconduct), but it happened every day.[80]

The second form of confiscation of public property was based on the police powers that every state has to protect the health and welfare of its citizens. Thus, it can "condemn" property whose use or condition poses a threat to public health and safety. It can close down houses of prostitution, order the moving of manufacturing plants or other businesses, and even raze buildings and dig up yards without compensating the owners at all. Under these powers, the city had brought down unsafe buildings and regulated (another form of restricting the use of property) various enterprises. Taking land to build sewers, ordering the placement of electrical and telephone wires underground, and cleaning up the docks all took property without compensation.[81]

A common form of police power regulation of property coming into prominence in these years was zoning. In zoning, the state or its agencies (including the city of Baltimore) limits how buildings and building sites can be used. For example, they could limit residential use or industrial use of the Inner Harbor by zoning it for one or the other. Setbacks of buildings from the street, reduction or enlargement of store frontage, and other forms of regulation to improve the quality of a district (for example, to reduce noise, prevent congestion, improve traffic flow, upgrade appearance, permit the movement of firefighting vehicles, and increasingly today, to protect the historical quality of a neighborhood or a particular block) are all legal purposes under zoning laws. The reformers did not resort to zoning, however. In fact, the constitutional test of zoning did not come until the 1920s, and the first city to extensively zone its industrial and residential districts was New York, in 1916.[82]

The committee work ran into a roadblock almost immediately. Small lot owners and tradesmen in the burned district could not afford to lose even the six feet of frontage that the committee wished to condemn and pave to widen the streets. Taking a stance reminiscent of the Boston tradesmen in 1760, they protested. If the land was to be taken by eminent domain, they wanted compensation. Some of them saw the prospect of compensation as a windfall. They went to the two branches of the city council, to the boards of estimate and public improvements, to the city engineer, and to the courts. They put a halt to all discussion of parks, public use piers, and open spaces. And they threatened to prevent any lasting change of the street plan.[83]

On March 11, McLane tried an end run around the protests. He named a six-member Burnt District Commission. Divided between reform Democrats and Republicans, it was Progressive through and through. The state government authorized the move, taking it out of local hands. The commission was to report its findings to the city council, not to work with it. Unlike the committee, whose purpose was to include the voices of area business and tradesmen, the commission was an administrative agency from the outset, and its members knew that improvement would mean winners and losers. That is to say, it was not a neutral forum for airing proposals and debate. It had an agenda and would use all of its members' private influence as well as its public authority to gain those ends.

Open spaces, harbor-front planning, the widening of streets, and revisions of building codes were all controversial issues, and the mayor and his commissioners were determined to ram those recommendations through. They "manufactured" public opinion when necessary and twisted arms when possible. They lobbied both branches of the city council when council members leaned in opposition to the plans. With the Maryland state legislature behind them and needing only the approval of the council, they had the advantage of initiative, secrecy, and organization over their opponents. Not that their opponents did not put up a terrific fuss or win over one or the other branch of the council at times, but the commission persisted.[84]

One of the opponents of the planned street revisions was the *Baltimore Sun*. The paper reversed itself in the course of making those objections. Put the electrical wires underground, the paper pleaded on February 11. On February 13, it supported the initial committee's "realignment of certain thoroughfares, whose crookedness and narrowness has along constituted a blemish as well as a serious drawback to the city's progress." Straightening and widening these would be "further proof that Baltimore is to rise from its ashes more substantial, more modern, and more imposing than before." Change the streets, the paper demanded, and stop trying to please everyone. But when, under the plans the commission contemplated, the *Sun* stood to lose footage on Baltimore Street, it changed its tune. "Outside agitators" and impractical "aesthetes" had taken over the process, the *Sun's* editorial page whined. Joining with the *Baltimore American*, whose frontage opposite the *Sun* on Baltimore and South was also at risk, the two papers initiated a publicity campaign. With "sledgehammer blows" the *Sun* and the *American* bludgeoned the "lobbyists and their cronies." The *Baltimore World* and the *Herald*, rivals of the *Sun* and the *American*, attacked them as opponents of reform, hinting that they were the tools of dark and corrupt forces. It was great fun for the political reporters and a good way to sell papers—there had been nothing like it since the fire itself.[85]

Worse for the commission was the problem of money. The state allowed the city to raise funds through a bond issue, but this smacked of (or could be made to seem like) fiscal irresponsibility. To counter such charges, the commission enlisted the aid of the liberal Roman Catholic leader James Cardinal Gibbons and rented the Opera House for a giant rally. There were bands and speeches, promises of more jobs and lower taxes. Meanwhile, the commission was buying up the land not in lots but by the square foot at fixed prices to avoid the fair compensation issue. It even convinced some holdouts to "surrender" their land before condemnation. After all, cash in hand was worth the rewards of a lawsuit in the bush. Nine months after its formation, the commission had "taken possession of all the land it needed for all the improvements."[86]

It should have been a triumphant moment for McLane. No city had ever recovered as well nor improved itself as much in so short a time as his. Even Chicago's boasted rebuilding was just that—not a remodeling at all. Burnham's plan for the lakeshore was still a piece of paper in 1904. But McLane's emotional reserves were drained by the fire, the political infighting that never seemed to end, and a marriage to Mary Bibber, "a socially prominent and attractive widow from Philadelphia." Marriage, no matter how happy, always increases stress levels because it involves new behavior patterns. A longtime bachelor, McLane had obviously fallen in love, but that did not make married life easier. Also, it increased this shy man's public notoriety. Indeed, the wedding ceremony was not held in the city because it would have been a major news event.[87]

Everyone has a certain store or reserve of equanimity. Into it we make deposits and from it, in times of trouble and pain, we make withdrawals. McLane's balance was running low. Were he a soldier in war, he would have exhibited the signs of combat fatigue. On the evening of May 29, 1904, McLane returned home from his office, exchanged greetings with his wife, and went upstairs to dress for an evening out. She heard a sharp report, rushed into his bedroom, and found him on the floor, his pistol by his hand and a bullet in his head. Though today's bloggers and tabloids would have proposed all manner of conspiracy theories about his death, and his wife and others insisted that it must have been an accident, the verdict of suicide is all but inescapable. McLane's Republican rival E. Clay Timanus, the president of the second branch of the council, finished out McLane's term. Personally opposed to much of the street-widening plan, Timanus nevertheless pushed all of it through the council, albeit using more traditional political methods.[88]

Baltimore realtors were delighted that the widened streets did not diminish their rental fees. Commerce simply replaced the lost frontage with increased vertical space. Downtown went up. The purpose of the remodeling of downtown was to increase retail and wholesale business and renew the urban values of community. Taller office buildings recaptured rental space in the center of the city. In September 1906, the city celebrated a weeklong Baltimore Jubilee with parades and concerts. The downtown never seemed more alive or happier. Speakers lauded the recovery—ninety percent of the lots in the burned district had new buildings on them. Cities are always renewing themselves (with or without fires), and twenty years after the fire Baltimore's productivity had increased fivefold from pre-fire levels.[89]

SAVING THE DOWNTOWN AGAIN

In an unintended way, the boundaries of the burned district redefined the cityscape. Because the widening of streets and the restoration of the waterfront was limited to the fire zone, the recovery effort turned the Inner Harbor into a distinct and coherent place. One can say that the fire made a downtown where one had not really existed. But in the years after the fire, the sense of common purpose that the reformers imposed on the downtown slowly dissipated. The memory of the determination to "win again" faded as the generation that rededicated the downtown area died.

The Inner Harbor prospered in the World War II years, but its identity—the identity the fire and the recovery fostered—decayed. By the 1950s, the downtown area suffered the same malaise of spirit and decline of real estate value as many older cities. So long as people came downtown to do their shopping, the gift of the Great Fire was safe. When shoppers looked elsewhere, the economic renaissance that followed the fire was imperiled.[90]

And that is what happened. "Between 1948 and 1954, retail trade in metropolitan Baltimore may have increased a strong 25 percent, but it sank nearly 2 percent in the downtown shopping district." The tax value of the downtown stores was similarly falling. In 1954, O'Neill's department store closed, signaling the retailers' retreat from the center city. The people with real buying power had moved to the suburbs. The great department stores closed their inner city locations and followed, to the suburbs. Offices and office buildings emptied out at night, as the clerks, managers, secretaries, professionals, government workers, agents, and bosses went home to the suburbs. More than 18 million people left the city to live in the suburbs in the 1950s, taking with them their shopping and their dining out. Public transit, the great advantage city folk had over the car-dominated suburbs, lost 700 percent of their passenger miles, costing the transit companies revenues. Cities took over the mass transit business, with the rider suffering from rising fares, periodic strikes, and reduced service. With the migration to the suburbs went the tax base for the city (a "ten percent drop from 1952 to 1957"), crippling police and fire services and delaying repair of infrastructure. Potholes in roads, water main collapses, reduced bus service, and increases in street crime were the marks of a decaying city. Baltimore had all of them.[91]

But Baltimore had not forgotten the gift of the Great Fire. Just as businessmen had created a committee to pool their resources and co-opted the city government and gained the aid of the state in the recovery from the fire, so they responded to the decline of the downtown. In 1954, the Committee for Downtown formed itself and a year later joined with the Greater Baltimore Committee, Inc. The chair of the executive committee of the larger body was real estate developer James Rouse. From the first, the businessmen worked hand in glove with city hall. The first objective was to upgrade downtown retail facilities, create incentives for people to visit downtown, and increase the number of jobs. Nothing had been added to the building stock since 1928. The committee's planning council hired David Wallace, an urban planner and architect, who knew that other attempts to rejuvenate the downtown areas of Eastern seaboard cities had led to empty streets and empty stores. He went back to the city beautification movement of the 1910s for inspiration. The idea was to bring the greenery and open spaces of the Olmstead plan to fruition, though none of the planners, including Rouse, cited Olmstead's plan.[92]

The Charles Center—their name for the downtown real estate development—would cover twenty-two acres in the heart of the Inner Harbor, from Lombard to Fayette and Charles to Hopkins Place.

The site was big enough to tie together the banking, insurance, and retail districts, and to provide attractive pedestrian walkways and hidden parking. A civic center, theater, and apartments were also central to the plan. The planners retained a number of older buildings, still occupied, so that the site would not look like a giant vacant lot as they developed the Charles Center. Finally, the site was divided into a number of smaller parcels and offered to a variety of developers. Federal funding, part of the 1960s urban renewal movement, helped, as did highly publicized design competitions.

The result was a combination of hotels, restaurants, office buildings, a sports arena, and retail outlets in the center city, and for a time lots of broken pavement in the roads through East and West Baltimore leading to the downtown area. But there was a downside: Much of the city's tax base was going into the Charles Center rather than into local projects, including schools and infrastructure in the poorer neighborhoods. Although a net increase in jobs resulted, and the businesses that relocated to downtown profited, the city itself (because of the tax breaks for the businesses) did not immediately gain. Still, the city recouped its lost income after 1975, when it reassessed taxes downtown.[93]

Who Will Win Again?

The business promoters were not done. Heirs to the energy, the confidence, and the acumen of McLane and the Progressives of 1904, Rouse and his comrades turned to the waterfront. The Inner Harbor was a busy port during World War II. By the 1950s, however, the harbor itself was vacant and the land immediately adjacent in Samuel Smith Park was open space for parking. The parking lot was the suburb's kiss of death for downtown—a Trojan horse that used valuable people space to store cars. "For a decade after that, the Inner Harbor lay neglected, its piers rotting and its buildings filling with vermin rather than cargo." Rouse, best known as a suburban mall developer, had already begun to redevelop areas of inner cities as "Festival Marketplaces." From the moment he joined the Greater

Baltimore Committee, he surely was thinking about how to reinvigo-
rate the decaying harbor front. "'Nobody believes in the American
city,' he once lamented, 'We have lived so long with old, worn-out
ugly places that we have become anesthetized to their condition.'"
He thought he knew the answer: Revive the old city marketplace and
wrap it in "'informality, diversity, color, texture, fragrances.'" Put the
new marketplace where people would go. From a lifetime of watching how people behaved—how they gathered, what they liked, the
patterns of their intercourse, and what attracted them—he felt certain that he could transform the waterfront.[94]

Rouse brought in a longtime collaborator, architect Benjamin
Thompson, and Thompson proclaimed that the key to rejuvenation
of the center city was food. "'The sight and smell of food, the corner-
stone of human commerce'" would bring people (and their wallets
and pocketbooks) back to the downtown area. Together the two men
had already completed the restoration of Boston's Faneuil Hall, taking a worn-out nineteenth-century Greek Revival shell and turning it
into a vibrant food court and restaurant center—an inner city mall—
when the prospect of doing the same for the west and north sides of
the Inner Harbor presented itself. Baltimore had condemned the
land at the edge of the Inner Harbor. Rouse obtained the leases in
1978, and within a decade, the shops, restaurants, hotels, and tourist
attractions on the Light and Pratt Streets crossing had become a
magnet for people from all over the world. The pavilions were multistory, split-level, glassed-in, so that the shop wares and restaurants
attracted the eye of the passerby. As Thompson described them, they
were "transparent, light, shimmering . . . in some ways invisible, a
non-building, a building of magic." Over 100 hundred merchants
rent space in these creations. Tourists from all over the country
(Harborplace is the number one attraction in the state) enjoy the
pavilions, the historical ships moored to the piers, and more recently,
the science center, state aquarium, bookstores, arcades, and other
restaurants along Lombard that followed.[95]

Not everyone benefited from Rouse's vision. Just as the small
businesses and shops lost out in the 1904 recovery plan, so the allocation of city resources to private enterprise in the 1960s and 1970s

diverted attention from the problems of the rundown neighborhoods of poor people. Early twentieth-century ordinances passed to "beautify" the city had as their not-so-secret second purpose confining blacks to ghettos. Zoning was cynically employed by reformers to ensure that those ghettos did not escape their existing confines. Racist covenants (contracts) to keep blacks who could afford better housing from buying in white neighborhoods added a private dimension to publicly mandated segregation. When these covenants were declared illegal in 1912, entire blocks, followed by neighborhoods, shifted racially as "blockbusting" pushed whites out. Row houses built in the 1910s and 1920s to provide affordable housing for integrated neighborhoods were stigmatized by residential segregation by the 1950s. Within the space of twenty years from 1950 to 1970, some areas along the east-west axis went from 99 percent white to 92 percent black. Housing discrimination was not peculiar to Baltimore; red lining was a common feature in Northern cities. But the impact on Baltimore was tragic.[96]

Though the highly visible physical symbols of progress downtown may have hidden a "two-tiered" city, the success of the renaissance of the Inner Harbor demonstrated that the spirit of 1904 retained its promise of continued renewal. The old power plant, the last building at the harbor to face the fire, is now a museum. The B&O Camden rail yards and station have become the Baltimore Orioles' Camden Yards ballpark. The museum and the ball park frame the width of the Great Fire. The widened streets of the old downtown are now filled with pedestrians.[97]

And Baltimore, like Chicago, has not forgotten its Great Fire. At the Power Plant Live there is a plaque—here is where the fire was beaten. The centennial remembrance, with walking tours and the Maryland Historical Society exhibition "Baltimore Ablaze," ran from February through the end of October. The Enoch Pratt Free Library exhibition "Footprints of the Fire" and the Johns Hopkins University lecture series in March 2004 were well-publicized events. The restoration of buildings that survived the fire is further testimony to the city's resilience. Tenants occupy One South Calvert (the Continental Trust Building frame refurbished), the Jefferson Building (the old Union Trust at Fayette and Charles), the Alex Brown Building at Calvert and Baltimore, the Mercantile Safe Deposit Building at Calvert and Redwood, the Safe Deposit and Trust at 13 South Street, and the International Trust at St. Paul and Baltimore. The thick layers of ceramic tiles that saved the steel columns and floor supports in the Continental Trust became the standard for all high-rises after the Baltimore fire. They protected the older buildings around New York City's World Trade Center when its innovative structures, without the heavy tile facings and wraps, succumbed to fire.[98]

The memory of the fire lives in another way. Charles Street at Fayette sharply narrows—returning to its pre-fire width. The city has taken up the sidewalk concrete and replaced it with red brick. The storefronts and the buildings on both sides date from the era before the fire, and these have been restored by a neighborhood association. Walk the steep blocks of Charles from Fayette toward the Washington Monument and you can go back in time. At the intersection of Liberty and Baltimore, you can still imagine a cold February Sunday morning a century before.

The wind picks up and the bitter, wet cold seeps into the buildings as it did a hundred years before. The sidewalk is almost empty at Hopkins Plaza, next to the Mercantile Building, as it was the morning of the fire. A few of the old alleys have survived the succession of renovations, and their windowless brick-and-mortar walls, separated by a mere forty feet of pavement, recall the pre-fire city. The call boxes are gone, but a modern fire engine's siren howls not far away. The firefighters know about the horrific explosion here, and the heroic stand their predecessors made at Jones Falls the next day; it is part of the lore of a proud department.[99]

THE GREAT FIRE OF BALTIMORE was the last of its kind, a citywide fire developing from a single fire source. Other cities would burn, some from gas main fires (San Francisco in 1906), some from exploding chemicals (Texas City in 1947), some from inadequate fire service to racially segregated neighborhoods (Tulsa, in 1921 and New Bern, North Carolina, in 1922), but no American city would again allow a single spark to reduce an entire city core to ruins. The greatest danger to cities from fires would not arise from carelessness, neglect, or accident in a single site, but from fires intentionally set for political or personal reasons or because people built their homes in a place that fire had already claimed and would reclaim.

DETROIT, 1967

The Baltimore fire of 1904 was an accident that brought a divided industrial city together. The Detroit fires of 1967 were arson that split a divided industrial city wide open. It pitted young against old, whites against blacks, the poor against the upwardly mobile, and the city against its own suburbs. It framed the story of a "rust-belt" city in a downward spiral, a wealthy metropolis stunned by violence, "white flight," and maladministration. Above all, it is a story about the corrosive power of hopelessness.

Elmhurst is a shady street on the West Side running from Twelfth Street to Cherrylawn. It is studded with working-class, low-rise apartments, attached housing, brick and wood frame stand-alones. In the immediate post–World War II era, it was home to Jewish families. When they left in the 1950s and 1960s, lured by hope for a better life and pressed on by real estate agents using "blockbusting" fear tactics (the blacks are coming, better move now before the neighborhood goes), hopeful black families from the South moved in. Mount Zion Baptist Church took over the B'Nai David synagogue building. Around the church the neighborhood grew. Mary Thomas, a deaconess, remembered "trees and children were everywhere on the street." Thomas thought that things "were up and coming." The police who walked the beat knew folks, and there was "little crime." For Choice Cooper, "who bought the house at 1926 Elmhurst in February 1962 . . . Elmhurst was pretty, quiet, close to work and safe."[1]

Go a mile south, down Twelfth Street to Clairmount, and there you will find a different story. In the 1960s, it was "a strip of pool halls, liquor stores, party stores, and illegal drinking establishments called 'Sin Street.'" On these corners, "sagging wooden houses with strips of peeling paint, two story homes where balconies had broken rails and missing uprights, houses with boards over the windows to keep out the wind" were home to a shifting collection of poor, periodically unemployed, and disaffected souls. "The timeless ebb and flow of corner life . . . rocked like kelp in the tide." Its people "had little power to shape events, and individuals could deal, generally, only with what came their way." On Elmhurst, hope; on Clairmount, ingrained resentment, growing anger, and lingering despair.[2]

On July 23, 1967, Sin Street came to Elmhurst in fire and fury. The Reverend Edith Johnson heard the sound of gunshots, saw crowds of young men pushing supermarket carts filled with looted goods, and smelled the smoke of fires set all along Linwood, Twelfth, and the other storefront thoroughfares. Nothing was ever the same afterward. "You are not going to find the colorfulness of the city, the culture, the way it existed before," poet and activist Kalema Hasan lamented, because the fire "destroyed not only the buildings, but it destroyed a basic foundation and fibre." Gregory Byrd, returning home to Twelfth from service in Vietnam in September 1967, recalled recently that "nothing was ever the same."[3]

And it could have been so different, if only people had not given in to hopelessness. If only whites had not found a target in blacks for their anger and anxiety, and blacks had not responded in kind. But even that meltdown took time. In the 1920s, the reform energy of the Progressive Era was waning. The so-called Lost Generation festered in a sense of betrayal. The sacrifices of the Great War to Save the World for Democracy had led nowhere but thousands of war dead and sick.

But not in Detroit. For Detroit was the home of the automobile industry, of Ford and all its competitors, and there were jobs. It was a factory city, with workshops lining the river. The profits poured into the city in skyscrapers, department stores, wide avenues, and monuments to culture like the Detroit Institute of the Arts and the Public Library, facing one another across the 5000-block of Woodward. Detroit was a city too busy to have race riots (though there were enough episodes of confrontation and sporadic violence to give wise people pause). So to it came, like the Jews of the Exodus, thousands of black Southerners seeking opportunity and fleeing oppression.[4]

In 1911, there were only 5,400 blacks in Detroit. By 1925, they numbered nearly 100,000. The young men came first, willing to pay more than whites for comparably bad accommodations, willing to work the "dirtiest and meanest jobs" that whites did not want. "Sweaty and dirty from their jobs in the foundries, they boarded street cars and so inadvertently reinforced the negative image of Negroes held by whites." They were not welcome, except as handymen and house labor, in the very wealthy enclaves, and the police, all white, rousted them, harassed them, and sometimes shot them with no one to say nay. The Ku Klux Klan had found a home in Detroit's West Side and busied itself burning crosses where black people could see them.

Still, the early 1920s were good times for the immigrants from the South, compared to the places they had left. The Urban League branch in the city provided housing tips and helped them look for jobs. Folks who had never lived in the city, with all its complicated etiquette (what to do with the garbage, how to use the mass transit, how to tell the quick-fingered thieves from the rest of the surging street crowds) learned quickly.

Blacks found places to live next to other blacks. For most, this was a matter of choice and expense—poor housing for poor people among other poor. But whites did not want blacks to live among them—they made it abundantly clear. A few middle-class blacks ventured out into the larger world, looking for a nicer house in a nicer neighborhood. Enclaves of black housing sprang up outside the old east "Black Bottom" ghetto. There was hope.[5]

Then came the Great Depression. The banks staggered and the factories curtailed their operations. Ford plant closings; line shutdowns at the other plants; too much borrowing and too easy credit left the working classes vulnerable to their own lack of savings. For the white immigrants who had come to the city with little but their willingness to work, joblessness was a terrible blow. They took it out on the blacks. Color meant they could not hide, and to their own economic plight others added displaced anger and racial prejudice. Novelist Jeffrey Eugenides imagined what race relations looked like in 1932:

> The trolley crossed . . . Hastings Street. At that moment, every passenger, all of whom were white, performed a talismanic gesture. Men patted wallets, women refastened purses . . . the streetcar had entered the Black Bottom Ghetto . . . The light seemed to change, growing grey as it filtered through the laundry lines. The gloom of front porches without electricity seeped out into the streets . . . Sud-

denly children were running alongside the streetcar, waving and
shouting . . . Now in the alleys she saw men washing themselves at
open faucets . . . all the bodies filling the streets, nearly a half million
people squeezed into twenty-five square blocks.

But still no fires in the ghetto. Despite the unemployment, no fires.
"The basic achievement was the blend. Under conditions ripe for explosion and social upheaval, Detroit held on to relief, credit, and
confidence in democratic processes . . . The municipal government
in Detroit [under Mayor Frank Murphy] for all its groping, was one
of the few islands of sanity in the middle of confusion." Because
there was still hope.[6]

At mid-twentieth century, Detroit was again the poster child for a
city that worked. In World War II, Detroit was "the arsenal of democracy." Nearly 1.8 million people lived within the city limits. Unemployment was low. On the Detroit River, manufacturing plants
ran day and night, turning out tanks and jeeps. Loren Estleman's
evocative murder mystery, *Jitterbug*, imagined a 1943 car chase
along

the new expressway west. The four-lane sweep of white concrete
made him proud . . . American surveyors and engineers were building a network of shining highways . . . eleven short months from
groundbreaking to ribbon cutting, reducing the travel time between
Detroit and Ypsilanti from an hour and a half to twenty minutes.
[The suspect] swept past teams of yellow earthmovers with their
headlamps on, planing hills for yet more ramps and overpasses.

In the midst of war, Detroit anticipated a brave new world of auto-
mobiles and expressways.[7]

After the war, Americans embraced the car and the highway. Detroit was the automobile capital of the world. Machine and parts
shops supplying the factory lines employed those who could not get
the better-paying jobs in the auto factories. The United Auto Workers and other unions worked with industrial giants like Ford Motor
Company to prove that progressive policies benefited all workers.

Workers could buy their own homes, and the city sponsored family-owned detached housing that sprawled out to the west and north. Wages for factory work allowed blue-collar families to edge into the middle class. It was not the prettiest city in midcentury America, this vast grid of undistinguished neighborhoods sprawling out from a gray center city on an industrial waterway, but it was among the biggest, busiest, and most admired.[8]

The worm in the bud was still race, or rather, racial animosity. The contest for housing was still the breaking point. There was a chronic shortage of housing in the boom times. Wartime and immediate postwar public housing and urban renewal efforts threw together a succession of "Detroit Plans" to upgrade housing for the blacks; but where was the city to put the new units and who would get to occupy them? Blacks were 9 percent of the population of the city in 1940, a figure that rose to 16 percent by 1950. As more blacks moved into the city, blacks wanted to reduce their crowding. White residents demanded racially pure neighborhoods. They opposed public housing outside of the areas already heavily occupied by blacks and fought tooth and nail against blacks moving into their enclaves.[9]

There were incidents and assaults on both sides, days of anger like those leading to the explosion of racial violence on Belle Island, in 1943. In three days of gang fights and mob violence then, thirty-four people died. Only the introduction of federal troops ended the rioting. It did not matter who started what, for the riots were ignited by rumor and fueled by racial misconceptions. Much of the impetus came with the white immigrants from Europe and black immigrants from the South, a clash of people who might have seen common cause, had not ill fortune pitted them against one another. Most of the actual confrontation was between groups of young people—an important fact in light of later events. For the young had less attachment to the city, and easily redirected the frustration and impatience the young have for authority figures onto "others." Even so, the riot did not derail people's ambitions, or the city's growth.[10]

Progressives in the city were determined that the race riots would not recur, but white supremacists were running for office, too. Long before the "race card" was used to win acquittal of black defendants in criminal cases, it was dealt by white demagogues to deny blacks equal rights. Detroit was not segregated by law (segregation was against state law), but segregated in fact nonetheless. The wall between white and black that worked to stigmatize and keep down the blacks was high and well tended. In Detroit, during the height of the Cold War, conservative politicians won control of the city by convincing white voters that blacks and their allies were all Communists or Communist sympathizers. The "Negro invasion" of white residential neighborhoods thus appeared to be the opening breach of a Red invasion of America. When mayor Louis Miriani ordered his "crackdowns," it was on the heads of the blacks that the white policemen's batons fell.[11]

Blacks won some seats in the city council but could not change the pervasive racial tension. The U.S. Supreme Court had to order the ferries that ran to Bob-lo Amusement Park (on Bob-lo Island in the Detroit River) to obey the state's own laws against segregation in amusement parks, for example. The result was that official policies opposed redlining and discrimination, but unofficially, particularly in the white police department, racism flourished.

In the fight for racial equality in public facilities, the National Association for the Advancement of Colored People and other centrist civil rights groups had to separate themselves from their natural allies among leftist political groups to make headway in the war on Jim Crow. They succeeded on the state and city level, at the cost of the withering of genuine leftist political agendas. The ironic twist to the NAACP's leadership in the Civil Rights movement was that it became racialized. Instead of bonding together people of all races in the struggle for justice and fair treatment, it appeared to be a black interest group's demand for special privileges.[12]

The Civil Rights movement would revolutionize city politics, but that too came at a crushing cost and very slowly. The long night of discrimination continued into the 1960s. A reform mayor named Jerome Cavanagh, a lawyer and a liberal Catholic Democrat, reached out to the labor unions and the black churches in 1961. He started by integrating the city services, bringing in reformers such as

George C. Edwards, and then Ray Girardin, as police commissioners. He welcomed Martin Luther King, Jr. when the NAACP invited him to Detroit, and the black community poured out for a parade with King as an honored guest.

But progress was slow. The city was poor—tax revenues had not kept up with expenditures, including those for essential services. Help from the federal government was always just around the corner. President John F. Kennedy's "Great Cities" initiative and President Lyndon B. Johnson's "Model Cities Program" were not enough to get the city over the hump of its own failing economy. Industrial jobs were steadily vanishing, going abroad mostly, and the infrastructure, the schools, even garbage collection, were falling behind. Dirty streets were an omen. When money did come for the people who lived on those streets, it came with a patronizing attitude and the admonition that the poor really deserved their poverty.[13]

Still, for black leaders in the union movement like Roger Robinson, traditional politics was opening up for blacks who had paid their union dues, literally and figuratively.

> Detroit was the future in terms of Black politics . . . by World War II there was a sophisticated black industrial working class earning adequate money . . . the children of that black working class became teachers, management people in the post office, professionals . . . There was a black empowerment movement in the [Congress of Industrial Organizations] . . . In 1964, Detroit was the first urban area that elected two Blacks to Congress. Relatively proportionate complements of Blacks were elected to the Michigan state legislature. . . . Detroit was a generation ahead. Detroit was the future.[14]

And there was still hope. "Do you love me?" the Motown sound asked. It was a combination of rhythm and blues with jazz riffs, gospel choruses, and improvisational tonalities. It was "soul." Behind the artistry of such vocal performers as Smokey Robinson and Marvin Gaye and the promotional talents of Motown Music producer Berry Gordy was a mismatched but brilliantly talented collection of percussionists—keyboard, guitar, drums—and horn players called by

Gordy "The Funk Brothers." Some, like Richard "Pistol" Allen, came from the South to work in the factories, and others, like Philadelphia's Jack Ashford, came to Detroit for the music scene or because Gordy recruited them. Two were white, including Detroit native Joe Messina, the rest all the browns and blacks of America's African diaspora. Some, like drummer Benny Benjamin and guitarist James Jameson, lived short lives of great promise and lost a battle to their own demons. They played in the Motown Studio for hours, then let it hang out at after-hours clubs on the West Side. From their first recordings, in the later 1950s, through the 1960s, they gave Detroit and the world a wonderful gift. Their musicality launched the careers of Stevie Wonder and Martha Reeves, Otis Wilson, and Gladys Knight. The music touched the familiar themes of love found and lost, crying with joy, "You made me so very happy"; conceding, "You really got a hold on me"; wondering, "Where did our love go?" and finally lamenting, "What becomes of the brokenhearted?"[15]

While the Funk Brothers worked and partied, more militant and less gifted younger blacks contested the Civil Rights movement with the King generation and the union men of Robinson's coterie. The new generation of black leaders insisted that the people of the ghetto must determine their own fate. Mere legal equality was not enough. Cavanagh tried to accommodate these impulses, creating a committee to bring together black and white reform groups, block clubs, church leaders, and grass-roots leaders. The result was that "meetings frequently turned into acrimonious shouting matches during which fratricidal . . . feuds were continued." The center, fabricated from Cavanagh's progressive faith in reasoned discourse and glued together with the promise of federal funding, barely held.[16]

Throughout the country, black ghettoes began to erupt in fire, but Detroit only simmered. If the city could just get through the boiling summer of 1967, perhaps the new policies would take hold. Federal money was going to the war in Vietnam instead of the Great Society, but Detroit was not without its own resources, partly from the state, partly from foundation grants. If only Detroit's police department would let the fragile peace continue. One community activist remembered 1967: "We were all involved in the struggle against police brutality. A black would be killed in a community, either by a merchant or the police, and the police would plant a knife on the person who was killed. We would protest. The police would always be absolved of any blame by the prosecutor." Fred Williams, then a young beat cop, recalled, "the police were the catalyst . . . but it would have happened anyway. The lack of jobs, the despair, the bullshit by the politicians," all were underlying causes of unrest, including a sense of disempowerment among the younger blacks.[17]

Did Detroit have to burn? Was it inevitable? Was hope fated to give in to anger and despair? The story of Detroit's fires is a mystery—we know how; we know when; but we do not really know who set the fires, or why.

"Motown,
If You Don't Come Around,
We Are Going to Burn You Down"

Saturday evening, July 22, 1967. The muggy nights and windless, sullen days had come—another Detroit summer. The temperature topped 90°F and the dry southwestern wind—the same wind that drove the Chicago fire across the face of that city—only made the surfaces of the streets hotter. The newspapers forecast no relief. The city, flat and featureless, sliced into ethnic islands by superhighways and diced into an endlessly repeating street grid, baked in the sun. Few of the dwellings had air-conditioning, and at midnight the day's heat still had not dissipated. Smog, always a problem, grew worse in a lethal mix of industrial pollutants, automobile exhaust, and heat inversion. Ozone-related medical problems for the elderly and the very young made living in the inner city a little more dangerous than it usually was.[18]

LIVING WITH THE HEAT

Such heat can be deadly for firefighters working a fire. Wearing the old rubber-coated turnout gear that did not permit sweating, facing structural blazes that reached over 1000°F, riding in apparatus without air-conditioning—these made dehydration, heat exhaustion, and eventual heat stroke travel along with the crews to every alarm. The average summer day brought a little over 100 of these. Perhaps one-fourth were false alarms, almost all of them from ghetto street fireboxes, and that angered the firefighters. A rig responding to a false alarm was a rig not available to go to a real fire. The wear and tear on men and machines from false alarms caused the firefighters to look upon the ghettos as problem areas. But in general, relations between the firefighters and the locals were not nearly as hostile as they were with the police department.[19]

On an average day in June, 500 members of the Detroit Fire Department (DFD) manned the firehouses. Another 856 were on twenty-four-hour leave, part of the standard forty-hour-week shift system. The fire commission roster had 266 on extra leave, twenty-eight on furlough, and three suspended for various infractions of housekeeping rules. The total force numbered 1,724. Over the past week, the fire service had responded to 447 single alarms (an engine, a pumper, and a chief's car), three extended alarms requiring more apparatus and perhaps one of the special squads, 225 false alarms, 149 reports of smoke, and seven auto accidents in which passengers or drivers were trapped in their vehicles. Eight people had died as a result of fire in May alone, and thirty-three so far that year. All these totals would soon change.[20]

In a union town like Detroit, the firefighters had negotiating leverage with the city that other cities' fire services did not. The Detroit Firefighters Association wanted an "adjustment" to their pay in the budget. Mayor Cavanagh replied that they would have parity with the police but that they had the third-highest starting pay in the country. An issue simmering just below boiling temperature was Cavanagh's plan to base promotion to command slots on seniority with a merit system. But in general, relations were good between the unions and the mayor. He would need all the friends he could get, as the summer heated up.[21]

Another kind of heat baked the city. A few days before July 23, the *Detroit Free Press* hinted that race riots in Newark, New Jersey, could replay themselves in Detroit. There, "the city leaders obviously had no communication with Newark's poor and trampled." Before the explosion, Newark's mayor had boasted that violence would not come to his streets. But in the inner city, people were without hope, frustrated by poverty, and faced a rising unemployment rate: "[T]he fuse was lit." Cavanagh did not have to read the editorial to know how the wind was blowing. He had said as much himself to anyone who would listen.[22]

So did other visitors to the city. The Southern Non-Violent Coordinating Committee's Stokely Carmichael and other advocates of "Black Power" did not want partnership in the larger society or to share in its bounty. Black Power rejected the assimilation of white standards and the longing for belonging in a white society. In its place, the new movement accepted as a given what the leaders of the Civil Rights movement denied—that racism was natural, inevitable, and uncontainable. Given that, blacks would have to make a place for themselves, purging all whites from leadership positions in the movement. As Carmichael said, "[I]ntegration was a subterfuge for the maintenance of white supremacy."[23]

In the ghettos of the North, the SNCC's H. Rap Brown and others found young people ready for a revolution. Brown told a meeting of the SNCC in Detroit on June 29th: "'Let white America know that the name of the game is tat-for-tat, an eye for an eye . . . and a life for a life . . . Motown, if you don't come around, we are going to burn you down.'" Incendiary words, and prophetic. As Adam Shakoor, then a member of the League of Revolutionary Black Workers, recalled in 1994, "It was a leadership that had a sense of the rightness of the cause, and there was no compromise."[24]

On the commercial blocks of Twelfth Street, brick-fronted stores, cluttered sidewalks, and ranks of parked cars radiated the heat back into the atmosphere. Slow-moving cars belched exhaust gases that pedestrians inhaled. Still, Twelfth "hummed by day," with car and foot traffic. By night "it swung," as the clubs and bars filled and emptied and refilled.

In the area where Twelfth Street crossed Clairmount, the heart of the West Side ghetto, the displaced families of an ill-considered urban renewal project camped with relatives or boarded. Dense living conditions frayed tempers, piling temporary inconveniences on top of long-term uncertainty for young people. The summer, a time when unemployment hit its peak and young people were not in school, packed the streets. There, testy and tired young folks joined the usual mix of night people—drifters, grifters, gamblers, drinkers, and gang members.[25]

The small businesses shuttered early. One employee watched the door warily while another gathered the day's receipts. "Holdups were common," and merchants looked the other way when the prostitutes and numbers runners ran the streets. The owners no longer resided above their shops. White or black, they lived outside the ghetto, sometimes beyond the city limits. Samuel Lipson had owned a clothing and variety store on the block for years. Next to his store, between Pingree and Philadelphia, were "a fruit market, a drugstore, a hardware store, a fish market," and other small retail outlets. He "did not expect trouble," for after all, he and his customers shared a common interest, and he treated them fairly. Others did not—particularly drugstore pharmacists (whose prices for prescriptions were not posted)—according to a study in the black weekly newspaper. It was a common problem and a genuine grievance.[26]

Rumor ratcheted up the level of tensions on Twelfth. The residents of these streets rarely saw a white face, save for the official face of the city: the police, the process servers, the tax collectors. But the past few weeks had been different. The Detroit Police Department (DPD) was setting traps for prostitutes and their pimps along Twelfth. On the street, folks spread a story that one of the vice squad members had beaten up a prostitute, then shot her. Angry muttering about more police brutality added fuel to the fire of racial resentment, for the DPD was almost entirely white, and Twelfth had become almost entirely black.[27]

But like the Irish on DeKoven in old Chicago, ordinary people of color knew little about the difference between the Civil Rights movement and the Black Power ideology. For them, racialism was a matter of face-to-face contacts. Respect and decency earned respect and decency in return. Despite the heat and tension of the summer, most of the time folks simply got along with one another. On

Kercheval in the heart of Detroit's older ghetto on the East Side, the Moms and Tots Center was run by a white visiting nurse and black volunteers. Though it was across the street from the "Adult Community Movement for Equality," a hive of Black Power advocates, relations between the two centers of the community flourished in mounting mutual respect.[28]

For Aubrey Pollard, nineteen, a welder at the Ford plant, currently unemployed, white people were not the enemy. They simply had little place in his life. Whether he cared about the rumors or not, he surely resented the condescending attitude of the police toward the people in the ghetto. He had kept out of trouble—mostly (fifteen days in juvie, for hitting a teacher)—but some of his friends already had police records. His mother and father were trying to raise him right. They had strict rules, but he did not always follow them. He had a quick temper and did poorly at school. Federal money paid for his training as a welder, an advantage that few of his clique had. But not a lot of federal money had found its way down to Twelfth. These days he spent a lot of time lying around. Even a man with a little money could find a place to party and some friends to party with.[29]

It was just such a party that lit the Detroit fires of 1967. The police "cleanup" (vice) squad routinely busted up "blind pigs" (unlicensed speakeasies) and gambling dens. The blind pigs used a simple watch-and-warn system that did good service in the days of prohibition. Behind stout doors in basement or second-floor rooms misleadingly labeled as legitimate businesses (most were listed as community action groups or civic societies), young black men and women gathered for nighttime frolics. Someone kept watch on the street and someone else manned the peephole. There was money—money paid for the drinks, money in the games, money in the pockets of the habitués—and the blind pig owner was more worried about robbers than cops. But cops were still a problem. If they got in, they would report the illicit activity to headquarters downtown and the paddy wagons would carry off everyone in the room.[30]

That is what befell the patrons of the blind pig elegantly misnamed the United Civic League for Community Action on Twelfth and Clairmount, early in the morning of Sunday, July 23, 1967. The watchers had let down their guard, and the police nabbed them. Expecting to find a dozen or so late-night drinkers and gamblers, the police stumbled upon a party for returning Vietnam veterans and had to haul off eighty-two people. That took a number of runs. The police and the arrestees joked with one another. Many had been through the routine before, and knew they would be out of custody later in the day. But the crowd gathering across Twelfth began to grow restless and resentful. By the last of the police paddy wagon runs, neighborhood youths had started hurling bottles and stones at the police cruisers. The police mobilized their tactical squad and reinforced their presence on the street. That, in turn, brought out even more spectators and rock throwers.[31]

RIOT

Awakened in the early morning with the news of street violence he had long dreaded, Mayor Cavanagh had no choice but to alert the National Guard, the Wayne County sheriffs, and the FBI. At the same time, he mobilized his Summer Task Force, a coalition of local black leaders, including young U.S. congressman John Conyers, Jr., and Hubert Locke, a Wayne State University professor doubling as a police department assistant commissioner. They returned to the streets and told people to cool it—nothing was happening. Bravely, Conyers climbed up atop a car and begged people to leave the streets. He got a rude reception—heckled, shouted down, threatened, attacked. He retreated. The police returned to the scene in numbers (over 1,000 were called back to duty, and 500 of these had gathered at a nearby staging area). They found thousands of people (the immediate vicinity contained over 15,000 people), many of them women and children getting ready for church, who had come to watch or participate in the confrontation.[32]

Looting of stores along Twelfth had begun. Told by Police Chief Girardin, a former crime reporter and judge, not to use weapons, tear gas, or to charge into the crowd, the police waited with increasing impatience. Their restraint, read as incapacity by the crowds, led to the spread of looting and violence. On the other side of the coin, the police were getting restive themselves. Trained to keep order and arrest violators of the law (as well as regarding the street people of the ghetto as a little less than human), they saw their own inaction as unmanly.[33]

Pacing in the operational headquarters of the police department downtown, Cavanagh hoped that this was not "the bad one." Other ghettos far smaller than Detroit's sprawling sixteen square miles of mean streets had exploded in fire and violence in the previous four years. Perhaps he should have gone down to the streets and walked arm in arm with local black leaders. Hindsight is so easy.

Police Chief Girardin, later criticized for not taking to the streets himself, kept a leash on his men from police headquarters. He had a plan and it governed the first response of the city. It had worked the year before, when the East Side briefly erupted in violence. Massive police presence without massive police force had dissipated crowds of young people.[34]

On the 20th, three days before the outbreak of violence, the DPD had worked up a simulated riot scenario that began with a black on white traffic accident. The "intellectual war game" set everyone thinking about how to contain the programmed riot, not how to prevent it. There was no way that the police, fire, and other city services could prevent a riot. But when it did begin three days later, the police made sure that the troubles stayed within the ghetto. The streets were sealed off to prevent any attacks on motorists, as had worsened the riots in other cities. There would be no miniature race war, with black mobs in pitched battles against white mobs, Girardin determined. By 8:00 AM in the morning, the police manned key intersections at the edges of the western ghetto. No one would be allowed to enter except for an emergency or on official business. They were in no way imprisoning the blacks, but simply acting to quarantine the violence. Anyone who wanted to leave the burned district could. It was all part of Girardin's plan, and into the morning of the 23rd, it seemed to be working.[35]

Girardin's plan was rooted in past experience and recent events, including the explosion of race animosity in the Watts district of Los

Angeles, in the summer of 1965. A look at a map of the serious rioting then shows that it was concentrated on the major thoroughfares,
particularly at key intersections. Control these streets, one might ra-
tionally conclude from the Watts riots, and one controls the flow of
the crowd and its violence. So long as the violence is unfocused, so
long as it has no interior organization and advance planning, then
containment could follow by sweeps through the streets and should
end the riots. The authorities had to be patient, however, bring to
bear overwhelming force, control that force so the order keepers did
not become trigger-happy, and be able to time their movements
correctly.[36]

"WE ARE GOING TO BURN YOU DOWN"

Soon after the riots erupted, fires began to appear along commercial
streets on the West Side of the city. DFD chief Charles J. Quinlan
was a veteran firefighter. He had joined the force in 1927 and had
risen up every step through the ranks until his appointment, in June,
as chief of the department. His instincts were those of every first-rate
city fire department senior officer. In the words of Battalion Chief
Harry Carter of Newark, a city that erupted in riot and fire shortly
before Detroit: "The buildings were on fire, you arrived, stretched
the appropriate hose line, entered the buildings and extinguished the
fire . . . We made fun of the people who did not like to stretch the big
line [to the nearest hydrant]. We did not stage at a distance. We arrived and went to work." But Quinlan was also a realist. Stones, rocks,
bricks, and other projectiles rained upon the DFD as it raced from
scene to scene. By four in the afternoon of the first day, he ordered,
"All those without police protection, tell them to withdraw. Do not
try to get in and extinguish the fires." Police protection for the firefighters was required, but hardly possible—too many fires, too few
police, too many partygoing rioters hurling missiles.[37]

At the same time as he pulled his men out of the dangerous situation, Quinlan issued a general recall of off-duty firefighters and
formed an all-black rapid response squad. It did no good. Members

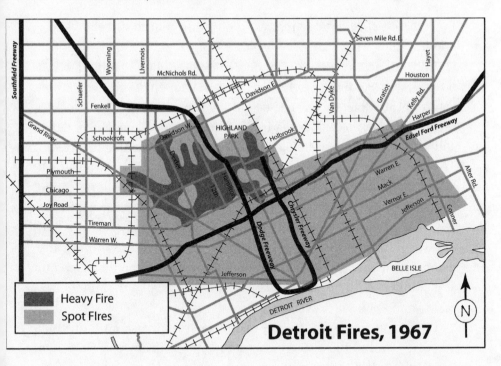

Detroit Fires, 1967

Heavy Fire
Spot Fires

of the crowd bombarded the black firefighters as they tried to put out the fires. Not everyone was throwing missiles. News photos at the scene, in fact, show that most of the people in the streets were simply watching the firefighters work. This is the same kind of spectator behavior as in Pittsburgh, Chicago, and Baltimore. In fact, some of the people in the street offered drinks and food to the firefighters. Later in the evening, groups of armed locals offered to protect the firefighters, and they accepted the offer.[38]

The "back step" firefighters who rode the apparatus had little sense of the overall picture. Indeed, if today one simply looked at the general distribution of fires, one might conclude that they resembled random spot fires thrown off by a wildfire. Such fires are elemental, natural, and without internal logic. Their growth and spread are determined by external forces such as the availability of fuel and the strength and direction of the wind. Had the blazes fit into the category of urban wildfire, driven by wind and available ground fuel, they would have been catastrophic. For Detroit was one great prairie. The results would have resembled the Chicago fire of 1871.

Fortunately, the Detroit fires were of a different and, believe it or not, less dangerous sort.

Putting each incident of fire on a time line shows that the Detroit burning was like the outbreak and spread of an epidemic. One street youth put it perfectly on the second night of the riots: "You know a rash? You know how it spread? Well this is a rash, and it spreadin' and spreadin'." In epidemiology, this is called the "contagion effect." The "vector" or carrier of the contagion may not be known at first. Whatever its cause, the fire is like a form of illness, a contamination that spreads like a plague. Not every building burns because even in the worst of plagues, not every potential victim actually gets sick, but the distribution of the cases does follow certain rules. To push the metaphor further, the police isolation of the ghetto can be likened to a quarantine of the outbreak. Isolated, the fires, like the number of cases in an epidemic, dwindle.[39]

Of course this is an analogy. The fires resulted from individual acts of arson. But the analogy is a useful one. As in any epidemic, one has to study the individual cases to understand causes. The headquarters "activity log" of the first day gives a first, vital clue. The fires did not begin with the rioting. They came later. What's more, they began slowly, then increased by leaps and bounds. This is the exact pattern of an epidemic.

The log tells the story: at 8:00 AM, a shoe store at Twelfth and Clairmount, then at 12:10 PM, a rubbish fire in the street at Twelfth and Taylor, then at 2:05 PM, a multiple alarm fire at Twelfth and Philadelphia. The fire line was moving down Twelfth, and by 3:20 PM it had reached a drug store at Twelfth and Virginia Park. A half hour later, a large fire had erupted at Linwood and Gladstone, and for the first time, the DFD asked for police assistance. At 4:17 PM, another fire at Twelfth and Blaine, then one at Twelfth and Euclid, from which the DFD was driven by a crowd. By 10:05 PM, Chief Quinlan asked the neighboring fire departments for assistance and at 10:25, he pleaded that gas stations (sources for firebomb fuel) be closed. By 2:10 AM the next morning, the fire had jumped over Woodward and the near downtown to the East Side, along Kercheval. Air reconnaissance found twenty-three fires burning at dawn west of Woodward and six to the east of the thoroughfare.[40]

The police "disorder log" for the first day takes up the story and offers another clue to the nature of the epidemic. At 1:22 PM, the first police dispatcher called "any vehicle, Twelfth and Blaine, help fire department," then at 1:33 PM: "All units, Twelfth and Clairmount, assistance for fire department." Through 4:28 PM the dispatcher relayed nineteen calls from the DFD to police units to assist, protect, and help the firefighters. Some of these were for "trapped" members of the department, or concluded "fireman in trouble." By then, Quinlan had ordered the fire department to take up and pull out of any site where there was trouble. But the DFD was still responding to calls when the police department, or later, the Michigan National Guard, rode with them. From 5:00 PM to midnight, the police dispatchers logged another eighteen calls for the police to assist the DFD. At the same time, locals were still calling the firefighters to assist people who had collapsed or were trapped in fires. In other words, in the midst of an arson epidemic, people in the area still looked to the firefighters as the first-due responders when something happened to them.[41]

Something in Detroit was sick, so ill that the symptoms burst through the skin in fiery pustules. Responses to such epidemics of unknown cause and unpredictable degree are different from responses to well-defined events. No one knew where the next fire would appear. Committing multiple companies to fires, even entire blocks of structures, dangerously overextended the DFD. Sending men to riot locations imperiled them and prevented them from doing their jobs. Recognizing their own limited resources, Cavanagh, Girardin, and Quinlan reached out for help from the state and the federal government.

Michigan governor George Romney arrived to assess the situation. So did President Lyndon Johnson's emissary, Under Secretary of State Cyrus R. Vance. Both Romney and Vance were appalled by the violence and the looting, but it was the fires that most worried them. Vance charted the course of the fires, and his report provides a third critical insight into the fire sickness. In the chart he made of the pattern of fires, one sees that they did not increase in linear fashion, or in true geometric fashion. Instead, they had a kind of punctuated shape, like a staircase going up. In fact, they increased in bursts as evening fell, then leveled off in the wee hours. So, too, the activity pattern of the fires—spreading between seven in the evening and eleven at night, then dying down—fit the pattern of fever in a diseased patient.[42]

This diagnosis suggests that the fires were not tied to the looting. In some cases, after breaking the windows with bricks and stones, and casually helping themselves to whatever was on the shelves and in the storeroom, some looters set fire to the premises. But many of the fires were not set by the looters. After all, their hands were full; their hearts were happy; and they had no particular desire to run and find gasoline cans, Molotov cocktails, or other accelerants and use them. "Help yourself baby, gets what you want," one observer recorded a looter saying to a hesitant friend. The street-corner society had turned into a self-help committee, carrying off armfuls of goods. When the store was emptied, and the loot carried off in cars, on foot, and even by bicycle, someone else torched the store. (Looters did not become snipers either. Although 2,498 handguns, rifles, and shotguns were taken from gun shops, and only a small proportion—542—of these were recovered during arrests, the number of snipers, while considerable, never came close to the number of firearms looted from stores.)[43]

What's more, the timing and spread of the fires on the first day demonstrates that the rioting was the occasion for the fires, not their cause. A plot of the fires laid over a plot of the rioting shows much overlap, but the rioters had left the streets by the time many of the night fires were set. Indeed, the course of the rioting did not match the course of the fires. At 3:00 PM on July 23rd, when the number of fires was still small, the riots had grown much faster. The mayor asked for state police assistance. Seven hundred state troopers were sent. A little after 4:00 PM, Cavanagh asked Romney to release National Guard troops to be added to the order-keeping force of police. By the end of the day, 750 guardsmen were on patrol, and eventually their numbers in Detroit swelled to nearly 10,000.[44]

The epidemic of fires the DFD confronted on July 23rd and in the following days was a compacted version of what other big-city firefighters all over the country called the "war years." In the period from 1965 to 1975, firehouses in the South Bronx, Harlem, and Brooklyn ghettos of New York City had three and four call outs every night. Whole blocks in the heart of the ghetto disappeared as vacant buildings were torched and people abandoned buildings after too many fires. On the way to fires, the men would be bombarded from the roofs, sometimes by the very people whose loved ones the firefighters would soon be trying to rescue. On one occasion, murderous pranksters set a car afire at the head of a street to pin down an engine company working a fire. The lieutenant ordered the driver of the rig to ram the car and escape the trap.

Some of the firefighters gained a unique reputation as a "ghetto fireman," hardly ever retreating from a fire; making heroic rescues; leading their crews by example. But even the most gung ho firefighter had to have doubts about this war. In one firehouse in the war zone, the men put up a sign that said, "This could be the night." For dozens of them every year in these terrible days, it was. Firefighting is dangerous enough without attacks from bystanders.[45]

Back in Detroit, on the early morning of the 24th, the fires inside the box of streets the police cordoned off stretched the resources of the DFD to its limits. The city was huge—a diffuse grid of 139 square miles—and nearly fifty square miles of its streets and blocks had at least one building involved in fire. Six months after the terrible events of July, Quinlan prepared detailed maps of fire-engaged blocks. The maps show how the arteries of the city—Grand River, Grand Avenue, Woodward, Jefferson had become fire courses. Within them, lesser commercial streets like Warren, Wilson, Fourteenth, Twelfth, and Linwood had lost entire blocks to fire. Samuel Lipson's store, for example, burned to the ground, along with every other shop or store on the block.[46]

Quinlan could not get his apparatus into position to put out individual fires, and even if he could put out one fire, ten took its place. He could only work to contain the plague. But containment was almost as difficult in sprawling Detroit. If the burned district could be squeezed into a limited area by natural boundaries, like rivers, or firebreaks built into the urban landscape, open spaces, or curved streets that could be blocked off, then the impact of the burners' acts could be confined. But there was too much ground to cover. Eventually, when enough blocks had been reduced to rubble, the absence of fuel would lower the numbers of fires, a kind of containment equivalent to defeat. The question was, how many blocks would the burners destroy before they confined themselves?

Governor Romney, in conversations with Cavanagh, understood the danger but came at it from a different perspective. He kept asking how the fire would be controlled. When Cavanagh told the governor that "the fire could exceed the fire department's capabilities," Romney went on and on about fire control. In part, he was worried, like Cavanagh and Quinlan, that the DFD could not put out the fires in the ghetto. In part, however, he was even more concerned that the fires (and the burners) would escape the box and start burning the wealthier parts of town and even move into the suburbs. Not only was the property there more valuable, but once a pestilence has broken out of confinement, its spread may be uncontrolled.[47]

For Romney, the evil was not just the fires but the motivations of the fire setters. As he said to Vance, in an effort to get Vance to release federal troops into the city streets, "[T]his is not civil disturbance, but lawlessness and hoodlumism." By early evening, looting and fire had reached out as far as Seven Mile Road to the north. Then it turned east, back toward the downtown along Kercheval in the older East Side ghetto. From the air, it looked as though "the city had been bombed."[48]

With the coming of evening's darkness, two new and even more frightening threats to the DFD appeared. First, gas stations in the ghetto were selling gasoline to pedestrians with open canisters and containers. Plainly, this would be used for Molotov cocktails to start fires. Chief Quinlan had little trouble convincing Girardin to order all gas stations in the ghetto closed. At about the same time, snipers began targeting the firefighters. The police "disorder logs" reveal a fire situation spiraling out of control. At 9:35 PM, the police dispatcher called "all units" available to respond to Twelfth and Lawrence, "for shooting at firemen." The sniping had spread to Twelfth and Colling-wood by 9:54 PM, and then to Dumbarton and Grand River. The fire-fighters "needed police protection" and crowds were "threatening the firemen." So it went, at Mack and Seneca, by 1:12 AM, then at Wa-verly and Dexter, then on Grandview, and on into the night.[49]

That night Romney asked for federal troops; but it proved hard to persuade U.S. attorney general Ramsay Clark that they were needed. Meanwhile, the night had brought some relief. The looters, anger slaked and celebration done, had to sleep; they had never meant to overthrow a government, merely to stock their larders and enliven their living rooms. The next day, however, was worse. Vance was at first hesitant to carry Romney's request to Washington, D.C. "In a few areas, fires were burning but they appeared to be coming under the control of fire fighting equipment on the scene." That night, however, the burners were back. Persuaded by what he saw, he agreed with Romney and Cavanagh to deploy the federal troops. The fires had convinced Vance, just as they had swayed Romney.[50]

On the 23rd, there had been 209 alarms. The next day, the total had skyrocketed to 617. On the 25th, 319 were logged, and on the 26th, 177. In normal summer days, the department could expect 119 calls. Overall, the dispatchers recorded 283 occasions of "harass-ment" so severe that the men had to flee, leaving the fire and their hoses behind. Worse, the DFD was losing equipment. The count was thirty-three pumpers, eighteen ladder trucks, six squad vehicles, and four chiefs' cars damaged by bullets, stones, bricks, and other projectiles. The men had been at it with little rest for nearly forty-eight hours. They reported back for duty after short rest periods. They were frightened, with good reason, and their patience, like their strength, had worn very thin.[51]

Outmanned and exhausted, the DFD and the fire departments that came to its aid from the surrounding towns still did not surren-der to the fires. Some men, John Ashby, for one, loved being fire-fighters and putting out blazes. Attached to engine No. 21, in the center of the ghetto, he knew about the simmering anger of the peo-ple in the ghetto. Early on the 24th, Ashby was one of a relief crew working with a ladder company on the near East Side. His wife later recalled that she had a premonition that this was the day that all fire-fighters' wives dreaded. Riding a tower ladder to put out a hot spot on top of a torched supermarket, his helmet touched an ungrounded high-power line. Resuscitated at the scene, he lingered in the hospital for nearly two weeks, then died on August 5 from his injuries.

Carl Smith would have understood how much Ashby loved being a firefighter. A five-year veteran, Carl had "gained the reputation of being a 'gung-ho' firefighter," and he loved to be the first man in when there was a four- or five-alarm fire. He volunteered for extra duty with a ladder company on Monday morning, when the assembly area—the fire station at Mack and St. Jean—was under sniper fire. Smith was caught between the snipers and the police, and someone shot him in the head. The bullet was a .30 caliber, a round from a carbine of the sort that police and guardsmen alone were using. Friendly fire had killed a fireman.[52]

The mayor had ordered everyone but emergency personnel off the streets in the burned region, and the governor had ordered that anyone carrying a flammable liquid in the open be arrested. But the burners were quick, sly, and dogged. Later arrest figures would show than fewer than thirty-four of the total 3,837 black males of all ages arrested were charged with arson. This was one more clue that the rioters and the burners were not one and the same. Most of the arson cases fit the National Fire Protection Association category of "vandalism." City vandalism fires are only prosecuted 7 percent of the time, in large measure because it is so hard to find out who the incendiaries are.[53]

Newsmen and television crews reported an entire city aflame. They were accurate. "Thick black smoke," one reported, during the day; as night approached, another reported that the sky took on "a red glow." From the top of the juvenile justice building in the center of the city, Judge James Lincoln recalled that "fires could be spotted everywhere and there were intermittent sounds of gunfire." The TV stations had remote crews on the scene, and as Eleanor Josaitis, a founder of one of the Catholic relief organizations in the city, recalled, "You turned on the television and you thought that you were in some foreign country that was on fire."[54]

Stills from newspaper coverage and taped versions of the television reports were filled with shots of burning buildings and hordes of spectators. There was nothing new in the numbers of spectators or how close they came to the peril—that is part of every city fire scene. But something else was missing from these fire scenes. Find any photojournalistic report of a city fire and in the foreground are what seems a swarm of fire engines, ladder trucks, rescue squad vehicles, and chiefs' cars. The hoses running from the hydrants to the pumpers and from the pumpers into the buildings are piled on the street like spaghetti on a plate. Firefighters and their officers confer around the apparatus, and men are laying external ladders, knocking out windows to vent the fire, helping victims out of the structures, and climbing up and down fire escapes like so many bees.

But in many of the fire scene photos in these days of Detroit's agony, there were few or no fire trucks, pumpers, firefighters, or coils of hoses. Under a Fred Plofchan photo for the *Detroit Free Press*, one reads: "[B]uildings blazed uncontrollably in the balmy blue air, while the curious collected on street corners." The shot included one engine company fighting what was obviously a multiple-alarm blaze. An Ira Rosenberg photo from a circling airplane showed "both sides of Linwood Avenue just north of Euclid were turned into smoking raging infernos," but only a few fire trucks were on the scene. At Grand River and Dexter, a line of cars were burning fiercely, with no apparatus in sight. That is what made the scenes, to some, seem to be from a Third World city in the throes of civil war. The fire service is one of the defining marks of the modern, technologically advanced city. Knowing that the fire department will go "like hell" to fires and "come when called" is one of the comforts of living in an American city.[55]

By this time, the fire sickness had even infected the order keepers. Tired and frustrated police and undertrained and nervous guardsmen began to use excessive violence, no longer concerned about the ultimate consequences of their use of firearms. Snipers shot at the police and guardsmen, and some of the rioters were armed, but most of the violence now came from officers pushed past their "breaking point," as Girardin admitted.[56]

That—and the residual animosities of a thousand slights and an equal number of arrogant displays—led to the Algiers Motel massacre during the riots. Police entering the motel after reports of snipers found a group of black males and two white women. One of the men was Aubrey Pollard. The building stood on Woodward Avenue and was, according to later police reports, a known "'haven for pimps, prostitutes, drug pushers, and addicts, gamblers, numbers operators, and other criminal elements.'" Three of the officers making the raid were young policemen who had been under fire, or believed they were, for many hours. They gathered the men and women in a room, beat them, took some of them to another roomand assassinated at least one of them, possibly all three. Pollard was the first to die.[57]

Others were trapped in the area of rioting and burning and died from misadventure; or because they looked out a window at the wrong time; or were simply unlucky; or refused to stop when an officer commanded it; or simply because the police and the guardsmen did not care who they shot. Young Willie Hunter and Prince Williams had come to Detroit from Cincinnati looking for a new start. Detroit was always a city of immigrants. On this day they had seen cars going by "with couches casually tied across the roofs . . . the west side of Detroit became a vast department store without checkout counters. Everything was for free." People who would not have dreamed of stealing became looters because everyone was taking something. For people without a lot, the sanctity of property was a loosely held concept. Messing around in the burning drugstore on Twelfth, the two young men learned that fire can kill without burning. Their bodies as close together in death as the two friends had been in life, the two were found three days later, dead from asphyxia.

Sheren George was riding with her new man when they came upon a mob beating a white man. A pistol shot from someone in the crowd tore through the car and her. Firemen tried to save her life, but she died in a hospital emergency room. Just when her life was coming together, a hooligan with a handgun ended it. He probably never knew where his round went.[58]

Fortunately for the DFD and the city, the supply and pressure of the water from the hydrants was adequate to fight the fires and the

wind did not pick up. First, the Detroit River supplied the water for
the city, and new plants and pumping stations, including high-lift
pumps at the water works completed in 1961, "increased the city's
capacity to one billion gallons a day" by the year before the fire. Second, except for downtown, Detroit was not a city of high-rise buildings. Instead of the six- to ten-story apartment houses one found in
New York City or Chicago ghettos, Detroit's lower-class black population lived in one- and two-story houses, often detached from one
another. This in turn meant that water streams from the land lines
did not have to reach far from the street or high in the air. Even the
commercial structures along Linwood, Twelfth, and other streets
were rarely more than two stories high. Fires in low-rise buildings
may get as hot as fires in high-rises, but there is not as much fuel in
them and they do not produce the fire swirls—the updrafts of heat
and burning debris—that come out of a high-rise fire. Thus, the low-
rise fire does not spread its embers as far as the high-rise fire, except
when there is a high wind. And the wind did not pick up until the
end of the day. More important, it never went above ten miles per
hour. Had it gusted to the twenties, the fire might have spread
throughout the city.[59]

By the 27th, the total number of fires had dipped to ninety-four,
below the pre-riot average. The ordeal was over. When the fire tally
was complete, its extent became clear. The city had narrowly averted
a firestorm like those in Tokyo, Japan, Berlin, Germany, and other
urban war zones from 1939 to 1945. Setting aside the somewhat inflated estimates in the immediate wake of the fires, rumored to
range all the way up to $500 million in damage, lost revenue, inven-
tory, and the like, the damage was still substantial. There were 564
damaged or destroyed taxable items, some of which were entire
blocks of houses or stores. The value assessed was $22,542,380 ($131
million in 2005 dollars). Insurance would cover about two-thirds of
the total. That does not sound like a lot of money, given the number
of fires and the area burned. Indeed, it demonstrates how little the
property owners of the ghetto actually owned. The burners had
wiped out people only one or two rungs above them on the social
and economic scale.

The actual number of structures that were destroyed or had to be pulled down because they were dangerously compromised was 690. These included forty-six apartment houses, 139 one- and two-family dwellings, seventy-four groceries, twenty-six drug stores, twenty-seven cleaners, nineteen clothing stores, thirteen bars, twenty-six furniture stores, twenty warehouses, and fifteen restaurants. The DFD had responded to 3,034 calls in the week between July 23rd and 30th. Two DFD members had died. Eighty-four had reported injuries that required medical attention. Another 200 or so were injured but did not report unfit for duty. Forty-two other fire departments had helped contain the fires.[60]

THE BURNERS

With smoke visible for miles and fires burning all around them, none of the DFD officers had time to stop and ask: Why fire? Who were the burners? I asked those questions to a thirty-year FDNY veteran of some of the most fire-riven districts in Brooklyn. He had seen the worst of the war years from the "back step" of a fire engine and later as an officer. He replied, "I never knew. I just put them out." But to understand fire in the American city of the riot years, we have to know who the burners were.[61]

The riots were not hard to explain. In fact, many explanations compete for adherents. This much is clear: Angry people cannot contain their frustration and alienation forever. In Detroit, as in other city ghettos that erupted in rioting, the rioters and the minority onlookers interviewed at the time overwhelmingly agreed that the violence was a form of protest.

On-the-spot studies of arrested rioters by professors uncovered what anyone might have surmised already. The detainees were young, angry, came from lower-class one-parent families, and thought that they had little to look forward to. Many had recently come by themselves or with their families from the South. They had comparatively little formal education. They were frustrated people with no future, or no faith in their future.[62]

Looting had its rationale as well. It expressed both a sense of entitlement and a feeling of grievance. Stores whose owners were perceived to have defrauded or gouged black customers were the targets. In particular, the adhesion or buying-on-time contract, which inflated the price of a consumer durable far in excess of its actual value and gave the seller the right to repossess the item for a single nonpayment, was a special grievance. In a sense, for the people of the Detroit ghetto, looting was an almost legitimate, respectable way of adding to a family store of goods. Looters did not resell what they took. One historian of these events has suggested that looting is simply an extension of Americans' obsession with consumerism. None of the families in the immediate area were wealthy, and just about everything that was taken was put to use. Looting was appropriation, whether one saw it as crime or as recouping what discrimination in salaries and job opportunities had taken.[63]

Setting fires was a horse of a different color. Fire does not transfer wealth or redistribute goods. For those in the ghetto who do not have the wherewithal to rebuild better or a way to lure development capital into the neighborhood, fire has no upside. After the fire, residents could not do what Rouse and the Baltimore businessmen accomplished for the Baltimore downtown, for no one was going to take a chance and rebuild and reopen when the danger of arson was so obvious.[64]

Burning down a store not only cost the owner, it denied to the neighborhood future access to the store's goods. Food stores, clothing, liquor, and drugstores led the list. So whatever had made the goods attractive to looters, the fire reversed. Henceforth, ghetto residents who wanted shoes, or pharmaceuticals, or liquor would have to travel farther. Unlike looting, fire made no economic sense.[65]

Perhaps another sense, then—as a popular entertainment? The fires took place in what some described as a "carnival atmosphere." Pictures of the street scenes at the fire sites show young people in the same poses they might have taken at an amusement park or during festivals like the Mardi Gras in New Orleans. But what kind of carnival destroys the celebrants' own community? People who lived on Twelfth, Pingree, Linwood, and other residential streets had lost homes, treasured keepsakes, furniture, and livelihoods. The old, who could not replace a lifetime of hard-earned personal belongings, the very young, who had to be taken to shelters, and the parents, bewildered by it all, asked the same question—why? Gregory Byrd, serving in Vietnam at the time, returned to his parents' home near Twelfth and Philadelphia to find nothing the same as when he left. His parents embraced him and said, "It's a good thing you were away." From apartments and homes, locals peered out, frightened and angry. "Why are they doing this to me," they asked, but no one had an answer.[66]

For a time during the riots, black-owned stores, shops, and businesses kept themselves safe. Owners painted "Soul Brother" or "Brother" on the windows or doors. Later, black shop owners were the most insistent on police intervention and criminal punishment of the burners, a crackdown with the use of police "firepower" if necessary. They formed patrols, sometimes arming themselves, and warned potential burners off. They were not successful, however, and blacks' homes and shops suffered the greatest losses from the fires.[67]

In a small number of cases, class animosity within the black community played some role in the burning of black-owned homes or businesses. The pyramid-like social and economic structure of the ghetto, with many more poor than middle class, might have engendered envy or anger at the black shopkeepers. But the hierarchy of class in the ghetto was truncated. The black owners had only a little more to their names than their neighbors. Moreover, the fires destroyed much of the capital of the middle classes, and with that, the chance for capital investment within the black community. One cannot conclude that the burners were class-conscious rebels fighting against an oppressive local elite.[68]

If setting fires was political, the beginning of a bottom-up revolution, or some demonstration of Black Power, it should have taken place where it would threaten whites. True enough, Governor Romney was worried that it would spread, and it could have, but only on the wind. Rumors circulated that busloads of black rioters were heading for the city line, but no evidence ever supported the rumors.

The burners were not seeking to clear land for more profitable development. True, arson of this sort was part of every inner city's life in the twentieth century. In New York City, apartment-house owners were suspected of hiring arsonists to destroy properties the owners no longer wanted to manage. Around the country, the Federal Emergency Management Agency (FEMA) reports, "Greed is often the most important motivation for the arsonist. Landlords have burnt their own buildings for insurance settlement, to scare tenants out of rent-controlled apartments, or to empty the apartments and gentrify the building." But the ghetto arsonists of Detroit that July were not landlords or organized crime lords or their minions. Nor were they hired to torch the buildings.[69]

Another kind of arson has revenge as its motive. For some injustice or insult, the burner avenges himself with fire. The DFD chief of arson, Charles Evancho, explained how arson was "[a] weapon . . . Revenge is the primary motive, including drug turf wars and domestic violence. Other motives are insurance fraud, pyromania, juvenile mischief and concealment of a crime."

Arson-as-revenge becomes a kind of political act. That is, it gives power to people who have little access to the formal apparatus of self-government. Slave arson, the most frequent crime that slaves committed against the master class in America, took this form. Because arson was relatively easy to perform, particularly at night, slave owners created "patrols" to ride around the plantations and insure that slaves did not go about at night. The patrols were not successful. In the few cases of large-scale slave insurrection in North America, fire played a major role.

Powerless as the arsonists in Detroit may have perceived themselves, they were not slaves and their acts did not send a message to their masters. Nor, by analogy, were they revolutionaries, for they did not seek to burn out government buildings. By the end of the day, most of the stores and homes they burned belonged to their neighbors and kinfolk.[70]

Personal animus did play a key role in an earlier epidemic of fires in Detroit, but the burners were organized, and they were white. In the 1950s and early 1960s, there was a plague of arson, along with defacement of houses, assaults, and threats. Lower-class whites' resentment against black home owners exploded in Molotov cocktails hurled against walls and through windows. In 1963 alone, there were sixty-five "incidents" of vandalism and arson. They were not random or the product of frenzy, mere entertainment or mindlessness. They were set after meetings of white home-owners associations targeted black newcomers. They were, in short, political actions of a conspiratorial vigilante sort. There must have been some of this in the July riots, but no evidence of well-organized conspiracies was uncovered.[71]

Who then were Detroit's fire raisers? If not the snipers, the looters, the rioters, the revolutionaries, the advocates of black separatism, the paid arsonists, the fanatics, then who? *New York Post* columnist Jimmy Breslin visited Detroit the first night of the fires. In front of a drugstore fire, he spoke with a group of boys. When he said "bad fire," they corrected him. "Good fire, the toothpaste burning now." They were "Negro youth."[72]

By setting buildings afire, breaking the curfew, traveling freely at night, confronting the fire crews (but not, note, the police—they had weapons), the young people of the ghetto challenged all adult authority. The shopkeepers they burned out were the ones whose goods they could not afford, not the ones who overpriced their goods; the bars and clubs they targeted were the ones that they could not patronize. They did not care if their incendiaries fell upon private homes, so long as it was not their home. Irresponsible because they were young, they did not foresee the consequences of the burning for their own future. They had little attachment to the city or its reputation. The burners were young vandals.

Vandalism is the single largest category of fire setting, over 30 percent of the total in urban environments. And nearly 40 percent of the incendiaries in this category are under the age of eighteen. Their most common targets are vacant buildings, cars, and trash collections. This fits the Detroit case. Most of the arson cases involved buildings that were already trashed or vacant, cars, or trash barrels. Very rarely was anyone occupying a building the arsonists torched.[73]

Given this realization, one can understand why the Detroit arsonists burned their own neighborhoods, then attacked the fire department when it arrived to save lives and property. Young people saw no distinction between the fire departments and the police departments. They were men in uniform. Older people, people who have seen or called the fire department for assistance, people whose property and lives had been saved by firemen, people who knew they could trust firemen, would not act in this way. When the firemen arrived at active fires, local teens taunted them—what were trucks and engines doing there? Adults knew why—putting out fires, rescuing the victims, aiding the sick. Acting Detroit battalion chief Marcene Taylor was black, but when he led the engine companies to Twelfth, he found, "[W]e [black firefighters] seem to be their favorite target." The black firefighters were older men; the taunters and the burners were teenagers. There was a rebellion in Detroit, but insofar as it involved arson, it was not a rebellion against poverty, discrimination, and the white power structure. It was a fire-born rebellion of the young against their parents. The "urban guerrillas" with Molotov cocktails in their hands wanted to burn down their parents' world.[74]

But when adults reasserted their authority, the young vandals went home. For example, when word of the burning reached the women of Moms and Tots, they decided the center must stay open. They would care for whoever brought their children. They would find food for whoever came—old or young—because the local supermarkets and corner stores were all burning or denuded by the looters. The center did not burn because the women who ran it made it clear that they would not tolerate adolescent antics.

Adult members of the black community were much more effective at preventing burning than official order keepers precisely because their presence undercut the cause of the fire sickness. Private home owners took out their rifles and banded together to protect firefighters when their homes were endangered. These were middle-class blacks, and they stood and faced the looters. "'We saw [the firefighters] needed some protection, and we're damned well going to give it to them.'" The home owners' attitude was simple—this is our property; and we will defend it. But the subliminal message to the burners was "behave yourself—we are your parents and enough of this nonsense." The *Michigan Chronicle* editors understood that the young people were the root cause. "These young people need some-thing to do," they editorialized. All the photojournalism confirms this verdict—when adults in the community stood up to the burners, the burners stood down.[75]

THE RIOTS, the burning, the disorder went on for four days, but by the 27th of July, relative calm was achieved. The regular troops' dis-cipline and serious demeanor seemed to have a "calming effect." It helped that nearly a quarter of them were black. By the end of the ri-ots and the fires, on July 28, forty-three people were dead and 1,189 injured, almost all of them African-American. The police had ar-rested over 7,200 citizens, 95 percent of them black and the vast ma-jority of these between the ages of fifteen and thirty. The final tally showed that 582 of those blacks arrested were juveniles; 4,683 of the blacks were adults. White detainees numbered 590. Fewer than fifty of the total number of arrested were convicted of offenses requiring jail time. On the 28th, Cavanagh walked up Twelfth Street and chat-ted with the locals. They appreciated his appearance. The fires were out. Their consequences were just about to be felt.[76]

"New Detroit"

The contagion of fires in July 1967 could have been much worse. The looting was local; the riots were limited; but the fire could have spread throughout Detroit just as the Pittsburgh and Chicago fires had. Jerome Cavanagh was not exaggerating when he wrote to Charles Quinlan: "[T]he evidence is abundant that the DFD has added a brilliant new dimension to the professionalism of fires." Cavanagh was relieved that "during a dangerous civil disturbance, [the DFD demonstrated] skill, efficiency and resourcefulness." But once was enough for catch-up, invent-on-the-run, and hope-for-the-best firefighting in the riots. The city implemented a new plan for fire during civil disturbances. It called for more equipment—especially fifteen new pumpers; upgraded communications, including new radios for commanders and firefighters; a formal mutual aid plan with all the surrounding departments; and "security measures to protect vital fire department installations."[77]

With the smoking ruins of entire neighborhoods still smudging the sky, the inevitable finger-pointing began. Watching from California, Governor Ronald Reagan denounced the "riffraff" of society, little more than savages. H. Rap Brown blamed Lyndon Johnson, an "outlaw from Texas." Black newspapers criticized both "hoodlums" and the police for "writing off" the streets when they should have swooped in and arrested violators. There was room on the list of culprits for "young Turks" who ran their mouths, then vanished, leaving black politicians without a following and their followers without a plan. For the victims of the burners, the morals of the entire black community seemed to have collapsed—a complaint that older folks were making about young people all over country during these years of sexual revolution and youthful demands for autonomy. Judge Lincoln, after hearing the cases of hundreds of accused rioters, decided that the tipping factor in 1967 (absent in prior years) was that ghetto folks had lost patience with legal means of improvement, and were beginning to advocate lawlessness. White newspapers saw a conspiracy of "well trained groups," gangs of a new kind—proto-revolutionaries armed and alienated from society. They quoted a dispirited Cavanagh when he complained of a culture of lawlessness, and a bewildered Romney when he pointed to lawless "elements."[78]

The truth that hovered over all these accusations was that the same conditions for catastrophic outbreaks of arson existed the next summer, and every summer thereafter. Unlike the fires in Boston, Pittsburgh, Chicago, and Baltimore, Detroit's did not cleanse the city's dilapidated housing stock, nor did it renew the people's confidence in their own ability to overcome natural disasters. The gutted buildings and empty lots did not become memorials to human courage, endurance, and creativity. Instead, they were mute witness to the impoverishment of the spirit. Rain came on July 28, 1967, and cleared "all the smoke" of the fires, but when the smoke was gone, what remained?[79]

The fires of 1967 had a corrosive effect, beyond the burned and then demolished buildings, beyond the vacant lots, beyond the incapacity of the city's first responders to respond to the deeper causes of the fires. The conflagration left a poisonous cloud of mistrust in the air. Young burners grew old filled with yet unburned particles of racial animosity, frustration, and hopelessness. Not all combustion gives off the heat and light of fire. In slower types of burning, the reaction continues so long as the fuel remains. Detroit did not burn again; it rusted.[80]

In 1973, the city's black majority elected the fiery and feisty Coleman Young as the city's first black mayor. He vowed to curb the racism of the police, and did. When, in 1977, the huge Detroit Renaissance Center opened on the waterfront, privately financed by a

combine of the city's business and realty leaders, one Young supporter waxed eloquent: "Cities have died. Have burned / yet
phoenix-like returned / to soar up livelier, lovelier than before. Detroit has felt the fire / Yet each time left the pyre / As if the flames
had power to restore." But the Renaissance Center did not revitalize
downtown. The monuments he and the business community erected
were surrounded by empty spaces and emptier rhetoric.[81]

Instead, in the agony of a bankrupt and crime-ridden city, the
Motor City had become "Murder City" in the press, and for good
reason. From 1940 to 1966, the city had averaged slightly under 100
homicides a year. In a steep ascent, the number rose to nearly 800 in
1975, and averaged over 600 per year through the 1980s and 1990s.
As one journalist called it, the 1980s seemed "a riot . . . in slow motion . . . steady relentless corrosion." White flight was reducing the
city's population by half, whites going from nearly 60 percent of the
city in 1950 to less than 10 percent in 2000, reducing the total population from nearly 2 million to under 1 million. Worse, the refugees
were the white and black professional and business classes. For the
final offering of the fire was "white flight." The city dipped below
800,000 residents as the greater Detroit region grew to 3 million.
The DFD was "out of service," a tragic mirror of the city's own debility, and one final proof of the impact of the fire, playing itself out
over the long course of time.[82]

A New Detroit?

Within days of the departure of the federal troops, the business community, as in Baltimore, gathered to discuss the disturbances. The
conversation in these meetings did not focus on repair of the physical destruction the fire wrought. With some self-sacrifice, that damage could have been repaired. Indeed, recovery from catastrophic
fire would provide a visible and unifying experience for people of all
color and classes. Chicago and Baltimore had suffered more and had
risen from their ashes. But those ashes covered vital downtown business districts. In Detroit, the fire damage lay mainly in the ghettos.

Prime real estate sites were not lost to the burners. Had the fire destroyed lower Woodward and the riverfront, then the bankers, corporate leaders, and city and state government would have to rebuild. In other words, the recovery effort would have become an opportunity to renew the city. Instead, they turned their attention to the far more intractable and divisive issue of the rioting.

Still, the "New Detroit" movement looked promising at first. On July 27, 1967, a conference of business and community leaders met, and on the 28th, the Detroit Chamber of Commerce, with Cavanagh's backing, created the New Detroit Committee. Its self-defined task was to find jobs for those disadvantaged by unemployment in the ghetto. The plan for recovery had the same impulse as in Chicago—no relief without work—modified by progressive ideas of government–private industry cooperation, as in Baltimore. Cavanagh wanted corporate assistance for a financially beleaguered city. General Motors and Ford executives promised to help. The committee reached out to the militants. Some wanted nothing to do with the white power structure, but others were willing to serve. The committee membership emerged from its gestation thirty-nine strong; nine members were black.[83]

No one from Twelfth Street came to the founding meeting, and no one from the committee toured the fire sites. Charles Butler sat on the board of New Detroit. He was no "power broker," and he did not think much of the quick "fixes" that the committee recommended. True, New Detroit "quieted things down." No more riots. But nothing fundamental changed. Maggie DeSantis, one of the members of the committee, recalled that the "same corporate structure" that ran the city before was still running it. She thought everyone who did their bidding was a puppet. They did nothing for the poor who needed housing, for example, a particularly exigent issue after the fires. All manner of local and voluntary associations butted their heads against a city hall and an entrenched landowning elite on behalf of the poor renters, winning individual battles and losing the war against indifference, decline, and decay. DeSantis quit.[84]

Had the fires of 1967 at least changed general attitudes—paving the way for a new Detroit to emerge? The answer was no. For the fires had only torched the ghetto, allowing ordinary whites to see it as a problem that blacks brought on themselves. If anything, in the months after the fire, white attitudes toward blacks grew harsher and more uncompromising. Blacks surveyed after the fire still wanted to be part of a larger society. Only 1 percent wanted a complete separation of the races. Nearly 17 percent of whites would have preferred total separation and only 24 percent favored genuine integration, as opposed to 88 percent of the blacks.[85]

Nor had the fires altered black attitudes. In 1968, a *Free Press* poll showed that black resentment of "police brutality, poor housing, lack of jobs, and poverty" had increased. By now, ghetto folks knew that whites had not become more sympathetic to black struggles because of the riots. Quite the reverse was true. Whites agreed in record numbers that Detroit was "worse off" because of the events of July 1967, and running on an anti-crime platform, Wayne County sheriff Roman Gribbs succeeded Cavanagh as mayor. By 1971, polling data indicated that blacks' pessimism about the city's prospects equaled whites'.[86]

Behind the failure of the New Detroit program was the fact that the fires did not clear valuable property for development or make property available for more profitable use. They simply took ghetto building stock out of circulation and left voids in its place. The ultimate irony was this: Had the burners left their own neighbors alone and gone downtown to do their mischief, New Detroit might have been more successful. Such dramatic ironies, however, only indicate how dreadful the options were for the city.

The election of Coleman Young in 1973 changed the city's official attitudes toward its black citizens and might thus have imparted new value to the vacant lots in the ghettos, but Young did not seize that opportunity. Instead, he cultivated an "us against them" politics. In his favor, one might say that he was a "risk taker" who was willing to go to the brink in difficult situations. Lower-middle-class Catholic in background, he keenly felt the barbs of institutional racism and found in the organized labor movement and the left-liberal wing of the Democratic Party an aegis for his political career. He weathered the Red Scare days of the 1950s and rose with the Black Power agitation of the 1960s. Most important, he was not tainted by the riots of 1967. By the early 1970s, he had established a record as a state senator who did right for Detroit and as a leader to whom blacks in the city could relate. He won with solid black support.[87]

Young would win reelection four times, but the city was crumbling and he could not save it. When black politicians criticized or challenged him, he dismissed them as the "Great White Hope" and "Aunt Jemimas." He did not polarize the city, but he played on the polarization to stay in office. Indeed, he acted the role of the turn-of-the-century city boss, giving out favors and swiping at those who did not tow his line. He borrowed money and unwisely invested it in industrial plants in an economy that was deindustrializing. The result was not only the waste of state and federal grant money, it was greater indebtedness for a city already in debt with declining means to pay.

Some observers compared the city government to an African nation whose leaders live well and whose ordinary people suffer everyday indignities of joblessness and decay. Errol Henderson, a black community leader, advocated Afrocentric cultural ideas but worried, "Just like in Africa, Detroit has a gerontocracy—rulership by the elders. That leadership has to move over." According to journalist Ze'ev Chafets, under Young, "Detroit [became] . . . a black metropolis, the first major Third World city in the United States. The trappings are all there—showcase projects, black-fisted symbols, an external enemy [the white suburbs] and the cult of personality [Young's own]." The vacant lots remained as well. Soon the city was the largest property holder within its own borders, but the value of the property had so declined that there was no sense in building anything on the lots. After, all, the population of the city was shrinking drastically; housing was not a problem any more.[88]

WHITE FLIGHT

The most direct and devastating consequence of the fires was white flight. As historian Thomas Sugrue has written, the city was residentially segregated from the beginning of the black migration. Residential segregation meant de facto school segregation. The city school board made de facto school segregation worse by continuously redrawing the "catchment" lines of schools so that no whites had to go to schools in black areas and no blacks could attend schools in white areas. Official desegregation in 1970 was met with white boycotts and a campaign to oust school board members who supported the plan. Whites whose opposition was strongest simply left the city. "In the short period between 1967 and 1978, the Detroit public School District lost 74 percent of its white students . . . by 1995, only 6.2 percent of Detroit public school students were white." For whatever reason, by the end of the 1990s, Detroit and its metropolitan area constituted the most segregated urban area in the United States. In other metropolitan areas with large black populations, the degree of separation was slowly declining. In Detroit, there was little relaxation of color lines.[89]

As whites left, the city unemployment rate climbed. Jobs in the industrial sector declined as many manufacturing enterprises, among them automotive assembly, shipbuilding, and textiles, were outsourced. It had once been easy to get a job in industry in the city. But when a new plant to manufacture Mazdas opened in 1987, 100,000 people applied for 2,000 openings. Industrial, retail, and wholesale jobs had just about vanished. Worse, "Detroit has simply not been competitive in planning, management, financing, marketing, legal or accounting services." All these require the kind of labor force that had left Detroit, "the income and educational mix to complete a transition to a service oriented economy."[90]

The result was a downward spiral. Landlords and home owners had no money to put into renewal of their own areas, and outside investors had no reason to favor Detroit. The city demolished the burned-out buildings, but nothing appeared in their place. In 1982, political scientists George Kelling and James Q. Wilson called this the "broken windows" syndrome. Broken windows in a factory or an abandoned building were signs of neglect. The same year, Detroit novelist Loren Estleman depicted a street in the old East Side ghetto: "[W]arehouses and tenements wallowed in the mulch of decades, their windows boarded up as if in an effort to shut out the world around them. Yellow mortar oozed out of brick walls covered with obscenities sprayed in black and candy-apple green." In 1988, James Risen, a *Los Angeles Times* reporter, toured the same streets: "In the tall weeds among the thousands of abandoned buildings and vacant lots in this city, along vast corridors of once-bustling streets, now reduced to urban wilderness . . . nature seems to be reclaiming sections of this city that man is abandoning." *Detroit News* columnist George Cantor agreed: "'I can't quite fathom the level of devastation that is going on. There is just block after block where nothing is remaining.'" Andy Bull, a London *Independent* features writer, visited in 1991. He saw "an alien, hostile landscape, a flat plain on which almost everything is crumbling to dust." A ride down East Jefferson in the summer of 2005 was only a little less appalling. Such visible signs actually became causes of further disorder and social dissolution. More and more vacant buildings lead to more and more blight.[91]

Ironically, the vacant lots were the direct result of city policy. By the 1990s, the city was demolishing 2,000 buildings a year, but only building 370. Housing density was decreasing as well, as the overall population dropped. Motown decamped for sunny Hollywood in 1972.

But it was not just people who were leaving. The vacant lots surrounded once thriving institutions, and now they were closing. At the end of 1982, the ninety-one-year-old J. L. Hudson Department Store, the queen of the downtown shopping area, closed its doors. A full block and many stories high, one of the three largest department stores in the country, it was to Detroit what Macy's was to New York City and Marshall Field was to Chicago. Indeed, its model was Marshall Field, for at Hudson's shopping was more than just buying. There were restaurants and a bookstore, "platoons of uniformed and gloved elevator operators, carpeted floors, wood-paneled corridors, tall chandeliers and a brass buttoned doorman." The store brought people into the core city. Hudson's sponsored the city's Thanksgiving Day parade, ran the city's bridal registry, and was home to people who simply liked to walk its floors. Now gone, the building's once valuable real estate (and its tax payments) were lost.[92]

Before the fires of 1967, in the heart of Detroit one could find a

Roman Catholic church in every neighborhood. Blacks and whites came to worship together, and the church was a vibrant part of the community. For example, in the near East Side, Sweetest Heart of Mary had seen hundreds of thousands of masses, weddings, christenings, and funerals. By the end of 1988, only the funerals filled the pews. Surrounded by vacant land, the largest Catholic church in the city was shutting its doors. Edmund Cardinal Szoka had announced the closing of forty-three parish churches. Those parishioners who remained protested, and the priests were bewildered, but the economics were plain—the people who came to worship were driving into the city from the suburbs.[93]

In the summer of 1990, University of Pittsburgh sociologist Robert Mast returned home to Detroit and spent over three months talking to community organizers there. He called the project, "Who Cares About Detroit?" and he found out that three generations of activists did. But something had happened to their city, their communities, their people. A light had gone out. Labor organizer James Boggs: "[I]t's devastating . . . a crisis in society" when the old pride in working the whole week, in having a job that paid decently, in belonging to a place had vanished. No one saw it coming; the giant wheels of history grinding so small and so far away that when Detroit factories slowed down or shut down, the people were shocked. His wife, Grace, understood how the crisis could have come upon them—"I have learned over the years that there are very few people who can move from one stage into the next." James agreed: The political reforms in the city, the civil rights victories, the triumphs of the labor unions—these paled in people's minds because "they got hooked on racism . . . There ain't no sense of class in them at all."[94]

Even the national boom times of the 1990s did not restore the city to its earlier preeminent position. As a whole, the prosperity of the greater Detroit region grew during the 1990s, vaulting it to number twenty-one in the country, past Dallas and Cleveland. The metropolitan region diversified its economic pattern, shifting from heavy industry to service and more specialized manufacturing. It even assayed a return to early nineteenth-century Detroit riverside development plans. Still, even after the boom times of the 1990s, nearly one-third of the city proper's population was under the age of eighteen and lived in a one-parent household, and the city itself ranked eighty-eighth among the top 100 cities in average household income. Segregation in schools and housing remained the most egregious in the nation.[95]

DEVIL'S NIGHTS

The brooding omnipresence, the dark cloud that hung over the city, was smoke from its fires. The city was still burning. Absentee landlords paid arsonists to burn out deadbeat tenants. Tenants tried to burn out rack-renting landlords. Landlords torched their own property for the insurance. On March 13, 1987, just such an arson in an abandoned warehouse killed three firefighters. Two were victims of a roof collapse, the third, their officer, was blown out of a window. The declining population and decreasing housing stock in the city did not diminish the frequency of arson. In 1997, Fire Commissioner Harold D. Watkins told the media that the city had had 6,557 "suspicious fires" the previous year, costing nearly $82 million in damage. Insurers took note. Premiums in the city were much higher than in the surrounding suburbs.[96]

Each year, in the days before Halloween, Detroit's "Devil's Night" revived the incendiary vandalism of 1967. It began in 1983, when a new generation of young men and boys in the ghettos set off 610 fires on October 29, 30, and 31. In 1984, the DFD rushed to 810 deliberately set blazes. The next year, 400 firefighters raced from Dumpsters to abandoned buildings, vehicles, trash cans, and vacant lots. Arsonists even set occupied buildings on fire as residents fled. Lots all over the city's poorest neighborhoods blazed into the night. Mayor Young promised an "all-out offensive" against the burners, called out volunteers and even put the city's sanitation men to work, but only seven young men were arrested for arson, and the DFD could not keep up with the burning. In the meantime, "throughout the night, fires were being photographed and commented on by television crews from other cities, national network news crews, and at least one television news crew from Japan."[97]

The next year, Young again promised a decline in the fires, announced another major campaign to deal with them, and then begged the newspapers not to cover the story. The burners were young men, many of them teenagers and some even younger. At least the number of fires had diminished, or so the reports the city released said. But the DFD was so busy that it took an engine a half hour to reach one garage fire, by which time the house next door had become involved. People were using their garden hoses to prevent fires from spreading.[98]

Roving bands of young black men used "homes for kindling" and old folks "with long coats over their bathrobes, standing grimly on their porches, armed with shotguns and water hoses," watched the streets like hawks. Firefighters, protected by the police, raced from blaze to blaze, followed by crowds of onlookers and television crews. Sometimes they left too soon, failing to pull down walls or ceilings where the fire hid. The burning before Halloween had become a Detroit tradition, as one observer put it, "like some grotesque urban horror film." In 1987, thousands of citizen volunteers helped the firefighters and the police control the arson contagion, and the city's curfew on young people kept the perpetrators off the streets, but two years later, the total number of fires had risen again to nearly 500.

A massive campaign to reduce the number of arson cases through the 1990s, including the "adopt a house" initiative, the renaming of the night Angel's Night (along with city-sponsored activities for young people), and cash rewards for informants, quieted the problem. By 1995, the three-day period before Halloween only had 158 fires, lower even than the normal three-day total of 185. The curfew remained in effect. The city expedited the prosecution of curfew violators, imposing community service on the offenders. The state of Michigan footed the bill.[99]

OUT OF SERVICE

The history of the DFD in these years was a microcosm of the history of the city. The heroism of July 1967 could not hide the ill will many Detroiters held toward their fire service. Accused then of racism, later reeling from the effort to quell Devil's Night blazes, trying to find its way as the first truly integrated public service agency in Detroit, the DFD rode a roller coaster. But the scars of the fires of 1967 would not heal. Understaffed, unappreciated, overlooked (except when it failed to perform), the DFD mirrored the declining fortunes of the city it served.

The DFD had resisted hiring and promoting blacks for many years, finally allowing three men to join the force in 1938. They ate in segregated quarters. By the 1970s, those barriers were long gone. They were taken down by an "affirmative action" program that recruited black firefighters and expedited their promotion to officers.

A fire department lieutenant or captain works alongside the firefighters, standing right behind the nozzle of the hose or leading the inside search of a building. Firefighters must have confidence in their officers, and officers must be superbly trained, knowledgeable, and able to lead if they are to gain the confidence of their crews. Official spokesmen for the DFD beamed, "Many white officers who vigorously opposed the influx of these minorities at first, have come to accept the phenomenon because it often makes it easier for them to operate in minority communities." But a serious morale problem reasserted itself when it came to promotion. "We became very arbitrary when it came to promotions,'" Mayor Young admitted. For every white promotion, a black was promoted.[100]

The selection system, based on evaluations and personal ties, had once worked to keep blacks from getting ahead. Now it worked to promote them sooner. Fire Commissioner Melvin Jefferson, the first black to hold the civil command position (fire commissioners are not necessarily firefighters), put it simply: "'[W]e want the Fire Department to look like the city.'" The affirmative action plan held up in court tests, despite a suit by thirty-eight white firefighters who claimed they had been unfairly bypassed by less qualified and more junior blacks. Neither the suit nor its outcome boosted morale. In 1988, Harold Watkins jumped over thirty others to become the first black chief of operations in the DFD, its professional commander. In

1996, Charlene Graham, also black, became the first woman division chief.[101]

The new DFD's civilian commissioner and top brass set out to repair its public image with a media blitz of press releases, open houses, and staged events. When a new aerial ladder truck arrived in April 1989, the DFD held a dedication ceremony and Commissioner Jefferson told the media, "[T]his fire ladder truck is of unique design . . . enhanced by the use of stainless steel in the construction of its cab and body." In fact, the Seagrave 100-foot ladder truck was hardly novel (it was already in service in a number of other cities). Still, Jefferson made it seem that the city had been delivered from its fire demons by a machine descending from heaven. The press release continued, "Detroit's newest addition to the fleet of firefighting apparatus can be viewed by interested citizens, any day of the week between the hours of 10 AM and 4 PM" by calling the "Community Relations Division."

The sophomoric hype continued the next year, when a Seagrave pumper arrived to keep the ladder truck company. The city again rolled out the red carpet. The pumper was the first in the city to provide indoor seating for the firefighters and it had an automatic transmission. It was to join forty-seven other major pieces of apparatus. For a city (at the time) of over a million souls, this was hardly an impressive array. Nevertheless, the latest addition would be feted at its own ceremony: "Refreshments will be served." Over and over, with the "pilot fire-safety program," the employment of a new kind of fire suppressant foam, the accession of more equipment, the introduction of an emergency management course, the distribution of 8,000 smoke detectors, and each class to graduate from the fire academy, the city trumpeted the progress of its fire service.[102]

Festivities and hoopla aside, the measure of a city fire department is twofold: How well does it maintain its apparatus, and how quickly does it respond to alarms? Drive by the local firehouse during the day and you will find the firefighters cleaning, repairing, and checking their equipment. They may be unrolling the hoses to prevent the cracking that comes when they are left rolled too long. Or they may be testing the pumper to be sure that it can sustain the landline water stream for an hour. Safety inspections of personal equipment and the apparatus are mandated and standards set by national organizations, but every fire service, every firehouse, and every company takes pride in the spit and polish appearance and operation of its gear. Safety checks save lives. A cracked hose that bursts will kill a firefighter who no longer has a working line in his hand. A first-attack hose line that fails kills victims who cannot be reached safely.[103]

While the city of Detroit was congratulating itself on its new apparatus, the tower ladder truck of ladder company No. 7 was falling apart. That did not stop the DFD from sending it on runs. Its history, traced by *Detroit News* investigative reporters Melvin Claxton and Charles Hurt, reveals a very different DFD from the city's press releases. Tower ladder No. 7 came into the fleet in 1985. In 1990, "the system supplying air to firefighters in the aerial's bucket" failed, and the paper reported that "the problem is never fixed." A year later, the tower ladder could no longer be raised quickly and the front end began to shimmy. Again a report: "Neither problem is corrected." The next year, the chauffeur (driver) reported that the truck would not go faster than twenty-five mph. Two years later, a crack in the windshield went unrepaired. In 1996, the hydraulic lift for the tower malfunctioned, spewing fluid. The crew tried carrying extra fluid containers because the repair shop could not or would not fix the problems. Yet another report: "On March 21, the truck's commander [the ladder company captain] writes to his boss, the chief of the fire department, outlining 19 specific problems with ladder 7. The truck stays in service and the problems are not fixed."[104]

On April 1, 2000, ladder No. 7 was first responder at the Pallister Plaissance apartments. The tower was vital in enabling the "outside ventilator"—the ladder company firefighter who checks for victims by going through windows—to evacuate victims from the upper floors. But the aerial ladder did not elevate and the truck company watched in agony as residents on the eighth floor hung out windows and screamed for help. Four residents died. After the tragedy at the Pallister, the DFD bosses put the truck back into service, broken ladder and all.

Unfortunately, the breakdown of ladder No. 7 was the rule, not the exception. The repair shop kept trucks and engines for months, in effect shutting down firehouses for a total of 286 days in 1999, and "More than 2,000 of the city's fire hydrants were out of service in 1999, some for more than four years." In the same period of time, seventy-five times, companies could not complete their runs to alarms because their apparatus broke down. Over the previous four years at least twenty-one people died because the firefighters did not get to fires within ten minutes.[105]

The time that it takes a fire department piece of equipment to respond to an alarm is a measure of the functional capacity of the department, and hence of the investment of the city in its services. Fire departments do not determine allocation of resources on the basis of the wealth or status of the person seeking help. They respond to an alarm in the ghetto as fast as to an alarm in a middle- or upper-class neighborhood. The key variables are not personal attitudes (particularly when a department, like Detroit's after 1973, is fully integrated), but the efficiency of the alarm system and the state of readiness of the men and equipment. If the engine or truck takes more than ten minutes to arrive, lives will be lost that could have been saved and fires will spread that could have been contained. Slow response may also derive from firehouse closings, layoffs or furloughs of men, and faulty equipment. Too few skilled mechanics could also trigger a domino effect, delaying repairs, idling companies, and slowing response time. The DFD experienced all of these. Worse, it had "ignored national firefighting standards." Over and over, mismanagement led to needless deaths and damage.[106]

Claxton and Hurt embedded their tale of ladder company No. 7 and its defective tower ladder truck in a series on the woes of the DFD. "Out of service" ran for a week in early November 2000, and its top-notch reporting chilled readers. The mayor and the fire commissioner said they were grateful for the revelations (though readers were left to wonder why they did not know the statistics and the problems already). Instead, the bosses blamed "firefighters and low level fire department officials who failed to bring problems to [their] attention." Reverting to the celebration style of media spin that had characterized its relationship with the press in earlier days, the DFD responded to the stories "with a demonstration of the aerial ladder at the station near Detroit's New Center area. But fire officials had to close that fire company for three hours . . . so department mechanics could fix hydraulic problems on the rig before the demonstration. Officials made no mention of the repairs during the briefing. Inside the firehouse, rags sopped up hydraulic fluid that leaked from the ladder truck before it went into the shop." Typical, and not mischance. Evidence of sloppy management and absent supervision were everywhere: in the decision not to use the city's two functional tower ladders on any but major fires, so they sat idle when apartment house fires raged and tower ladders were needed; ordering pumpers with the wrong connection, so that they could not spray foam on gasoline fires (in a city crisscrossed by superhighways); firehouse doors that were too small to admit newly purchased rigs; and a parts supply shop that was closed on "weekends, evenings, and holidays," the very times when fires are most common and parts most needed.[107]

The series sparked a strong response among readers. They knew about the breakdown of the DFD firsthand, but they expressed gratitude that the *Detroit News* had uncovered the city's complicity in the debility of its service. Two letters stand out. Raymond Hanka, a member of the DFD, wrote the first: "As a nine-year veteran of the Detroit Fire Department, I have seen rigs being held together with duct tape and ropes, companies riding without proper manpower [three men instead of the four or five necessary to do the job] firehouses literally falling down around my ears because the city has not properly maintained them for 30 years. Sometimes we go months waiting for uniforms because the city hasn't paid a bill." Don't blame the men, he said, "when the bell goes off, we still show and do the best job" we can.

A second letter went further. Lou Angeli, a battalion chief with the Chester County Fire Department in Pennsylvania (a department that sees its share of serious fires) wrote, "Why? Municipal officials reward political supporters—their friends—with the job of running this nation's fire departments. Such ill-trained appointees should not be charged with safety of the general public or firefighters . . . The

News's 'Out of Service' series clearly indicates that the administration of the Detroit Fire Department is unable to manage its day-to-day operations." The answer: Take the DFD out of politics and put it in the hands of professionals.[108]

But that answer was one that ran against the entire grain of recent Detroit history. When new fire commissioner Charles Wilson appeared before the city council to answer the charges in the series, he fumed, "'I'm going to do what I think is best.'" No apology and no acceptance of responsibility for past errors. Just more of the same. One week after Wilson stiff-armed the city council, a pumper dispatched to a fire at the Brewster-Douglas homes in the old Black Bottom ghetto broke down at the scene. Other companies had too few men riding on their apparatus to force entry into the burning buildings quickly, and two of the nearby hydrants turned out to be inoperative. Six children died. Later investigations by reporters (rather than inspections by the city) found that the hose on many pumpers was so old it cracked and leaked. One such hose was in play at the Brewster-Douglas fire until it burst. The fire bosses countered that the "children killed in the fire could not have been saved anyway," a remarkably callous (though probably accurate) reflection on the value the city placed on its own children as well as its services. In sum, the DFD was no worse, and no better, than the city government itself.[109]

TRAVEL ABOUT THE CITY and you will see that Detroit is still divided by the fires of 1967, but the division is no longer between black and white. It is between reality for the black city dwellers and illusion for the white corporate leaders. At street level, the corner of Twelfth and Clairmount no longer resembles the photos from before the fires. Low-rise housing developments set back from the street and edged with picket fences have replaced many of the brick up and down two-flats. On a hot Sunday morning in June 2005, the cars fly by on the divided thoroughfare that has replaced the commercial avenue. The once busy foot traffic of the old community has been reduced to occasional passersby. On buses that run irregularly whose air-conditioning does not work, the poor ride to nowhere. In the Motor City, the great highways have sucked the life from the streets. But in the riverfront Renaissance Center, all steel and glass nearly 750 feet high, the reality of the streets vanishes. The base of the central tower, the headquarters of General Motors and a high-rise Marriott Hotel, features a glitzy display of upscale cars that the vast majority of the city's citizens cannot afford.

Does Detroit remember the fires of 1967? Undoubtedly yes. They cannot be forgotten in a city where empty lots dot just about every block along the major streets. Is there a memorial to the heroism of the firefighters? No. They had worked tirelessly and in great personal danger for four days, extinguished hundreds of fires, and saved the city from ruin. Their reward was cuts in funding and staffing. There is no monument to them or to the fires. Where would one put it?

The East Bay:
Oakland Hills, 1991

Nestling at the top of the ridge that runs along the eastern side of San Francisco Bay, Grizzly Peak at 1,500 feet is about twice the elevation of the top of the Renaissance Center in Detroit. No two vistas could be more different. From the foot of the Radio Tower on Grizzly Peak, one looks down on a gardened world of twisting single-lane roads, sharp escarpments, and almost hidden hollows. The skyscrapers of the city of San Francisco rise across the bay like turrets of a castle. The weather, usually mild in winter, pleasantly warm in summer, with a refreshing wind that carries the moisture of the bay up into the hills, is a joy. Even the fog that envelopes everything on some evenings is more mysterious than menacing.

The mist is part of what meteorologists call a "microclimate." The low-lying bay shore region is damp and cool. The western-facing slopes of the Oakland Hills, nearly 1,500 feet above sea level, are drier and windier. But there are compensations to living in these hills. One forgets the bustling city streets and the flatlanders who live but a few miles below. Indeed, residents of the Oakland Hills such as *San Francisco Chronicle* editor Tim Neagle boast, "'[T]he infamous Oakland is down on the flat with all the crime and poverty. When you get back up in the hills it's completely different.'" Richard Paddock, a Los Angeles reporter visiting the hills, agreed: "this is where the elite of Oakland and Berkeley lived, along with refugees from the urban clamor of San Francisco: doctors, lawyers, judges, professors, star athletes, corporate executives, writers, artists, and elected officials."[1]

There have been people in the hills for thousands of years, fishing, hunting, and more recently harvesting crops. Did they enjoy the natural delights of the coast? Did they feel the earth move and wonder if the gods they worshipped were angry? The folded ranges of hills of Northern California kept the clans of Native Americans separated from one another and they developed their own idioms. But waves of Europeans—Spanish, Russian, English, German, Irish, African-American—all spoke the same language of economic opportunity when they moved into the hills. They came for the money and stayed, sometimes dirt poor, sometimes fired by anger and frustration to prey on those who were there first (Indians, and later Mexicans) and those who came later (Chinese and Japanese). Ranchers and farmers killed off those Indians who survived the diseases the Spanish friars brought. There was a bounty on Indian scalps just like the bounty on wolf skins and coyotes. The discovery of gold in 1848 doubled and redoubled the population, and the San Francisco Bay area was its major port of disembarkation. Its Chinese immigrants lived in rickety squalor, worked long hours for a pittance, and faced relentless discrimination.[2]

The east side of the Bay was the entry to the gold fields. There, a city sprang up overnight. Oakland was a boomtown with pretensions. In 1853, the College School opened its doors. It would later become the University of California at Berkeley. By 1860, the recorded population passed 1,500, but the census was notoriously inexact. Uncounted gold seekers stayed awhile before they headed for the interior. Five years later, Frederick Law Olmstead designed the city's cemetery, the finest of its kind in the state. The city soon introduced horse-drawn trolleys to carry visitors from the terminus of the transcontinental railroad to the center of town. In 1891, the first electric trolley car rolled out of the barn and carried passengers up to Berkeley. On the shores of Merritt Lake, a former marsh transformed into a lovely tidal basin, tycoons built elegant mansions. Oakland began to attract an artist community. They found in the hills vistas to inspire the spirit and refresh the flesh. By 1910, the city boasted 150,000 residents, skyscrapers, and a city hall that was for a time the tallest building west of the Mississippi.

To the city came the multitudes yearning to be free and employed. Asians, Latinos, and African-Americans found jobs in the railroad industry and the city's many factories. The city annexed nearby hill towns, tripling its size. With its deepwater port regularly dredged by the federal government, Oakland became a leader in World War II shipbuilding. After the war, the city invested in parks, street lighting, better sewers, and an expanded library system. With the Bay Bridge connecting it to the San Francisco peninsula and later the Bay Area Rapid Transit, Oakland became part of one of the most prosperous of American metropolitan areas. The growth of the city attracted the Raiders football team in 1960 and the Athletics baseball team in 1968.[3]

For some, progress was not so apparent. Blacks occupied the bottom rung of the economic ladder, carting, hauling, collecting, and sweeping. Employment discrimination was everywhere and police brutality a common subject in the black community. In October 1966, Bobby Seale and Huey P. Newton founded the Black Panther Party in the city and demanded far reaching reforms. Some of their objectives were entirely within the mainstream of progressive ideals: the end of racism in education, employment, housing, and politics. Other aims were more militant, and they would lead to violent confrontations with police forces.[4]

Real panthers did not roam the hills, but—just as predatory—real estate developers did. Starting at the beginning of the twentieth century, the rail and traction companies, the developers, and their bulldozers carved streets and house plots out of the treeless chaparral of the East Bay. The Realty Syndicate Company, the creation of developers F. M. Smith and Frank C. Havens (also briefly the owners of the Claremont Hotel) promised "a perfect setting . . . which nature gave" to the hills. They sold over 13,000 acres of homes before the enterprise went under in the 1920s. Around the Victorian gingerbread, old California haciendas, and eclectic style houses, owners planted Monterey pines, eucalyptus, and other non-native but elegant trees (the eucalyptus came from another chaparral ecology—Australia), as well as a myriad of bushes and flowering plants. In the 1960s, the combination of natural and landscaped greenery, lovely, breathtaking panorama, and architecturally sophisticated dwellings attracted an upscale clientele.[5]

For a first-time visitor, the ride from the port of Oakland to the Oakland Hills is hair-raising. You travel on California Highway 24—at its widest an eight-lane expressway—and get off just before the Caldecott Tunnel at Old Tunnel Road. The gentle roll of the Montclair and Rockridge districts south and west of the expressway is cut into small valleys by the low shoulders of hills. As you follow Tunnel Road's winding course upward, hair-raising switchback curves dare gravity as they jut out from steep grassy slopes. Once these roads were a challenge to undergrads at the University of California at Berkeley, less than a mile to the east. They would push themselves to "get to the top." Later, the bicyclists took over the roads. They are too narrow for all that traffic, unless people drive very slowly.[6]

The most striking topographic feature is the hills themselves. The foothills merge into the ridgeline. The slopes and dales turn small pieces of land into miniature neighborhoods, sometimes only a single winding street long. Near the top of the ridge, a few roads run parallel to the ridgeline. Most travel a snaked spiral downward. You need a map to find your way. There are no clear sight lines and no hint of a grid. It is more like a children's game maze on the back of a restaurant place mat. God forbid you need to find your way out of the hills in a hurry. The lanes in and out of miniature developments are barely wide enough for two cars. When residents and guests double-park on them, a common practice, only one car at a time can navigate them. The only way out of the hills entirely is over Grizzly Peak onto Fish Ranch Road or, to the south and east, Tunnel Road. Where Tunnel becomes Route 13 in Berkeley, it narrows into a paved arbor of greenery-bordered houses that almost touch the road. Going south, Tunnel Road cuts Highway 24. The entrance to the expressway westbound, toward the city, is a narrow and tight one-lane access road. A wonderland, and like the original, treacherous.[7]

All the beauty and solitude comes at a cost. Natives are not shy about telling visitors about "the big one" that is coming. They have all been through earthquakes, fires, and mud slides. In fact, they seem to have an obstinate pride in the danger that lurks in the hills. The Hayward Fault line runs right under these hills. As disaster chronicler Ted Steinberg has written, Americans are drawn to risk-prone residential settings. The Hayward Fault is overdue for a major quake. As with the mud-slide terrain of the Pacific Coast housing developments west of Los Angeles, the retirement communities on the edges of national wilderness lands in Arizona, Nevada, and New Mexico, the sand dunes of the outer banks of the Carolinas, and the hurricane-path condos on the Florida shoreline, the lure of natural beauty outweighs environmental caution.[8]

When the earth shakes, fire is never far behind. On April 18, 1906, the earth shook for nearly a minute along the fault lines in the Bay region. The quake ruptured water lines and set gas lines afire. Half the city of San Francisco was gutted. In 1923, a firestorm swept out of the Berkeley Hills, devouring 600 houses and barely missing the city center and the university campus. On October 17, 1989, the Loma Prieta earthquake hit 7.1 on the Richter scale. Only eleven people died and only a hundred buildings fell or were later condemned in San Francisco, but thirty-six fires, primarily from gas lines, led to property losses exceeding $2 billion. The same quake killed forty-two people in Oakland, leveled much public housing, and cost business over $90 million. Even the Caldecott Tunnel can be a fiery trap, as it was for seven civilians on July 4, 1982. A collision between a gasoline tanker and a passenger car set the tanker's cargo on fire. The half-mile-long tunnel burned for hours.[9]

Fire loves the Oakland Hills. The neighborhood's flora, particularly the eucalyptus, whose bark is shed yearly, is especially fire prone. The saddle-shaped terrain (saddles and swales act like wind chutes) and the dominant dry and hot weather pattern in late summer and early fall make the region a particularly inviting target for fire. Left undeveloped, the chaparral, or "Mediterranean scrub," ecological system of the Hills can handle periodic burns. But when people move on the "urban-wildland" edge, even a controlled fire is an invitation to disaster. The Oakland Hills communities are right in the middle of one of these fire regimes, the "chaparral firebelt." In the housing subdivisions and apartment complexes, firefighters cannot rely on traditional, urban "structural" firefighting tactics—stationary posts and heavy equipment—because the blazes spread too quickly. They cannot deploy traditional wildfire-fighting techniques, because they cannot dig trenches or set backfires and retreat without surrendering valuable homes to the fire. To fight ground-cover fires in populated areas on the urban-wildland edge requires introducing a new kind of firefighting entirely.[10]

And when the wind called the diablo comes over the hills in the fall, the danger of a brushfire becoming a firestorm increases exponentially. The diablo is a "Froehn"-type wind created "when a high pressure weather system is located over the great basin [of Nevada and Utah] . . . accompanied by an off shore low pressure system. The high pressure system imports chilled air from the far north, with extremely low moisture content." At the two mighty weather systems' intersection a powerful wind is generated, and it sweeps in over the hills from the northeast. The wind is dry and hot, sometimes bringing temperatures over 90°F. The diablo gusts well into the fifty-mile-an-hour range and can reach near hurricane force at its worst. When forecasters predict a diablo, the National Weather Service issues a "red flag" warning. This tells fire departments that conditions for a serious wildfire are present. Red flags in the national parks mandate evacuation of fire-prone areas. But home owners in upscale East Bay subdivisions are not going to abandon their property just because the wind is blowing from the east.[11]

They should know better. In September 1923, the diablo turned a careless smoker's discarded cigarette in the hills north of the Berkeley campus into a three-mile-wide path of destruction. In 1931, and again in 1933, 1937, 1940, 1946, 1955, 1960, 1961, 1968, 1970, 1980, and 1990, significant fires raged over the hills. In seven of these cases the diablo was blowing. When it blew, the fire raced faster than an Olympic sprinter can run and literally blew up houses in its path. Every one of these fires took place in September, October, or November, and the average area scourged was over 500 acres.[12]

Heaven and hell, in the same place, that is the coast of Northern California. But on a lovely early fall morning, for someone sitting out on their redwood deck in the Oakland Hills, surrounded by lush scenery, the inherent danger of fire seems distant, a phantasm that dissipates like the previous evening's mist. Until the first wisp of smoke . . .

A Perfect Firestorm

Sunday, October 20, 1991, in the hills on the eastern edge of the Bay Area started out unseasonably warm. A light breeze drew people outdoors; they were walking dogs, sitting on patios and decks, in a quiet morning prelude to a lazy afternoon. Linda Fletcher was especially pleased that a grassfire on the steep slope alongside Marlborough Terrace at the top of the hill had been quelled the day before. She wondered idly what might have happened had the diablo awakened. Deirdre English, looking out her window on Vicente Road in Claremont Canyon on the Oakland Hills–Berkeley Hills border, smelled smoke. She was reassured by the 911 operator that firefighters were already on the scene, overhauling the previous day's fire. She must be smelling the few remaining cinders. Muriel Varney, older and wiser, was more worried. She had seen the 1970 fire in the same place consume thirty-six homes. But her request that the firefighters stay over the previous night had been ignored.[13]

OVERHAULING

Assistant Fire Chief Don Matthews was well aware of the danger—he compared it to the 1970 fire in the same area. Interviewed for the Saturday papers, he sighed: "'We lucked out. The only difference between that day and today is that the Santa Ana winds were blowing then, and it was unstoppable.'" Neither English nor Fletcher knew that the California Department of Forestry and Fire Protection (CDF) had issued a "red flag" warning for the weekend. Conditions were ripe for dangerous wildfires. The warning only pertained to public lands and wilderness areas and only required that the CDF's wildfire prevention crews be on alert, but other Northern California fire departments decided to overstaff their shifts. Oakland did not. The interview Chief Matthews gave to the *San Francisco Chronicle* did not mention that he had heard about the "red flag" on his radio, but he was shift commander for Sunday morning, and he would send out crews to look for hot spots from the Saturday fire as soon as he came on duty.[14]

The Saturday hillside fire had probably begun with a rubbish pile construction workers left behind when they were done with the week's work. However it started, it consumed thirty-five acres of grasses on a slope between Buckingham Boulevard and Grizzly Peak Boulevard. Both of these lanes are misnamed. They are the very opposite of the grand avenues of Paris. The steep slope where the brushfire burned is not suitable for building, even for the most daring of developers, and the workers had no building permit. West of the site, on Marlborough and Buckingham, there are houses, but none of these was involved in the fire. As is most often the case in such brushfires, the fire rose up the hill toward Grizzly Peak.[15]

Before the fire service was done with it, however, the Saturday fire called out twelve engine companies and two trucks from Oakland and two engines from Berkeley. The East Bay Regional Parks district, representing the state, contributed three engines. The fire was not out until nearly 7:00 PM. Helicopters from the CDF dropped water as companies moved in from all directions, squeezing the fire zone and protecting the houses on either side. In all, it was as close to an "all-hands" as was possible, without calling in off-duty crews. In early evening, the crews dug out fire spots and by nightfall there were none visible. Still, the crews left their lines, attached to the hydrants, in place, "because of the tremendous fire potential." Experienced wildfire fighters know that such a blaze will go into the root structures and may continue to smolder for days or weeks. There certainly would be hot spots that would need watching and overhauling before the danger was over.[16]

Longtime home owners on the upper slopes of the hills recalled the 1970 Fish Ranch Road fire. Then, the wind had carried the fire along the eastern side of Grizzly Peak, across narrow and winding Fish Ranch Road, and burned out nearly forty houses. The Oakland Fire Department called on the aid of other Alameda County and Contra Costa County departments and just barely managed to prevent the fire from spreading. Residents helped—a tradition in the hills—spelling exhausted firefighters on the lines and using their own lawn hoses to wet homes and brush.[17]

No one who had experienced these red-zone fires would ever forget them. As Oakland firefighter Zac Unger wrote some years later, "On hot days [in the fire season] the wealthy hang off their porches and pace their well-manicured streets, eyes scanning the hillsides and noses twitching for the hint of bush smoke. A dozen frantic calls will come in anytime somebody lights a barbeque in a backyard and lets a puff of white smoke drift into the air."[18]

But remembering the terror and taking precautions against a repetition are different matters. In the fall of 1991, five years of drought had left dry brush everywhere, adding to the residents' own dried-out landscaping. A cold winter had killed brush, and financial problems in Oakland had delayed a cleanup. "Gutters got choked with dry leaves, and tinderlike annual grasses" added to the immense amount of fuel for a terrible fire close at hand. On public lands, California law required a "30 foot fire break around all structures and . . . fuel modification within a 100 foot radius." Applied to the slope beneath Grizzly Peak, that meant a complete cleanup of the dead brush and greater separation of homes. But so valuable was the real estate in the hills that no amount of persuasion and no warning, however dire, was going to convince the home owners to let Oakland copy the California public lands' regulations.[19]

The Oakland Fire Department (OFD) was back on the upper slopes by 8:51 AM on Sunday morning. The late arrival time, along

266

with the failure to post men and equipment through the night, would cause a major controversy later that day. The delay was no one's fault. The firefighters' shifts changed at 7:00 AM, and not every firehouse was fully staffed yet. Saturday night is a busy time for city fire services. Some of the companies in the densely populated black and Hispanic neighborhoods downtown had been called out a number of times that night. "Los Bomberos de Fruitvale" (a.k.a. engine No. 13) averaged over 3,000 runs a year, and the "Animal House" (the home of engine No. 20, truck No. 7, and Third Battalion headquarters) put in 6,000 runs a year.[20]

When engines No. 19 and No. 24 with four-man complements returned to the Saturday fire site, they noted some hot spots inside the site. The wind was picking up, and more important, it had shifted from a gentle westerly to a gusting easterly. Winds coming out of the east could become a diablo. The meteorologists thought so, and so did Assistant Chief Matthews. He decided to have a look for himself. He made it up to the top of the hill by 9:13 AM and saw that hot spots were popping up all over.[21]

Matthews called for reinforcements, and engine No. 16 was dispatched. East Bay sent its own engine company to pick up the hose lines they had left in place the previous evening, but they were soon using the lines to put down little fires. East Bay sent more units, without lights and sirens. There was no emergency, just a sense of urgency. The hot spots had to be smothered or cooled before the wind began blowing in earnest. "More than 25 firefighters were on the scene overhauling hot spots," Oakland Fire Department captain Donald R. Parker recalled. After an hour of hard work, units on the hillside reported the flare-ups under control. Engine No. 24 was left to patrol the area.[22]

But these men were tired, and tired firefighters make mistakes. Some were overdressed—cooking inside the bunker gear city firefighters wear to battle city structural fires. Others were untrained in fighting what was, in essence, a groundcover or wildfire. To fight a wildfire you dress light (if you have to run, you have to run fast), carry a canteen and a "piss bag," and have a "fire shelter" (aluminum-coated shelter half) in case the fire outruns you. Later reassessments of the department's performance would note the OFD units' lack of wildfire training. This morning, the department personnel on the scene initially underestimated the danger and recalled their rigs too soon.[23]

Such judgments are easier to make after the fact than at the time. The OFD served nearly 400,000 people in the city, with a state-of-the-art call-in alarm system. Still, the 911 operators were not professionals and could be testy if overworked. "I am not a doctor," one dispatcher told an elderly woman who wondered if the smoke from a fire miles away was causing her breathing difficulties. The department had twenty-three engine companies, seven ladder (truck) companies, a rescue squad, and a modern hazard-materials unit, but none of these were based in the upper portion of the hills. The financial woes of the city in the 1980s had cut its staffing nearly in half, with many of the cuts coming at the command level. The entire force had only one assistant chief and two battalion commanders on each shift. Battalion commanders have multiple exacting jobs—they must direct the companies on the spot and also coordinate the units in a major fire. Too few senior officers, and the firefighting effort becomes disjointed and resources are not directed to the places where they are needed.[24]

In a pinch, the city could call on neighboring Berkeley's seven engine companies and two trucks, as well as other companies in the Alameda County Fire Mutual Aid Plan, the Contra Costa County companies (including the Moraga-Orinda Fire Department), the CDF wildfire equipment and manpower (including helicopters and tanker aircraft), and if necessary the San Francisco and other West Bay departments under the regional mutual aid plan. But these were as hard hit as Oakland's department when it came to funding.[25]

Invoking the mutual aid plan would mean that an incident commander would coordinate the various departments' contribution to the overall effort. Oakland had implemented the "incident command system" (ICS) after the 1989 earthquake. ICS originated in Southern California in the 1970s. Various fire departments used a wide variety of terminology, communications equipment, and command structures that hindered a uniform, speedy, and effective response to large-scale wildfires.

After a series of serious fires, the cities, counties, and the state created Firefighting Resources of California Organized for Potential Emergencies (FIRESCOPE). The idea was simple: A qualified incident commander in touch with all the engaged agencies would gather information and direct operations. ICS could expand, reassign, and release cooperating agencies as they were needed, where they were needed. "An effective incident commander," according to the program as adopted and taught by FEMA's Emergency Management Institute, "must be assertive, decisive, objective, calm, and a quick thinker." He or she also had to be a realist, knowing when to attack a fire, when to fight it defensively, and when to retreat. Finally, the incident commander had know when to delegate authority to those in operational command and when to overrule operational personnel.

ICS also managed the release of information to the public, assessment of costs, and safety of professional personnel and civilians. (That is, ICS insured that sufficient emergency medical personnel and equipment were on hand, and that hospital space and medical support was available.) The first priority of ICS was people's safety. The second job was containment and reduction of the threat. The third job (and this is an important hierarchy to remember) was the protection of property.

On the scene, the benefit of ICS is immediately apparent. There is a unified command structure. Orders flow down, information flows up, resources are expended to maximize benefit, and no one is left out of the loop. But ICS was not imposed at the outset of the East Bay Hill fire's expansion. In fact, as late as early afternoon, various fire departments were still not operating under a single command. Berkeley had its divisions and command structure, East Bay and Oakland theirs. The CDF was communicating with Oakland on telephone lines instead of using a single-command radio frequency. In a major fire involving multiple departments, the potential for confusion was great without ICS.[26]

A PERFECT FIRESTORM

In the hills, the confusion grew worse after 10:30 AM. Home owners in the area were already awake. Dorothy Stein smelled smoke, then looked out to see little pockets of flames. Another resident called 911 to report fire on the hill next to Marlborough Terrace. The OFD engine officer replied to the dispatcher that the East Bay crew was dealing with the problem. Engine No. 24 headed home, leaving only one Oakland fire company in the vicinity of the fire. Meanwhile, the East Bay companies, unable to communicate directly with the Oakland companies on the scene, were rushing up and down the hill putting out spot fires.

The Saturday fire had not exhausted the available fuel on the hillside, and the drying, hot wind was carrying sparks all over. A groundcover fire or wildfire's rate of speed is not just determined by the wind. Fuel consumption actually slows a fire. Thus, a fire in grass or light brush or gardens will move much faster than a wildfire in heavy vegetation. Terrain matters, too. Canyons and hills draw fire to them. The East Bay Hills landscape fit these descriptions.

Still, the fire was moving downhill and heat currents from it did not have the chance to preheat the lower hillside. Quick response could still save lives and property. Had the OFD and the East Bay companies been able to coordinate their actions at this early stage, they might have brought to bear sufficient manpower and equipment to contain and then extinguish the hot spots. But the radio frequencies of the OFD and the East Bay fire service were not the same, and the two forces were not coordinating their activity.[27]

Then one of the East Bay firefighters raked up a hot spot and the wind carried the embers outside the Saturday fire site. Bob Roth of local television Channel 2 was on the upper slope doing follow-up coverage of the Saturday fire: "'Suddenly this huge gust kicked up, and it was like dropping gas on [the smoldering ground], flames suddenly were twenty to thirty feet in the air . . . We weren't concerned yet, but we couldn't see my car through the smoke and it was getting hot." In the nick of time, one of the East Bay fire patrol's four-

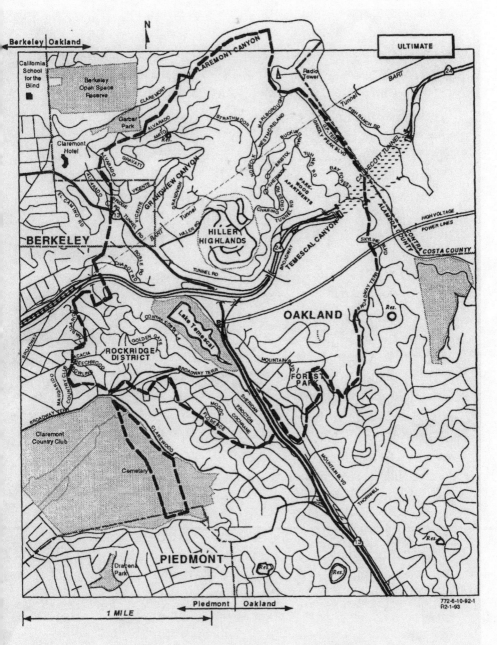

East Bay: Oakland Hills fire scene (FEMA)

wheelers scooted up, "'the driver said "hop in," and he gunned it out of there.'"[28]

The fire had moved outside the circle of the firefighters, found new fuel sources and was beginning to "crown"—the flame reaching high enough to ignite the tops of the Monterey pine trees. The wind carried the burning pine needles far beyond the fire line. Between 10:57 and 11:04 AM, firefighters on the scene called in three more alarms. The airwaves were now filled with the two fire departments' transmissions. The 911 system was also deluged with home owners reporting spot fires and smoke. The dispatchers were undermanned (Sunday staffing was usually light), so the recall of off-duty dispatchers began. They started arriving within a half hour, but sorting out the calls would take hours.[29]

The hillside dwellers were highly educated, individualistic, and self-motivated. They could see what the city fire service professionals had not yet concluded. Gregory Blais of Rockridge, a development on the other side of Route 13 from the upper hills, had spent two summers with the U.S. Forest Service fighting fires. He knew how fast a wildfire could move: "One moment it was a balmy, breezy, Sunday morning and the next an unimaginable inferno." From his home on Broadway Terrace, he could see the fire jumping the department's lines. Other home owners stared in amazement at the scene, "as if hypnotized." In the space of seven minutes, the firefighters had lost control of the blaze. Houses on all of the high terraces were threatened. Fire engines returning to the scene were deployed as they arrived, without any overall plan. The few commanders on the scene had too many tasks and too few hands.[30]

OFD battalion commander James Riley surveyed the fire as he drove toward the top of the ridge. At forty-nine, he was a twenty-five-year veteran and much liked by his men. "Quiet and tough," he must have known that this was going to be a big one. He had been a battalion chief for fourteen years, the youngest one ever to reach that rank in the OFD, and he had seen the 1970 and the 1973 fires in the area. But no single ground vantage point afforded a complete view of the hills. From the top, it is possible to see down into the canyon, but not over the smaller dividing humps of land. From the southern foot of the hills, where Tunnel Road leaves Highway 24, the upper hills are in view, but not the two canyons to the north. The incident commander at the bottom of the hill, Assistant Chief John Baker, could only see smoke. Riley, at the top of the hill, thus became operational commander on the scene.

"We have the most critical fire conditions in five years," he had radioed Oakland dispatch an hour before, but when he now asked for Contra Costa companies, he could not get through to them. Indeed, he was temporarily unable to use his command channels to reach the Oakland dispatch (they were already in use for a fire near the docks). At the very moment when cooperation among all the area fire departments was most vital because speedy interdiction might contain the fire on the upper slopes, communications had almost totally failed.[31]

At 11:33 AM, Riley radioed: "It's coming over. Probably can't hold. We are abandoning task." Live power lines came down and the fire started burning houses. Riley ordered a tactical retreat: "Don't get anybody killed," he told his men. He directed the evacuation. At 11:45: "Fire at both ends [of the hillside ridge]." Riley mounted his crew on their patrol vehicle and they roared toward the fire wall and safety beyond. But Riley had seen a woman trying to get to her car inside the ring of fire. He told his men to get themselves out, then went back on foot himself to assist her. It was the last his men saw of him. His wife and daughter would later agree that he would have preferred a death on the job he loved rather than to "just retire when he got old."[32]

With power lines down, cars and pedestrians had to be especially careful leaving the fire zone. Buckingham, for example, was blocked by parked cars and downed power lines. Architect Gail Baxter loved her home on Buckingham and delayed leaving it just long enough for the fire to catch her in her car. Kimberly Dakis-Robson and her husband, Brian, fled the fire in separate cars. She went up the hill and was trapped by the downed lines, dying in her car of smoke inhalation. He went down the hill and lived. At the same exact moment Riley was sending his final signal, Oakland police officer John Grubensky radioed to his dispatcher that he was getting out of his cruiser on Charing Cross to help sort out a traffic jam. Grubensky, a hero in the Loma Prieta earthquake highway collapse two years before, certainly knew the danger that the pileup on Charing Cross could cause. The fire was sweeping down the hills directly at the accident, blocking escape for the 2,000 people living in the seven-building, 431-unit Parkwood Apartments. These closely stacked two- and three-story, shingle-sided and -roofed dwellings nestled against the hillside. All of the units had windows facing the bay. A perfect Eden, about to become hell.[33]

By now the fire covered about fifty acres—a big fire, but containable. It was the speed with which the fire was spreading that amazed the OFD men, unaccustomed to wildfire. City fires simply do not cover that much ground as quickly. Their fuel slows them. The fire flew from the west-facing slope of Grizzly Peak down the mountain into the Parkwood Apartments in minutes. The area of the blaze had grown tenfold as the spot fires joined together into a 100-foot wall of fire.

At the same time that Riley and Grubensky were checking in, OFD chief P. Lamont Ewell arrived at the scene. Still optimistic that the fire could be contained on the upper slopes, he ordered the OFD to make a stand at Hiller and Tunnel Roads, below and just to the west of the Hiller Highlands. The OFD called for strike forces from Alameda County to mass about a half mile ahead of the fire. In effect, the OFD was conceding the property in the condos and the apartment complex to the fire in order to evacuate the area.

Engine No. 1 and trucks Nos. 1 and 3 tried to reach the Parkwood, but they were still blocked by the same wild traffic buildup that prevented residents from exiting the complex. The crews ran into the buildings on foot to rescue anyone still inside. As the buildings burst into flame around them, the fire alarms went off. The main body of fire by this time was less than a quarter mile away, and burning brands had set the roofs of the complex on fire. The OFD shifted its command post to the middle of Highway 24, at the Broadway Street exit.[34]

Over 100 acres were now fully involved. The wall of fire consumed everything halfway down the hillside and gathered itself to leap over

Charing Cross Road at the edge of the Hiller Highlands condo development. Meanwhile, in the Parkwood complex, people ran for their cars, then discovered to their horror that the only exit from the complex had become jammed with cars. The two-lane road beyond was blocked as well. Parked cars became insurmountable obstacles. Refugees abandoned their vehicles and ran beyond the blockage.

The Hiller Highlands "planned community" of townhomes and condos was the next bottleneck. It too had only one entrance and exit—Charing Cross—also at a standstill with cars jockeying for space. Frank Eakman rented there, later recalling that the cul-de-sac of "well-manicured lawns" turned out to be "a death trap." The CDF later calculated that structures with wooden roofs and fewer than thirty feet of cleared space would be totally destroyed ninety-six times out of 100. Built in the 1960s, with landscaping coming up to the buildings and without concrete walls and tile or other flameproof roofing, screens to prevent embers from flying into vents, and outside and inside sprinklers, the Hiller homes had no defense against the flames. Inside, telephones that were once lifelines to the outside world became carriers of terrified last words. Segall Livnah, a sophomore at Berkeley visiting her mother's condo in the Highlands, called her brother and left a message on his machine: "'Call me back quickly.'" Her body was found four days later, next to the phone.[35]

Hesitation is the great killer in fires. Victims found next to a door or window cause us to wonder, why didn't they get out? The answer is almost always that they had time but hesitated—they went back into the structure for something, or they could not make up their minds in time. Livnah's call to her brother killed her. Had she fled as soon as she recognized that there was a fire, she would probably have survived.

Those who could flee the Parkwood and the Highlands on foot were picked up by fleeing motorists. There was always a little more room in the car or van. One driver stopped to accommodate Matthew Soyster, a wheelchair-bound writer, and his neighbor, Catherine Campbell. She had dragged him up the steps to the street just ahead of the blaze. *Oakland Tribune* editor Robert Maynard, taking pictures for his paper from his roof, grabbed the dog and one of his cats before the flames reached him. His wife drove by and picked them up; then they stopped to let others clamber aboard. "Evacuate! Evacuate!" Deirdre English yelled from her vehicle at people still hypnotized into immobility. "Run, jump in, let's go!"— that was the new mantra of the burning hills.[36]

MUTUAL AID

The Berkeley Fire Department was listening in on the growing confusion by radio, but no one had called them out. They mobilized nevertheless. The California Highway Patrol jumped in to untangle the traffic nightmare. Joining with local police forces, CHiPs assumed the job of directing traffic out of the hills. CHiPs also relayed Oakland's call for assistance to Contra Costa. Communications had become a deadly serious game of telephone tag. But at last the Oakland and East Bay companies were able to explain the gravity of the situation on the ground to outside agencies. Above the fray, CDF command helicopters could see the whole fire and reported its rapid spread. Alameda County and Contra Costa were assigning units and calling back all shifts. Help was on the way. Would it arrive in time?

Firefighters are the least fatalistic of all our professionals. Training, instinct, and personality tell them to refuse to accept the inevitability of defeat. If they did, they would never run into burning buildings to save strangers, hump hoses up stairs into burning rooms, or race up hillsides to help people flee from a wall of fire advancing thirty to forty miles an hour straight at them. But wildfires like this one breed a certain respect for the will of nature in even the most aggressive firefighter.

Ordered to redeploy ahead of the fire by the incident commander, the drivers of the fire engines and ladder trucks were finding it almost impossible to maneuver around the sharp curves, evacuating vehicles, and parked or abandoned cars. Ladder No. 1, originally positioned at Marlborough, was to move down to Parkwood Apartments, but found itself hemmed in at Charing Cross Road. The fire sped down the hill faster than the ladder truck, which meant that the unit could not deploy to block the fire. The men had to veer away from the fire to save their equipment and their lives.[37]

As the situation in the center of the firestorm deteriorated, OFD assistant chief John Baker hoped that the eight lanes of Highway 24 would act as a firebreak and deny the fire the residential areas to the south of the expressway. Rockridge, Forest Park, and Piedmont lay in the lower slopes of the hills, and beyond them sprawled the heart of Oakland. In city fires, expressways do serve as natural firebreaks. Wildfires, by contrast, leap over wide stretches of road without taking a deep breath. But the incident commander simply did not have the forces at his disposal to guard against this eventuality. The callout of mutual aid had been too slow and catch up was a game that the diablo refused to play.[38]

Before the noon hour, a few Contra Costa units arrived at the top of the hillside and joined the OFD men aiding the evacuation. Fire suppression was out of the question. The safety of the firefighters and the civilians was paramount. Soon the entire force in the upper hill section was on the run or taking shelter in the few houses or swimming pools that offered refuge. Engine No. 19's lieutenant and a mixed group of OFD and Contra Costa firefighters retreated up the hill to the Gwin water tank and held off the flames there. OFD lieutenant Stephen Cuneo and firefighter John Dolan found Lynn Harrison trying to drive out of trouble on Buckingham. She didn't have a chance. The men yelled at her to jump into her pool. The three of them spent the next two hours in the water, periodically dousing the pool cover to prevent it from burning. The house was lost, along with every other one on the block, but Cuneo, Dolan, and Harrison survived.[39]

But some could not flee or find shelter. The fire caught them in the open. Two victims died not a block away from the heroic defense of 7140 Buckingham. Between 11:30 and noon, most of the other twenty-five fatalities occurred. Many were burned beyond recognition, so hot was the wall of fire by this time. The *Oakland Tribune* memorialized the anonymous victims each day of its magnificent coverage of the firestorm, adding identifications as they were made of the missing. Officer Grubensky died at the traffic jam on Charing

Cross, trying to help drivers and passengers extricate themselves from the wreck. Five civilians were found with him.[40]

With the firefighting units on the upper slopes falling back and mutual aid arriving piecemeal at the assembly grounds at the Broadway Street exit of Highway 24, nothing stopped the fire from moving whither the wind carried it. At noon, it leaped across Highway 24's wide expanse and landed next to Temescal Lake. A record leap— some 2,000 feet. The wind alone was not responsible for this feat. The heat of the fire had created a thermal convection column, a giant superhot horizontal wind tunnel. It raised the temperature of the ground fuel and the brush and trees ahead of the fire to near ignition point. Then the "tornado"-like winds became "flamethrowers" blasting houses and trees. But the wind was not blowing in a single narrow file; it swirled, and its whirling rotation carried fire across the entire face of the hills. It moved west into Grandview Canyon, south into Rockridge, and southeast toward Montclair. It was fanning out, spreading so swiftly and powerfully that it seemed everywhere.[41]

There are natural forces so overwhelming in their scope, so determined to have their way that no human action seems effective and no amount of resistance makes a difference. Great floods, hurricanes and tornadoes, earthquakes, volcanic eruptions, and tidal waves fit this description. They are the biggest killers among nature's predators. Fires in the city are horrific, but we feel they can be contained. This wildfire, let loose in the city, was testing the confidence and the competence of the East Bay area firefighting forces and the state's forestry firefighting teams.

At 12:29 PM, the OFD called the San Francisco Fire Department for aid. The call was expected. Residents of Berkeley and other cities on the bay, unable to reach their own fire departments, were calling the SFFD central alarm office for advice on whether to evacuate. In San Francisco itself, "hundreds of people gathered on rooftops to watch the vast smoke cloud rising above Oakland . . . ashfall in some places was in excess of three-quarters of an inch, in other places smoking pieces of paper and other burning debris fell in the streets." The diablo was blowing across the bay, and from all the way down the peninsula the rising smoke looked like a giant black thunderhead.[42]

San Francisco firefighters had noticed the ominous clouds piling up over the ridge. Lieutenant Gerry Trainor of the SFFD was in San Francisco at 10:00 in the morning. Driving back to Oakland, where he lived, he "saw a small amount of smoke in the Oakland Hills." Nothing to concern him—the OFD was overhauling the Saturday fire. He did what many other people in the Bay Area did—made himself comfortable at home watching the San Francisco 49ers game. But then, looking out the window, he saw something that did concern him: "All that black smoke . . . So I went to the garage and got my turnout coat and leather helmet and then jumped in my car" and headed where the smoke was thickest. SFFD chief Paul Tabacco's aide Leonard DeStefano was heading home, too, listening to the game on the radio. He remembered that from the backside of the ridge, "'I could see this cloud . . . and I thought to myself, Jesus, it must be awfully big.'" He arrived home and told a neighbor, "'I think I'll probably be going to this one.'" He was right.[43]

When the call for mutual aid did come, the largest city in the area had already started to mobilize its forces, calling up officers and off-duty shifts throughout the day. Oakland telephoned the SFFD alarm center to ask for a strike force. This military-sounding phrase is part of the ICS lexicon. It means a mixed contingent of companies. The SFFD's first two strike teams totaled ten engine companies. The total duty roster at that time in San Francisco was forty-one engines, eighteen trucks, and two rescue squads, along with a fireboat—a total of 296 uniformed officers and men. Fire Chief Frederick Postel immediately authorized the dispatch of the strike force. Before the day was out, the SFFD had sent five strike teams and over one-third of its entire force across the bay, some 144 officers and off-duty men, and over fifty on duty, as well as sixteen major pieces of equipment (including eleven fire engines), patrol buggies, vans, and even a motor coach.[44]

The first strike team, composed of five engine companies with Battalion Chief Jim Tracey in the lead, flew across the Bay Bridge, up the expressway to the Hills, and headed directly for the corner of Hiller and Tunnel Road—right into the maelstrom. Lieutenant Jim King of engine No. 29 was in the middle of it. On Broadway Terrace, the engine found itself wetting houses one step ahead of the fire, and then the fire jumped over them and it was time to scramble back. "The fire kept coming and we were losing water pressure . . . It grew dark because the smoke was so intense it blocked out the sun . . . I actually saw little balls of fire flying all around in the air." Engine No. 29 unhooked its supply lines from the now useless hydrants, folded its landlines and skedaddled, but not far. Along with the OFD crews, the SFFD men backed up facing the enemy and set a new line of defense. It went that way all afternoon and into the evening on the Rockridge–Forest Park flank of the fire. It was firefighting at its most dangerous and admirable.[45]

FOUR BATTLEGROUNDS

Strike team two of the SFFD, five engines, a hose tender (because hoses lost to fire put an engine out of commission), two battalion chiefs, and a division commander arrived at the marshaling ground on Highway 24 by 1:10 PM. Looming over the fire scene at the edge of Claremont Canyon was the magnificent four-story, wooden Claremont Hotel. From its terraces, facing west, the bay vista was breathtaking. Its gardens and grounds were world famous for their lush variety of vegetation. And it was a major fire risk. In fact, the hotel had already burned twice. Should the firestorm reach and consume it, its embers would set all Berkeley on fire. Residents on Vicente and Alvarado Roads, fronting the hotel, had already reported ash and sparks falling.

The Berkeley Fire Department recalled all its manpower and assigned an "all hands" to the hotel and the streets between it and Grandview Canyon. That is where SFFD strike team two joined the OFD's C division and the Berkeley force. Like the firefighters from New York City, Baltimore, Washington, D.C., and Philadelphia at the Jones Falls Canal in the turning point of the Great Fire of Baltimore, this line had to be held. It was a near thing. As one of the two SFFD chiefs at the hotel reported, nine hours later, "San Francisco Firefighters are in a very dangerous position behind [i.e., facing the fire] the Claremont."[46]

SFFD senior battalion chief Paul Tabacco climbed up Alvarado and saw the blaze coming at him like hell on wheels. Berkeley firefighters and OFD captain Parker were with him. They determined to evacuate everyone from the houses between Grandview and the hotel, as well as the guests at the Claremont, and slow the advance of the fire by attacking it frontally. Then they would fall back toward the hotel. In effect, this would create a suburban version of the wilderness backfire by denying the fire the fuel to advance. The CDF was higher up the canyon, plowing out a conventional firebreak with bulldozers. Communications between the two forces were haphazard, but both were working at a frantic pace.[47]

They were fighting an uphill battle, literally—pushing the lines up into Claremont Canyon along Alvarado. This is a steep slope, and climbing it even without humping landlines makes the calves ache and the heart race. The air temperature away from the flames was inching toward 90°F. Closer to the conflagration, the hot winds exceeded 100°F. The men could not use all their apparatus because the roads were increasingly blocked by falling power lines, but they did find functioning hydrants along Alvarado and hooked up to these as they moved farther up Claremont Canyon. By midafternoon they had run out 600 feet of hose.[48]

Residents and Berkeley students assembled to aid the undermanned fire department forces. UC Berkeley canceled its classes and shut its dorms, and students who ran or biked in the Oakland Hills along with those whose homes were threatened rushed to the fire scene to offer their aid. "Citizen volunteers," as they were called, had performed invaluable service helping firefighters during the earthquake and fire of 1989. These were mostly young and able men—Gary Strelow and Bill Lewis, for example—who were watching the San Francisco game when they saw television coverage of the fire nearby. When they arrived at the Claremont, they were assigned to fill out the engine companies.[49]

At first Chief Tabacco employed the volunteers as runners, carrying hose and couplings. The Oakland hydrants were not compatible with the SFFD hose couplings. (Based on the problems out-of-town fire companies had with the Baltimore hydrants in 1904, the National

Fire Protection Association adopted a "national standard of 2.5 inch width [threads] with 7.5 threads per inch." But twenty years after the fire, only 700 of the 8,000 cities in the United States had adopted the standard hydrants and fire hoses. Oakland was not one of them.)

Then Tabacco put the volunteers to work spraying the hotel's landscaping with its own water supply. Finally, the fittest of the volunteers joined in the attack on the fire itself. Matt Cord joined the fight at Vicente and Tunnel Road; for two hours his crew fought to save a home at a critical point on the defensive line. A single photograph among the dozens in the *Chronicle* account reveals that the regular companies allowed volunteers like Cord to control the nozzle of the fire hose. "The pipe" is almost always reserved to the senior men in an engine company. Letting the volunteers do this was both a compliment to the courage of the volunteers and a testimony to how exhausted the regular crews had become.[50]

Fremont Fire Department contingents from the Hiller Highlands–Tunnel Road command post (now abandoned in favor of the Highway 24 staging area) arrived at the Claremont, followed by an engine from Castro Valley, another from Hayward, and a Pleasanton rig. More units arrived from Berkeley and San Francisco. One of these carried the "Henry Gorter" nozzle, a piece of apparatus developed after the fire of 1906. It had a seven-inch opening and could throw streams very accurately a long way. Using the Gorter, the crews had some artillery of their own to battle the ordinance of the firestorm.[51]

At the rear of the hotel on Alvarado, the battle was now joined house to house. Seventy-mile-per-hour winds poured fire debris down the canyon, but the combined firefighting force saved most of the 600 block of Alvarado. In the midst of the combat, two of the volunteers, Nick Bamont and John Dove, saved the lives of two firefighters who fell through a burning porch. Each house saved was a victory; each house lost, a defeat that brought the fire closer to the Claremont. The eucalyptus trees were a fifth column within the firefighters' lines aiding the enemy, but they could not be felled without breaking the high-voltage lines supplying power to the water pumps. Had these been laid underground, the fight would have been easier.

In the meantime, the fire had climbed into trees, and they exploded. The fire jumped Alvarado, then was pushed back.

Chief Tabacco and his counterparts from "Hayward, Union City, San Leandro, Pleasanton, Freedom, Castro Valley, Novato, Berkeley, the CDF," and the volunteers, some 100 very tired, very determined men, refused to retreat farther. By 10:00 PM the fire had been denied the 700 and 800 blocks of Alvarado. By midnight, the fire was reduced to hot spots. Chief Tabacco was able to leave the field. With the wind abating and the cooling moisture-filled shore breeze arriving, the relief crews had only hot spots to put out.[52]

On the east flank, the fire was chewing up the high-voltage lines and poles that led back into Contra Costa County. The electricity powered the pumps that circulated water from the local reservoir through pipes that supplied the hydrants. Without working hydrants, the engine companies would be denied their most potent weapon in the battle. CDF helicopters with water buckets and Contra Costa fire teams reversed course and began fighting the new fires at Skyline Drive. Wildfires were developing all over the eastern slopes of the ridge, and they would not be brought under control until early evening. These fires diverted men and equipment from the East Bay fire at a crucial time—for the fire was swiftly moving into the residential developments west and south of Highway 24, and there were no firefighting units on the scene.[53]

Rockridge, the southern face of the battle, was just as important a front as the Claremont. Beyond it lay the city of Oakland. Its densely packed single-family homes shaded by old foliage was a perfect hostage to the fire. On Reata Place, at Chabot, just north of Highway 24, SFFD engine company No. 3's Joseph Cuff reported that "trees were blowing up and baseball sized embers" were landing on the wooden shingle roofs of the houses and setting them on fire. The hot wind was preparing the cedar and pine shingles for the burning brands, superheating the path in front of the fire. The company's lieutenant was blown off a roof but landed in the thick bushes. A dozen "college age kids" rushed to his aid, then ran up and down the hills carrying hose and other apparatus from the engine to the firefighters. When it was time to retreat, the volunteers were able to lead the firefighters to safety. The men were not relieved until 9:00 PM, most of them already dead on their feet.[54]

When SFFD strike team one arrived at Highway 24 and Broadway Street, Chief Tracey recalled, "[W]e were the only firefighting apparatus there . . . it was eerie." The heavy smoke obscured the sky. Redirected to Brookside Drive's intersection with tiny Eustace, the four engines and one hose tender positioned themselves around the college preparatory school. OFD and other SFFD units began to arrive. So did the fire. It set the median of the expressway on fire, burned through one old house on the corner in minutes, and threw embers into the air to join those already raining down.

Chief Tracey reckoned that the fire was "completely out of control" but did not order a retreat. In the tradition of all urban aggressive firefighters—a very different tradition from those who fight wildfires—he found working hydrants and fought to save buildings. But the fire dictated otherwise, and by 4:00 PM Tracey was staging his withdrawal. He told his command that "the safety aspects of the operation" outweighed the likelihood of gains from holding their ground. Still, it was a fighting retreat, down one residential street after another, preserving the integrity of the equipment.

By five in the afternoon the men were too fatigued to do more than stagger to the next hydrant and hook up. By seven that evening, more ominously, water pressure began to fail when a television news van ran over a supply hose. Then, just as the Rockridge battle seemed lost, the wind died away. By 9:00 PM, the scene was eerie once again, the smoke gradually dissipating and reinforcements moving into the burned area to put out hot spots. But who knew what the new day would bring?[55]

The southeastern front of the battle brought fire to the slopes of Montclair, due west of Caldecott Field. When police ordered the evacuation of the area, sometime around 1:30 PM, home owner Ed Yilek hid. As soon as the police had left, he unlimbered his garden hose and started to put out every burning ember that crossed Broadway Terrace and Pineneedle Drive. For ten hours he battled to keep the fire from crossing Broadway Terrace deeper into Montclair. Lieutenant Ted Aff of OFD's engine No. 4 arrived on the scene a few minutes after Yilek started his personal battle with the fire. Engine No. 4 had retreated down Skyline, expecting the fire to follow, and there was Yilek, hose in hand, rushing from side to side dousing fireballs as they fell. Mel Copeland, brother of a firefighter and fellow Pineneedle resident, joined Yilek, and other neighbors appeared as if by magic to lend a hand. Aff recalled, "[T]hey stretched hose, they tended line, they became additional members of my crew, they were tireless." Before the battle was over, three more OFD engine companies and other neighborhood citizen volunteers arrived. The fire never took hold in Montclair.[56]

Lieutenant Aff admitted that the firefighters' day "had been hell." He was not exaggerating. The heat away from the fire was over 90°F. Closer to it, the heat was now over 120°F. Inside the fire, Captain John Salse of the CDF estimated, the heat reached 2000°F. The Froehn wind blew steadily but did not cool. Instead, it was like a giant hair dryer. By early afternoon, it was a steady thirty- to forty-mile-per-hour force. Against this, and time, the firefighters had to haul the fully charged hand lines up the hills from the hydrants. Sometimes the slope was nearly 40°. Water-filled hose lines require two- and three-man teams. Even so, they are themselves hundreds of pounds of pulsating weight.[57]

The wind blew the underpowered spray back in the faces of the firefighters. The pumpers and squirters had their own water supply, and hose lines from them were shorter than from street hydrants, but the winding roads made it hard to get the big rigs close to the hillsides. Fighting in the open, the men did not use their air packs. Thus, they were gulping in huge amounts of toxic debris. Ash, smoke, and burning vegetable matter sucked in by the men's oxygen-hungry lungs stung and burned. Anxiety made all their hearts pump faster, and the firefighters had good reason to be anxious. They might face the worst nightmare of all—being trapped within the fire with no escape route. John Harrenhill, an Emeryville firefighter, overrun several times that day, remembered: "We had to abandon our hand lines and flee with several hundred feet of hose training behind us. As we were running for our own lives, I couldn't help but feel anger and helplessness in our inability to stop the fire spread."[58]

The most dramatic flight and survival story involved men from five engine companies of the OFD and five East Bay firefighters, along with one civilian volunteer who had stayed on Buckingham. They fought the blaze with a single landline until the hydrant was hit by a falling high-power line and the hose burned through. Unable to protect the civilians still on the street (the fire would not let them go down the hill), they herded everyone into a modern house with a sprinkler system. As the fire roared around them, the firefighters used every trick in the book and more to wet down the house. A backfire they set—standard wildfire fighting technique—burned up all the brush and grass at the rear of the house to prevent the fire from returning. Absolute discipline, superb training, and perfect cooperation among the professionals saved everyone's lives.[59]

In the meantime, the difficulties in communication continued. The ICS was not fully deployed until four in the afternoon. By then, there were fifteen command divisions, all of them mixed companies from various locales. Some units were in the field for nearly twelve hours. They lay down to grab a few minutes reprieve where they could. There was no organized effort to bring water to the firefighters, and dehydration among them further sapped their strength, though by midafternoon, Red Cross and Salvation Army volunteers were carrying food and drink to the firefighters they could find. On Alvarado Road, one home owner, grateful to the firefighters, was handing out Popsicles from a carton. Overheated and exhausted firefighter Charley Morrs greeted the orange ices as though they were manna from heaven.[60]

The end of the firefighters' ordeal came as suddenly as it began. When the wind suddenly died and moisture-laden currents from the bay surged in at ten in the evening, the advance of the fire halted. Mopping up continued well into the night, but the first-due crews could leave this to fresh forces. Firefighters who had spent twelve hours or more in the inferno were able to get some rest as fresh replacements arrived. Provisions were made for the morning, including bivouacs for a massive firefighting force at Alameda Air Force Base. The diablo did not return in the morning, allowing units with pumps, portable generators, and water tanks to reenter the vast burned area and overhaul hot spots. Still, some structures continued to smolder for the next two days.[61]

PARADISE LOST

Once proud owners of architectural marvels and treasured cottages mingled together with streams of refugees from rental property in fleeing all four fire-torn areas. They left not knowing the fate of their homes and apartments. Some refugees simply did not look back. Others stopped to watch their homes burn. Gone were some of the classic Bernard Maybeck pre–World War I homes, "a line of domestic architecture initially influenced by the indigenous buildings of the Bay Area: simple wood-framed and shingled houses half hidden by trees." Collections of Charles Eames tables and chairs, irreplaceable art work, and family heirlooms vanished in the ashes. Prized classic cars, expensive Mercedeses and Ferraris, along with family station wagons and vans melted where they stood.[62]

Some owners refused to go and fought with garden hoses until the last minute. Yilek was one. Martin Davis of Fairlane Drive, at the very top of the Hills, also stayed put as the fire moved away from his home. He was a home contractor and "should have known better," but his dander was up. As swirls of wind brought back embers, he hosed them down. When his house was out of danger, he started watering his neighbors' roofs and gardens. In all, he saved four homes on his street. Paul Stauduhar was not so lucky. He stood on his roof with two garden hoses until nearly overcome with smoke. "Covered with soot," he stopped long enough to give an interview to an *Oakland Tribune* reporter before both joined the more than 5,000 men, women and children who had to leave.[63]

The exiles were all stunned with the enormity of the events, but their reactions varied. One young man called his mother after his narrow escape and joked, "'You always said the house was too cluttered.'" His mother's reply was not recorded. Screenplay writer and critic Jeremy Larner was philosophical. He recalled: "[A]fter a moment, the terror drains from my body, and I see the immense devastation has a kind of wild, transcendent beauty." Most of his fellow refugees found neither gallows humor nor serenity in the scenes of devastation. Francis Rome remembered "a couple in their 40s standing clutching each other on the fringe of the crowd . . . the flames licked and raced at some houses not yet on fire . . . suddenly the couple both yelled out 'oh God, that's our house' . . . the woman was wailing now, and tears drenched the man's face." The onlookers had all lost something special, and understood the couple's grief. "We joined in . . . and it became a dirge . . . a chorus of 'we're sorry, so very very sorry.'" Dorothy Lage cried for her lost home of forty years and remarked to a reporter, "'My husband passed away last year. It's good he did not live to see this.'" The evacuation area exceeded the burned district, but even those who left before the flames reached their houses were wracked with worry.[64]

The police kept thrill seekers out of the area, though some tried to break the police lines to see the fire. Reporters were another story entirely. Determined to get the best stories firsthand, and perhaps scoop one another, the *Oakland Tribune*, the *San Francisco Chronicle,* and the *San Francisco Examiner* emptied their newsrooms and flooded the hills with reporters and photographers. H. L. Mencken would have been proud of the coverage and the aggressiveness of the reporting. Two dozen staff, news, feature, and editorial writers got bylines.

Local television stations sent crews to the edge of the fire as well. After his narrow escape at the top of the hill, Roth kept on following the fire until it was time to file his report, about 5:00 PM. After a stop at the emergency room for a checkup and some oxygen, he went to the television studio and gave his on-camera report.

Eddie Ledesman, a freelance photographer covering the fire for the *San Francisco Chronicle*, arrived at Tunnel Road around noon, just in time to see cars exploding. One minute he was shooting pictures in the middle of a crowd of spectators; the next he was all alone, his fellow onlookers having fled. In the great tradition of disaster photojournalism, he had gotten as close to the story as he could, but "'I thought I'd pushed my luck too far this time,'" he recalled later.

Matt Lee, a photographer for the *Oakland Tribune*, was assigned to the 49ers game, but he saw the smoke and drove toward it. On Chabot Road, just above Highway 24, he ran right into the ashfall. With only a scarf to cover his mouth and garden-hose water to wet himself down, "'I got some pictures, but that was as scared as I'd ever been.'"

Tony Russomanno, a television reporter, was better prepared: "'I learned a long time ago to carry fire gear with me in my car.'" He was a veteran of the region's wildfires, but he "'got worried . . . when the fire crews started scurrying around, looking for small depressions in the ground . . . I knew from covering forest fires that these holes were the places you dive into when it's getting really bad.'"[65]

IN THE END, twenty-five people died, another 150 were seriously injured, and 2,843 homes were totally destroyed. Perhaps as many as 30,000 people evacuated their homes and businesses for at least part of the day. The fire perimeter stretched over 5.25 miles, and the damage was estimated at slightly over $1.5 billion (in 2005 terms, $2.14 billion). One visitor to the area a week later, Lloyd Calder, described the ruins as reminiscent of pictures of Hiroshima. The forlorn hillside landscape of bare chimneys and foundation stones was still hot, and those who walked the winding streets felt the heat through the soles of their footware. But by that time, recovery had already begun.[66]

The fire had "played no favorites." Indeed, the higher up the hillside the home, the greater the loss. City councilwoman Marge Haskell, state senator Nick Petris, television personality Betty Ann Bruno, and former Oakland Athletics outfielder Reggie Jackson lost their homes. The human infrastructure of the Bay Area—city and state officials, harbor and transportation regulators, and fire and police officers—took part in the firefighting and rescue operations knowing they might have no home waiting for them at the end of the day.[67]

The "Quality of Life"

How do we measure the quality of life? On a lovely spring morning in the Oakland Hills, over a decade after the firestorm, the scars of the holocaust are barely visible. The power lines are underground. The hydrants have all been retrofitted with standard 2 1/2-inch couplings. The houses are even more lovely than before, and certainly more pricey. If one knows the history of the Hills, one can see that the old timbered and wood-shake structures have been replaced by concrete and tile; there is a little more room between houses, and most have indoor and outdoor sprinklers. The roads still wind and twist, and the vista is just as spectacular.

That spring day, a single stalled moving truck, unable to navigate a steep driveway on Tunnel Road, blocked one visitor's vehicle for nearly a half hour. What would have happened if others had needed the road to evacuate from a wildfire? That day, hikers paused to admire the view from the top of Buckingham. A single carelessly tossed cigarette butt, in the right circumstances, might have started a deadly blaze. Conditions before the 1991 firestorm were unusual—five years of drought; a harsh winter with resulting buildup of highly flammable eucalyptus bark and pine needles; a wildfire still smoldering under the ground; and then the arrival of the diablo—a set of unfavorable but not unlikely contingencies. The conditions for a catastrophic fire remain.[68]

COMING TO GRIPS WITH LOSS

Unlike the fires in Detroit, the Oakland Hills inferno destroyed some of the most desirable property in the state of California. The victims were not the poor people of the Oakland ghetto a few miles down the hill, but the advantaged in their lofty dwellings. But their grief, different from that of the downtrodden in Detroit, was still real, expressing itself in longing for treasured heirlooms and expensive material possessions. Grief-counseling professionals arrived on the scene soon after the holocaust. Psychologist Richard Feinberg warned that "[a] person's home is a very personal part of themselves. Right now people are in shock and having trouble accepting the reality that a part of them has been lost."[69]

Returning to their former home was the hardest part for many victims. Clara Oliveras sneaked back into the burned-over streets of her old neighborhood and was overcome by memories. D. A. Simpson convinced the policeman escorting her to let her stand awhile and look at the ruins of her house. There were no landmarks, but she knew where it had been because the number painted on the curb was still readable. Jeremy Larner came back two days later and was astounded that Alvarado looked unscathed. Then, "I turn a corner and hit the vast black slopes." A "silvery white ash" covered the spot where he had lived. "Steel skeletons" of cars hung "upside down" in ditches. Further down the block, a couple stared at the rubble of their former home. "'You never expect this to happen to you,'" the young wife and mother blurted. "'You read about other people in the news, but it's never you.'"[70]

Arriving in small groups at burned-over lots, wandering or simply standing and staring, people turned physical remainders into reminders of past days. Gerald Frank and Joan Tanzer "sifted through ashes and shards of pottery." The fired clay had survived the holocaust. Not so their house. Governor Pete Wilson, touring the area, remarked that the chimneys, standing alone, looked like "tombstones." Others gaped at the blackened street signs that were once familiar markings of their coming and going.[71]

Writing poetry seemed to help some victims adjust to their loss. The themes in this therapeutic literary exercise were encapsulated in Michael Shorb's lines—"charred beams and singed stone / Bramble of burned and half-burned / things that remained. . . ." A longing, a sense of loss, the desire—the need—to remember, or be able to remember. It is sentimental and highly personal poetry, and often it compared the loss of the physical things to the absence of a loved one or the end of a relationship. The lines, rarely more than two or three stanzas, cannot fully convey the enormity of the events, but they do reveal the strength of the authors' feelings. Nina Levil: "Out of control / Out of my hands / Lost in fear. . . ."[72]

Schools in Oakland closed the day after the fire, but when they reopened, teachers encouraged students to write short essays (for extra credit) about their fire experiences. The teenagers remembered larger issues—the displacement and the sadness of their parents, for example. Younger children retained more intimate details—a missing pet or the size of the firefighters. "We got in the car"; "It was very dark." Even older children had no sense of the scope of the fire. Their fire, like their world, was confined to a house, a block, a street, a family. For many, like Ali Lawrence, "it's all a blur now."[73]

Pets were just as important to their adult owners. Dogs were terrified by the fire and sometimes refused to leave a car, a house, or a garage. Some dogs fled over the mountain or down the bay shore and were found by Contra Costa and other county animal rescue crews. Cats were more adaptive, hiding from the flames in ditches, culverts, and other safe places and then returning to the rubble of their former homes. Owners found them sitting on what remained of stoops and porches, waiting. Alameda animal control had patrols searching for house pets, and animal shelters were overflowing with over 400 frightened dogs and cats. Owners reunited with their pets were overcome with emotion, as were some of the pets. An Oakland pet hotline was helping owners and pets find one another.[74]

A new species of survivor syndrome appeared—guilt because one's house was saved or survived unscathed. No one could explain why some houses remained untouched on streets totally burned out. One stucco house on a street in Montclair "looked like a spaceship on the face of the moon." The owner experienced a new kind of anxiety: "'When you're inside with the curtains shut, it's like life as usual. But you step outside and there's this,' he said, pointing to gutted house after house." Tom Haw of Montclair "said he considered himself blessed to still have a home, 'but when I came round the bend this morning I felt so guilty.'" Who would help the old people on the block "'who don't have money to build again?'" Susan Ito recalled a neighbor whose house had miraculously escaped damage. Unwilling to reveal her good fortune to her neighbors, she pretended that it was a total loss. She joined in community activities with a kind of manic fervor: "[T]he lie [that she was homeless too] had been completely absorbed by then. She believed that she had lost her home." Alan Rinzler's home on Alvarado was one of those saved. "'I'm having survivor's guilt,'" he told a reporter, "'all of our friends lost their houses.'"[75]

As complacent as the Hill home owners had been before the conflagration, they now were as easily panicked. There was fear of smoke inhalation (well founded), fear of cancer from the flame retardant the CDF tankers dropped (unfounded); fear of staying and fear of leaving. Everyone was afraid that fall rains, so long delayed, would bring catastrophic mud slides. Heavy rains were forecast for the weekend. The city promised aid. We want "the dirt to stay put," the city manager's office announced. But experts were worried. According to the director of the National Landslide Information Center, after serious fires in Southern California, mud slides carried off entire hill exposures. The Geological Survey chipped in that the East Bay area was prone to landslides. Fortunately, the rains were light and the city acted quickly. Volunteers, the California Conservation Corps, and U.S. Coast Guard troops based in the port of Oakland erected mesh fences, placed sandbags, and used hydro-seeding to restart grasses.[76]

The same degree and spirit of cooperation was not extended to the leadership of the OFD. In the wake of the fire, the news media roasted the OFD for its lack of preparedness, its tactics on Saturday, and its lack of leadership early on Sunday. Although most reports lauded the firefighters' courage, some home owners were upset that the Saturday fire was not thoroughly suppressed and the Sunday fire not properly addressed. The complaints began the day after the fire and competed for space in the newspapers with stories of loss, heroism, and hope. Should not firefighters have been stationed on the hillside during the night to overhaul hot spots before the sun, and the wind, came out? The terrain was steep and there was some danger letting city firefighters work there at night, OFD assistant chief Andy Stark retorted, joined by city fire chief P. Lamont Ewell: "[T]here was nothing that firefighters could do . . . even if we had 20 units on the scene." Oakland's mayor, Elihu Harris, agreed that only "Monday morning quarterbacking" could second-guess the OFD's conduct.[77]

Speaking only for themselves (and not casting explicit blame), other fire department officials such as the Park Service's Tom Hutchinson, stationed in Los Angeles, suggested, "[M]y personal policy anytime there is a fire, whether it's 20 acres or a quarter of an acre, is we will go through and [overhaul] up to the point that there is no smoke showing for a six hour period of time." San Jose's fire chief, Robert Osby, was also guarded in his criticism, but he had seen plenty of these fires and he knew how easily they "rekindled." In an unguarded moment, even the East Bay Regional Park District conceded, "'[W]e would leave people there [overnight] sitting on it.'" Jeff Hawkins at the CDF was also cautious, but he confessed that he did not understand why the full resources of his agency were not called upon until midway through the afternoon. In fact, the most outspoken of the critics of the OFD were the CDF air tanker pilots. They were certain that their 800-gallon tanks of fire retardant would have slowed or stopped the advance of the fire, had OFD not "dithered" about asking for help.[78]

The real culprit was the budget cuts—a loss of nearly one-third of its manpower and equipment over the period from the early 1970s to 1991—but in the wake of the firestorm, Oakland fire department chief P. Lamont Ewell faced a firestorm of criticism. Although he was a veteran firefighter, he did not arrive on the scene until 11:45 AM, a half hour after the fire had leaped the bounds of the original blaze and had his department on the run, and a full hour and a half after his assistant chief and his senior battalion commander had called in multiple alarms. It is not only traditional for a chief of service to go to major fires, particularly those endangering his crews, but in this case it was mandatory that someone who could speak for the entire OFD be on hand to coordinate the mutual aid request. That morning Ewell was giving out awards at a Special Olympics ceremony in Alameda, a city adjoining Oakland. This was a children's event—a political gesture of the sort that politicians enjoy. In fact, he would later go on to a career in politics as city manager in Oakland, then on to Durham, North Carolina, and eventually to San Diego.[79]

But surely, had he lifted his eyes for a moment to scan the ridgeline to the east, he would have seen the smoke billowing, and just as surely he could have checked in with his department to learn that the blaze was out of control. People across the bay, from San Francisco all the way down to San Jose, could see the smoke rising. Even after his belated appearance at the Highway 24 command post, Ewell did not authorize calls for mutual aid until the fire had broken out all over the hillside. The "good chief," according to former FDNY deputy chief Vincent Dunn, takes a leadership role in every fire scene, gaining information by direct inspection, working closely with subordinates at the scene, and in general letting everyone know that he is there and in command. Lamont's claims that criticism of him was in reality criticism of his men was misplaced (no one was criticizing their performance or their courage), and his contention that criticism of him was lowering morale in the OFD was a clumsy effort to deflect attention.[80]

His subsequent hints that the fire was "intentionally set" by arsonists (whose identity he knew but could not reveal) was laughable. Despite police and fire marshal investigations on a grand scale, no connection between construction workers burning trash on Saturday and the Sunday fire was found. He issued his final word on the "lessons of the firestorm" three months later in the *News*, the mouthpiece for Oakland city employees: "My goal is to get more proactive in preventing fires. Public education is the key," as if people in the hills were not already aware of the danger of fires. In addition, he wanted "more off the street parking" in the hills, as if owners, developers, and realtors were going to set aside valuable land for parking lots.[81]

NEVER AGAIN?

In 1992, FEMA and the U.S. Fire Administration made their own assessment of the OFD's conduct. It absolved the chief and his officers of negligence: "The most significant factor that should be recognized from this incident is that the fire was beyond the capability of fire suppression forces to control." It was a wildfire in a city, not a city fire. "The spread of the fire during the first hour is virtually unprecedented for an urban conflagration, including wildland-urban interface fires." Mistakes were made, but these became fatal because the fire moved so quickly and unpredictably on so many fronts. The 911 center, understaffed, had trouble going back and forth between telephone calls (with residents) and radio transmissions (to units in the field). In addition, some dispatchers were ill-trained to deal with CDF and other units' requests for information. In particular OFD commanders in the field asked for air drops of fire retardants as early as 10:49 AM, but a series of mistakes delayed the tankers' arrival until early afternoon. Better communications, particularly between different departments, between the OFD and the CDF, and between commanders and their crews would have prevented injuries, particularly injuries to over 150 firefighters, but would not have extinguished the fire.[82]

As postmortem of the events of October 20, 1991, this assessment was more or less fair; as a comment on the arrogance of putting expensive homes on the edge of natural fire courses, it was totally inadequate. For the Oakland Hills fire was a warning bell that was going unheeded. More and more cities extended their outer edges into areas prone to burn. When people, drawn to scenes of natural beauty or wildness, build houses, towns, and streets along natural wildfire courses, they put themselves in fire's path. The Oakland Hills' ecology included periodic fire episodes. The well-to-do red-zone migrant may carry with him the urban home owner's zero tolerance for fire, but there is no way to prevent fire in a place like Oakland Hills.[83]

The historian also knows that more than professional tactics, training, and ability was at stake in these controversies. Harris and Ewell, like much of the city administration, were African-American. The vast majority of the Hill residents and many of the reporters were white. Ewell was disturbed that his department was "already beset by charges of racism and reverse discrimination." Every California city politician held race cards in his hands, and in Oakland, they had long been laid open on the table. The vigor with which the mayor and the chief defended themselves hints that they may have seen a racial undertone to the criticism. Even the complaint that Ewell was favoring his own race in appointing officers was already a familiar one in urban fire departments with black mayors and black fire department heads. White Detroit firefighters had already lost their federal suit against their own department.[84]

Politics aside, the displaced of the Hills needed to get on with their lives. Living in rental quarters, with friends, or in hotels, they wanted to begin the rebuilding process. The city pledged to help. City Manager Henry Gardner promised. "[W]e will absolutely cut through the red tape." The city was moving quickly to restore water and electricity to the area. Governor Wilson promised that real estate taxes on new homes would not be excessive. In the meantime, real estate agents were doing a land-office business in rental properties. "Profiteering" had begun. Oakland could help with that, too—at least to a point. Mayor Harris warned landlords not to gouge dispossessed home owners and the city council passed an ordinance placing a ninety-day moratorium on raising rent for single-family homes. The moratorium exempted apartment buildings and complexes, making clear that the intended beneficiaries of the ordinance were not the poor people of Oakland.[85]

Builders were champing at the bit. For them and their subcontractors, the firestorm was a huge opportunity. General contractor Edward J. Levitch of Berkeley promised that homes could be completed within months—as soon as the building permits were issued.

He had built houses in the hills after the 1970 fire—some of them no doubt lost this time. But the newspapers advised caution in choosing a general contractor: "Choosing that person is arguably the most important decision you will make during the entire building process." Custom builders offered their own advice: Shop around, listen carefully, don't always take the low bid, examine the sample materials yourself, and don't spend more than you can afford. "Be prepared to spend a year" before commissioning a contractor. "Consumer advocates" suggested hiring an architect. In the meantime, the fire would "boost the Eastbay economy," pouring insurance money into the construction industry.[86]

INSURANCE WARS

The home owners expected their insurance to pay the cost of rebuilding. Fire coverage is a standard item in every home-owner policy, often covering interim expenses like rental housing. But many in the Hills were underinsured, particularly for their possessions. But then, everyone who owns a home is underinsured for fire damage to personal goods. The simple fact is that we own more than we realize and we rarely keep the fire insurance up to date. The rule of thumb was that insurance for chattels should equal 30 percent of insurance to rebuild or 70 percent of the face value of the policy. In fact, the insured were likely to collect about 50 percent of the face value for furnishings and other valuables, unless their worth was documented.

Worse, the homes were insured for replacement value, but this did not include the actual costs of building, in particular bringing the new home up to modern electrical, plumbing, and construction codes. A "guaranteed cost replacement" policy was extra, and even then, home owners would find that it might not include code updates. For the renter who did not have a rental policy covering personal belongings, and for the owner without comprehensive coverage, the loss was uncompensated.[87]

Hills home insurers put advertisements in all the local papers promising quick settlement of claims. The "catastrophe squad" of

"Fireman's Fund is Mobilized to Help in the East Bay." Don't worry, the message explained, "Fireman's Fund has a long history of helping people recover from disasters such as the East Bay fire. Rest assured, we'll help you get back on your feet as soon as possible." On the next page, "A Special Message to State Farm Policyholders" announced the arrival of "special units to process your fire related claims." State Farm was California's largest home insurer and had offices in the East Bay Hills. Safeco's hotline and "a team of adjusters" set up headquarters in the fire area.[88]

The key word in the advertisements might slip by an unwary eye. Insurance agents sell policies. An insurance "adjuster's" job is not just to authorize payment on the policy but to determine what payment is due a policyholder. The U.S. Department of Labor's *Occupational Outlook Handbook* spells out the adjuster's duties: "[T]heir main role is to investigate the claims, negotiate settlements, and authorize payments to claimants . . . They must determine whether the customer's insurance policy covers the loss and how much of the loss should be paid to the claimant." They inspect the site, gather information, including written and other forms of evidence, consult with others than the policyholder (for example, construction experts), and then "evaluate" a claim. The discretion they have is not uncurbed—both federal and state law prescribe boundaries—and "when claims are contested, adjusters will work with attorneys and expert witnesses to defend the insurer's position." In other words—they do not work for the policyholder. They work for the insurer. As soon as the policyholder notifies the agent of loss or damage, the agent "assigns it" to an adjuster. Agents live in the locality where they sell policies. Adjusters arriving from out of town were soon vying with displaced East Bay Hills renters and home owners for hotel space.[89]

Adjusters in California had to live with Proposition 103. Passed as a referendum in 1988, the reform turned the state insurance commissioner into an elective office and replaced the open system by which insurers sold policies and set rates "without prior approval or subsequent approval" with a regulated system. Those changes meant that as of 1988, rates had to be preapproved. The new regulations also affected fire insurance for dwellings. John Garamendi was the first of the elected commissioners. He served until 1994. To his office came complaints about insurers' alleged misconduct, refusal to pay, harassment of policyholders, and similar concerns. The insurers opposed the new system, in part because it guaranteed complainers access to the commissioner, though the reasons publicly given were red tape and "associated costs." The commissioner heard almost immediately from the Hills owners on his hotline.[90]

A disaster like the East Bay Hills fire could break an insurer, costing it, and its investors, hundreds of millions of dollars. Adjusted to 1991 dollar values, the East Bay Hills blaze insurance bill rivaled the Chicago Fire of 1871. That made the Oakland disaster the worst to date in modern urban history. Rightly, the insurers anticipated a flood of claims. On top of that, they still had to finish paying off claims arising from the 1989 earthquake. Finally, Proposition 103 had imposed rollbacks on auto insurance rates backdated to 1988. The insurers were already singing the empty pockets blues.[91]

With owners looking over the fine print on their policies or calling their agents to get a copy and consumer protection groups warning against settling for too little, insurance company adjusters had their hands full. Safeco had insured one-tenth of the home owners, and one of its thirty or so "contents" specialists, Michael Calder, spent six weeks hearing and examining claims. He began paying out interim awards. By this time, he recalled, evidence of construction firms gouging the owners (and the insurance companies) was pouring in. Henceforth, his company would urge its policyholders to expect to pay two and three times as much as the current assessed value of their homes to cover replacement costs. He recalled that a second innovation grew out of the media coverage of the fire. No firm wanted its insured telling the media that the company was holding out. So firms raced one another to satisfy claims. This required broad and generous initial estimates of the value of the contents of the homes, instead of going through detailed inventories with each owner and insisting on evidence of the value of each loss. Calder found himself writing $10,000 checks out of hand for his company's insured just to keep them happy until the claim was finalized.[92]

By October 14, 1993, according to figures presented to the California State Senate Committee on Insurance, 1,927 claims for total losses and 387 rental claims had been processed, 78 percent of the total claims had been paid, some $1.359 million of $1.733 million. But this was far short of the total—and a sign of many unhappy policyholders. They went to Commissioner Garamendi and he reported to Senator Art Torres that some insurance companies had "engaged in outrageous and despicable practices which brought the full weight of [Garamendi's] department on them." Allstate had to pay over $1 million in penalties for its misconduct.

Garamendi's department counseled angry policyholders, speeded payments, and otherwise mediated disputes, but the real problem was "lack of adequate insurance coverage." It was simply below the cost of actual replacement. He used the Senate hearings to urge companies to sell policies reflecting reality—but he also scolded them: "[C]ompanies must handle claims as though the scrutiny of the whole world is upon them. And it is." Or at least so it must have seemed, for "policy holders [in the Hills] had strength of numbers" and were organized.[93]

They had to be, according to Peter Dempsey, one of the victims of the fire and insurance companies' foot-dragging. The Department of Insurance was "a toothless dog." Even Allstate had not altered its approach to its customers. Other double victims testified before the committee that the insurers practiced "low ball," delay, and harassing tactics. For example, they refused to pay for steps, porches, and decks because these were not part of the house. State Farm, according to Jim Serais, would not accept the actual costs of bringing a home up to code, even though the "firestorm people" could not rebuild at all without code clearance. State Farm even harassed the builders. Above all, according to one witness, State Farm was the master of the "broken promise." The adjuster would agree to pay for an item, but the paperwork would not reflect that agreement. Robert Bruce accused TransAmerica of refusing to process paperwork in a timely manner, and Brenda Reed denounced Safeco for refusing to pay when one contractor refused to finish the work and another had to step in.[94]

Most of the insurers simply wrote letters explaining their practices, but Clark Holland, representing State Farm, told the committee, "State Farm remains proud of the effort it has made in the claim handling." No doubt, with so many claims of such complexity and scope, State Farm had exerted itself to the utmost. It paid an "average of $770,000 for its 470 claims of total loss," coming to $360 million. Holland denied that his adjusters harassed policyholders, and of 1,100 statements, only three were so suspect that they had to be taken under oath.[95]

Holland's defense of his company to the contrary notwithstanding, the experience of adversarial tactics of their own insurers was foreign to the victims. They bridled at being called liars. Taking statements under oath, in a quasi-legal proceeding, was a violation of California law, as Senator Torres reminded Holland. Torres went on to lecture Holland about the law. A lawyer and consumer advocate as well as a leader in the state Democratic Party, Torres would run for insurance commissioner the next year and was building up a record to support that campaign. He could not have found a more inviting target.[96]

THE "QUALITY OF LIFE"

While Mayor Harris was engaged in political damage control, and Hills landowners were looking up the telephone numbers of contractors and architects, and negotiating with the insurance adjusters, City Manager Henry Gardner, staring at the $250,000 cost of the city's firefighting effort, was thinking about the next fire. This one had not only damaged private property, it wrecked infrastructure. On November 5, 1991, Gardner published an update on the cleanup. Owners could view their property with a police escort. No building contractors, and no spectators were allowed in the burned area. Because President George H.W. Bush had declared the East Bay Hills a disaster area, FEMA had agreed to help, although its funds were limited.

On November 12, 1991, Gardner issued the second of his reports. He wanted the removal of all abandoned cars, timelines for building permits, and a one-stop permit center. Two weeks later, he circulated formal "Policy Specifications for the Rebuilding of the Fire Damaged Oakland Hills." It would have mandated fire-resistant roofs and siding, vegetation management for homes and open spaces, more fire hydrants, wider streets, and sprinklers in and out of all structures had it remained in place.[97]

Why such stringency? Perhaps Gardner had taken notice of David Brower's op-ed piece on October 27, 1991, in the *Examiner*. Brower was a child when the 1923 firestorm threatened to level Berkeley. As an old man, he got to see a straight replay. His observations were chilling. The diablo wind would blow again. There would be another drought. In a series of predictions, he said another fire "will start somehow." Many sites will be largely inaccessible to the firefighting equipment. The lovely trees will turn traitor and bear the fire on their shoulders. Water will be insufficient. And many will suffer. But Brower admitted also, "I am a hypocrite." His house in the Berkeley Hills, constructed after World War II, was a firetrap— lovely wood, lovely heavy vegetation, shaded by overhanging trees, filled with cartons and books, and "we had better take our own advice."[98]

Or perhaps Gardner was aware of a remarkable fact—as hot and as furiously fast as it was, the fire left in its wake unscathed the Hillcrest Elementary School on Marguerite Drive in Rockridge, and the Kaiser Elementary School on South Hill Court, just off Hiller Drive. All around them, homes were little more than piles of debris and collapsed walls and roofs. Why had the schools survived? They were built of brick and concrete, with fireproofing outside and inside. They were surrounded by open playgrounds and parking, clear of vegetation. The schools survived because their planners and builders did not want the children inside them endangered by fire. They were fireproofed.[99]

But the Hill dwellers wanted their wood-shake roofs, so rural and restful, and they wanted their eucalyptus, so familiar and comforting, and they wanted their redwood decks, without which one could not enjoy the "three bridge view" of the bay. No matter if the trees and shingles were "giant matchsticks" and the decks conveyed fire from one level of the hill to the next. Firefighters might report the dangers, but the timber lobby and the owners' voices were all the louder for the murmured warnings. The Cedar Shake and Shingle Bureau, based in Bellevue, Washington, was willing to make a concession—the company would be happy to sell fireproofed materials (at a slightly higher cost). They would even back legislation making the more expensive shingles mandatory. Even the Canadians got into the act—for they were the manufacturers of the red cedar shakes that had, until recently, graced many of the hillside residences that did not have the Washington State brand. The Sierra Club was equally worried about a plan to cut down thousands of eucalyptus trees.[100]

Gardner was no match for the cacophony of petitions, demands, and pleas. The city caved in to the demands for the unique "quality of life" in the Hills. In a January 14, 1992, memo to the city council entitled, "Amendments to Emergency Order," Gardner, like Mayor McLane and his reformers in Baltimore, dropped plans for widening all of the streets in the "fire hazard area." Only emergency routes needed to be two-lane, and this meant widening only Charing Cross, Strathmoor, and Drury. Roofs were to be fireproofed, but they could be wooden. The "aesthetic appearance" and "aesthetic roof lines" that architects and their clients wanted had prevailed.

And then there was the matter of the redwood decks. "There is no question . . . that an encroaching fire to a property will seek out a redwood deck as a combustible fuel." Still, Gardner surrendered. "The redwood deck is a staple commodity for hill dwellers seeking view enjoyment, a countrylike environment, and functional living space." How the deck improved the view or gave the main structure a countrylike environment was unclear to Gardner. The view was the same with or without the deck (though an obtrusive deck might actually obscure a neighbor's viewing), and few truly country cottages had redwood decks.

The real reason for making this concession was that the "hill dwellers" had organized into a variety of associations and all of them were used to getting what they wanted. "Prohibiting redwood decks for fire safety reasons would substantially diminish the quality of life for those residents and would not be in parity with all of the other non-fire damaged homes . . . in the area." In other words, why should people who were lucky enough to escape fire damage be allowed to keep their redwood decks when homes lost to fire could not be rebuilt with decks.[101]

A task force of community leaders approved Gardner's concession. Mayor Harris and Berkeley mayor Lani Hancock chaired the "Task Force on Emergency Preparedness and Community Restoration." The task force made clear what had to be inferred from Gardner's memo: In all planning, "homeowner assistance, suggestions, and proposals should be considered." Presumably considering those proposals already received, the task force urged minimal tree removal (to prevent erosion), regular clearing of brush but no targeting of particular species, including the eucalyptus and the Monterey pine. "Regular maintenance" would do—whatever in the world that meant. A "special fire assessment district," presumably coincident with the Hills, would monitor fire dangers—though that is exactly what the CDF and the U.S. Park Service already did and the OFD ignored. The task force also recommended sprinklers (hardly a new idea) and "encouraged" community planning and guidelines. (Whenever a task force calls for guidelines, it has already rejected guidelines.) The task force did order very practical reforms, but the OFD was already implementing these: retrofitting the hydrants to the national standard 2 1/2-inch diameter receptacles, adding backup generators for the water pumps, and upgrading radio and other communications equipment. But an incident command center was too "expensive," they said, and all other reforms in the future would have to take into account the lack of funding.[102]

The "Whatever-Lola-Wants-Lola-Gets" theme of Oakland's bow to the taxpayers and voters in the Hills had a lovely coda. On April 11, 1994, the city's municipal services center sent "Dear Property Owner" letters to its ratepayers. The city was installing new street lighting. "Property owners in the firestorm area have expressed a desire for decorative or ornamental fixtures." They got what they wanted.

The North Hills Phoenix Association continues to monitor the Hills—as its mission statement explains: "[T]he North Hills Phoenix

Association is a non-profit organization of home owners in the area
(north of highway 24 and east of highway 13. An area with about
1500 homes) some of which are represented by smaller neighborhood groups. The association was created after the 1991 Oakland
Hills fire in order to help residents rebuild and to insure that fire
safety would serve as a guiding principle in rebuilding." One would
think that would mean voluntary compliance with the strong version
of City Manager Gardner's emergency plan, but the association was
also a lobby. It represented the home owners at "city hall" and in
Sacramento and Washington in the effort to pave streets, put utilities
underground, and manage vegetation. What the association wanted
was improvement of city services, including regularly scheduled collection of "yard waste." In the meantime, those home owners in the
Wildfire Prevention Assessment District would be allowed to put out
"unlimited yard trimmings."[103]

IN THE YEARS AFTER the firestorm, The North Hills Phoenix Association pleaded with locals to join them in preventing a recurrence
of the 1991 holocaust. In particular, the high-power lines that still ran
along the streets had to go. But historical memory is the preserve of
the victims, and as they moved away, their precious store of wisdom
departed. Newcomers to the Hills built bigger houses, some resembling fortresses with towers and forbidding concrete turrets. Other
homes were three and four stories, little villas of stucco, or steel and
glass. The residents, proud of their gardens and greenery, are even re-
planting the exotics along their steps, terraces, and porches.

Oakland Hills is once again an upscale residential community,
with wider streets and a better water supply. But the basic ecological
lesson remains unlearned. Lovely multistory mansions near the top
of the ridgeline are surrounded by trees. There is too little defensive
space around the homes. Despite the Oakland Wildfire Prevention
Assessment District ten-year plans to clear brush, the Oakland Hills
will never be truly safe from fire.[104]

LOWER MANHATTAN, 2001

Everyone who has ever visited the East Bay Hills has come away delighted with the view. Looking up, the hills invite. Looking down, the vista of San Francisco Bay excites. Not so the towers of the World Trade Center. You loved them or you hated them. Still, the twin pillars could not be ignored. From whichever direction you came, the "Twin Towers" (technically World Trade Center One and Two) thrust themselves into your view. Rising from the Austin Tobin Plaza, dwarfing the other office buildings of the WTC and the Marriott Hotel, 110 stories above the ground (some 1,368 and 1,362 feet, not counting the 330 feet of the communications antenna on top of the North Tower), the two towers had achieved landmark status from the moment of their completion in 1973. King Kong and millions of tourists visited them. As Pulitzer Prize–winning architecture critic Paul Goldberger, no friend to the towers, wrote, "[T]he towers . . . appear almost everywhere that an iconic view of the skyline was called for—covers of the *New Yorker*, television commercials, travel posters, and little souvenir replicas."[1]

In purely material terms, the towers regenerated Lower Manhattan and symbolized the "noble, grand, and majestic" ambitions of the elite commercial interests of Gotham. By contrast, architects and urbanists derided their unadorned, boxy faces and moaned that they brought congestion to an already densely packed neighborhood. "A sheer disaster," critic Lewis Mumford called them. A "fiasco," urbanist Jane Jacobs agreed. "Out-of-date," Goldberger complained. City University of New York political scientist Marshall Berman concluded, "The Twin Towers were purposefully isolated from the downtown street system [on an above-ground plaza], and designed to fit [French architect] Le Corbusier's dictum, 'We must kill the street.'" And they had. Within the largest, biggest, most populous, and wealthiest city in the world, they were "a city within a city," a vertical layer cake of commercial neighborhoods connected by three internal stairways and nearly 100 elevators, a magnet to as many as 40,000 workers and 200,000 visitors a day.[2]

Lower Manhattan has always exhibited this Janus-like face: a dream of wealth; a nightmare of congestion, grime, and crime; an aspiration of the new; a dogged refusal to accept change without complaint. From the moment that the Dutch set foot on the tip of the Indian island of "Manahatta" and purchased the use of the land for themselves, they dreamed of a great trading empire radiating out across the Atlantic and down the coast of North America. But the Dutch version of globalism could not conceal the ragtag little village they threw together, its canal filled with refuse, its walls in perpetual disrepair, its guardians drunk, quarrelsome, and ineffective. Three hundred years later, F. Scott Fitzgerald, a New Yorker by adoption, called it the "incalculable" city, "feverishly active" and "generally inarticulate." The port of entry for the "multitudes yearning to be free." At midday, the Lower Manhattan streets resembled Babel.[3]

When I moved to Manhattan in 1974, I tried to master its rules, "a combination of touchiness and generosity, street smarts and worldly perspective." Manhattanites clung to an elaborate, almost mannered concern for privacy in the midst of jostling crowds, and to a civility that a single smile or a kind word could instantly elicit. For example, in a city full of celebrities, it was okay to stare, but only tourists asked for autographs. In 1974, when my wife and I lived in the Lincoln Tower Apartments on the Upper West Side, we happened to sit next to New York Knicks star Bill Bradley at a Vivian Beaumont Theater performance of *A Doll's House*. Everyone peeked his way—a professional basketball player in a city gone basketball crazy was a celebrity—but no one interrupted his enjoyment of the play.

There were other kinds of stars that no one noticed. The city was Mecca for intellectuals, artists, writers, and academics, but we joked to one another that no one would have noticed if Arthur Schlesinger, Jr., America's most honored historian and another New York City notable, plopped down in the front row that night. The very next evening, at a performance of S. J. Perelman's comedy *The Beauty Part*, we were dumbfounded as we watched Schlesinger enter and take a front-row seat. No one else looked his way.[4]

Some years later I took our firstborn, now a historian in his own right, to visit Hester Street. The horses, pushcarts, and throngs of woollen-clad children of the Lower East Side ghetto were gone, but the tenements, artifacts of the first generation of New York City urban renewal, remained. Once the home of teeming masses of Jews from Central Europe, Italians, Irish, and Poles (with a greater density of population than modern Bombay, India), they now housed immigrants from other faraway parts. One sturdy former synagogue had become a Buddhist temple. We visited the excavation for a new courthouse, under which city archeologists had found evidence of an African-American graveyard. The lesson was plain: The city had always been home to a mixed multitude of peoples.[5]

The discovery of the graveyard taught another lesson about the city. A political battle over the fate of the disinterred slaves quickly developed. The city was notorious for its political melees. From the moment that the Dutch and the Indians decided that they could not get along—through a Dutch-English war that turned New Amsterdam into New York City (the duke of York got the Dutch colonies of New Netherlands as a prize of war), two major slave rebellions in the 1700s, three pitched Revolutionary War battles, four days of anti-draft riots in 1863, and countless political scandals involving such colorful party crooks as the Tweed Ring, the Tammany Hall gang, and Mayor "Gentleman" Jimmy Walker—New York City has been the cockpit of political partisanship. So it should have come as no surprise when in 1966 Austin Tobin, longtime boss of the Port of New York Authority established by the states of New York and New Jersey to manage the waterway between them, and newly elected New York Mayor John V. Lindsay squared off over the tax revenues from the World Trade Center in a war of television spots, press conferences, and legal battles.[6]

The city even harbored its share of political terrorists. At lunch hour on September 16, 1920, in front of the J. P. Morgan bank at 23 Wall Street,

> a horse-drawn cart exploded in a spray of metal and fire . . . Survivors remembered a flash, a roar, then silence. Wall Street seemed to freeze in a tableau vivant. Runners [carrying goods and packages] lay flattened like ten pins . . . Then windows for blocks around burst from their frames, launching a panicked run for cover . . . Veterans [of World War I] likened the scene to a battlefield during the Great

War . . . an overturned touring car snapped and sizzled beneath a tower of flame.

Anarchists had made the city their home, and the bomb would lead to a roundup of suspected terrorists (almost all of them immigrants) and the intensification of our first Red Scare. The actual perpetrators were never caught.[7]

Dreamers found their way downtown, too. In 1904, the Municipal Art Society wanted to cut the grid below Fourteenth Street with a trapezoidal array of avenues. They were not deterred by the vast demolition project their street renovation would require, only hopeful that a "more imposing architectural and artistic" plan would emerge. Crowded streets were a worse problem in the 1920s, when Harvey Wiley Corbett proposed to the Regional Plan Association that sidewalks on the major avenues and streets be double-decked and all rail lines go underground. The idyllic above-ground walkways with pedestrian overpasses (no need for stop signs or lights) prefigured the design of indoor malls, an idea before its time according to Corbett of "a higher sense of beauty in the building of the city." In any case, the Great Depression ended that dream. Robert Moses had his own design for the tip of the island, a maze of concrete ramps and superhighways that would have wiped out the Battery and the shoreline.[8]

Lower Manhattan had to have the biggest fires, too. The first great New York City fire nearly wiped out the place. On September 21, 1776, according to one account, "a most horrid attempt was made by a number of wretches to burn the town of New-York, in which they succeeded too well, having set it on fire in several places with matches and combustibles that had been prepared with great art and ingenuity." Much of the Lower West Side of Manhattan was gutted. General William Howe, the author of the report, accused patriot incendiaries left behind when George Washington and the Continental Army retreated. Even so, the Crown's loyalists were among the 300 new applicants for almshouse relief. Washington, watching the flames from the other side of the Hudson River, called the conflagration an accident, but "had I been left to the dictates of my own judgment, New York should have been laid in Ashes before I quitted it." The Continental Congress had stayed his hand. The fire probably began in a tavern brawl.[9]

Nothing stayed the hand of the fire that consumed much of Manhattan below Wall Street on the night of December 16th, 1835. So cold was the city that night that the hoses froze, and so hard was the wind blowing that the fire could not be contained until the dawn revealed the destruction of Wall Street from one side of the island to the other. In all, 674 buildings vanished. Gone was the elegant Merchants Exchange, along with banks, offices, and warehouses. The volunteer firemen, exhausted, cold, and thoroughly disheartened, could only watch. The "rapidity with which house after house, range after range of buildings, was wrapped in flames was astonishing." Eyewitnesses recalled a night of "awful terror and indescribable grandeur . . . large flakes of fire were borne whirling aloft through the dark vault of heaven." People took refuge in Brooklyn, across the East River, or fled north on the island. There was no refuge from fire, however: From the "Great Fire" of 1835 to 1855, there were six more major fires (involving at least an entire block) and forty-eight other fires requiring fire department response—all in Lower Manhattan.[10]

Even the city's most elegant buildings seemed to beckon fire. In 1853, the city opened a grand imitation of the London World's Fair "Crystal Palace." The Crystal Palace occupied an entire block at Forty-second Street and Fifth Avenue, a massive octagon of iron and glass on the landfill of Reservoir Square. Construction took four years and stopped passersby in proud amazement. The 100-foot-diameter central dome and the seventy-five-foot-high high turrets could be seen from all over the city. It was a major tourist attraction, a huge exhibition hall of cast iron beams and trusses, and huge panes of glass. Into the palace went a half-year-long exhibition of art and industry, including picture galleries and priceless sculpture. The exhibition closed, in debt, but the building remained. After all, it was "fireproof." But on October 5, 1858, the Crystal Palace went up like a fireball and in one-half hour was totally gutted. Two thousand people were in the building when the fire started, but because it had many exits and was on a single floor, and the fire department arrived in sufficient numbers and good time, no one died. The Currier and Ives lithograph of the scene was a best-seller that year.[11]

Some Manhattan fires were horrific accidents. On June 15, 1904, in plain view of horrified spectators, the recreational steamer *General Slocum* burned to its gunnels. The fire and the waters of the East River took the lives of 1,021 people, many of them children on an outing. A newspaper reporter was one of the witnesses: "'No artist, unless he dipped his brush in the colors of hell, could portray the awful scene of a majestic vessel, wrapped in great sheets of devouring flames.'" The steamboat had seen better days, and inspectors, paid off, overlooked rotting life buoys and other fatal defects. The fire began accidentally, a spark lit the "cans of kerosene for the boat's lanterns and jars of polish for its brass fixtures." Leaving such perfect accelerants stacked in a cabin, however, invited an accident to become a holocaust. Five years later, "For ten terrifying minutes . . . nearly eighty manhole covers launched as high as forty feet into the air along Tenth Avenue . . . Pedestrians fleeing from the 'tongues of flame shooting from the earth' collided with the frightened occupants of stores, factories, and tenements, who, convinced that the shaking signaled an earthquake, were running into the streets for safety." The "gasoline and grease" routinely dumped into the sewer system had backed up during a high tide and someone's careless cigarette, "or a spark from [an electric] trolley" had set the fumes above the pooled effluvia on fire. The Triangle Shirtwaist Factory fire only killed 146 people—most of them young women workers who preferred to jump to their deaths eight stories below rather than be burned. It was a choice that some in a later generation of city workers would also make.[12]

Other fires, like the Crystal Palace's, were set. Arson was a New York City specialty. During the anti-draft riots of 1863, firemen set fire to the provost marshal's office. When the fire spread, other firemen rushed to the scene and fought the rioters while laying hose to put out the fires. In the labor-capital wars of the textile industry in which Jewish labor leaders and workers were pitted against Jewish factory owners, "Arson was another common crime, so much so that it was nicknamed 'Jewish Lightning.'" In the 1950s and 1960s, tenement owners routinely paid arsonists to destroy buildings for the insurance.[13]

What saved the city from its own pyrophilic tendencies was its proximity to water. Manhattan is an island surrounded by the Hudson River on the west, the Harlem River in the north, and the East River. The relationship between the water and land has been contentious. Ship traffic between New Jersey and Manhattan and Brooklyn and Manhattan required deepwater port facilities and navigable channels. Real estate and manufacturing interests on the island wanted more land, straighter streets, and easier crosstown access. Once upon a time, the shoreline was "flat and marshy . . . gentle flowering meadows sloped to the water's edge." Save for a poet or two, a sentimental love of nature does not seem to have been a New York trait, however, and as soon as private companies, individual shoreland owners, and later the state and the city, could clear off legal obstacles, raise funds, and (occasionally) do some planning, the shoreline became a jumble of wharves, piers, warehouses, jetties, and seawalls.

The city hired engineers to insure uniformity, but without political clout and independent funding, the plans never resulted in A Plan. General George McClelland, late of the Army of the Potomac, had no more success as the city's waterfront designer than he had in the Peninsula Campaign ten years before. Refuse piled up along the shallows, clinging to the piers as if reluctant to bid the city farewell. The railroads claimed the edge of the island next to the wharves until they were supplanted by a ribbon of raised motorways. The city even had city planners who attacked the idea of city planning, scoffed at "vision," and rammed through pet projects. Meanwhile, on the shoreline, willy-nilly, bigger and bigger berths for bigger and bigger ships demanded more of the harbor front. The Hudson and East Rivers vanished behind all the masonry, ironwork, and abutments. By 1980, the island's contractors had added nearly 2,300 acres of refuse, stone, and dirt to its edges.[14]

Of course individuals, companies, and even public agencies had plans for all that landfill. In 1811, a new city plan proposed a grid system of rectilineal streets (east-west) and avenues (north-south) consecutively numbered, all the way to the Heights at the northern tip of the island. That plan, save for Central Park, Riverside Park, and a number of other, smaller, grass and tree set-asides, still rules. In 1958, a Lower Manhattan hungry for development in a nation mired in the worst post–World War II recession, looked once again to its landfill. The sense that doom was just around the corner was the brooding omnipresence: "Downtown was in danger of complete eclipse . . . the irregular jumble of downtown's narrow streets and limestone corridors. Choked by traffic and challenged in every way by its congested physical conditions, downtown was in jeopardy."[15]

Lower Manhattan was merely following its own credo: "buildings went up" and then "came down, to be replaced by newer, more audacious, more arrogant structures . . . there was no point . . . in permanently bemoaning change. This was New York." A world trade center reflecting New York City's role in postwar global finance and commerce would surely rescue the old commercial district—but the dream, or rather "whose dream"—kept tripping over competing realities.

In New York, bankers, manufacturers, and realtors argued that rebuilding Europe should begin in America, and nowhere better than the busy port of New York. Port Authority bigwigs agreed. They could not push the project (they were a public entity, not a private investment company), but they could plant the idea for it. With director Austin Tobin prodding, the PA found surrogate advocates. The state of New York gave its blessing in 1946, and New Jersey joined in 1962. In the city, the Downtown Lower Manhattan Association, with Chase Manhattan Bank's David Rockefeller at its head, paid Skidmore, Owings, and Merrill, architects, to plan for development of a suitable area. The only problems were deciding where downtown to put the center, the removal of the current denizens, financing the construction, and finding tenants. And, of course, building the new trade center's structures.[16]

This was the heyday of "urban renewal," and who could stop the city from taking what it wanted? Well, the residents could try. When Mayor Robert Wagner decided to "level several square miles of manufacturing buildings and tenements south of Washington Square Park," locals raised the roof. "Neighborhood organizations . . . rallied to save [Greenwich] Village and Soho." South Village also escaped the wrecking ball. The merchants on Fulton Street saved themselves and Chinatown. The losers were the denizens of "Radio Row," an array of electronics stores, warehouses, and a myriad of "florists, fruit and vegetable shops, and restaurants" located on the sixteen acres of landfill between West and Liberty, Vesey and Church. Before the radio stores came, the same landfill had another name: "the Syrian Quarter," a host to a variety of Eastern Mediterranean shops. Others of the streets had their own specialties to offer. Liberty, bounding the site on the south, and Vesey, on the north, boasted some of the poshest gambling dens in the country, while Church Street, the eastern border of the parcel, housed "discreet" bordellos.[17]

The result was a plan for "razing most of the outmoded structures in Lower Manhattan to permit expansion of the financial district and other types of redevelopment." For "outmoded," read low-rise, low-occupancy, low-space buildings. As a scion of one of the great steel contractors in the city later wrote: A "shrug," and "there's goes the neighborhood." This was New York City and neighborhoods changed from one generation to the next. The plan, revised from 1958 to 1962, kept calling for higher and higher office buildings to "'strengthen the economy.'" Fifty stories, seventy-five stories, one building, two towers, higher and higher. It would "bring round the clock activity to the district around some of New York's most expensive real estate," or so said the *New York Times*.[18]

Tall buildings in cities are more than short buildings with overactive pituitary glands. They represent something beyond additional office space and greater human density. Cities build upward, when the technology permits, because space is at a premium or is not available horizontally. That could hardly be news to a New Yorker. The occupants of Radio Row put up a wonderful but doomed fight. They discovered that the land could be taken by eminent domain if the taker could show a public interest. That is why the Port Authority, a public agency, rather than the realtors, the bankers, the contractors, and the future occupiers of the space who waited in the wings, got the zoning clearances (necessary in New York City for high-rises) and took the land. Oscar Nadel, "with a tiny radio shop" in the middle of the plot, complained, "'The Port Authority will tear down my business, and I have not yet been heard. If it were for the betterment of the city [in other words, truly a public purpose], that would be one thing. But this is simply big business running over us.'"[19]

The "big" part was right. The PA selected a giant, Tishman Realty, to handle the general contracting, and Emery Roth and Sons, a huge firm, would join in the architectural planning. Even when Uptown realtors like Lawrence Wien (who ran the Empire State Building) intervened to protect their own interests, the momentum of the WTC could not be stopped. The small businessmen of the area would be relocated and the big realtors of Midtown placated (New York City takes care of its own), but thirteen square blocks of what the PA derisively termed "an antiquated . . . area full of firetraps" was going to become "a symbol of international business."[20]

Such dreams did not pause at ordinary people's concerns, or even the objections of a great city. Studies show that people like to look at skyscrapers from a distance. Closer, looking up or down, people fear giant buildings. City governments take a longer view of skyscrapers— so long as the tax benefits are there. But like Baltimore's Harborplace, the gainer in the proposed WTC would be the private interests. New York City could not tax the sixteen acres and the buildings on them because they were the domain of the Port Authority.

The city was not opposed to the development of the site. "With international trade becoming an increasing activity, this also behooves Lower Manhattan to carry out its potential to the maximum extent. . . ." It just wanted its share of the booty. As the feasibility studies progressed, however, some realtors (who would be renting out space in the high-rises), began to get cold feet. How could the new buildings attract tenants when tens of thousands of square feet of office space elsewhere in the city were vacant? The Port Authority went to the market cup in hand, begging for lessors. Then the cavalry arrived—the state and federal governments agreed to rent. In the end, New York State, the U.S. Bureau of the Customs, the Port Authority itself, and other government agencies rented more space than all other tenants combined.[21]

With the city and the Port Authority deadlocked, the city's unions—the fourth branch of government in New York—stepped in and demanded that construction begin. Thousands of jobs and hundreds of millions of dollars in salaries were at stake. Payrolls were expected to top $200 million. The combatants finally compromised their differences (actually splitting the difference between what the PA was willing to pay and what the city wanted). Hard feelings continued—they continue to this day—but the way was cleared to dig a very big hole down to bedrock, lay foundations, and raise up from it towers that touched the heavens and brought down their fire.[22]

Towers that pierced the sky; that was the ultimate allure and the glory of the World Trade Center. They symbolized the conceit and aspiration of the twentieth-century American city. Higher was better, whatever the cost, whatever the risk. A metropolis unto itself in the clouds, the Towers' construction seem to foretell the direction of the future cityscape.

"The Worst Day"

W here were you on 9/11? is a question that has become part of America's folk memory. Many in New York City remember exactly where they were at 8:46 AM that day. Ray Feurst, an ironworker, was straightening an American flag caught on itself above the renovated AT&T building, a block northwest of the WTC. He had to climb up a ladder inside the antenna at the top of the building, then up the "spikes jutting from the [antenna] needle to get to the flag. As soon as he unfurled it, he saw [a commercial wide-body jet] pass just four hundred feet overhead." In shock, he ducked, as though the plane might clip him. Then he heard whoever was flying the plane accelerate and saw the plane bank into the upper face of the North Tower.[23]

Mark Obenhaus, an ABC network news producer, said he "heard this tremendous sound behind me. I turned around and caught sight of this plane which appeared to be flying extremely low. It was a massive, massive plane. The plane was suddenly looming over the building tops . . . Your eye just tracked it directly down West Broadway and right into the North Tower. It seemed in a second to just vanish in the building . . . You could see this cavernous hole in the side of the building . . . Then the smoke starts billowing out." The impact set off an explosion. The fuel in the Boeing 767 had caught fire and was spreading throughout the structure, from the ninety-third floor upward and downward. The blast killed the hijackers, passengers, and crew, as well as everyone in the portion of the building the plane struck. Parts of the plane burst through the far wall of the building, spreading the death and dismemberment ahead of the flames. Pieces of the plane also rained down on the street.[24]

Joanne Lipman was an editor of the *Wall Street Journal* on her way to its offices next to the WTC. "All of a sudden people started stampeding. People started saying that a plane hit the building. Typical New Yorkers that we are, we assumed that somebody clipped an antenna . . . But people were really running." She left the concourse by the exit onto Church Street, where "it was snowing plaster." On the street, people were staring up, "transfixed," the same state of bewitched astonishment as the home owners in the Oakland hills and the spectators in Baltimore, Chicago, and Pittsburgh. The *Journal* office was on the other side of the street, but Lipman could not get there. "Burning debris and twisted metal," along with "pieces of the plane and also pieces of the passengers," blocked her way. Todd Maisel, a *New York Daily News* photographer, "raced to Liberty Street" to get shots of the North Tower on fire and found that "there were body parts and luggage scattered on the ground. A human hand pointed at me on the pavement."[25]

The building absorbed the huge shock wave of the collision, but inside the North Tower, on the eight floors the plane struck, the blast either killed everyone or injured survivors so badly that they were unable to call for help. No messages reached the outside world from the impacted floors. The elevator shafts were fractured and the stairwells made impassable by debris.

We can imagine, if we dare, what those moments were like for those on the impact floors. Everything that could move became a projectile weapon—bits of steel, pieces of furniture, human body parts. Concussion and blast killed on their own. The heat from the exploding jet fuel seared those it touched, and the combustion of oxygen from the flames suffocated those not already dead. The smoke ball, a cloud of deadly particles that rose and then banked down, filled the lungs of anyone still breathing and choked them. Perhaps it is well that we are spared the details of the fire itself, though it would be the same story—with a thousand variations—when terrorists slammed another wide-body jet into the South Tower, at 9:02 AM.

All we know for certain is what happened around the edges of the fire—above and below. Above the flames, victims called down to the lobbies for help, dialed 911, and reported that they were trapped or used cell phones to say good-bye to their loved ones. "There is a lot of smoke," they told fire department dispatchers. Then, "the floors are buckling." Some jumped rather than cook in the mounting heat. Below the holocaust, people asked one another whether they should try to leave, or stay and wait for rescue. They could not see the fire, but they tasted the smoke and heard the whoosh of falling debris. Smoke "'billowed out through the freight elevators' doors.'" Some people became hysterical, others exhibited an almost supernatural calm. A few became heroes, helping others to evacuate. Some were martyrs, putting others' safety ahead of their own.[26]

JUST ANOTHER WORKDAY AT THE WTC

September 11, 2001, had dawned bright, almost cloudless, in New York City. The city within a city that was the World Trade Center was already busy. The sixteen-acre plot bounded by Vesey Street on the north, the broad expanse of West Street that separated the WTC and the World Financial Center on the west, old Church Street to the east, and Liberty Street on the south would have been home to nearly 40,000 workers that day, not counting the visitors staying at the Marriott Hotel on the northeast corner of Liberty and Church. The special aluminum alloy Alcoa had provided for the skin of the Twin Towers reflected the sunlight in dappled shades of silver and gold.

Not everyone of the 14,000 people who went to work before 9:00 AM in the towers saw this display of metallic wonder. Rather than enter from Church Street and the Austin Tobin Plaza, most came up from the bowels of the earth. The cavernous space beneath the plaza opened to the New Jersey–bound PATH trains and the New York City subway system. Deep down, a multilevel garage served those who insisted on bringing their cars.

The plan for the center facilitated either approach. The plaza led to a mezzanine and elevator level, with escalators going down to the

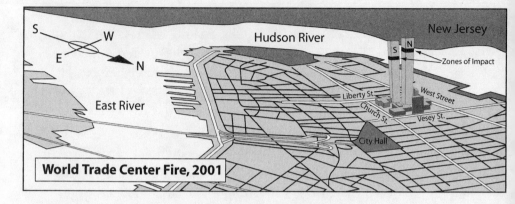

S
W
E
N

Hudson River

New Jersey

S N
Zones of Impact

Liberty St.
West Street
Church St.
Vesey St.

East River

City Hall

World Trade Center Fire, 2001

main and below-ground levels. There were upscale national outlets, some smaller boutiques, and fast-food restaurants on the lower levels, but the "concourse" (later renamed the "mall") was frenzied, like a train station, and uninviting. Only a pinprick of sunlight at the top of the escalators reminded pedestrians of the sunlit day above. People flashed their passes at the Port Authority police before getting on the elevator, or they went to the visitor's table to get a temporary pass, color coded for the day. Inspection was sometimes thorough, but most often perfunctory.[27]

On the early morning of 9/11, through the mall, up the escalators, "folded newspaper under their arms," people poured into the Twin Towers. The terror of a 1993 bombing was not forgotten but, like all finite agonies, had been put into a box on the shelf. Everyone was brave. The people who worked in the towers braved risks every day, like stepping into the elevators, looking out the windows, bracing against the wind, and thinking about the unthinkable. There were ninety-nine elevator shafts, 208 elevators flying up to the sky lobbies, moving people like packages in pneumatic tubes. Many offices had no windows, not a place for the claustrophobic. The towers' windows were small and strategically placed, designed to reduce the fear of heights. This morning, the two behemoths wobbled only a little in the wind. On gusty days, the towers wobbled noticeably. No bomb threats yet today—though they were so common that one security officer said they were phoned in "all the time."[28]

THE TWO TOWERS

The design of the Twin Towers had been controversial. There was no particular need for great height. Public facilities were often horizontal. Great train stations, for example, McKim, Mead and White's Penn Station in New York (1910, demolished 1963), was "'a civic vestibule to the world metropolis.'" Shortly before he died in 1977, critic and scholar Ernst Schumacher made a persuasive case against the Twin Towers: "Take the question of the size of a city . . . In places like London, or Tokyo, or New York, the millions do not add to the city's real value but merely create *enormous* problems and produce human degradation." Schumacher rebuked those who worshipped at the shrine of "giantism," men deluded by "modern technology, particularly in matters of transport and communications." But that was exactly what the PA had in mind for the World Trade Center. Schumacher had anticipated director of the WTC Guy Tozzoli's bold assertion that "the only way to achieve [income] was to build the world's biggest project." In Lower Manhattan, size would maximize the benefits of transportation (under the Hudson to New Jersey) and communication.[29]

In light of later developments, the choice of Minoru Yamasaki as chief architect by Tobin and Tozzoli turned out to be critical. Minneapolis-based, he too had dreams that withered before hard realities. His St. Louis "Pruitt-Igo" high-rise low-rent apartments had just been demolished (they bred crime, even if they had a certain austere elegance). It was a terrible mistake, he confessed, but not his last. He preferred low-rise, but when the PA wanted the tallest building in the world, he complied. He later recalled, "My particular reason for agreeing to build 110 stories high is that I stood under the Empire State Building and stared at it a long time. Really, unless you look like that, you're not conscious of the height. As far as the skyline of New York goes, that's going to change all the time. They screamed when the flatiron building was built . . . and the Chrysler Building, and the Empire State Building." In any case, the higher the building, the more plaza space one could put beneath it.[30]

The cost of construction began to rise apace with the towers—from the estimated $355 million, to $575 million, to over $1 billion. But what a magnificent project. The numbers were staggering—thousands of feet of steel supports in a seven-foot-high cage to frame the basement of the two towers alone. Over 1 million cubic yards of dirt to remove, then 6,000 cubic yards of sand to fill each of the cofferdams supporting the concrete and steel that in turn supported the towers. Three levels of elevators to serve three zones of occupancy. The "sky lobbies" on the forty-fourth and seventy-eighth floors became interchange platforms for the three elevator lines. There were also express elevators to the top.[31]

The towers themselves entailed a rethinking of all construction conventions. All the elevators would go in a core of the building, surrounded by steel girders, cages within a cage. "The structure was new and different from other conventional high rise buildings." Each tower would be a giant "framed tube, a kind of web of metal." A core of steel girders would surround the elevator shafts and three stairways. The external walls, a "curtain" of hollow steel panels, would bear 60 percent of the load (weight plus wind resistance) of the towers. The core would be tied to the external steel panels by floors composed of triangular "trusses," lightweight crisscrossed steel frames embedded in concrete. Under each floor truss assembly would go horizontal shafts for the electricity, ductwork, and repair—in short, a kind of miniature subway system running under each story.[32]

Koch Steel, a family firm in the city with a vast store of experience, good union relations, and able management beat out U.S. Steel and Bethlehem Steel for the job. The low bidder, Koch got the job for $20 million, a tiny portion of what the steel itself would cost. The company also bid for and got the all-important floor sections—some 5,760 truss and concrete prefabs that had to fit perfectly. In fact, everything was prefab, numbered for assembly. The towers would go up (the North six months ahead of the South) in lockstep from the "footings" in the basement to the observation platforms at the top, numbered piece fitted to numbered piece.

The towers were deceptively huge at their base (209 feet per side), and all told, each had 1 1/2 times the cubic volume of the Empire State Building. The exterior wall "panels," each three stories high, for the external curtain wall weighed tons. Still, weight was the enemy in such a tall structure, so the floor trusses had to be light as well as strong. The aluminum skin on the outside of the curtain members (the columns) was also light. Four "kangaroo" cranes, one at each corner for each tower, did the heavy lifting. Seven thousand construction workers welded, bolted, fitted, hoisted, and finished the assembly. Eight of them died.[33]

The curtain that Koch Steel erected was not a facade but a load-bearing element, giving the entire tower a giant hollow cubical plan. Therein lay the genius of the design—for without heavy structural members inside the building (except for its core), each floor offered an acre of almost entirely open "rentable" space. Narrow windows, a hollow core in the "load"-bearing outside members, and serration of the curtain provided additional strength. The primary concern of the designers and builders was wind resistance, but tests with models proved that the towers should survive a level three tornado—"the equivalent of a large ocean freighter" hitting the building at full speed, or a fully loaded 707 jetliner, for that matter.[34]

But what about fire safety? Fire in a high-rise is an occupant's dread and a firefighter's nightmare. Smoke and heat rise, making escape from the upper floors essential, but the higher the building, the more isolated, exposed, and endangered the people on the uppermost floors are. Fireproofing gives the occupants extra time to make that journey down, but only if the escape routes are adequate for the number of people using them and fireproof themselves. The New York City fire code of 1938, based on the many lessons of fires like Baltimore's, prescribed thick fireproof concrete and ceramic tiles, six stairways scattered throughout a building of the towers' size, wide stairwells and exit doors, and high standards for structural members' ignition temperatures. Based on the old code, firefighters estimated that even a fully burning high-rise would stand for at least three hours before the steel started to lose its shape and collapse became likely.[35]

But the PA did not have to conform to New York's fire code. The PA voluntarily adopted some of the provisions of a proposed 1968 code into design specifications for all the WTC buildings, but these were a step back from the 1938 code. They allowed for only three internal fire escapes, stairwells grouped at the core of the buildings instead of distributed throughout, narrower doors and stairs (too narrow for all occupants to fit in), and reduced fireproof ratings for the structural members. In fact, the stairs were so narrow that they could only accommodate two lanes of traffic. If firefighters were trying to reach upper floors by ascending the stairs, occupants evacuating the upper floors could only proceed down in single file, at the speed of the slowest person. Fireproofing was one-half inch of spray-on for the floor trusses and steel beams, and on the drywall surrounding the core. The WTC did not feature the heavy and expensive fireproof ceramics that graced the neighborhoods' other high-rises, such as the Woolworth Building. The towers did not have a sprinkler system at first. One was added later.[36]

Another key to preventing fire's spread in high-rises is compartmentalization—that is, confining a fire to a closed space on the floor. No one at the time seems to have addressed the special problems of compartmentalization that the wide-open design of the towers' floors presented. They were giant oxygen tanks. In addition, the underfloor ducts were perfect conductors of heat from a major fire, much like the raised sidewalks of Chicago in 1871. On top of everything else, no one tested the spray-on fireproofing for the steel floor trusses. Perhaps because fire is not considered one of the structural issues (like weight and wind), it is not a central concern of designers from the inception of their work. The towers were not fireproof. Indeed, in the right conditions, they would become the world's tallest smokestacks.[37]

Shortcuts in the design and construction—both planned and unplanned—resulted in jammed elevators, locked stairwell doors, and plumbing failures. It cost too much to use all the lights and keep the air-conditioning or heat running at peak demand. To prevent theft, stairwell doors were locked. (Keys could be obtained from office managers—not a particularly expeditious process in case of a fire and evacuation.) The PA spent time and money on fireproof carpeting and furniture, but problems in communication between the fire marshals in each building and the various floors went unsolved. The floor volunteer fire marshals could never be found when you needed them. Not everyone took the fire drills seriously. The stock market traders were the worst offenders, always sneaking back to their computer consoles.[38]

TERROR STALKS THE TOWERS

On February 26, 1993, plans for evacuation of the towers got their first real test, and flunked. That morning, everything seemed normal in the "bathtub cathedral of the routine" at the base of the towers. Security did not worry about a yellow van parked against the south wall of the North Tower. No one was alarmed when the driver and his passenger emerged and got into a red car and left. The occupants and visitors at the towers on that day did not know that a truck bomb was ticking away in a parking area three stories beneath the main level. For fifteen minutes fuses in the van burned, then ignited 1,500 pounds of nitro. At 12:18 PM, the bomb burst was "150,000 pounds per square inch" of exploding air pressure and a fireball of 2230° Fahrenheit. At that temperature, concrete dissolves and steel melts. Walls collapse. People anywhere near the blast die from explosive forces, blunt trauma, concussion, impalement, smoke inhalation, and burns.

A conspiracy of Islamic terrorists plotted to destroy the towers, for them symbols of Judaism, modernity, liberality, feminism, and the global economy. It was a holy war conducted in the way that holy wars have been conducted throughout history—pitilessly indifferent to the suffering of the unbeliever. The enemy were faceless unpersons, unworthy of life.[39]

The bomb placed against the retaining wall should have turned it to dust, toppling the North Tower down on the South Tower. The blast shot up three floors and down into the bowels of the building, then vented itself out the parking lot ramp. The building shifted and the debris from the blast flew up the elevator shafts to the upper floors, but the top of the building barely moved and the towers remained standing.[40]

Fire engines, summoned by people inside and outside the towers, raced to the scene, followed by ambulances. Ladder No. 10 and engine No. 10, right across Liberty Street from the plaza, were the first responders. In the garage, they reported a monster fire whose smoke made it impossible to see beyond their hose nozzles. Smoke had already killed one man in the basement garage. There was enough smoke on the forty-eighth floor to frighten people there, but the FDNY fire dispatcher urged them to stay on the floor and "cram something into the vents." Don't panic.

That was the drill. Block the smoke and flames and wait for the firemen who were already in the building. Firefighters moved up the stairwells in ragged conga lines of men and equipment. As they dispersed along the corridors of the higher floors, they escorted the frightened occupants from their offices. It was early evening before the last stragglers were evacuated from the towers. Even had the order to evacuate been given immediately and just as immediately obeyed, it would have taken four hours to empty a tower full of people completely. The three stairwells were too narrow to permit speedier evacuation.[41]

After spending millions to restore the towers after the bombing, the PA finally agreed to lease the WTC to Silverstein Properties, one of the city's preeminent realty firms, for $3.2 billion on a ninety-nine-year lease. On September 11, 2001, the lengthy negotiations had just ended, but the PA staff still occupied its eighty-eighth-floor offices in the North Tower and was assisting in the transfer of operation. In fact, that morning PA staff were waiting for a trolley load of forms needing review and signature. The PA was still in charge of safety at the facility and most of the PA regulars were at their posts, though reporters later discovered that the staff members were anxious that morning about their job security under the new arrangements.[42]

THE BRAVEST

At 8:50 AM on 9/11, the WTC director, Guy Tozzoli, was on his way to work in his North Tower office. Held up in traffic at the New Jersey entrance to the Holland Tunnel (the first PA project, completed in 1927), he looked up to see "waves of thick, oily smoke billowing from a gash" in the face of the North Tower. "'Its going to take us a long time to fix that,'" he thought out loud. Tozzoli was a brave man who did not think of himself as a hero. But his heartbeat raced as he sped through the tunnel. "On the Manhattan side, a uniformed policeman stopped him and ordered him to turn around. Tozzoli pulled out his credentials. 'Listen, I built that place . . . I've got to get down there to help.' The policeman's reply was curt. 'I don't care if you're the Pope. You turn this car around.'"[43]

When off-duty FDNY firefighter Dan Potter saw the smoke, he raced into Manhattan. The police let him pass—"'I held my badge up to the windshield and the cops just flagged me through.'" He found the 10/10 firehouse on Liberty Street filled with emergency personnel and firefighters from all over the city. The men pulling on their bunker gear and readying themselves to enter the towers were the bravest of the brave. No city in history ever had a fire department, police department, or emergency medical services that compared to New York's in sheer size, training, or commitment. Shaken by what they saw in front of them but still confident, they prepared to do battle with their old adversary. Others would find out who was responsible and deal with them. The firefighters and other first responders would rescue the people trapped in the towers and put out the fire.[44]

Immediately after the Civil War (in which its firefighters had joined the Union forces in great numbers), New York City reorganized its thirty-four engine companies and twelve ladder companies into a modern force—complete with horse-pulled steam engines and a military-type system of ranks. By 1870, under the city's control, the FDNY expanded its operations to cover all of Manhattan. After the 1898 consolidation of the five boroughs into the present city, the fire department grew into the largest in the country. It introduced rescue and breathing equipment, motorized apparatus, and fire boats, a "Fire College" for training recruits and continuing education, a fire-prevention bureau to educate young and old and promote fire safety, and the "shift" system, putting crews on twelve-hour and later eight-hour shifts. The FDNY survived the cutbacks of the Great Depression and the loss of manpower during World War II to emerge a stronger and more efficient organization.

In the early 1970s, during the inner-city "war years," the FDNY responded to an average of over 130,000 fires a year—more annually than Los Angeles, Chicago, and Philadelphia combined. Nearly 5,000 of these fires each year were serious—requiring at least a third alarm. The veterans of these fires came to regard the ghetto fire-setters' slogan of "Burn, baby, burn" with grim cynicism. Sometimes the arsonists left a special calling card—a gasoline bomb or a trap hole in the floor disguised with a linoleum cover. FDNY firemen suffered heart attacks, anxiety attacks, and depression. They died in floor collapses, wall collapses, and roof collapses, from burns and concussions, and they drowned in the water-filled basements of burning buildings.

The collapse of a building on fire is not an extraordinary event, as every firefighter knows—for at temperatures over 1000°F, brick and stone begin to melt, steel expands and buckles, and wooden joists and crossbeams thin and then turn to ash. Collapses killed more on-duty firemen than all other causes combined. In the meantime, the FDNY covered its rigs with bulletproof roofs, and carried on.

Although the "war years" had ended by the 1980s, and the number of fires dropped to five figures per year, the city's fires remained deadly battles. Nineteen firefighters died in the 1980s, and twenty-two in the 1990s. The number of fires declined through the 1990s, from an average of 100,000 a year, of which about 4,000 were serious enough to require four fire companies or more, to an average of 60,000 fires per year at the end of the decade, of which 3,000 were serious. False alarms declined as well, from over 100,000 per year to a little more than 5,000. As the yearly number of fires lessened, so did the deaths of civilians, falling from 160 to 110, on average, and the injuries to firefighters from over 1,545 in 1993 to 402 in 2000. With its 205 engine companies and its 163 ladder companies spread throughout the five boroughs, added to its five elite rescue and seven special operations squads, and a computer-assisted alarm system that reduced the average response time to under five minutes, the

FDNY's performance had reached a pinnacle of professionalism and expertise.

By the new millennium, the Fire Department of New York City was unparalleled in its training and experience. As Cherry Hill Fire Department Captain Kevin Kenniff told me, riding with them was "another country." Pride, camaraderie, devotion to duty, and a sense of fun marked the members of the FDNY. Robert Galione of Brooklyn's Rescue 2 said it best—where else did grown men get the chance to pull down walls, cut holes in roofs, and break windows? In the culture of the members of the FDNY firefighters, the man who "did the right thing," who stayed calm in the face of danger, who mastered himself, was the model for all his brothers. (There were only twenty-six women in the FDNY, despite over twenty-five years of recruitment efforts.) Officers—company lieutenants and captains—led by example, as close to the fire as they could get. Leadership was based on a simple motto: "First in, last out." In a reality show segment for *The Bravest*, filmed a few months before 9/11, Rescue 1's David Weiss gently boasted, "[W]hatever it is, we can handle it."[45]

The rituals of firefighting were deeply ingrained as well. From formalities like mind-bending written tests for promotion, to the ordinary things, like proper wear of turnout gear, pride in scuffed and blackened helmets, practical joking in the firehouse kitchen, and even the ceremonies of mourning for those lost in fires, customs and pride imposed order and reassured men facing the chaos and danger of fire. As William Lake of Rescue 2 put it, "[F]ire has a way of humbling you." He knew from experience that no matter how confident and prepared his elite company might be, they never knew what they would find once they arrived at the scene.[46]

"THE WORST DAY"

The first FDNY unit on the scene of the North Tower fire was First Battalion Chief Joseph Pfeifer on "a run" with ladder No. 1 checking out a suspected gas leak. With the chief and the company was a

French documentarian, Jules Naudet. Hearing the low-flying plane, Naudet scanned his camera up and caught the moment of impact on the face of the North Tower. Pfeifer ran for his battalion car and called in the first and second alarms as he raced downtown, followed by the ladder truck. His call went to central dispatch and then out again to the nearest units. By the time he arrived at the North Tower and saw the damage, he had transmitted a third alarm. He selected Vesey and West as the staging area for the arriving apparatus and went into the lobby of the tower. The lobby of the North Tower became the first operational command center.[47]

The South Tower was hit at 9:02 AM. In its lobby, the FDNY set up another operational command post. From it, the chiefs sent the men up the stairs to rescue civilians. Dennis Smith, on his way to the site, imagined what the incident command response must have been: "Each [chief] will have a specific job, each will direct personnel to preassigned duties in evacuation, rescue, or firefighting. The chief in charge, probably Peter Ganci, the chief of department . . . will be setting up his command post in accordance with prefire plans at the fire control panels in the lobby of the first building hit . . . There will be lists of each of the three engine companies and two ladder companies that will respond to each alarm as it is transmitted." The citywide computer system and the dispatchers would be assigning more companies to the site, up to "ninety engine companies and forty ladder companies." It seemed like chaos—but controlled chaos, almost choreographed, as more men and apparatus were being fed into the emergency.[48]

In the streets surrounding the WTC and in the plaza, firefighters climbed out of their rigs and walked into the maelstrom. Routine, repetition, training, discipline, and coolness of men and officers imposed a hurried order on chaos. Lieutenant Dominick Maggiore of Battalion 50 recalled, "[I]t was mayhem . . . but what did get my attention . . . the people, maybe not the higher ranking, but the people who were down in the trenches cops, firemen. It was that they worked like they had worked together forever like two good partners." Drivers maneuvered the apparatus on the streets—getting the engines as close to hydrants as possible, while leaving room for the trucks to deploy their ladders. The "can men" swung their fire extinguishers out of the truck compartments and put out car fires, always dangerous jobs. Weaving in and out of the ranks of heavy equipment, the rescue squad vans and the Emergency Medical Service vehicles disgorged their crews. Victims of falling debris needed immediate attention. EMS members took on all manner of tasks, sometimes on their own: "Nobody was in charge [but] [e]verybody kept their head. Everybody worked as a team."[49]

The men had to swivel their heads skyward, for anything falling from ninety floors above the street hit the ground like shrapnel. Victims leaping to their deaths became bombs. *New York Post* photographer Bolívar Arellano: "I was taking pictures of people jumping . . . I was praying inside my mind, 'God, give them wings so they cannot touch the ground.'" Paramedic Richard Erdey blocked out images of the body parts, but he would never forget them. His comrade, Mark Harris, saw five people die in front of him, as people from the upper floors landed on them. One firefighter running into the building literally exploded as he was hit. Another "firefighter was struck by something that fell from the building, his head and chest bloodied. Fellow firefighters were dragging him away from the danger, one screaming, 'Hold on, brother, hold on.'" Danny Suhr, a firefighter, had been struck by a woman jumper. He had massive injuries but his brother firefighters would not abandon him or give up hope. "Danny, Danny, Danny," they yelled, trying to revive him. Suhr died on the way to the hospital, the first FDNY member to lose his life at the WTC.[50]

Within an hour, half of the fire crews on duty in the city (elements of more than 200 units) were either at the site or on their way. In addition, off-duty firefighters and officers who saw or heard about the attack began arriving on the scene. They came because dispatch called them, because their brothers were in danger, because their city was on fire, or because that is what the FDNY members do. In the North Tower, floors ninety-three to ninety-nine were fully involved in fire. Firefighters trooped up the stairs passing evacuees marching down. The smoke billowed up 1,000 feet over Lower Manhattan. Police helicopters taking pictures recorded a scene of war, and some on the ground agreed, "[W]e are at war." In the South Tower, smoke still poured from the seventy-eighth to the eighty-fifth floors.[51]

Only on-site visual inspection would tell the FDNY what to do, and it was thus necessary to send men up the stairs to reach the burning area. Able commanders always send men on "reconnaissance missions." When Pfeifer's bosses, including Peter Ganci, Jr., Deputy Chief of the First Division (Lower Manhattan) Peter Hayden, Ray Downey, the legendary head of the Special Operations Command, Bill Feehan, a deputy commissioner and the living storehouse of the department's memory, and Assistant Chief Joseph Callan, the citywide tour commander who would act as operational commander in the North Tower, arrived on the scene, they decided that there was no way to put the two fires out. Too much was burning. As he and other chiefs in the lobby assigned floors to the arriving companies, Callan recalled, "I gave them instructions that we are not going to be extinguishing fire. What we were going to do is assist in evacuating the building."

The mission of the FDNY, along with the Emergency Services personnel of the New York Police Department and the Port Authority police on the scene, would be confined to rescue. The department's standard operating procedure (SOP) for structural fires were clear—protecting life came first. As Deputy Chief Hayden said, "'[W]e have to get those people out.'"[52]

That decision meant sending enough men up the stairs to rescue the hundreds of victims on the burning and impacted floors. Rescuing an injured person may require four firefighters. The classic "fireman's carry," dragging a victim by his clothing or wrapped in a blanket, may require only one rescuer, but placing an injured person on a backboard, a litter, or in the body-shaped Stokes basket used to transport the seriously injured demands coordinated effort from two to four rescuers. It was also understood that there might be a limited collapse of the upper floors, killing those trapped above the fire unless they could be evacuated. Thus, the chiefs ordered a speedy ascent by as many men as possible to clear a path to the trapped civilians and guide or carry them down to safety and away from the site. If a building collapses, it not only endangers those inside, but anyone within the "collapse zone" of the building will be imperiled by falling debris, thus the need to evacuate civilians from the immediate area as well as from the upper stories.[53]

The FDNY's SOP put life safety at the top of the list of priorities—and that included the safety of the men going into the buildings. First responders, including the FDNY, PA police, and emergency service units of the NYPD, helped evacuate civilians from the lower floors and the lobbies. Many more were injured on higher floors. A search for victims of a high-rise fire takes time—the primary search is not enough—every nook and cranny will be examined on a secondary search. But buildings will collapse when left to burn for a time, and getting up to the fire floors, much less searching above them, would take hours. It had in 1993, and it would again.[54]

The chiefs were aware of the risks—all firefighting command involves a constant calibration of risk to the men versus rescue of civilian victims. They decided that the risk was manageable. A defensive strategy, in effect "conceding the building to the fire," was part of their thinking—they did not intend to put out the fire. The key problem was when to pull the men out. The department had had more than enough tragic experience with collapses to keep them in mind.

One of the critical warning signals was "vibrating floors that are sagging at the center." Civilians above the fire would report such conditions in both towers, but these reports did not go to the chiefs. The chiefs knew that the floors were trusses, and they hated truss construction because it buckled and collapsed without much warning. So they sent the men up, and waited and watched with increasing concern down below.[55]

On the scene, the men had no illusions about what awaited them. Daniel Nigro, chief of operations under Chief Ganci, took one look and said, "'This is going to be the worst day of our lives! . . . The order of the day [was] 'Let's get the people out as fast as we can.'" No one underestimated the difficulty of that task or the disciplined courage needed to perform it. Jerry Nevins, from Rescue 1, told a colleague, "'Oh man, we're going to be lucky if we survive this,'" then he headed up the stairs. The entire Rescue 1 crew died in the collapse. Dennis

Tardio, captain of engine No. 7, following hard on Pfeifer's heels into the North Tower, later recalled, "'How proud I am of the men. At no time does anyone turn around and say, 'I ain't going up there.' . . . They just keep going on and on."[56]

But inside the buildings, the FDNY was losing control of its personnel. Some battalion commanders' transmissions from the South Tower sky lobby were reaching the command center, but others could not hear a thing on their radios. The police who had helicopters in the air monitoring the scene and officers on the streets around the towers who could see the progress of the fires could not communicate directly with the fire chiefs. Their radios did not share the same frequencies, and they did not "pair up" to share radio information. The FDNY could not keep communications open with their own men in the towers, because the small handy-talkies the men wore and the command radios the officers carried did not work well in high-rises—too much interference. The "repeater" system installed after 1993 to amplify signals was not much help. Thus, there was at best a lag between the time the chiefs made decisions and when these reached their men. Some key orders simply did not reach the firefighters.[57]

In the South Tower, Battalion 7 chief Orio Palmer's radio transmissions to the ladder No. 15 crew close behind him indicated that the most important concern for all of them was getting the injured out of the towers. The report of "a lot of bodies" on the seventy-eighth floor spurred him and his men to climb high and fast. They sent the injured down to the lower sky lobby, where the men were trying to run an elevator shuttle to the ground floor. Meanwhile, Palmer was talking to the "irons" and "roof" men from ladder No. 15: "We're going to have to hoof it." No elevator would take them nearer the burning floors. Palmer, in superb condition, was huffing now. "Boy, boy," he gasped. His aide, fifteen floors below, radioed, "I got to rest. I'll try to get up there as soon as possible." Palmer pressed on, and so, around him in the other stairwells, did the rest of the FDNY. When the elevator evacuation stalled, he radioed down, "Its imperative that you go down to the lobby command post and get some people up to 40. We got injured people up here on 70. We got injured people all the way up here." At 9:58, he keyed his radio, but the transmission was not recorded. The tower was collapsing on top of him. It killed every firefighter in the building.[58]

Listening to Palmer and his comrades on the recovered tape, one can hear the urgency of men working at high efficiency, but there was never a hint that the clock was running out on them. The communication problem had proved deadly. Before the collapse of the South Tower, at 9:32, Chief Joseph Callan in the North Tower radioed to his men, "'All units down to the lobby.'" This was a call for a complete withdrawal, and should have been followed immediately. In fact, such calls are rarely obeyed instantly, because they are so rare. As retired chief Vincent Dunn wrote, before 9/11, "It's usually accompanied by confusion and delay once the order is given."

Callan made the proper call—he based it on "the conditions in the [North] lobby, large pieces of plaster falling, all the 20 foot high glass panels on the exterior of the lobby were breaking. There was obvious movement of the building." He gave the order on his radio, but Palmer in the South Tower did not hear it, nor did the men on the upper floors of the North Tower. The police in helicopters saw the South Tower begin to lean and sag, and told their superiors, who relayed the message to the NYPD men in the towers, but it did not reach the firefighters because their much older radios did not work in the towers, and the chiefs' radios did not share a command frequency with the police radios. When the South Tower collapsed, at 9:59, chiefs at the West Street command post had to retreat into an underground garage and were unable to communicate with anyone in the North Tower for a time.[59]

Thus, many of the firefighters in the North Tower did not learn about the collapse or receive the order to retreat from the building. Even Deputy Chief Hayden, in the lobby of the North Tower, did not know the South Tower had come down until "somebody told me. We felt it. We didn't know what it was right away." A great cloud of dust and debris swept through the lobby of the North Tower, and Hayden and Pfeifer took shelter under the escalators. Pfeifer transmitted another order for an emergency withdrawal: "'All units, tower 1, evacuate the building.'" But again, not everyone heard. Up on the fortieth floor, Battalion 11 chief Richard Picciotto recalled, "There was no one on the radio, no hard information, just the simple daunting fact that the South Tower . . . had collapsed, and the all but certainty that whatever brought that building down was going to bring this one down also. And soon."[60]

The upper portions of the stairs in the North Tower were by now devoid of civilians. Firefighters were still clumped at various landings, mixed companies that had been leapfrogging one another up the stairs, then resting. By this time, a number of the men were suffering from angina pectoris—severe chest pains due to lack of oxygen. Indeed, so many men huffing and puffing up the narrow stairwells were using up the available oxygen faster than it could be replenished from below. Lieutenant Gregg Hansson, on floor twenty-seven, "heard urgent messages with firefighters reporting chest pains." On the thirty-fifth floor, he ran into an entire ladder company stopped for a break. Then the building started to shake and he heard a chief yelling into a bullhorn telling them to get out. It was Chief Picciotto.[61]

Picciotto heard and felt the collapse of South Tower as he moved up the stairs in the North Tower. He was later quoted as shouting, "get the [blank] out of here" to everyone in earshot. Captain Jay Jonas, twenty floors below, looked out a window and saw a great cloud of ash where the South Tower had been. Jonas quietly told his men, "'It's time for us to go home.'" Firefighter Mike Cancel heard the order to evacuate on his radio. It must have been Pfeifer. Why his message got through and Callan's earlier order did not remains a mystery.

As Chief Dunn had predicted, it proved hard to get the men to reverse direction and abandon the building. Lieutenant William Walsh, from ladder No. 1, one of the first companies to enter the North Tower, passed on the order to withdraw and then moved down the stairs, but firefighters resting on the lower floors of the North Tower blew him off: "Yeah, yeah, we'll be right with you, Lou [the NYC shorthand for lieutenant]." Picciotto, coming down behind Walsh, employed a variety of motivational tactics to get the men up and moving. Though he was the senior officer on the scene, he had to curse, shout, threaten, lie, wheedle, and bully the crews at every landing in the stairwell.

According to firefighter Steve Modica, Picciotto "was yelling quite a lot" when they met on the stairs. Modica was waiting for his boss, Chief John Pailillo, who had gone ahead up the stairs, but Picciotto was having none of it. Modica had little choice but to turn around and head down. Because Picciotto insisted, Modica survived. Had Picciotto not come upon Captain Tardio and the engine No. 7 crew, they might never have gotten out, Tardio later recalled.

But as Tardio and others poured out of the building into the ash-fall from the South Tower collapse, Picciotto's flight stalled. He came upon Jonas's men and a civilian, Josephine Harris, who simply could not go on any longer. As the men encouraged her to continue, the whole North Tower came down on their heads. Remarkably, all Jonas's men and Ms. Harris survived.[62]

The French documentarian Naudet stayed at Pfeifer's side in the North Tower throughout the crisis. When the South Tower came down and the order went out to abandon the North Tower, Naudet recorded it. When the ash and debris from the South Tower collapse turned the lobby of the North Tower dark as night, Naudet's video cam light became a beacon to the survivors. Both men made it out alive over the covered walkway to the World Financial Center, minutes before it, too, came down. Pfeifer threw his body over Naudet to protect him from the falling debris.

Outside, Fire Marshal Michael Smith was running for his life: "'[A]ll you hear was this thundering train . . . ba-boom, ba-boom, and then loud thunder . . . all you could do was look up, because all you saw was one floor after the other floor" crashing down. Then "I turn around real quick . . . all I see is this monster, concrete dust bowl coming up the street."[63]

SHOCK AND AWE

People far away from the WTC often knew more, sooner, about the collapses than did the firefighters going up the stairs in the towers.

"According to a Pew Research Center poll, approximately 81 percent of Americans" were watching television or listening to radio accounts. In an unprecedented step, network, local, and cable companies shared feeds and footage. Coverage was round the clock and commercial free.[64]

New Yorkers, wherever they happened to be, were alerting one another to the evolving disaster. In Athens, Georgia, preparing for my nine o'clock lecture in American history, I got a telephone call from my wife, in Cherry Hill, New Jersey. "Are you listening to your radio?" my wife asked. "A plane has just hit one of the towers in the World Trade Center." I logged on to CNN.com and there was the North Tower, billowing smoke.

People inside the city were getting calls from people far away. Brooklyn's Rod Dreher, a columnist for the *New York Post*, first heard about the explosion from his dad, who was watching television in Louisiana. Dreher's father was not the only Louisiana man transfixed by the images. Guy Massaro, a New Orleans district fire chief, was in Emmitsburg, Maryland, at the National Fire Academy for a two-week course on fire and arson investigation.

> We were in class for 7:30 AM, and we were studying high-rise construction, and how fire affects the structural members of a high-rise building. We took a break at 8:30, and when I returned to the classroom I noticed that on the large projection screen there appeared to be a very difficult fire scenario in one of the Twin Towers. Within a minute of my returning to the class, the second airliner hit the second tower. Like everyone in the class, I was shocked to see such an unbelievable event. I asked the instructor, "How were you able to generate a scenario as complicated as this?" He informed the class that he had patched the TV into the big screen and that this was real and it was unfolding as we watched. Needless to say, the room fell silent.[65]

At the scene, news photographers and reporters knew that the attack on the Twin Towers was the most important event they had ever covered. Mika Brzezinski of CBS News saw the North Tower burning on the monitors in the newsroom, and "I thought, 'I need to be there.'" When she and her producer were caught in the gridlock in the street, she took off her shoes, hopped out of the cab, and ran down West Street. Fear and desire drove her toward the story of her life. News photographer William Biggart and his wife were walking their dogs when they looked up to see the dark cloud from the first impact. It was 8:45. Biggart ran home to get his cameras. In a lifetime of taking chances to get the best shot, this was his best shot at an event that would change world history. His snaps of the burning North Tower from below were the closest anyone got. The *Post's* Arellano watched his freelance counterpart in anxious envy. "I saw Bill Biggart . . . taking pictures in the middle of the street. I said to myself, 'This guy is too close. It's too dangerous. . . .'" Biggart died in the collapse of the North Tower.[66]

Daily News photographer Susan Watts "was too close [when the South Tower collapsed]. I never thought you could ever be too close. Moments before the building fell, cops had been pushing the photographers back. I argued with them saying, 'You can't push us back. You're censoring us. This story is too big.' . . . You know what? The [police] were right." Just after the South Tower was hit, David Handschuh, a *Daily News* photographer, saw the smoke and heard the fire department dispatcher on his car radio. The dispatcher was calling a citywide "all hands." "On the way down[town] I hooked up behind a fire rescue unit that was driving on the wrong side of the [West Side] Highway.'" It was Rescue 3, from the Bronx. All five rescue squads, elite units, responded to the fire. Their job is to handle difficult rescue operations, including those of firemen trapped in a building. "'I followed his rear bumper, driving right behind. I've covered the police and fire beat in New York City for over 20 years, so many of these men and women . . . are friends. Two of the guys are putting on their gear in the back of the truck . . . and they're waving out the back window. It was their final run.'"[67]

It was almost Handschuh's last run, too. "'I'm across the street from the South Tower when all of a sudden, it collapses . . . I start to bring my camera up to my eyes, but something said to me, 'Run, just run.' I've never, ever, run from an assignment in more than 20 years of doing this, but running from that saved my life . . . I looked over my shoulder and saw a wall of debris flying in my direction—bricks, rock, water, glass. It was almost the approach of a tornado.'" Handschuh was partially buried under the "thick" muck. "A group of firemen, themselves likely running from the same dust storm, 'dug through the rubble and pulled me out.'"[68]

Reporters and photographers repaid the compliment. Todd Maisel helped save a firefighter from suffocation under the debris pile. Lieutenant William Ryan was one of the other rescuers. He recalled, "[the driver of the truck] was trapped in it, 'He was under about two or three stories of I-beams . . . It was a nightmare.'" Then the two men saw ladder No. 35's Kevin Shea, motionless. Maisel detected life, and he would help bear Shea, the only survivor of ladder No. 35, away from the ruins.

Many of the firefighters who escaped the collapses were disoriented, in part from the shock, in part because the "blizzard" of ash hid all signposts. Captain Michael Donovan later remembered, "[T]here was nobody. There was nobody" in sight. In the gray world of ashfall, victims and rescuers were indistinguishable from one another.[69]

The collapse not only showered the streets with lethal debris, it created a windstorm in the streets. Firefighters ran for their lives. Paramedic Mark Harris reported that as the North Tower started to come down, firemen rushed his van, broke the windows, and piled in. "This was like keystone cops . . . five of them, six, in back. Two on the bumper. One on the windshield wipers, one holding the mirrors." They were screaming, "f—king drive, drive," and he hit the gas. "Because behind us was the black cloud of the building collapse." The sweep of the debris out from the collapse created a partial vacuum. The wind sucked back into the void, like a tidal wave's return to the sea. Rescue and fire personnel had to dive under their vehicles or find shelter in doorways and storefronts. Carol Marin of CBS remembered the scene: "I turned and ran, and fell. A fireman grabbed me by the waist and threw me back on my feet, and we ran as fast as we could . . . Somewhere, the fireman threw me up against a wall and covered me with his body. All you really have at a moment like that is this giant sensory overload. It's what you smell, feel, and hear, not what you geographically see in a large picture." There was no sound—no screaming or sirens or bullhorns. "Ash was falling, two, three four inches deep on everything and on people . . . the [police] emergency and [fire] rescue teams were looking for each other, looking for their colleagues because they got swept away."[70]

In the midst of the chaos, civilians, reporters, and emergency personnel reached out to one another. With pieces of the building still bouncing off the pavement and the wind howling, Ruth Fremson, a *New York Times* photographer hiding under a vehicle, said hello to the man next to her. "I'm Ruth Fremson from the *New York Times*. He says, 'Hi, I'm Dan Mullin, I'm a cop.' We were both calm and having a conversation like we'd just met in a bar." Then they heard glass breaking nearby and it was time to run again.[71]

The collapse leveled ranks in the fire service. Gone was the entire Rescue 1 crew, including Nevin and Weiss. Gone, too, was Deputy Commissioner Feehan, almost impervious to harm in his forty-two years in the department. He had seen everything in his seventy-one years (six years past active service mandatory retirement age), a living history of the department as it modernized and diversified. No one could tell a story or comfort a grieving brother firefighter like Feehan. Gone was Downey, who entered the service in 1962, three years after Feehan and was much the opposite in his demeanor: "He wasn't much of a talker." He was a prodigious worker, however, a man who learned and taught everything there was to know about fighting fires. "He was decisive and smart" and understood how to keep his gung-ho charges in line. But in a fire, no one kept cooler than Downey. Gone was Chief Ganci. He left a safe area to warn the men at the Vesey Street command post to move back and was pinned under debris from the North Tower. Ganci's bravery was legendary, his composure and "gregariousness" infectious. He was a man whom other men trusted and loved. Though he had become chief of the department, he remained unpretentious. He still "put in eighty hour weeks" visiting the firehouses, "hanging out with his men."[72]

Tricks of fate saved other firemen's lives. Lieutenant Bill Wall of engine No. 47 was responding with his men to the fifth alarm at the

South Tower. He was supposed to go to the fortieth floor to assist in the rescue, but his guide, a WTC employee, led him to the wrong tower: "Saved our lives. Wrong place at the right time." Then he and his men got stuck in an elevator in the lobby of the North Tower just as the South Tower was collapsing. Two of his men were injured, and he and the others carried them out of the North Tower just before it pancaked.

At the staging area, after the collapse of the South Tower, Lieutenant Ray Brown told his men to go back to their rig to get an extra "bottle" for their air packs because, "it's going to be a long day." The ladder truck was parked on the other side of West Street from the WTC. The men checked their escape ropes and masks while they were there, and missed the collapse of the North Tower. Because firefighter John Breen's lieutenant told his men in the Marriott Hotel at the WTC to use Stairwell A instead of another, they survived the collapse of both towers. Ray Brown's men were able to extricate Breen and his brother firefighters from the flattened Marriott.[73]

The command structure of the FDNY had suffered a terrible but not a mortal blow. Although many officers were lost and a general retreat ensued, the discipline of the department held. Within minutes of the collapse of the second tower, firefighters resumed rescue operations in the street and other buildings in the area. City paramedic Roger Smyth recalled, "[A]s soon as the smoke [from the second collapse] started to clear, I saw people getting up and going toward the rubble to get whoever they could out." Firefighter Arthur Myers was the chauffeur of an engine company, and his company left him to enter one of the WTC buildings. He could not contact them after the collapse and started thinking, "Where are the guys?" When they appeared out of the ash cloud, he rushed to them, all of them "hugging and crying" in front of the West Street command post. Then they went back to work the pile.[74]

In the minutes after the collapses, the losses and destruction seemed almost unbearable, but the city's people had already begun to respond. As if by magic, a fleet of boats appeared at the edge of the seawall. Deputy Chief Robert Browne: "[A]ll kinds of boats were pulling up. The fire boat had pulled up and docked. Several other boats—a police boat. There was a tug boat there. There were civilian boats pulling up, willing just to take people, hand them off over onto the boat, and they were going to take them off on over to [New] Jersey for us."

Citizen volunteers—first aid, construction, military—all found ways to evade the police barricades or talk their way past the cops into the danger area. Nick Gerstle, a construction tech at Verizon headquarters next to the WTC, left a job in Brooklyn to get to the site: "'I'm a pretty big guy. I knew they'd need people who could move things.'" Gerstle stopped at a makeshift medical facility for a mask, found a turnout coat lying on the floor of a Burger King, donned heavy-duty gloves, and went to work alongside firefighters, a detachment of U.S. Marines, and ambulance technicians. They saved two PA policemen. The debris was still smoldering and choking ash was still in the air, but "'there was so much camaraderie you didn't feel the fear.'" Gerstle was overcome by the pollutants and ended up in the hospital. There he became something of a celebrity. The next day he was back at the debris pile.[75]

THE BIG PICTURE GRADUALLY BECAME CLEAR. In the city, the dead amounted to 2,973, of whom 343 were FDNY firefighters and officers, thirty-seven members of the Port Authority police, and twenty-three members of the NYPD, almost all of them elite Emergency Service Unit personnel. Fourteen EMS technicians died as well. The seven buildings of the World Trade Center complex were totally destroyed. Other terrorist attacks that morning left a portion of the Pentagon in flames and killed sixty-four people on the jetliner and 125 in the building or its grounds. Estimates vary, but as many as 10,000 people were successfully evacuated from the WTC. It was "the worst day" in many ways, but the conduct of the FDNY's rank and file in the crisis bespoke the best traditions of American urban firefighting.[76]

They "Ran In
As Others Ran Out"

The artistic traditions of city fire photography going back to the Chicago Fire of 1871 reached a peak of perfection on 9/11 and the following days. Perhaps the most striking of these photographs looked the fire right in the eye. NYPD photographers in helicopters circled the doomed buildings as they poured smoke thousands of feet into the air, and other members of the same remarkable special unit captured the collapses from ground level, in the midst of the maelstrom. Their photography reveals the immense scale of the tragedy. But for me, two far more intimate stills captured the determination and the despair of the FDNY. Neither was beautiful in a composed, aesthetic sense, but that did not detract from their emotional impact.[77]

The first is the back of a single member of the service in bunker gear, later identified as Lieutenant Ray Murphy of ladder No. 16. He is walking toward the plaza after the collapse of the South Tower. Grey ash covers everything, so that the engine to his left is barely visible, and only indistinct shapes loom ahead of him. He is going to rescue whomever he can from the debris. His carriage is erect and his stride long, though he must already know that the collapse has maimed many of his brother firefighters. A carpenter by avocation and a husband and father of simple, traditional virtues, he will die in the second collapse. Like his brother firefighters, he "ran in as others ran out."[78]

The second photograph appears to have been taken the afternoon after the collapse. Dennis Smith selected it for the cover of his deeply moving *Report from Ground Zero*. Again, the subject is a single firefighter, Joe Higgins of the Training Division. He sits on a piece of the steel curtain panels, head bent into his hands. We cannot see his face. His turnout coat is open and his helmet off. Perhaps he is simply too weary to deal with all his emotions. Perhaps beneath his hands tears run. He "had just realized he lost his brother Tim, a firefighter from [Chief Downey's] Special Operations Command." Perhaps he is also wondering if anything will be the same, ever again.[79]

There were other pictures, of course, hundreds of thousands of stills and video. Once busy Lower Manhattan commercial streets strewn with paper and piled with ash, a still life of twisted and burned vehicles and shattered storefronts. There were pictures of pictures—panoramas of the photos of missing loved ones that family and friends posted on the walls of Lower Manhattan. The image of a city in shock and mourning radiated out from Ground Zero. The fire and the collapse had touched many more than the immediate families of victims and care providers.

The tragedy was not just Manhattan's or New York City's, but the country's and the world's. Everyone in the country was watching or listening to the unfolding story of the tragedy, for in the towers and the WTC people from every continent worked in harmony. The terrorists were correct—the site not only symbolized the global economy, it proved that the city was still a haven for the oppressed multitudes seeking to be free.[80]

But for the history of urban fire and firefighting, the WTC fires had another message, far less ennobling or reassuring than the rhetoric that flowed from Ground Zero. The fires raised the unanswered question of whether the fire services could contain high-rise conflagrations. The ruins of the towers, mountains of twisted steel and powdered concrete, might be any of the thousands of American city skyscrapers that could be assaulted by catastrophic fires.

Mourning

With the fire still burning that early afternoon, the FDNY issued its first general recall of all off-duty, vacationing, and sick personnel in thirty years. As the men arrived at their firehouses, they heard rumors passed by word of mouth about who had gone to the fire. Rumor soon solidified into tentative lists of the missing. Every company that responded to the emergency had riding rosters posted in the houses—the officer and the firefighters assigned to each piece of apparatus. But some of the night shift men had ridden along on the apparatus or had swapped places with others listed for duty.

Each FDNY firehouse is an extended family; the men and their families know one another well. Loved ones at home had watched the fire on television. Many of them knew that their firefighters would go to the scene. They called the firehouses, where off-duty firefighters manned the phones. The questions had a kind of uniform anxiety. The callers knew that their men would want to be at the scene. Over and over, they had insisted, "I'll come home," but this time they hadn't. Did Kevin ride with the apparatus, his wife wanted to know. Did he go up into the towers? Did he get out? People kept turning up at the firehouses, so there was hope. There are always "voids"—small but stable empty spaces—in all collapses, even a "pancake" collapse like the Twin Towers. Captain Jonas, Chief Picciotto, and Josephine Harris, along with a dozen others, ended up in one void. Firefighters working the pile rescued them. Hope for others drove the rescuers' exertions and kept the callers' spirits up. Surely there were more men and women buried alive in the ruins.[81]

The massive, silent steles of the WTC only reluctantly gave up their secrets. By the evening of September 16, the rescuers grudgingly accepted that they would not find anyone else alive. The men on the pile turned their efforts to recovery of the bodies of the victims. Firefighters and their officers, along with emergency medical service personnel from all over the country, journeyed to the pile to help. Relatives of victims appeared in solemn groups. Fathers, brothers, and sons of missing firefighters worked the site, while other loved ones simply watched, sometimes edging perilously close to the danger area.

The commanders at the site had to cajole, plead, threaten, and restrain the rescue force. Battalion Chief John Norman: "By that point [24 hours after the collapses] a lot of the families were there . . . just trying to deal with them was very hard . . . we're trying to reassure them . . . we haven't given up hope . . . it was tough trying to explain that . . . [but] we got as far as we could until we were stopped by solid rubble." Heavy equipment arrived and deployed, but much of the searching was still eye and nose to the ground. Sniffer dogs prowled the pile and became noticeably upset when they could not find any more living victims. The cost ran to hundreds of millions of dollars to remove the debris, though at first no one was counting. "It will take a year to dig through . . . the pyramid of smoking rubble," the firefighters wrongly assumed, nevertheless planning to be "at the site" whenever they could.[82]

Author and former FDNY member Dennis Smith went to the site every day for nearly two months. He later reported: "This is how it works . . . if something is discovered that belongs to a firefighter [missing in the rubble] a small army of his brothers comes in to dig out the area." If the article belongs to a policeman, the police moved in to recover the body. Firefighters with charged hoses stood by; like a wildfire, there were hot spots and sometimes they flared up. In the "middle of the site itself," the men moved about like ants on a hill, poking, carrying off debris, "looking for signs of past life . . . If a body part is found, everything will stop and the men will begin to lift and sift by hand." They were there to "take our boys home." Remarkably, given the danger of more collapses and the rickety debris pile, none of the recovery crew died.

There were burials of the recovered firefighters every day, and Smith attended as many as he could. He watched crews marching in slow step behind the flag-draped apparatus. For Chief Ganci, thousands came. But every firefighter had a formal interment and every company that could turned out, decked in their class A uniforms. On October 6, 2001, twenty-six funerals and memorial services marked the flood tide of mourning. Mayor Rudy Giuliani and Commissioner

Tom Von Essen rushed from one to the next, hopscotching with Smith. The pipers played the tunes of glory as the dead were borne to their final resting place. Smith noted: "The bagpipers are a special breed of firefighter . . . in fact most of them come from the busiest firehouses." They played for the families who next time might be their own. It would go on for nearly a year, until a final formal ceremony on May 30, 2002, at Ground Zero "marked the end of the recovery effort."[83]

Later, documentaries recorded the voices of the men of the FDNY who survived the collapse of the towers and those who worked the debris pile. Journalist Pete Hamill and firefighter-turned-documentarian Mike Lennon's documentary, *Brothers on Holy Ground,* captured the men's optimistic fatalism. The firefighters they filmed all agreed that if the towers were burning again, they would run in as civilians ran out. The men on the rigs that tour; the men who happened to be going off duty; the men who had arranged to do a shift for someone else—they would all run in. It was what they did.[84]

But in the wake of so many deaths, grief and anger fed on one another. The firefighters are tough, clannish, and loyal, and it was in that character, at Ground Zero on November 2, 2001, that the "prolonged wake" became a violent melee. There were too many near accidents at the site, and too little command and control of the seekers. This was particularly true of the fire company contingents searching for their dead. Von Essen proposed that the sixty-four firefighters on each shift at Ground Zero be reduced to twenty-five. Mayor Giuliani, with advice from his appointees, particularly Police Commissioner Bernard Kerik, agreed. The FDNY contingent would be matched by twenty-five police officers and twenty-five PA policemen. In effect, this both reduced the number of firefighters engaged in the recovery effort and placed it under the control of the police department. Officers' union president Peter Gorman and firefighters' union leader Kevin Gallagher protested. It led to a confrontation at the site, fisticuffs, the arrest of eleven firefighters, a captain, and three other officers, followed by a FDNY march on City Hall. The arrests were later reduced to misdemeanors and the detainees released.[85]

The resentment between the two forces ran deeper than an argument about whose bodies would be recovered first. The dispute is an old one, going back at least two generations of firefighters and police, to the 1970s. The rivalry between the FDNY rescue squads and the NYPD emergency services units was the tip of a very large iceberg. The two proud and superbly staffed units did not train together, nor did they cooperate at emergency scenes. The rivalry turned bitter in the 1990s and had not been reconciled, much less remedied, on 9/11. Police in the North Tower knew from their officers that the South Tower had collapsed and that the North Tower was leaning to one side, but "with some lower level" and individual "exceptions," this information was not systematically shared with their counterparts in the FDNY, either in the tower or at the FDNY command post.[86]

The nub of the dispute remains which of the two forces will command at an emergency. In May 2005, the mayor's office announced that the NYPD would command at hazardous materials sites and other suspected terrorist actions. The FDNY would take orders from the police. Peter Hayden, by this time the chief of the department, was livid. He told the city council that "police helicopters [on 9/11] observed that one of the trade center towers was near collapse, 'but police commanders became so focused on their own tasks that they neglected to perform the critical task of information sharing.'" Hayden put the case for the preeminence of the FDNY in stark terms: "'The agency that is responsible for saving lives at a terrorist incident and for the rest of the city is not equally responsible for command . . . this does not make sense.'" The firefighters and officers filling the balcony gallery at the city council chamber in City Hall clapped and shouted encouragement. Hayden, a hero at the site, was a hero again. Police Commissioner Raymond Kelly was not amused, but then, he had won what new fire department commissioner Nicholas Scoppetta admitted was a "behind the scenes" dispute.[87]

There was nothing "behind the scenes" about the serious morale problem that infected Scoppetta's troops. FDNY members' assignments take them to different firehouses, and they get to know firefighters and officers in other companies. Everyone in the department on 9/11 lost friends in firehouses all over the city. City University professor Michael Berman dropped by his local firehouse late in the fall of 2001. The companies had not lost a man, and he told them, "I was so glad they had all survived. 'We shouldn't have,' a fireman with moist eyes" replied.[88]

There is a huge literature on "survivor syndrome," the guilt that overtakes individuals when their close friends are lost in a catastrophic event. The tears in the firefighter's eyes were genuine indications of the stress and sense of emotional loss that accompany helplessness. They are made worse by fatigue (particularly among those working the site of the collapses). The worst-case scenario among the FDNY involved terrifying "re-experiencing" among those who got out of the buildings in time. Their symptoms included anxiety, depression, and dissociation (memory loss or staring into space without connecting with one's surroundings). One could walk past any firehouse in the city and see these symptoms on the faces of some of the firefighters. The FDNY suffered from survivor syndrome.[89]

Such massive and easily documented emotional distress was not included in the compensation package that Congress, and its chosen administrator of the fund, offered to the firefighters. As the administrator, Kenneth Feinberg, later recalled, "[T]his was a tough call. A strong argument could be made that such mental injury and emotional trauma should be compensable, but I was worried about an open-ended run on the U.S. Treasury." In effect, if the firefighters could make claims, why not the rest of the city?[90]

Some FDNY survivors wondered why they had not perished along with their brothers. Kevin Shea was the only survivor of ladder No. 35 and engine No. 40 that went to the towers from his firehouse. He was nearly killed by falling debris at the site but had gnawing doubts about his own conduct. He could not remember—had he run away when others "ran in"? Had he let his fallen brothers down? No, his captain told him, the men were overjoyed that he came back. It turned out that he was putting out car fires in the street behind the South Tower when it came down.

Malachy Corrigan directed the FDNY counseling service unit. He knew that the mantra of the firefighter is "'I'm a tough guy and I can't be weak emotionally,'" and that it no longer worked. He and his forty peer counselors heard thousands of cases, and 80 percent of them derived from 9/11. The men had nightmares when they tried to sleep and hallucinated when they awoke. For the men of Rescue 2, "there's no one moment" when things are back to normal. "After a while, the guys start to make fun of themselves, of their own sadness ... but even making fun doesn't make the sadness disappear."[91]

Senior officers took early retirement in droves. In the nine months after 9/11, 213 officers retired, a figure more than 50 percent higher than in the previous year. Daniel Nigro, serving as Ganci's successor, was going, and so were the heads of the fire prevention and safety divisions. The flight of the company commanders was even more vexing, for they were the officers the fighters worked with every day. Emotion played a role. So did the lingering lung injuries that the firefighters had suffered because of exposure to toxic pollutants in the collapse and at the site over the following weeks. Altogether, like veterans of any combat zone, the firefighters were "sick of their own pain."[92]

SELF-CRITICISM

For the command of the fire service and the elected officials of the city, there had to be a more thorough and analytical response to the WTC fires. No one in peacetime could condone and no one would be willing to concede the kind of losses in personnel that occurred on the morning of September 11th. Two days into the recovery efforts at the World Trade Center, Rescue 1's captain, Terry Hatton, was still missing, along with his entire squad. His father, Kenny, an FDNY veteran, called commissioner Von Essen, and asked, "How could this happen?" Everyone was asking the same question. Von Essen didn't have an answer.[93]

In part, finding that answer meant reexamining the creed that sent firefighters into burning buildings to save civilians. There is no doubt that the FDNY members were as well trained, led, and motivated as any emergency service in the twentieth century. As Battalion Chief

John Salka wrote, some years after he took part in the recovery operations at Ground Zero, "[T]he story of the FDNY is, at heart, the story of an organization whose tradition of phenomenal leadership has always enabled it to meet and overcome any challenge, no matter how daunting." That attitude toward fires is necessary if the primary focus of firefighting is to protect life. But imbued with this creed, had the senior commanders committed their men to a fatal and useless effort to rescue those beyond help?[94]

Another part of the inquiry entailed the FDNY's internal review of its SOP. Everyone recognized that critical misjudgments had occurred. The question was, how basic were these to the operational tactics of the FDNY? Many fire departments, the National Fire Academy, and the U.S. Fire Administration, have adopted the incident command system and incident management guides. According to former FDNY chief Vincent Dunn, the FDNY subscribes to these norms when the occasion demands. The SOP in ICS begins: "[F]irefighter safety is the first consideration for all procedures." Plainly, that commandment was stretched to the limit in the towers. SOP requires "information, [firefighter] safety, and liaison . . . the ability of all units or agencies to communicate at an incident." Staging— managing resources—and deployment of personnel at the incident are also essential preliminaries to firefighter safety and effective operations. Men and apparatus must be staged in a safe area and committed to the danger area only as needed. In fast-moving or highly dangerous conditions, SOP mandates easily movable command posts.[95]

Had these SOPs been followed at the Twin Towers fire scene? There seemed to be little effective liaison. True, there were two police forces and a myriad of other first responders to coordinate, but the fact remains that fire chiefs did not have senior PA and NYPD police liaisons standing with them at the command post. Staging and personnel deployment were not well controlled. Apparatus parked at the foot of the plaza disgorged their companies in the shadow of the towers. For example, Lieutenant Brian Becker of engine No. 28 responded with his company to the fire in the North Tower and no one told the chauffeur where to put the rig. Becker asked him where he wanted it (chauffeurs are experts at parking near the hydrants), but on this occasion neither officer nor driver knew where to park. They decided on a spot under the West Street pedestrian overpass from the North Tower to the World Financial Center because they did not want jumpers from the towers to hit the crew. The engine was destroyed when the collapse brought down the overpass.[96]

In addition, no one told the crew what to do once they alighted from the engine. They simply moved to the lobby and reported their arrival. When they entered the North Tower, a chief sent them up the stairs. Becker could not recall who it was: "[T]here was no command. It was chaos in the lobby." Even arriving battalion commanders had no clear idea of the priority of tasks or the whereabouts of equipment. When Battalion Chief John Pailillo arrived with his aide Mike Modica in the lobby of the North Tower, Pailillo went over to the commander in the lobby and after a moment returned to where Modica was standing. "What do we do?" Modica asked. Pailillo replied, "[S]tart up and wherever we can find ourselves useful, we'll help." That was the sort of man Pailillo was and that was the reason he had gained such esteem in the department, but the two had no assigned tasks in the building. They should not have been there. Pailillo never came down.[97]

Vital information did not reach the men in the towers, and they were not able to communicate with their commanders. When the buildings came down, "a dazed force that had lost many of its leaders initially struggled to respond before rousing itself to plunge into the debris pile in search of survivors." The senior leadership had done what the FDNY always did—lead by example, close to the danger. They were killed at the West Street command post after the collapse of the North Tower because they remained too close to the peril even when it had shown its face.

"Many of the surviving chiefs had been scattered by the debris clouds," and some had concluded that they alone survived. The enormity of the tragedy spurred the remaining command cadre to climb onto the debris pile to search for lost colleagues, though the debris pile was hot, unstable, and shrouded in dangerous haze. "Chief Thomas McCarthy [recalled] . . . that some firefighters were so determined to find people that they took dangerous chances scrambling about in unstable areas of the debris pile." The would-be rescuers had to be treated for smoke inhalation, damage to eyes, and assorted bruises.[98]

With the new year, newly appointed fire commissioner Scoppetta and Mayor Michael Bloomberg asked an outside consulting firm to examine the conduct of the FDNY in 9/11. Almost a year after September 11, after extensive consultation with other fire services and within the FDNY, McKinsey and Company issued its recommendations for improving FDNY performance in major incidents.[99]

McKinsey, in the words of one student of business history, "is huge." In fact, by repute McKinsey is the world's leading consulting firm. The company's Web page spells out its approach: "We aim to help the executives of leading companies and organizations make significant improvements to their overall performance by tackling their most challenging issues. We do so by taking a top-management perspective, bringing innovations in management practice, and building our clients' capabilities." The McKinsey report provided its recommendations in the most tactful but clear fashion. "As our work progressed, we found many examples of actions by the FDNY that saved lives, but we focused on identifying procedures, organization, and technology that should be improved to increase the Department's preparedness in the future." One cannot get more tactful than that.[100]

For all its studied understatement, the report was devastating. So-called 20/20 hindsight is always suspect, and it is easier to pronounce what should have been done than to adapt to rapidly changing conditions at a fire scene as they unfold. No one at the time was certain exactly what had happened. Unfolding events did not give a clear picture beyond the obvious airplane strikes. As the fire control center in the South Tower transmissions stated, "[W]e don't know what it is here." Nevertheless, the McKinsey interviews revealed a disturbing pattern. The FDNY set up operational command centers in the lobbies of the towers, embedded rather than mobile sites. The firefighters did not stage properly. The buildings were full of firefighters and officers whose units were not assigned to the fire by dispatch but came on their own. Soon after the first alarm was sounded, the FDNY lost track of its own personnel deployment. The photographs of West Street behind the towers before the collapse show that apparatus was all over the street. After the collapse, the apparatus was buried under tons of debris.[101]

Adding to the mishandling of staging and personnel assignment, the department did not supply its men with necessary information during the time the towers stood. The communications problem was long-standing, and in the spring of 2001 new radios that would have improved communications at the towers simply sat while lower-ranking officers refused to learn how to use the equipment. Commissioner Von Essen later recalled, "[W]e had spent millions of dollars" for the new radios, "but the implementation was badly botched." On 9/11, radio transmissions to the men from their commanders were garbled. In the end, the chiefs and their men returned to nineteenth-century methods of word-of-mouth and line-of-sight command. Chief Picciotto's bullhorn may have been the most effective piece of equipment in the communications arsenal that day.

A second failure of communication was even more devastating: "Inter-agency coordination was minimal. For example, there were no senior NYPD chiefs at the incident command post [on West Street] established by the Fire Department." The result was that police department information about the imminent collapse of the towers did not reach the fire chiefs.[102]

For the McKinsey investigators, what had made the FDNY so magnificent in an age of small-group, traditional firefighting was maladaptive to large-scale incidents. What had kept morale so high in the past was an obstacle to correcting the flaws in future. In particular, "When units failed to stage properly in the past, the Department did not follow up systematically . . . and, if necessary, sanction their [those units'] officers, and their commanders." The symptoms of on-site institutional malpractice were so serious that McKinsey recommended the department engage in thorough self-examination: "The FDNY must make a renewed commitment to leadership, accountability and discipline at all levels, in the field and at headquarters."[103]

Only "profound change" in the management of the department would insure that the losses of 9/11 never recurred. Although the FDNY supposedly "uses the incident command system taught at the National Fire Academy," elements of that system were significant by their absence on 9/11. The department would have to embrace the incident command system, and that meant full cooperation with the police as well as retraining of the senior fire officers. In more concrete terms, the FDNY needed an operations center rather than a semi-amateur dispatch system, incident management teams instead of hastily arrayed conglomerations of chiefs and deputy chiefs, and strict control over who in the department did what at major emergencies. Ninety-seven pages of even more detailed instructions followed.[104]

The report was compelling reading and thoroughly professional, but in one sense it may have been incomplete. It rested upon the same assumptions about firefighting and the fires of 9/11 that had directed the FDNY's response. It assumed that every firefight can be won if tactics, training, and manpower are appropriately utilized, and it assumed that the towers fires were simply very big and very dangerous structural fires. If neither of these assumptions were true, then one would have to reassess the events in a very different way.[105]

Technically speaking, the "chain" of ill fortune that leads to firefighter injury or death begins with the "environment." Misread the fire environment, mistake the dangers in the environment, and the risk of injury or death comes a giant step closer. When the experts reassessed the decisions that led to the 9/11 disaster, they—like the chiefs on the scene at the fires—assumed that the towers were simply big structures and the fire was simply a structural one. The environmental link in the "accident chain" that led to 343 FDNY deaths then focused on the unexpected speed, severity, and nature of the collapse. In short, the chiefs anticipated that the towers would hold up a lot longer, and if they collapsed, they expected the collapse to be a local rather than a total one. Even if the last horrific eventuality befell the men, the chiefs assumed that the collapse would leave many "voids" in which the men would find refuge. Given this reading of the environment, the decision to send the men up the towers to the fire scene turned out to be a mistake, but an entirely understandable one. In fact, given the assessment of the number of civilians needing assistance and the mission of the fire service, one could hardly second-guess it. But what if the basic assumption that the towers were simply very big buildings badly misread the environment of the fire?[106]

How could so experienced, able, and well trained a leadership cadre as stood that morning on West Street have misread a fire scene? As the risk management course at the National Fire Academy explains, fire chiefs have in their minds a kind of "hard drive" of prior experience: "When [they] are presented with a situation, such as a structural fire, [they] unconsciously take what [they] see and attempt to match it with a situation that [they] have seen before." This mental matching system of tactical response runs into problems with high-risk, low-frequency events: "High risk, low frequency situations where there is no time to back off and make decisions pose the most extreme levels of risk to responders and response organizations." No one in America had more experience of structural fires than the FDNY chiefs assembled on West Street that morning. That experience included an SOP about collapse—that "prolonged burning of a serious fire on several floors" was grounds for complete withdrawal from a building.[107]

But the unexpected and total collapse of the towers need not have been the critical issue, had the fires been regarded as wildfires rather than structural fires. After his rescue from a void in the North Tower debris, Lieutenant Mickey Kross came back to work recovery at the site. He noticed, "It's kinda' like being on a mountain range. You need to be careful of your footing. In a way it's a survival game. I don't mean to make fun of it, but it's the WTC reality show." Kross had glimpsed something about the site that had escaped the notice of the McKinsey assessors and the chiefs the morning of 9/11.[108]

The distinction between a structural fire typical in the city and a canyon wildfire is one that runs all through the story of the Oakland Hills firestorm of 1991. The OFD came equipped to fight a city fire and found itself in the middle of a wildfire. Urban fire departments are not accustomed to fighting wildfires and do not plan for firefighter safety based on the characteristics of wildfires.

Wildfires are not without precedent in New York City. The borough of Staten Island has some largely undeveloped areas. These have experienced groundcover fires, but training to combat them was never part of the command course. When fires ripped through the brush and scrub on the island in 1962 and 1963, the FDNY was stretched to its limit to contain the blazes. Over 200 pieces of heavy apparatus had to be ferried to the island to help the FDNY companies stationed there. Pictures from the fire show that the men were tied to their pumpers and the pumpers' effectiveness tied to the water supply. The fires raged almost uncontrolled for days.[109]

Can it be that the towers fires were also groundcover fires? Although the fires were structural in the sense that the building itself was on fire, other characteristics of the fire were more like those of wildfires. Return to the WTC the morning before the catastrophe and compute the space and distances involved. The site was sixteen acres. That is a perimeter of .625 miles at the base of the plaza. A visit to "the tub" today reminds one of how huge the site is in two dimensions. Each floor of the towers was about an acre in horizontal space. Multiply that by 110 stories of the two towers, for a total of 220 acres. Add to that the huge spaces beneath the buildings, the equivalent of another six acres for each building, a total of 232 acres. An acre is 43,560 square feet. In two dimensions only, the area of potential fire in the towers was thus 10,105,950 square feet. But the towers were not flat surfaces. They were giant rectangular solids. Each story in them was ten feet high. Thus, the buildings contained 100,105,950 cubic feet of potential burn. Because of the unique construction features, there was no way to confine the fire within one part of the floor. The floors were like little valleys between walls of canyons. Seen in this light, there is just too much ground to cover even for hundreds of firefighters.

Consider what the two wide-body jets filled with airplane fuel did to this space when they smashed into the towers' external walls. The first plane ripped a diagonal rent in the North Tower's north face seven floors wide, from the ninety-third to the ninety-ninth. The impact of the collision and the fireball destroyed the stairwells and the elevator shafts in the core of the building, cutting off the water supply to the standpipes and sprinklers. The explosion blew away the thin layer of fireproof drywall protecting the core. The fuel exploded and splashed all over the floors, pouring down some of the elevator shafts. This enabled the fire to spread far more rapidly than in a normal city structural fire. The burning fuel acted the role of the eucalyptus and pine cinders in the Oakland Hills fire.

In the South Tower, the collision ripped the south face from the seventy-eighth to the eighty-fifth floor, smashing most of the columns supporting the core and spreading fire through the entire southern and western sides of the building. The wide-open ("rentable") space designed into each floor supplied the tower fires with plentiful oxygen, more like a wildfire than a city fire, where closed spaces compartmentalize and slow the spread of fire.

Now think of the distances the firefighters had to go to get to the fire on the upper floors or to rescue victims below the fire. The elevators were not safe. The men had to go up the stairs. They were so narrow that the firefighters going up and the evacuees going down had to pass one another single file. That slowed the responders' pace. The towers were over 1,300 feet in elevation, but the stairs were a far longer walk than that. Assuming the stairs were 45° (though they were not quite so steep), if they were laid out, they would be 1,850 feet long. But the steps were not laid out. They were an uphill climb. Going up, the men were wearing fifty-nine pounds of gear (helmet, bunker coat and pants, boots, gloves, hood, flashlight, air pack) and carrying up to another forty pounds in Halligan tools, axes, saws, lanterns, and the like. Many of the engine company men were carrying sections of hose.

Estimates of the time it took for a fully equipped firefighter to go up a single flight ranged from one to two minutes. Thus, going up ninety stories would take an hour and a half—if the men could maintain the pace over the entire distance. In fact, by the nineteenth floor, many were laboring. By the thirtieth floor, they were having severe chest pains. Rescue 1 was treating FDNY members for angina.

The men who joked about the distance they had to go to fight the fire had made a rough calculation of the fire's size and the space involved. In retrospect, it appeared to be quite accurate.[110]

With all this in mind, one can see that going up the stairs in the towers on 9/11 was like walking into the center of a canyon filled with flammable brush and scrub where the winds are already kicking the blaze into fire whirls. Nothing could be more fatal to firefighters. The major groundcover or wildfire kills less through its heat than through its extent and its speed. It gets behind the firefighter and traps him, then sucks the oxygen out of the air and strangles him. The Forest Service's smoke jumpers know that such a fire can catch the fastest and fittest member of the team. For example, the crew of engine No. 28 only escaped from the North Tower because of their "mad dash" down the stairs.[111]

Hindsight is always 20/20, and my analogy may only amuse veteran city firefighters, but conceived as a wildfire, the towers' blazes on 9/11 should have been fought entirely differently. One simply cannot approach wildfires too closely, whether to extinguish them or rescue victims. They cover too much space and move too fast. In wildfires, the distance between the firefighter and the fire is the margin between life and death. One can only try to prevent the fire's expansion into the surrounding countryside.

Had the chiefs treated the WTC fire as a wildfire instead of a conventional structural fire, the FDNY would have assisted the NYPD and the Port Authority police in escorting civilians from the buildings from the lower floors and clearing the entire plaza area and the other WTC structures. FDNY apparatus would have been deployed in a wide ring around the WTC site to prevent the spread of the fire, putting out fires in adjacent buildings. The men would never have been committed to the upper floors at all, nor would they have parked and climbed off their rigs under the towers. In 2004, Commissioner Scoppetta told the 9/11 Commission that the FDNY had consulted with "the U.S. Forestry Service, which has extensive experience using ICS at complex, long duration incidents," and was sending officers assigned to the FDNY's newly created Incident Management Teams to get "hands on training at major incidents in the western United States." In wildfire management, one assumes.[112]

THE FDNY RECOVERS

In the days after the disaster, despite the decline in morale and the retirements, the FDNY began its institutional recovery. The department reasserted the very values that had led its commanders, their officers, and the men to go up into the buildings. As Lieutenant Kross recalled, "'[W]e got off the rig and I had a little pep talk with the guys right in the street. It was something to the effect of, 'Okay, guys, this is going to be tough. It's going to be tough, but it's another fire—the main thing is, we just stay together and watch out for each other.'" That's what the FDNY did after the fire.[113]

First, it raised memorials to the dead. The rituals of mourning helped. At the Fire Academy on Randalls Island, a "5-foot high, 40 pound scroll" with six smiling faces honored the probationary firemen who followed their officers into the holocaust. For that is what officers tell the probies—stick close to me and you will be safe.

Every firehouse in the city became an impromptu memorial site as well. Neighbors festooned the walls outside the apparatus bays with flowers. Inside, the men put up pictures and plaques reminding the living of the dead. Lockers whose owners would never return to claim the personal gear inside became miniature shrines. The city's Fire Museum on Spring Street dedicated a wall of honor to the 9/11 fallen. The *New York Times* and *Newsday* profiled the men. On the web, memorial sites such as www.bravestmemorial.com listed every man who died and provided a picture and brief obituary.[114]

The extended FDNY family staggered but healed its own wounds in time-honored fashion. As Commissioner Von Essen told the mourners at David Weiss's funeral, "[T]he fire department has a broken heart . . . but it will mend." At the funerals, the brass and the grieving families consoled one another. One widow said to Commissioner Von Essen, "'[T]his isn't your fault . . . don't even think that for a minute." Her husband, who had just come back to duty after months of rehab from a collapse, could not have been stopped from going into the buildings "'even if'" the commissioner had wanted him to hold back. Families told one another that the loved one "had been a fireman, and he had always known the risks"; he "loved the life"; and "had died doing his duty." At Chief of Department Peter Ganci, Jr.'s funeral, Von Essen told the chief's family, "Pete would never ask anyone to do anything he hadn't . . . that is what happened . . . as he took charge of rescue and firefighting efforts at the World Trade Center." Battalion Chief Salka tried to explain to a civilian friend why so many of the FDNY dead were officers. "First in, last out . . . sums up the leadership philosophy of the FDNY. It's the guiding principle behind everything we do . . . We lead out front, where everyone can see us."[115]

The department recruited heavily to return its numbers to pre-9/11 levels. It promoted rapidly to fill the ranks of missing officers. In fact, some 170 men were immediately raised to officer rank. The elite squads, decimated by losses at the WTC, were refurbished with eighty qualified men from the other companies. Rescue 3 lost eight men on 9/11, but a bare four months later their places at the firehouse were taken. Firefighter Jeff Cool, a newcomer to the squad, told a reporter, "I lost a friend here, and I felt like I had the experience to fill a void . . . You never really fill it, I guess."[116]

Some men just needed to remind themselves how good the FDNY was at fighting fires. "In January, 2003, [Rescue 2 caught] a good job during a blizzard." They saved a ladder company officer who had fallen through a hidden hole, then "drag[ged] out two other firemen overcome by the heat." With acetylene tanks going off all around them, they helped put out the flames. Rescue 2 Captain Phil Ruvolo recalled thinking, "'This is nothing. This is easy. Hell, this is fun.'"[117]

Firefighter Cool also accepted the special dangers facing rescue squad members. On January 23, 2005, he and five other men were searching the upper floors of a Bronx apartment house when "a fireball burst through the floorboards." He was trapped between the burning room and a high window with no way to get back out the door. Four men jumped before him, and two died from their injuries. He and a buddy tied the personal safety rope he carried to one of the child safety bars and scaled down, both falling a short distance when the rope gave out. Cool was released from the hospital on February 19, 2005, with Rescue 3's men lining the sidewalk and cheering. "'Jeff's a tough guy,' his captain told a reporter, 'always has been, always will be.'" At a May 10, ceremony honoring his partner, Joseph L. DiBernardo, Cool sat in the audience. "'It's like a roller coaster ride,' Battalion Chief Edward Moriarty told the audience, 'We go up and we go down.'"[118]

It was hard for the firefighters and their officers to digest criticism of their traditions, but in a thousand little ways, the FDNY began to do just that. As Von Essen said at firefighter Weiss's funeral, the FDNY was going to "fix, rebuild, retrain, and regroup." Firefighters who were rock climbers developed a new kind of personal escape rope made of Kevlar, with a folding hook attachment. The city agreed to buy one for every member of the department, at a cost of $11 million. The rescue squads started to think more seriously about terrorist attacks and how to counter them. There were new training courses at the Fire Academy every month, expanding on programs that Chief Downey had introduced. Hazardous materials and terrorism response courses were added to the academy curriculum and to the department's continuing education program. New equipment arrived to replace the apparatus lost at the site—eighteen pumpers, fifteen ladder trucks, and two rescue squad vans, not to mention the ambulances; all told, a total of ninety-one vehicles. Tools, air packs, bunker gear were all replaced. Even the new radios were finally distributed and mastered. The firefighters and officers worked out routines for dealing with chemical and radioactive scenarios. The next time, they told themselves, they would be ready.[119]

The FDNY recovery was inspiring, but not out of the ordinary. Firefighting in America is bound by tradition but is open to improvement. When city builders introduced concrete skyscrapers, fire departments like New York City's and Philadelphia's introduced special rescue squads "'with the newest sort of apparatus to fight the modern fire. Buildings are made stronger and are, therefore, more difficult to tear down when necessity arises. . . . Specially picked and trained experts'" were the answer. They had to have experience in construction, attend extra classes at training school, and learn to work as a team. And this was 1926.

In New York, the McKinsey report had made its weight felt. Commissioner Scoppetta told the 9/11 Commission that the FDNY "fully subscribes to the letter, policy, and principles of ICS," and "currently, the Department's IMTs [Incident Management Teams] are on-call and ready to respond to any large-scale incident at the direction of the Chief of Department."[120]

WHY THE TOWERS COLLAPSED

For engineers and design consultants asked to determine the reasons for the towers' collapse, there was no guilt, no survivor syndrome, no apologies, and no doubt. Their mindset was entirely different from the fire service. They clinically examined the burned trusses and panels removed to a New Jersey dump site to answer the question, "Why did the towers crumble?" They played with numbers, test results, and modeling, then agreed it all came down to "rentable space" and cutting corners to save money.

From their inception, skyscrapers were giant heavy-limbed cages—lattice works of steel, concrete, and tile many feet thick. A remarkable photograph of the Singer Building at 149 Broadway taken during its construction in 1907 demonstrates the point. The 612-foot-high building was for a time the tallest in the city, and to prevent collapse the builders put larger cages of steel around smaller cages of steel until the shell looked like an impenetrable maze of columns and girders: "The point was structural integrity." The columns had to be placed every twenty feet or so to anchor the floors. Redundancy provided strength. If there was a local collapse, the rest of the building could support the fallen floors.

Not so in the Twin Towers. Leslie Robertson, working with Yamasaki, found a way to replace the multiples of interior columns with load-bearing external panels and heavy core supports. At the top, only thin steel was needed in the columns and the floor trusses, the other major innovation. It was the floor trusses that were the target of inquiry, and the culprit turned out to be the bolts that held the floor trusses to the core and the curtain.[121]

In 2002, the Federal Emergency Management Agency released its preliminary findings from its "World Trade Center Building Performance Study." The report concluded that the external panels on both buildings withstood the shock of the collision. The fireball from the airplane fuel was hot enough to start structural fires, and ultimately softened and weakened the floors. The culprit in the avalanche or pancake type of collapse was not the walls, but the floors. In the final minutes of each of the towers, victims on the upper floors called down to the lobbies, saying that the floors were buckling. The explosion blew away much of the sprayed-on fireproofing on those trusses. In fact, no one had tested the fireproofing on the steel trusses that held the floors in place. When they were tested, after the fire, they passed—but only for seventeen-foot lengths of steel. However, the steel trusses under the buckled floors were twice that in length. Whatever parts of the buildings the explosion did not blow away were thus from their inception inadequately protected from fire. After the Baltimore fire, the standard for all high-rises was wrapping the steel beams and cross members in many feet of concrete, tile, and brickwork. This standard was intentionally abandoned in the design and construction of the towers and the rest of the WTC complex. The report also criticized the absence of fireproofing around the exit stairs and the failure to distribute exits around the entire building.[122]

At the same time that FEMA was issuing its preliminary findings, the man who built the towers announced his own conclusions on why they collapsed. He did not need to see the FEMA results:

> The exterior walls performed beautifully as long as the floors were intact. About thirty-one columns were knocked out in the South Tower when the plane hit and the load simply spanned around the lost section . . . It was the ensuing fire that weakened the floor systems and then caused them to collapse as if they were imploding . . .

in both [the North and South] cases the intense heat weakened and
deformed the trusses, causing them to collapse and eliminating the
lateral support for the exterior wall and the core columns.

The trusses had softened in the heat, "deflecting" or bending, pulling
out the bolts that connected them to the exterior curtain and to the
core columns. In short, the very unique design features that had
made the towers so open and created so much "rentable" space—the
features that depended upon lightweight trusses bolted to external
panels and the core vertical supports—had been a mortal flaw from
their inception. "Heavy structural beams [instead of the trusses]
spaced at perhaps ten foot intervals and fully fireproofed, would
have in all likelihood resisted the fires for hours, not minutes, perhaps allowing firefighters to reach them and put them out."[123]
On August 22, 2002, the federal government inaugurated a $23-
million investigation of the collapse of the towers and WTC Seven,
across Vesey Street. The National Institute of Science and Technology (NIST) completed this study in February 2005 and announced
its findings on April 5, 2005. The FEMA study was wrong—the design was not at fault. "These fires, in combination with the dislodged
fireproofing, were responsible for a chain of events in which the
building core weakened and began losing its ability to carry loads.
The floors weakened and sagged from the fires, pulling inward on
the perimeter columns," causing the columns to buckle and bow inward. "Collapse then ensued." Not so hidden was the message that
the Port Authority and the designers wanted to hear—the towers
were not "doomed" by design flaws. The impact of the planes, the
heat of the fuel, and the fire itself had led to the collapse. The director of the study insisted that "'the buildings performed as they
should have,'" neatly avoiding the hypothetical question—Would
more traditional design and construction methods have stood longer
in the face of the same impact and fires? The fire was the culprit, the
NIST concluded, and had it not been caused by the planes' impact, it
would have been merely a bad office fire.[124]
But the engineers had missed the mark. The real question for
American cities and American firefighting was not whether the fire

or the impact was responsible for the collapse, but whether the American city and its obsession with open space in commercial towers posed unacceptable fire risks. The debate over the replacements for the Twin Towers similarly avoided that question, an evasion that brings together all the lessons of urban infernos in America.

New Towers, Old Mistakes

When all the engineering and architectural verdicts were in and the site cleared, there remained "a pit, a hole, a void." From the site, construction workers had carted 190,500 tons of steel and 1,450,140 tons of concrete, a total of over 110,000 truckloads. In the meantime, the sixteen acres had taken on a life of its own. The site had become a holy place for the families of the victims. On the sixteen-foot-high wire and mesh fence along Church Street, markers recounted the minutes of agony and two plaques recorded the names of the victims. Busloads of visitors stopped to pay their respects. On a lovely late summer day in 2005, much like 9/11, tourists from all over the world took one another's pictures with Ground Zero as a background. For the commuters who poured out of the PATH commuter trains from New Jersey and the Eighth Avenue E trains, the almost normal routine of the workday had reasserted itself.[125]

If the grieving families wanted the empty space to remain a memorial to the dead, Lower Manhattan real estate was too valuable to leave vacant, even for memorials. So Governor George Pataki created a Lower Manhattan Development Corporation (LMDC) and taxed its president, John C. Whitehead, with filling up the hole. Whitehead—a financial mogul with Republican connections—had been around for a long time. Critics were quick to point out that Whitehead and the LMDC looked too much like the PA. To allay some of these suspicions, the LMDC opened up its deliberations as the PA never had. The resulting competition for architectural designs recapitulated the achievements, and controversies, of the past century.[126]

Seven designs were finalists, and the architects behind them revealed their creations at the Winter Garden, part of the World

Financial Center adjacent to the big hole, on December 18, 2002. None of the designs addressed the fatal flaw in the original towers. Fire safety was simply ignored. None of the presentations in the Winter Garden stressed the fire dangers of high-rises or how fire-prevention measures in the proposed structures would distinguish them from the original towers. There were no members of the FDNY on the LMDC. No officers or firefighters advised the developers how to allocate funds to prevent the new designs from having the same fire-prone characteristics as their predecessors.

The anti-terrorist federal architecture of the post-9/11 era features concrete barriers around all federal buildings, but no one was talking about concrete and fireproof tile around the airy spires and luminescent filigree of the proposed WTC II. Fear of terrorism has spawned an industry in surveillance cameras, security checks, a vast new federal bureaucracy, and even a "no fly" ban on people with the wrong names, but no one in the competition puffed their design as the most fireproof.[127]

PERHAPS MANY BELIEVED that "there was not only no precedent for dealing with the enormity of the loss, there was no system for figuring out what should happen next." Insofar as the 9/11 attack was global terrorism, perhaps that was so, but not if one considers 9/11 as a catastrophic fire. Cities such as Boston, Pittsburgh, Chicago, Baltimore, Detroit, and Oakland had all confronted enormous losses and not succumbed. Why should Gotham be different? As New York City historian Max Page wrote shortly after the fire, major city fires in the past provided opportunities for cities to rethink "urban design and economic development." The fires of 9/11 gutted sixteen valuable acres but left the infrastructure, the economic foundations, of the city intact, and thus, its mindset.

The years after the catastrophe have seen the same political controversy and business jockeying for advantage as followed the other urban infernos, and one can predict that some version of the towers will again rise. When they burn, men like FDNY deputy chief Robert Browne will arrive, determined to get as close to the danger as possible, to "see what we could do . . . to take care of the people who were injured." He'll say, "C'mon, guys," and his men will follow him, just as the firefighters in Boston, Pittsburgh, Chicago, Baltimore, Detroit, and Oakland followed their officers. May it always be so.[128]

CONCLUSION

W hat the frontier was to America's West, the city has been to America's core. In the city, the economic heart of our country beats most strongly. City property is worth far more than rural land. City lights illuminate our progress. Cities are the hubs of our transportation and distribution systems. Our march to independence began in the cities. They made room for immigrants, sponsored education, paid for industry, and promoted culture. The city embraced innovation and experiment. When "lusty growth" in the cities led to slums, urban planners invented new kinds of dwellings and marts.[1]

Thus, when our cities were attacked by fire, we rushed to defend them. Their smoldering ruins become the fertile ground for renewal. Firefighting in the city matched and mirrored the rise of professionalism in our land. The amateur gave way to the professional; bravado deferred to fire science, and hand power accepted the aid of machines and computers. Perhaps most important of all, firefighting and fire prevention became public duties rather than private matters. The city, the state, and the federal government invested in fire suppression.

Nevertheless, the great urban fires tested our will. Colonial city fires seemed to be a judgment of an angry God upon wayward sinners. Patriot spokesmen saw in the Crown's indifference to victims irrefutable evidence of corruption and tyranny. If fire did not bring on the American Revolution, the fire wardens and firefighters certainly took the lead in agitating for it.

Nineteenth-century cities such as Pittsburgh and Chicago were simply too important to surrender to fire. Fire prone, they burned. The risk taking that permitted fires also inspired an almost reckless confidence in restoration. The city that emerged from the ashes became the model of the metropolis—bigger, taller, and more ambitious than before the fire.

The Baltimore fire was the last of its kind—an inferno that threatened to destroy an entire city. But just as the city's polyglot population, factories, and neighborhoods reflected the industrial metropolises of the early twentieth century, so the suppression of its Great Fire proved that once warring sections had become a great nation. Firefighting forces from all over the Northeast coast arrived to battle the flames. Firemen who spoke with the drawl of western Maryland joined firefighters with New York City accents at Jones Falls, engine men and ladder men of all colors and national ancestries stood shoulder to shoulder to save East Baltimore.

The epidemic of arson during the Detroit riots of 1967 was likewise symptomatic of the nation's condition. The troubled American city of the 1960s reflected a racially divided country. Cities burned because fire had become one tool of political incendiaries, unthinking native terrorists. Detroit was the worst case, and its lingering agony reminds us that the postindustrial city cannot prosper if its fire service is allowed to rot.

Fires in a city like Detroit serve warnings. History teaches lessons. The next fire is already upon us. Groundcover fire at the interface of natural fire courses and suburban neighborhoods is not limited to the California coast, but the Oakland Hills fire of 1991 was a spectacular example of how devastating such fire could be. The cost of such fires dwarf their predecessors. They challenge the way that insurance companies are managed and cities are planned.

The high-rise inferno is another kind of wildfire. Spreading swiftly up and down rather than horizontally, fires like those in the Twin Towers imperil more people and damage more property than conventional urban building blazes. Forget for a moment the origin of 9/11 in the acts of terrorists. The dangers that high-rise fires pose to our cities demonstrate once more that the very acts that enable a city to prosper also increase its susceptibility to fire.

Put simply: A city's growth will always be accompanied by increasing population density, more buildings, stocks of goods, and mechanical activities. From a fire standpoint, this translates into more opportunities for fires to start, more fuel for fires to burn, and more fire-prone sites. It is less a contradiction than a simple fact: If cities cannot exist without fire for heating and cooling, manufacturing, cooking, and carrying on businesses, then cities cannot progress without adding fire. The lesson of the seven fires is that city fire is inevitable; it can be contained, fought, and controlled, but not eliminated.

There is another paradox the seven fires present. It also goes to the marrow of our national experience. Fire events and recovery from fire reveal this paradox in its starkest form. Major urban fires are an enemy of all, but can be a friend to some. Fire wreaks havoc on rich and poor alike, but in the burned districts of Boston, Pittsburgh, and Chicago, cheap housing stock was replaced by pricier dwellings and commercial structures or left abandoned and empty. Poor people had to find other places to live as real estate values soared.[2]

Developers were well aware that burning buildings in downtowns made real estate more valuable, the way that burning brush fertilizes gardens. After the earthquake and fire of 1868 in San Francisco, the city's *Real Estate Circular* for October reported, "Since it occurred, hundreds of property owners have been anxiously watching to see what effect it would have upon our real estates. While many persons prophesied death and disaster to the city generally . . . events have proved that it did not have a depressing effect upon property for even a day." After the Great Fire of 1991 had scorched the East Bay communities of Alameda and Contra Costa counties, median home prices rose, and have kept on rising. In fact, the fire was a boom time for construction firms, and the average price of a home rose from $200,000 to over $700,000.[3]

Indeed, those who could take advantage of the rising real estate values discovered that they could exchange substandard structures for larger and more profitable ones. Such benefits might redound to an entire city. Fire enabled the repair and expansion of port facilities in Baltimore and lakeshore property in Chicago. Fire rubble became landfill. The debris from the Wall Street fire of New York in 1835 became the foundation for "the extension of West Street from Cedar to the Battery." On that landfill, many years later, a World Trade Center would rise.[4]

These kinds of ironies, contradictions, and puzzles run all through the seven fire stories. We want fire safety, but not at the price of profit. The endeavor to make high-rises fire safe after the Twin Towers collapsed epitomizes this self-immolating refusal to face reality. After three years, 10,000 pages, millions of dollars, and much expert thinking, the National Institute of Science and Technology issued its recommendations for making high-rise buildings safer. They included more sprinklers, wider and more fireproof stairwells, as well as the wider incorporation of measures the WTC took after the 1993 bombing. Had these been in place on 9/11, hundreds, perhaps thousands of victims, might have survived.

But NIST's suggestions for code changes were met with skepticism and opposition in some quarters with a familiar refrain—too costly, not necessary in every building, high-rises were already the safest kinds of structures. Some of the suggestions will undoubtedly find their way into new city building codes, and others will be voluntarily adopted. Too little, too late? Or a slow but steady process of learning? In fact, both. The report and the response are a perfect example of our city government and private enterprise embracing paradox—weighing profit and loss against the likelihood of human and property damage.[5]

One last paradox sums up all the lessons. Our fire science professionals have adopted a "firefight-as-battlefield metaphor," a battle that we are supposed to be able to win. Fire protection, fire safety, and fire prevention are staples of our vocabulary. Fire department public education offices instruct public officials, private enterprises, and even school children. But in our cities' history, and our nation's, fire is not always the implacable enemy. Fires pose challenges and demand responses that renew and reform urban landscapes. The first of the seven fires sparked the American Revolution and led to American independence. The last of them may well convince us to recast our entire concept of urban living. Whatever the cause and the outcome, urban infernos have reshaped America.[6]

NOTES

PREFACE

1. John Demos, *The Unredeemed Captive: A Family Story from Early America* (New York: Knopf, 1994), 23; Peter Charles Hoffer, *Sensory Worlds in Early America* (Baltimore: Johns Hopkins University Press, 2003).

INTRODUCTION

1. James George Frazier, *Myths of the Origins of Fire* (London: Macmillan, 1930), 195; *New Larousse Encyclopedia of Mythology* (London: Hamlyn, 1959), 93–95.

2. Alfred Crosby, *Throwing Fire: Projectile Technology Through History* (Cambridge, UK: Cambridge University Press, 2002), 40–49; Stephen J. Pyne, *Fire: A Brief History* (Seattle: University of Washington Press, 2001), 46–101.

3. Neil Hanson, *The Great Fire of London: In That Apocalyptic Year, 1666* (New York: Wiley, 2002), 58; Stephen Porter, *The Great Fire of London* (Thrupp, UK: Sutton, 1996), 46.

4. John Evelyn, *The Diary of John Evelyn*, ed. William Bray (London: Dent, 1907), 3; William Penn, on the plan for Philadelphia, 1677, quoted in John W. Reps, *Town Planning in Revolutionary America* (Princeton, N.J.: Princeton University Press, 1965), 208.

5. Dennis Smith, *Report from Engine Company No. 82* (New York: Pocket, 1972), 42. Ricard Picciotto, with Daniel Paisner, *Last Man Down: A Fire-fighter's Story of Survival and Escape from the World Trade Disaster* (New York: Berkley, 2002), 163; Mike Kelleher, Troy (N.Y.) Fire Department, in Frank J. Miale, "Fire Behavior," *The Firefighter's Handbook: Essentials of Fire-fighting and Emergency Response* (Albany, N.Y.: Delmar, 2000) [hereafter

FFH], 73; Vincent Dunn, *Command and Control of Fires and Emergencies* (Saddlebrook, N.J.: Pennwell, 1999), 23–24.

6. John Salka, with Barret Neville, *First In, Last Out: Leadership Lessons from the New York Fire Department* (New York: Penguin, 2004), 44; Gregory Blais, personal recollection, Oakland Public Library, History Room, Oakland fire, 1991; Jack Fanning quoted in Andrew Coe, ed., *F.D.N.Y: An Illustrated History of the Fire Department of the City of New York* (New York: Norton, 2003), 75.

7. Mark Tebeau, *Eating Smoke: Fire in Urban America, 1800–1895* (Baltimore: Johns Hopkins University Press, 2003), 324.

8. Earl Emerson, *Vertical Burn* (New York: Ballantine, 2002), 19; Wally Malone, interview at the New York Fire Museum, June 22, 2005.

9. Norman Maclean, *Young Men and Fire* (Chicago: University of Chicago Press, 1992), 5; Stuart O'Nan, *The Circus Fire* (New York: Anchor, 2000), 91; Simon Winchester, interview in the *New York Times Magazine*, January 23, 2005, 13.

10. Student papers in George Stratton's college psychology course, 1919, quoted in Philip L. Fradkin, *The Great Earthquake and Firestorms of 1906: How San Francisco Nearly Destroyed Itself* (Berkeley: University of California Press, 2005), xvii, xviii; Tom Downey, *The Last Men Out: Life on the Edge at Rescue 2 Firehouse* (New York: Holt, 2002), 49; D. A. Simpson, D. Kessler, and Linda Fletcher, personal recollections, Oakland Public Library, History Room, Oakland Hills fire, 1991.

11. This and the following paragraphs from Robert J. Whelan, *The Ecology of Fire* (Cambridge, UK: Cambridge University Press, 1995), 8–56, and the entries in David E. Newton, *Encyclopedia of Fire* (Westport, Conn.: Oryx, 2002).

12. Miale, "Fire Behavior," *FFH*, 91–94.

13. Miale, "Ventilation," *FFH*, 519–525.

14. Maclean, *Young Men and Fire*, 37.

15. Pyne, *Fire*, 102–115; FDNY Fire Safety Education, "Fire Safety in High Rise Residential Buildings"—"Two things not to do. Never use the elevator during a fire! Never leave apartment doors open if you flee a fire," http://www.ci.nyc.ny.us/htmlfdny.

16. Pyne, *Fire*, 106.

17. Mike Davis, *Ecology of Fear: Los Angeles and the Imagination of Disaster* (New York: Random House, 1999), 95–147.

18. Pyne, *Fire*, 115.

19. Firefighting skills, management of companies and departments, technical know-how, and fire science are expanding and demanding fields. Once based solely on experience and a kind of apprenticeship, modern fire services have added a vast amount of schooling to on-the-job training. The following

paragraphs only hint at the amount of information a firefighter and officer must know.

20. The concept of a fire department as a business comes from Thomas J. Wutz, "Fire Department Organization, Command, and Control," *FFH*, 24. The paramilitary concept appears in Ronny J. Coleman, "Overview," *FFH*, 14.

21. National Institute of Standards and Technology, U.S. Department of Commerce, World Trade Center Investigation, April 5, 2005, "Executive Summary," 7. If you don't believe me about the complexity of all this, try taking the Firefighter Exam cold. Then see Norman Hall, *Firefighter Exam Preparation Book, Revised and Updated,* 2nd ed. (Avon, Mass.: Adams Media, 2003). And that is just the entrance exam.

22. Thanks to Kevin Kenniff and Eric Frey for these remarkable facts.

23. David Halberstam, *Firehouse* (New York: Hyperion, 2002), 47–61; Thomas Von Essen, with Matt Murray, *Strong of Heart: Life and Death in the Fire Department of New York* (New York: Regan, 2002), 87–97; Joseph Natale Schneiderman, *The Firefighting Buff's Guide to New York City* (San Jose, Calif.: Writers Club, 2002), 7; Ze've Chafets, *Devil's Night, and Other True Tales of Detroit* (New York: Vintage, 1990), 217.

24. Eric Frey, Sergeant, Athens (Ga.) Fire Department, to the author, June 17, 2005.

25. Dunn, *Command and Control,* 97–98, 101.

26. Geoff Miller, "Salvage, Overhaul, and Fire Cause Determination," *FFH*, 608–610; Dunn, *Command and Control,* 31, 5–6; Picciotto, *Last Man Down,* 158 ("too hot"), 122 ("Firefighting 101").

27. Terry Golway, *So Others Might Live, a History of New York's Bravest: The FDNY from 1700 to the Present* (New York: Basic, 2002), 244–246; Von Essen, *Strong of Heart,* 179–183; Melvin Claxton and Charles Hurt, "Detroit Fire Department: Out of Service," *Detroit News,* November 5, 2000, A1; Bill Dedman, "Slower Arrival at Fires in U.S. Is Costing Lives," *Boston Globe,* January 30, 2005, A1.

28. U.S. Fire Administration, "Firefighter Fatality Figures," January 5, 2005, http://www.usfa.fema.gov/about/media/2005releases/010505.shtm; Zac Unger, *Working Fire: The Making of an Accidental Fireman* (New York: Penguin, 2004), 57.

29. Miale, "Fire Behavior," *FFH*, 84; Dennis Smith, *History of Firefighting in America: 300 Years of Courage* (New York: Dial, 1978), 172–173.

30. "Detroit Warehouse Fire Claims Three Firefighters" March 12, 1987, U.S. Fire Administration, Report No. 3, Major fires investigation project, FEMA; Philip Schaenman, "Schomberg Plaza Fire, New York City, March 22, 1987," U.S. Fire Administration, Major fires investigation project, Report No. 4, FEMA, quotation on p. 9.

31. "Chicago High-Rise Fire Injures 37," Tuesday, December 7, 2004, http://www.cnn.com/2004/US/12/06/chicago.fire/index.html. The fire on the twenty-ninth floor left twenty-two firefighters injured seriously enough to be taken to emergency rooms. Jim Dwyer and Kevin Flynn, *102 Minutes: The Untold Story of the Fight to Survive Inside the Twin Towers* (New York: Times Books, 2005), 188–189; Jay Jonas account in Dennis Smith, *Report from Ground Zero: The Story of the Rescue Efforts at the World Trade Center* (New York: Viking, 2002), 95; Picciotto, *Last Man Down*, 74.

32. Dunn, *Command and Control*, 9–10.

33. Max Page, "Creatively Destroying New York: Fantasies, Premonitions, and Realities in the Provisional City," in Joan Ockman, ed., *Out of Ground Zero: Case Studies in Urban Reinvention* (Munich: Prestel, 2002), 168.

BOSTON, 1760

1. Francis Parkman, *Montcalm and Wolfe, the French and Indian War* [1884] (New York: Da Capo, 1995), 348; Fred Anderson, *Crucible of War: The Seven Years War and the Fate of Empire in British North America, 1754–1766* (New York: Knopf, 2000), 373.

2. John Winthrop's lay sermon on board the ship *Arabella*, 1630, in Perry Miller and Thomas H. Johnson, eds., *The Puritans*, rev. ed. (New York: Harper, 1963), 199; figures on first year's losses from Edmund S. Morgan, *The Puritan Dilemma: The Story of John Winthrop*, rev. ed. (New York: Longman, 1998), 56.

3. Benjamin Colman, *"It Is of the Lord's Mercies that We are Not Consumed" A Sermon Preached . . . March 4, 1736* (Boston, 1737), 10.

4. Darrett B. Rutman, *Winthrop's Boston: A Portrait of a Puritan Town, 1630–1649* (Chapel Hill: University of North Carolina Press, 1965), 31; Ola Elizabeth Winslow, *Meetinghouse Hill, 1630–1783*, rev. ed. (New York: Norton, 1971), 61; Peter Charles Hoffer, *The Devil's Disciples: Makers of the Salem Witchcraft Trials* (Baltimore: Johns Hopkins University Press, 1996), 118; Richard Cullen Rath, *How Early America Sounded* (Ithaca: Cornell University Press, 2003), 107–113.

5. William Cronon, *Changes in the Land: Indians, Colonists, and the Ecology of New England* (New York: Hill and Wang, 1983), 109, 119; Rutman, *Winthrop's Boston*, 37.

6. G. B. Warden, *Boston: 1689–1776* (Boston: Little, Brown, 1970), 16–20; Arthur H. Hayward, *Colonial and Early American Lighting* (New York: Dover, 1962), 36, 59, 75; Gloria L. Main, *Peoples of a Spacious Land: Families and Cultures in Colonial New England* (Cambridge: Harvard University Press, 2001), 4.

7. "The Itinerarium of Dr. Alexander Hamilton," reprinted in *Colonial American Travel Narratives,* ed. Wendy Martin (New York: Penguin, 1994), 284. Pudding Lane ran east-west for one block between Water Street and King Street. See William Burgis, Map of Boston, 1728.

8. Colman, *"It Is of the Lord's Mercies that We are Not Consumed,"* 2. The National Heritage Museum in Lexington, Massachusetts, and the American History Museum of the Smithsonian Museum in Washington, D.C., both have splendid displays of colonial-period eastern Massachusetts housing and street scenes. The Freedom Trail in Boston, administered by the nonprofit Boston Freedom Trail Foundation, includes a number of surviving period structures complete with tours and costumed reenactors. National Park Service Rangers also run tours of Faneuil Hall and other sites in Boston National Historical Park.

9. Hugh Morrison, *Early American Architecture: From the First Colonial Settlements to the National Period* (New York: Oxford University Press, 1952), 71–75; Porter, *The Great Fire of London*, 43.

10. Rutman, *Winthrop's Boston*, 215, 219; Carl Bridenbaugh, *Cities in the Wilderness: The First Century of Urban Life in America, 1625–1742* (New York: Knopf, 1968), 59, 210–211; Arthur Wellington Brayley, *A Complete History of the Boston Fire Department, Including the Fire-Alarm Service and the Protective Department, From 1630 to 1888* (Boston: Dale, 1889), 4–5, 18; Tebeau, *Eating Smoke*, 16–18, 25–27.

11. Paul Ditzel, *Fire Engines, Firefighters: The Men, Equipment and Machines from Colonial Days to the Present* (New York: Crown, 1976), 16–20; Bridenbaugh, *Cities in the Wilderness*, 57, 59. Fire ordinances were never obeyed, though they might be repeatedly passed. See, e.g., Hanson, *The Great Fire of London*, 36.

12. Kenneth Stampp, *The Peculiar Institution: Slavery in the Ante-bellum South* (New York: Knopf, 1956), 127–128; Michael Meranze, *Laboratories of Virtue: Punishment, Revolution, and Authority in Philadelphia, 1760–1835* (Chapel Hill: University of North Carolina Press, 1996), 31; *The Diary of Samuel Sewall, 1674–1729,* ed. M. Halsey Thomas (New York: Farrar, Strauss, and Giroux, 1973), vol. 2: 683 (March 26, 1712).

13. My reconstruction of the progress of the Pudding Lane fire is based on the available documentation, a study of other colonial town fires, and more speculation than I would otherwise prefer. Unfortunately, the missing details have to be filled in by imagination and surmise.

14. David W. Conroy, *In Public Houses: Drink and the Revolution of Authority in Colonial Massachusetts* (Chapel Hill: University of North Carolina Press, 1995), 131–139, 227; Sharon V. Salinger, *Taverns and Drinking in Early America* (Baltimore: Johns Hopkins University Press, 2002), 166–167, 191–194.

15. Nancy S. Seasholes and Amy Turner, "Diagramming the Growth of Boston," 17, and Seasholes, "Gaining Ground," in Alex Krieger and David Cobb, with Amy Turner, *Mapping Boston* (Cambridge: MIT Press, 2001), 118–145, 174.

16. This and the following description of the 1711 fire from Brayley, *Boston Fire Department*, 29–31, and Stephanie Schorow, *Boston on Fire: A History of Fires and Firefighting in Boston* (Beverly, Mass.: Commonwealth, 2003), 1–4.

17. David Von Drehle, *Triangle: The Fire That Changed America* (New York: Grove, 2003), 170; Pyne, *Fire*, 104.

18. Increase Mather, *Burnings Bewailed . . . in a Sermon* (Boston, 1711), 2, 3, 9, 10, 11, 34.

19. Increase Mather, *The History of King Philip's War* [1676], ed. Samuel G. Drake (Boston, 1862), 46.

20. Robert Blair St. George, *Conversing by Signs: Poetics of Implication in Colonial New England Culture* (Chapel Hill: University of North Carolina Press, 1998), 249; Michael P. Winship, *Seers of God: Puritan Providentialism in the Restoration and Early Enlightenment* (Baltimore: Johns Hopkins University Press, 1996), 139–140; Robert Middlekauf, *The Mathers: Three Generations of Puritan Intellectuals, 1645–1739* (London: Oxford University Press, 1971), 279.

21. Cotton Mather, *The Voice of God, Crying to the City . . .* (Boston, 1711), 1, 19.

22. *Diary of Samuel Sewall*, vol. 2: 669 (October 7, 1711); Increase Mather, *Burnings Bewailed*, 23, 33; Cotton Mather, *Voice of God*, 23.

23. Cotton Mather, *The Voice of God*, 26. On women and witchcraft accusations, see Carol Karlsen, *The Devil in the Shape of a Woman: Witchcraft in Colonial New England* (New York: Norton, 1987), and John P. Demos, *Entertaining Satan: Witchcraft and the Culture of Early New England* (New York: Oxford University Press, 1982). For Cotton Mather's role in bringing on the Salem tragedy, see Hoffer, *Devil's Disciples*, 144–148.

24. Bridenbaugh, *Cities in the Wilderness*, 210.

25. Increase Mather, *Burnings Bewailed*, 34; Cotton Mather, *Voice of God*, 32.

26. Some of this shift was led by the appearance of Anglican chapels in Boston and other cities. These invariably more refined structures were brick rather than wood. Richard L. Bushman, *The Refinement of America: Persons, Houses, Cities* (New York: Knopf, 1992), 169–180. On the meetinghouse of the First Church, Abbott L. Cummings, "Meeting and Dwelling House, Interrelationships in Early New England," in Peter Benes, ed., *New England Meeting House and Church: 1630–1850* (Boston: Boston University, 1979), 4; on painting, Peter Benes, "Sky Colors and Scattered Clouds: The Decorative and Architectural Painting of New England Meeting Houses," in ibid., 51–69.

27. I have adapted these iron laws of indifference to fire safety from Christine Meisner Rosen, *The Limits of Power: Great Fires and the Process of City Growth in America* (Cambridge, UK: Cambridge University Press, 1986), 12–19.

28. G. B. Warden, "The Distribution of Property in Boston, 1692–1775," *Perspectives in American History* 10 (1976): 81–130, quotation at 100.

29. Ibid., Table III, 121–122.

30. Ibid., 100; Bridenbaugh, *Cities in the Wilderness*, 211–212; Schorow, *Boston on Fire*, 4–12.

31. The difference between a phase 2 fire, singeing and smoldering without flames, and a phase 3 fire, burning with flame, is that simple open door. Edward T. O'Donnell, *Ship Ablaze: The Tragedy of the Steamboat General Slocum* (New York: Broadway, 2004), 98–99.

32. Malcolm Gladwell, *The Tipping Point: How Little Things Can Make a Big Difference* (Boston: Little, Brown, 2000), 9–14.

33. Porter, *Great Fire of London*, 18; Bridenbaugh, *Cities in the Wilderness*, 367; Ditzel, *Fire Engines*, 10; Smith, *History of Firefighting in America*, 7–8; Brayley, *Boston Fire Department*, 14, 15.

34. Bridenbaugh, *Cities in the Wilderness*, 369; Benjamin Franklin, *Autobiography of Benjamin Franklin*, ed. Leonard W. Labaree et al. (New Haven: Yale University Press, 1964), 174. Amy S. Greenberg, *Cause for Alarm: The Volunteer Fire Department in the Nineteenth Century City* (Princeton: Princeton University Press, 1998), 11, gives 1718 as the year of the first volunteer company, as opposed to 1678. The difference may be that the volunteer companies organized themselves and selected their own chiefs.

35. *Pennsylvania Gazette*, February 4, 1735; Franklin, *Autobiography*, 174; John Bainbridge, *Biography of an Idea: The Story of Mutual Fire and Casualty Insurance* (Garden City, N.Y.: Doubleday, 1952), 41–47.

36. Newsham broadside reproduced in Carl Bridenbaugh, *Cities in Revolt: Urban Life in America, 1743–1776* (New York: Knopf, 1955), 46; Carl Read advertised in the Boston *News-Letter* as did Houghton, both reprinted in George Francis Dow, *Everyday Life in the Massachusetts Bay Colony* (Boston: Society for the Preservation of New England Antiquities, 1935), 129, 131; Tebeau, *Eating Smoke*, 18–33.

37. *These Presents Witness, That We As Subscribers . . . When in Danger By Fire, Do Agree to the Following Articles* (Boston, 1742); *Rules and Orders to be observed by a Fire Club . . . instituted at Boston, March 4th, 1762* (Boston, 1762); *Rules and Orders . . . of the Anti-Stamp Fire Society . . . Instituted at Boston, 1763* (Boston, 1776). The 1741 organization's articles seem to have been widely circulated, even though the society had a watchword that, when whispered to the clerk, allowed the individual to take part in the quarterly meetings. All of these sets of articles are almost identical.

38. Samuel G. Drake, *History and Antiquities of Boston* (Boston: L. Stevens, 1856), 649. For prophetic visions of disaster: Andrew Johonnot, *A Poem on the Rebuke of God's Hand* . . . (Boston, 1760), and Joseph Fisk, *Reflections on the Sins of the Times* (Boston, 1761), 6. For the more mundane account of the October 17 and 18 fires, Boston *News-Letter*, March 21, 1760.

39. William Pencak, "The Social Structure of Revolutionary Boston: Evidence from the Great Fire of 1760," *Journal of Interdisciplinary History* 10 (1979): 268; Drake, *History and Antiquities of Boston*, 651. Cooper and Savage identifications in Ditzel, *Fire Engines*, 10.

40. John N. Maclean, *Fire and Ashes: On the Front Lines of American Wildfire* (New York: Holt, 2003), 54, 55.

41. Boston *News-Letter*, March 21, 1760; Boston *Post-boy*, March 24, 1760; *A Particular Relation of the Great fire of Boston . . . March 20, 1760* (Boston, 1760), 46–47. Brayley, *Boston Fire Department*, 60, attributes the unsigned account to Cooper.

42. Boston *News-Letter*, March 21, March 27, 1760.

43. Not the Boston fire, but another equally devastating inferno in a colonial port city. Barnet Schecter, *The Battle for New York: The City at the Heart of the American Revolution* (New York: Penguin, 2002), 204, 206, 208.

44. Boston *News-Letter*, March 27, 1760; Thomas Pownall, *A Brief* (Boston, 1760). Calculation of the extent of the fire is based on William Price, "A New Plan of ye great town of Boston" (Boston, 1743). Estimates of modern equivalents of colonial money are very rough. These are based on the formulas and data in "Consumer Price Index (Estimated) 1800–2005, http://www.minneapolisfed.org/research/data/us/calc/hist1800/cfm, and "How Much Is That Worth Today" http://www.eh.net/ehresource/howmuch/poundq.php. The modern housing market figures come from Boston Indicators Project, "Housing Highlights," http://www.tbf.org/indicators2004/housing/overview.asp.

45. John A. Schutz, *Thomas Pownall: British Defender of American Liberty* (Glendale, Calif.: Clark, 1951), 85–152, 175; James Melvin Lee, *History of American Journalism* (Boston: Houghton, 1917), 65, 67; Frank Luther Mott, *American Journalism: A History, 1690–1960* (New York: Macmillan, 1962), 11–14; Sidney Kobre, *The Development of the Colonial Newspaper* (Gloucester, Mass.: Peter Smith, 1960), 29, 44, 49; Brayley, *Boston Fire Department*, 69; Adrian Tinniswood, *By Permission of Heaven: The Story of the Great Fire of London* (New York: Penguin, 2003), 54, 55.

46. Thomas Pownall, *A Brief* (Boston, 1760), and Benning Wentworth, *A Brief* (Portsmouth, N.H., 1760); Horatio Sharpe, *A Brief* (Annapolis, Md., 1760).

47. Boston *News-Letter*, March 27, 1760.

48. Thomas Hutchinson, *History of the Colony and Province of Massachu-*

setts Bay, ed. Lawrence Shaw Mayo (Cambridge: Harvard University Press, 1936), vol. 3: 80.

49. James A. Henretta, "Economic Development and Social Structure in Colonial Boston," *William and Mary Quarterly* 3rd ser. 22 (1965): 75–85.

50. Gary B. Nash, *The Urban Crucible: Social Change, Political Consciousness, and the Origins of the American Revolution* (Cambridge: Harvard University Press, 1979), 246, 247, 253; Allan Kulikoff, "The Progress of Inequality in Revolutionary Boston," *William and Mary Quarterly* 3rd ser. 28 (1971): 381.

51. Pencak, "Social Structure of Revolutionary Boston," 269.

52. Reports of petitions for relief in this and subsequent paragraphs from *Records Relating to the Early History of Boston* (Boston: Municipal Printing Office, 1900) 29: 1–88. On women and tavern owning, Conroy, *In Public Houses,* 103–104, and Salinger, *Taverns and Drinking in Early America,* 167.

53. Andrew Oliver, Report of the Selectmen, November 29, 1760, *Records of the Early History of Boston* 29: 100–101.

54. Richard L. Bushman, *King and People in Provincial Massachusetts,* rev. ed. (Chapel Hill: University of North Carolina Press, 1992), 11.

55. *Records Relating to the Early History of Boston* 29: 103, 104, 113, 114.

56. Ibid., 112, 117.

57. Ibid., 113, 116, 117–118, 121, 127–128.

58. Ibid., 106, 107, 108, 110, 112.

59. On older ideas of deference, Edward M. Cook, Jr., *Fathers of the Towns: Leadership and Community Structure in Eighteenth-Century New England* (Baltimore: Johns Hopkins University Press, 1976); on the Hutchinson circle, Bernard Bailyn, *The Ordeal of Thomas Hutchinson* (Cambridge: Harvard University Press, 1974), 30–32; Nash, *Urban Crucible,* 273, 274.

60. *Boston Town Records* (Boston: Record Commissioners, 1886), 16: 54, 55, 58.

61. *Boston Town Records,* 16: 107, 167, 177, 199; Benjamin Carp, "Fire of Liberty: Firefighters, Urban Voluntary Culture, and the Revolutionary Movement" *William and Mary Quarterly* 3rd ser. 58 (2001), 794–795; Edmund S. and Helen M. Morgan, *The Stamp Act Crisis: Prelude to Revolution,* 2nd ed. (New York: Collier, 1962), 160; Warden, *Boston,* 157; Nash, *Urban Crucible,* 296.

62. Roe to Peter Hubbert, March 24, 1760, in *Letters and Diary of John Rowe, Boston Merchant . . . ,* ed. Anne Rowe Cunningham (Boston: Clarke, 1903), 346.

63. John W. Tyler, *Smugglers and Patriots: Boston Merchants and the Advent of the American Revolution* (Boston: Northeastern University Press, 1986), 16, 17; Carp, "Fire of Liberty," 798.

64. For this and the following paragraphs on the writs of assistance cases, I

rely on M. H. Smith, *The Writs of Assistance Cases* (Berkeley: University of California Press, 1978), 126–230.

65. Otis's arguments are traced in Peter Charles Hoffer, *Law and People in Colonial America*, rev. ed. (Baltimore: Johns Hopkins University Press, 1998), 136.

66. Bernard Bailyn, *Faces of Revolution: Personalities and Themes in the Struggle for American Independence* (New York: Knopf, 1990), 126.

67. Jonathan Mayhew, *God's Hand and Providence . . . in Public Calamities* (Boston, 1760), 5, 6, 14, 15, 23, 26.

68. Ibid., 18, 23; Charles W. Akers, *Called unto Liberty: A Life of Jonathan Mayhew, 1720–1766* (Cambridge: Harvard University Press, 1964), 139–148; Bailyn, *The Ideological Origins of the American Revolution* (Cambridge: Harvard University Press, 1967), 35, 37, 38, 40, 42, 99.

69. My account in this and the following passages derives from my own *The Brave New World* (Boston: Houghton Mifflin, 2000), 429–475.

70. Warden, *Boston*, 114; Pauline Maier, *The Old Revolutionaries: Political Lives in the Age of Samuel Adams* (New York: Knopf, 1980), 27.

71. Alfred F. Young, *The Shoemaker and the Tea Party* (Boston: Beacon, 1999), 31; Nash, *Urban Crucible*, 293, 296–297; Morgan and Morgan, *Stamp Act Crisis*, 157–230; Carp, "Fire of Liberty," 808. Carp, on p. 806, agrees with Warden that the speed and dexterity with which the mob pulled down the stamp office indicates there were firefighters among them.

72. Mayhew, *The Snare Broken . . . A Discourse preached at the Desire of the West Church, May 23, 1766* (Boston: Edes and Gill, 1766), 12, 13.

73. Ibid., 17; Carp, "Fire of Liberty," 798, 806: Jesse Lemisch, *Jack Tar vs. John Bull* (New York: Garland, 1997), 78–82; Edward Countryman, *A People in Revolution: The American Revolution and Political Society in New York, 1760–1790* (Baltimore: Johns Hopkins University Press, 1981), 38, 62. The street design is clear in "A Plan of the City and Environs of New York in 1743 . . ." [1813], New York City Historical Society; Paul Gilje, *The Road to Mobocracy: Popular Disorder in New York City, 1763–1834* (Chapel Hill: University of North Carolina Press, 1987), 44; Maier, *From Resistance to Revolution*, 83–100. Carp, "Fire of Liberty," 802, argues that the New York City mob had few firefighters among it, but this may be due to the fact that New York City did not have the fire wardens to mobilize the firemen.

74. Pencak, "Social Structure of Revolutionary Boston," 275; Robert V. Wells, *The Population of the British Colonies in America Before 1776* (Princeton: Princeton University Press, 1975), 83–84, 86–87; Billy G. Smith, "The Vicissitudes of Fortune: The Careers of Laboring men in Philadelphia, 1750–1800," in Stephen Innes, *Work and Labor in Early America* (Chapel Hill: University of North Carolina Press, 1988), 234–235; Morgan and Morgan, *Stamp Act Crisis*, 159–160; William Pencak, "Play as Prelude to Revolution:

Boston, 1765–1776," in Pencak, Matthew Dennis, and Simon P. Newman, eds., *Riot and Revelry in Early America* (University Park: Pennsylvania State University, 2002), 127–129; Jackson Turner Main, *Social Structure of Revolutionary America* (Princeton: Princeton University Press, 1965), 39, 134.

75. Brayley, *Fire Department of Boston*, 74, 66–76 (names of fire company members); *Records of Boston* 16: 176; Carp, "Fire of Liberty," 785, 798.

76. Quotations in Carp, "Fire of Liberty," 810; his evidence, among other sources, comes from David Hackett Fischer, *Paul Revere's Ride* (New York: Knopf, 1994), 301–307, and John W. Tyler, *Smugglers and Patriots: Boston Merchants and the Advent of the American Revolution* (Boston: Northeastern University Press, 1986), 253–277. To the men named in these, Carp has added John Ballard, of No. 1 engine, Gibbons Sharp, of No. 2 engine, and Thomas Uran, of No. 4 engine, who were firemen in the early 1760s and after 1775 became fire wardens.

77. Richard D. Brown, *Revolutionary Politics in Massachusetts: The Boston Committee of Correspondence and the Town, 1772–1774* (Cambridge: Harvard University Press, 1970), 60; Benjamin Woods Labaree, *The Boston Tea Party* (New York: Oxford University Press, 1964), 132–148.

78. Charles Bahne, *The Complete Guide to Boston's Freedom Trail*, 2nd ed. (Cambridge, Mass.: Newtowne, 1998), 20–21; Labaree, *Boston Tea Party*, 132–148; Young, *The Shoemaker*, 43.

79. *Letters and Diary of John Rowe*, 74, 76, 113, 116; Brayley, *Boston Fire Department*, 74–75; on potash: Alan Taylor, *William Cooper's Town: Power and Persuasion on the Frontier of the Early American Republic* (New York: Knopf, 1994), 180–181.

80. Over the course of a weekend in October 2004, I asked the park rangers and the local bookstore owners, as well as the interpreters along the Freedom Trail, if they knew of the fire. None did. Gary Gregory is sole proprietor of Lessons on Liberty, "dedicated to accurately teaching the foundations of independence" at http://www.lessonsonliberty.com. On January 18, 2005, he wrote to the author that none of the people with whom he worked on the Freedom Trail were familiar with the fire.

PITTSBURGH, 1845

1. Joshua Gilpin, *Pleasure and Business in Western Pennsylvania: The Journal of Joshua Gilpin* [1809], ed. Joseph E. Walker (Harrisburg: Pennsylvania Historical and Museum Commission, 1975), 86; Anne Royall, *Mrs. Royall's Pennsylvania . . .* (Washington, D.C.: Printed for the author, 1829), vol. 2: 39, 40, 52; Edward K. Muller and Joel A. Tarr, "The Interaction of Natural and Built Environments in the Pittsburgh Landscape," in Joel A. Tarr, ed., *Devasta-*

tion and Renewal: An Environmental History of Pittsburgh and Its Region (Pittsburgh: University of Pittsburgh Press, 2003), 19–20.

2. François André Michaux, *Travels to the West of the Alleghany Mountains* [1805], excerpted in Roy Lubove, ed., *Pittsburgh* (New York: Franklin Watts, 1976), 3, 4.

3. Richard C. Wade: *The Urban Frontier: Pioneer Life in Early Pittsburgh, Cincinnati, Lexington, Louisville, and St. Louis* (Cambridge, Mass.: Harvard University Press, 1959), 12, 13, 43; John Melish, *Travels in the United States of America . . .* [1812], quoted in Wade, *Urban Frontier,* 43.

4. Pittsburgh *Gazette,* January 27, 1816; Pittsburgh *Mercury,* May 11, 1816; Michaux, in Lubove, ed., *Pittsburgh,* 4, 5.

5. Timothy Flint, *Recollections of the Last Ten Years* (Boston: Cummings, 1826), 17; John Kudlik quoted in Edward K. Muller, "River City," in Tarr, ed., *Devastation and Renewal,* 46.

6. Wade, *Urban Frontier,* 45, 46, 47–48; Laura Frey, *The Land in the Forks: Pittsburgh, 1753–1914* (Philadelphia: Dorrance, 1955), 69–75.

7. George W. Ogden, *Letters from the West . . .* [1823], excerpted in Lubove, ed., *Pittsburgh,* 6, 7; *Thomas's Travels Through the Western Country* [1816], Carnegie Library of Pittsburgh Centennial collection.

8. Royall, *Mrs. Royall's Pennsylvania,* 52.

9. O'Nan, *The Circus Fire,* 66–67.

10. Charles F. Danver, "Mrs. Brooks Did It," *Pittsburgh Post-Gazette,* March 31, 1945; "The Story of the 'Big Fire' In Pittsburgh . . . Written Down by Miss Wilma Owens," n.d., Carnegie Library of Pittsburgh; George Swetnam, "Who Was Pittsburgh's Mrs. O'Leary?" *Pittsburgh Post-Gazette,* April 6, 1952, Heinz Historical Center, Historical Society of Western Pennsylvania Library and Archives.

11. Samuel Jones, *Pittsburgh in the Year Eighteen Hundred and Twenty-Six . . .* (Pittsburgh, 1826), 50, 57; Wade, *Urban Frontier,* 46; Frances G. Couvares, *The Remaking of Pittsburgh: Class and Culture in an Industrializing City, 1877–1919* (Albany: State University of New York, 1984), 9, 10.

12. James Hall, *Letters from the West* (London, 1828), 29. Furnace and forge descriptions from Charles B. Dew, *Bond of Iron: Master and Slave at Buffalo Forge* (New York: Norton, 1994), 10–11, 30; Couvares, *Remaking of Pittsburg,* 19.

13. James J. Davis, *The Iron Puddler,* Project Guttenberg e-text no. 1297, http://www.gutenberg.net/dirs/etext98/tirnp10.txt, p. 25; John N. Ingham, *Making Iron and Steel: Independent Mills in Pittsburgh, 1820–1920* (Columbus: Ohio State University, 1991), 33–35, citing the work of David Montgomery.

14. United States Census Office, *Sixth Census* [1840] (Washington, D.C.: T. Allen, 1841), 148–153; Royall, *Mrs. Royall's Pennsylvania,* 89–124.

15. Charles Dickens, *American Notes: A Journey* [1842] (New York: Fromm, 1985), 154.

16. Hall, *Letters*, 28.

17. Donald E. Cook, "The Great Fire of Pittsburgh in 1845," *Western Pennsylvania Historical Magazine* 51 (1968): 128–129; Rose Demorest, "Pittsburgh, The Great Fire, 1845," manuscript in Carnegie Library of Pittsburgh, 1–3.

18. *Sixth Census*, 142; Oscar Handlin, "The City Grows," in Stefan Lorant, ed., *Pittsburgh: The Story of an American City* (New York: Doubleday, 1964), 104, 107; Leland D. Baldwin, *Pittsburgh: The Story of a City, 1750–1865* (Pittsburgh: University of Pittsburgh Press, 1937), 223–227; David Brody, *Steelworkers in the Non-Union Era* (Cambridge, Mass.: Harvard University Press, 1964), 81; McAlister Coleman, *Men and Coal* (New York: Farrar and Reinhart, Inc., 1943), 36.

19. Peter Way, *Common Labour: Workers and the Digging of North American Canals, 1780–1860* (Cambridge, UK: Cambridge University Press, 1993), 163–164; Charles C. Arensberg, "The Pittsburgh Fire of April 10, 1845," *Western Pennsylvania Historical Magazine* 28 (1945): 13.

20. Davis, *Iron Puddler*, 17.

21. Sara E. Wermiel, *The Fireproof Building: Technology and Public Safety in the Nineteenth-Century American City* (Baltimore: Johns Hopkins University Press, 200), 5; sketches of Seventh Street, the courthouse, and the city market and reproduction of the regulations in Handlin, "The City Grows," 84–88; Virginia K. Bartlett, *Keeping House: Women's Lives in Western Pennsylvania, 1790–1850* (Pittsburgh: University of Pittsburgh Press, 1994), 57. On stable fires, David Dana, *The Fireman: The Fire Departments of the United States* (Boston, 1858), 258–259. On the Third Presbyterian Church, William Wilson McKinney, *Early Pittsburgh Presbyterianism* (Pittsburgh: Gibson, 1938), 264–265.

22. Elizabeth Ruffin, in 1827, quoted in Mark M. Smith, *Listening to Nineteenth-Century America* (Chapel Hill: University of North Carolina Press, 2001), 28; Flint, *Recollections*, 17; *Darby's Emigrant Guide*, 1818; *Commonwealth*, November 19, 1816, in Carnegie Library of Pittsburgh, Centennial Celebration collection; Wade, *Urban Frontier*, 91, 92, 293.

23. This and later paragraphs describing the fire from "Further Particulars of the Great Fire," *Pittsburgh Daily Morning Post*, April 12, 1845, and "Awful Conflagration," *Pittsburgh Gazette and Advertiser*, April 11, 1845.

24. James Waldo Fawcett, "The Quest for Pittsburgh Fire Department History," *Western Pennsylvania Historical Magazine* 49 (1966): 39–55; Ronald M. Zachrychta, "Municipal Reorganization: the Pittsburgh Fire Department as a Case Study," *Western Pennsylvania Historical Magazine* 49 (1966): 58 (1975): 471–473; Charles T. Dawson, *Our Firemen: The History of the Pittsburgh Fire Department* (Pittsburgh, 1889), 43 and after.

25. *New York Times*, January 28, 1859, 5; Dana, *The Fireman*, 12.

26. Ibid., 12, 13.

27. Greenberg, *Cause for Alarm*, 85–95; Tebeau, *Eating Smoke*, 25–29. On the mental traits of Civil War soldiers, James M. McPherson, *For Cause and Comrades: Why Men Fought in the Civil War* (New York: Oxford University Press, 1997), 46–61, 77–89. The analogy is mine.

28. Bryan F. LeBeau, *Currier and Ives: America Imagined* (Washington, D.C.: Smithsonian, 2001), 18–19. I have based my rumination on the image of the firefighter on Greenberg, *Cause for Alarm*, 19–40.

29. Robert McKnight, Diary, April 10, 1845, Heinz Center, Historical Society of Western Pennsylvania; Dorothy Kantner, "Old Diary Reveals Spark-by-Spark Account of Blaze," *Pittsburgh Sun Telegraph*, March 26, 1955, Historical Society of Western Pennsylvania; Further Particulars of the Great Fire" *Pittsburgh Daily Morning Post*, April 12, 1845; "Awful Conflagration" *Pittsburgh Gazette and Advertiser* April 11, 1845.

30. *Sixth Census*, 24–26.

31. William G. Johnson, *Life and Reminiscences from Birth to Manhood of Wm. G. Johnson* (Pittsburgh: Knickerbocker, 1901), 179–181.

32. Ibid., 181–183.

33. Personal account quoted in Fradkin, *Great Earthquake*, 10.

34. This and the following paragraphs rely on J. Heron Foster, comp., *A Full Account of the Great Fire at Pittsburgh, on the Tenth Day of April, 1845* . . . (Pittsburgh: J. W. Cook, 1845), 3–7.

35. Ibid., 47.

36. Josiah King to his parents, April 12, 1845, Carnegie Library of Pittsburgh.

37. "Pittsburgh in Ruins," *The Mystery*, April 16, 1848; *Gazette and Advertiser*, April 11, 1845.

38. Henry Marie Brackenridge correspondence to *National Intelligencer*, April 14, 1845; William F. Keller, *The Nation's Advocate Henry Marie Brackenridge and Young America* (Pittsburgh: University of Pittsburgh Press, 1956), 368.

39. Cook, "Great Fire," 141; calculation based on "consumer price index (estimate) 1800–2005," http://www.minneapolisfed.org/research/data/us/calc/hist1800.cfm.

40. Brackenridge, *National Intelligencer*, April 14, 1845; Owens, "Story of the 'Big Fire,'" Carnegie Library of Pittsburgh.

41. Foster, *Great Fire*, 48.

42. Figures from Edward C. Goodman, *Fire! The Most Devastating Fires and the Heroes Who Fought Them* (New York: Black Dog and Leventhal, 2001), 24, 34, 56, 68, 151.

43. "Dear Brother," September 28, 1845, Carnegie Library of Pittsburgh; Dana, *The Fireman*, 258–259.

44. Dana, *The Fireman*, 259–261.

45. Ibid., 40–53, 176–178, 60–62, 83–86; Paul Kens, *Justice Stephen Field: Shaping Liberty from the Gold Rush to the Gilded Age* (Lawrence: University Press of Kansas, 1997), 16.

46. E. P. Swift, *The Calamity of Pittsburgh: A Sermon Delivered in the First Presbyterian Church Allegheny City, April 24, 1845* (Allegheny, Pa.: Kennedy, 1845), 15.

47. Ibid., 8, 9, 10.

48. On the burned-over district, Whitney R. Cross, *The Burned Over District: The Social and Intellectual History of Enthusiastic Religion in Western New York, 1800–1850* (New York: Harper, 1965), 3–54, 252–268.

49. Linda K. Pritchard, "The Soul of the City: A Social History of Religion in Pittsburgh," in Samuel P. Hays, ed., *City at the Point: A Social History of Pittsburgh* (Pittsburgh: University of Pittsburgh Press, 1989), 332–338; McKinney, *Pittsburgh Presbyterianism*, 257–259.

50. Quoted in McKinney, *Pittsburgh Presbyterianism*, 267.

51. Handlin, "The City Grows," 120.

52. James H. McClelland to his sister, April 27, 1848, quoted in Cook, "The Great Fire of Pittsburgh in 1845," 143; Common Council and Select Council (Pittsburgh), letter to Governor Francis R. Shunk, April 12, 1845, in Foster, *Great Fire*, 15, 16; Francis R. Shunk to the Senate and House of Representatives of . . . Pennsylvania, April 14, 1845, in Foster, *Great Fire*, 14.

53. Frederic Henry Hedge, on "Schiller" [1834], in Perry Miller, ed., *The Transcendentalists: An Anthology* (Cambridge: Harvard University Press, 1967), 80; Elizabeth B. Clark, "'The Sacred Rights of the Weak': Pain, Sympathy, and the Culture of Individual Rights in Ante-bellum America," *Journal of American History* 82 (September 1995): 484.

54. R. C. Grier et al., Message to Governor Shunk, April 12, 1845, in Foster, *Great Fire*, 15; Thomas J. Bigham, address to Pennsylvania House of Representatives, April 14, 1845, in Foster, *Great Fire*, 18, 19.

55. Board of Assessors, list of losses, 1845, in Foster, *Great Fire*, 30–42.

56. Tebeau, *Eating Smoke*, 54–84.

57. Foster, *Great Fire*, 50–51; Henry Oliver Evans, "Notes on American Fire Protection and Insurance," in *A Booklet Published on the Occasion of "The Big Fire" of 1845* (Pittsburgh: Historical Society of Western Pennsylvania, 1945), 31; Cook, "Great Fire," 142.

58. Lawrence W. Friedman, *History of American Law* (New York: Simon and Schuster, 1973), 476–477; Peter Charles Hoffer, *Law and People in Colonial America*, rev. ed. (Baltimore: Johns Hopkins University Press, 1998),

79–85; Wayne V. McIntosh, *The Appeal of Civil Law: A Political-Economic Analysis of Litigation* (Urbana: University of Illinois Press, 1990), 43.

59. *Hillier v. Allegheny County Mutual Insurance Company,* 3 Pa. 470 (Supreme Court of Pennsylvania, 1846); *Hackney v. Allegheny County Mutual Insurance Company,* 4 Pa. 185 (Supreme Court of Pennsylvania, 1846).

60. *Bruner v. Sheik,* 9 Watts & Serg. 119 (Sup. Ct. Middle District, 1845); *Magaw v. Lambert,* 3 Pa. 444 (Supreme Court of Pennsylvania, 1846); *Hannen v. Ewalt,* 18 Pa. 9 (Supreme Court of Pennsylvania, 1851).

61. Robert Bremner, *American Philanthropy* [1960] (reprint Chicago: University of Chicago Press, 1982), 45, 61, 70; Bremner, *The Public Good: Philanthropy and Welfare in the Civil War Era* (New York: Knopf, 1980), 23; Kathleen D. McCarthy, *American Creed: Philanthropy and the Rise of Civil Society, 1700–1865* (Chicago: University of Chicago Press, 2003), 81.

62. Foster, *Great Fire,* 20–28.

63. Senate and House of Representatives of Pennsylvania, April 14, 1845, in Foster, *Great Fire,* 20; Friedman, *A History of American Law,* 182. On the relationship between the active state and the business community, see James Willard Hurst, *Law and Markets in United States History* (Madison: University of Wisconsin Press, 1982).

64. William J. Novak, *The People's Welfare: Law and Regulation in Nineteenth-Century America* (Chapel Hill: University of North Carolina Press, 1996), 80, 81; Greenberg, *Cause for Alarm,* 131–136.

65. Foster, *Great Fire,* 43–45.

66. 1872 Atlas of the City of Pittsburgh, Plate 15, First Ward, http://digital.library.pitt.edu/maps.

67. "The Smoking Chimneys," *Ballou's Pictorial Drawing-Room Companion,* April 14, 1855; Andrew Carnegie, *Autobiography of Andrew Carnegie* [1920], ed. John Van Dyke, with a new foreword by Cecilia Tichi (Boston: Northeastern University Press, 1986), 39, 40; Carnegie quoted in Joseph Frazier Wall, *Andrew Carnegie* (New York: Oxford University Press, 1970), 145–146.

68. Fred B. Schell, drawing reproduced in J. Cutler Andrews, "The Civil War and Its Aftermath," in Lorant, ed., *Pittsburgh,* 150–151; Willard Glazier, *Peculiarities of American Cities* (Philadelphia, 1883), 333; Robert A. Woods (1909), quoted in Joel A. Tarr, "The Pittsburgh Survey as an Environmental Statement," *The Search for the Ultimate Sink: Urban Pollution in Historical Perspective* (Akron: University of Akron Press, 1996), 88.

69. Greenberg, *Cause for Alarm,* 128–131; Dawson, *Our Firemen,* 65; Andrews, "The Civil War and After," in Lorent, ed., *Pittsburgh,* 152.

70. George Tucker, *The Progress of the United States in Population and Wealth* . . . (New York, 1855), 127; Samuel Miller quoted in Thomas Bender,

Toward an Urban Vision: Ideas and Institutions in Nineteenth-Century Amer-ica (Baltimore: Johns Hopkins University Press, 1975), 9.

71. Glazier, *Peculiarities*, 332; I base this musing on Leo Marx, *The Machine in the Garden: Technology and the Pastoral Idea in America* (New York: Oxford University Press, 1964), 145–226. The quote is from Marx, *The Machine in the Garden*, 260.

72. On Wall, see "The Artist Reports on the Fire of 1845," *Carnegie Magazine*, March 1945, 300–301.

73. Currier and Ives, "The Great Conflagration at Pittsburgh" 1845, Print No. 4220.

74. Alexis de Tocqueville, *Democracy in America* [1840] (New York: Knopf, 1994), vol. 2: 187, 190; Brackenridge, *National Intelligencer*, April 14, 1845; C. W., letter from Pittsburgh, June 12, 1845, to *Cincinnati Gazette*, reprinted in Foster, *Great Fire*, 9, 10.

75. O. Ormsby Gregg, *Pittsburgh, Her Advantageous Position and Great Resources . . . Embraced in a Notice of Sale of Real Estate* (Pittsburgh: Johnston and Stockton, 1845), 1–3, 34.

76. Ibid., 16, 22.

77. David Blight, *Beyond the Battlefield: Race, Memory, and the American Civil War* (Amherst: University of Massachusetts Press, 2002), 1,2.

78. George T. Fleming, "Great Conflagrations that have changed the appearance of the city," *Pittsburgh Gazette Times*, June 28, 1914; "Today Is the Seventy-fifth Anniversary of Pittsburgh's Great Fire," *Pittsburgh First*, April 10, 1920.

79. Joseph M. Kesslinger, "Since 1845 many great fires damaged Pittsburgh," *Pittsburgh Dispatch*, June 5, 1921; William G. Lytle, Jr., "Washerwoman's fire starter of blaze which swept through Pittsburgh in 1845," *Pittsburgh Press*, April 5, 1925.

80. "Disastrous Fire of 1845," *Pittsburgh Post-Gazette* September 26, 1936; "Washerwoman's Tiny Fire Developed into Pittsburgh's Greatest Catastrophe," *Pittsburgh Press*, December 11, 1935; "Building Is 'Stop' Sign for Fire or Flood," *Pittsburgh Post-Gazette,* November 18, 1936.

81. "Commemoration Planned of Big Fire of April 1845," *Pittsburgh Post-Gazette,* November 16, 1944; "Historical Society Exhibit to Feature Big Fire of 1845," *Pittsburgh Press*, November 19, 1944; "Fire Ceremonial Observance Hits Snag," *Post-Gazette,* March 26, 1945; "Fire Pageant Change Made," *Pittsburgh Sun-Telegraph*, March 26, 1945; "Parade and Pageant Mark Historical Fire Here," *Post-Gazette,* April 11, 1945; Playbill, "One Hundred Years Ago: An Historical Sketch, by Madge Miller and Margaret Townsend Scully," April 10, 1945, Carnegie Library; Ann Weiss, "Old Family Names Mark Committees for Fire Centennial," *Pittsburgh Press*, April 8, 1945; Historical Society of

Western Pennsylvania, *1845–1945 An Historical Commemoration* (Pittsburgh, 1945), 10; Mary Ensign Pardee, "Story of the Fire Centennial," *Western Pennsylvania Historical Magazine* 28 (1945): 6.

82. Kenneth Speer, "Big Fire of 1845," *Pittsburgh Sun-Telegraph,* April 10, 1953; "112th Anniversary of City's Big Fire," *Pittsburgh Sun-Telegraph,* April 10, 1957.

83. Roy Lubove, *Twentieth Century Pittsburgh: Volume 2, The Post-Steel Era* (Pittsburgh: University of Pittsburgh Press, 1996), 4, 19; Samuel P. Hays, "Beyond Celebration, Pittsburgh and Its Region in the Environmental Era—Notes by a Participant Observer," in Tarr, ed., *Devastation and Renewal,* 193–219; Tarr, "The Pittsburgh Survey," 98.

84. Franklin Toker, *Pittsburgh, An Urban Portrait* (Pittsburgh: University of Pittsburgh Press, 1986), 16–17, 36; Arthus Ziegler quoted in Lubove, *Post–Steel Era,* 234.

CHICAGO, 1871

1. Nelson Algren, *Chicago: City on the Make,* introduction by Studs Terkel (Chicago: University of Chicago Press, 1983), 10.

2. James L. Merriner, *Grafters and Goo Goos: Corruption and Reform in Chicago, 1833–2003* (Carbondale: Southern Illinois University Press, 2004), 27, 26; Herman Kogan and Lloyd Wendt, *Chicago: A Pictorial History* (New York: E. P. Dutton, 1958), 24.

3. This and after from Bessie Louise Pierce, *A History of Chicago, Volume I: The Beginning of a City, 1673–1848* (Chicago: University of Chicago Press, 1937), 15–74. The inspiration for much of this paragraph is William Cronon, *Nature's Metropolis: Chicago and the Great West* (New York: Norton, 1991), 23–27.

4. Cronon, *Nature's Metropolis,* 126–127; 414; Pierce, *A History of Chicago: Volume II: From Town to City, 1848–1871* (Chicago: University of Chicago Press, 1940), 5; William G. Ferris, *The Grain Traders: The Story of the Chicago Board of Trade* (East Lansing: Michigan State University Press, 1988), 13–16.

5. Pierce, *Chicago,* vol. 2: 245, 247, 255, 504–505; Donald L. Miller, *City of the Century: The Epic of Chicago and the Making of America* (New York: Simon and Schuster, 1996), 113–114.

6. Upton Sinclair, *The Jungle* [1906], with an introduction by James R. Barrett (Urbana: University of Illinois Press, 1998), 25.

7. Frank Norris, *The Pit: A Story of Chicago* [1902], ed. Joseph R. McElrath, Jr., and Gwendolyn Jones (New York: Penguin, 1994), 55, 56.

8. Hamlin Garland, *The Rose of Dutcher's Coolly* (New York: Harper, 1895), 170, 178, 156.

9. A description of the weather in the region for the weeks preceding the fire appears in Denise Guess and William Lutz, *Firestorm at Peshtigo: A Town, Its People, and the Deadliest Fire in American History* (New York: Holt, 2002), 45, 48, 50, 51, 65, 82–88, 99, 100, 154. The quotation is Joseph Kirkland, "The Chicago Fire," *New England Magazine* 12 (August 1892): 726. On fireballs: Dixie Franklin, *Michigan* (Oakland, Calif.: Fodor, 2001), 128.

10. E. J. Goodspeed, *History of the Great Fires in Chicago and the West* (New York: H. S. Goodspeed, 1877), 121.

11. A. T. Andreas, *History of Chicago from the Earliest Period to the Present Time* (Chicago: A. T. Andreas, 1889), vol. 3: 120. The idea of the city as "nature's metropolis" and its connection to fire in the countryside is explored in Cronon's *Nature's Metropolis*, 202.

12. Harold M. Mayer and Richard C. Wade, with the assistance of Glen E. Holt, *Chicago: Growth of a Metropolis* (Chicago: University of Chicago Press, 1969), 44; Cronon, *Nature's Metropolis*, 171, 179, 198.

13. Goodspeed, *Great Fires*, 121; Carl Smith, *Urban Disorder and the Shape of Belief: The Great Chicago Fire, the Haymarket Bomb, and the Model Town of Pullman* (Chicago: University of Chicago Press, 1995), 19; James W. Sheahan and George P. Upton, *The Great Conflagration: Chicago, Its Past, Present, and Future* (Philadelphia: Union, 1871), 63–64.

14. Goodspeed, *Great Fires*, 121.

15. Paul M. Angle, "Introduction," *The Great Chicago Fire*, new enlarged ed. (Chicago: Chicago Historical Society, 1971), 1–2; Andreas, *Chicago*, vol. 3: 121–122.

16. Tebeau, *Eating Smoke*, 162–166; *F.D.N.Y.*, 36–37.

17. Andreas, *Chicago*, vol. 3: 120–126; Richard F. Bales, *The Great Chicago Fire and the Myth of Mrs. O'Leary's Cow* (Jefferson, N.C.: McFarland, 2002), 11–20; Rosen, *Limits of Power*, 95, 110.

18. Kurt F. Nietze, "Early Days Recalled," http://www.lafire.com/stations/archive/EraoftheHorses_1886-1921; Marty, "A History of Horses in the Fire Service," http://www.firefightersrealstories.com/horses.html. On famous fire horses, http://www.publicsafety.net/dalmatian.htm, and http://www.ci.detroit.mi.us/fire/history.htm. The classic work on fire horses is Alfred M. Downes, *Firefighters and their Pets* (New York: Harper, 1907).

19. Tebeau, *Eating Smoke*, 141–164, 214; Bales, *Great Chicago Fire*, 18–20.

20. Tebeau, *Eating Smoke*, 214–215.

21. Goodspeed, *Great Fires*, 83–84.

22. Ibid., 115; Bales, *Great Chicago Fire*, 17; Andreas, *Chicago*, vol. 3: 120; Mabel McIlvain, "Introduction," in McIlvain, ed., *Reminiscences of Chicago During the Great Fire* (Chicago: Donnelly, 1915), xviii; Von Essen, *Strong of Heart*, 165.

23. Joseph Edgar Chamberlin, 1871, in McIlvain, ed., *Reminiscences,* 1.

24. Perry Duis, *Chicago: Creating New Traditions* (Chicago: Chicago Historical Society, 1976), 14; Kenneth T. Jackson, *Crabgrass Frontier: The Suburbanization of the United States* (New York: Oxford University Press, 1985), 124–128.

25. This and the following narrative from Bales, *Great Chicago Fire*, 51 and after.

26. Oliver Wendell Holmes, Jr., "The Path of the Law," *Harvard Law Review* 10 (1897): 458.

27. Bales, *Great Chicago Fire*, 112–138.

28. Catherine O'Leary testimony, November 24, 1871, in Bales, *Great Chicago Fire*, 217–221.

29. Bales, *Great Chicago Fire*, 140–143; "Report of the Board of Police and Fire Commissioners of Their Investigation of the Origin and Spread of the Great Fire," *Chicago Times*, December 12, 1871, reproduced in ibid., 295–296. After a brief period of public praise for what was obviously a heroic if unrewarded effort to contain the fire in the West Division, newspapers, city government, and popular opinion shifted to blame the fire department. The old accusations of "drunken and stupefied" firemen and bumbling and loafing officers appeared in public print. As the accusations grew to a crescendo, the city decided on an open investigation, the first of its kind into a city fire. On November 23, the city council began its official inquiry. In the end, the investigation involved fifty-one witnesses, took two weeks, resulted in over a thousand pages of evidence, and neither cleared the department of negligence nor managed to find anyone to blame. It was less a cover-up than a muddled conversation among bewildered inquisitors and tightlipped residents.

30. Kogan and Wendt, *Chicago*, 10–19; William J. Brown and Matthais Schaefer, testimony, November 24, 1871, in Bales, *Great Chicago Fire*, 213–216.

31. Chamberlin, in McIlvain, ed., *Reminiscences*, 2; tactical situation in fire suppression: Dennis R. Childress, "Fire Suppression," *FFH*, 558, 559; Williams account here and in following paragraphs, Robert A. Williams, testimony before the commission of inquiry, December 2, 1871, transcript reproduced in Bales, *Great Chicago Fire*, 271–276.

32. David Swing, "A memory of the Chicago Fire," *Scribner's Magazine* 11 (June 1892): 692.

33. Andreas, *Chicago*, vol. 3: 684, 695. The Chicago fire books industry was only surpassed by books on 9/11.

34. James M. Perry, *A Bohemian Brigade: The Civil War Correspondents* (New York: Wiley, 2000), 174, 175, 176; Ernest Crozier, *Yankee Reporters, 1861–65* (New York: Oxford University Press, 1956), 362–365; Smith, *Urban Disorder*, 30; Sheahan and Upton, *Great Conflagration*, 64, 65.

35. Sheahan and Upton, *Great Conflagration*, 75, 76, 77, 78.

36. Ibid., 67, 69, 74, 75; Elias Colbert and Everett Chamberlin, *Chicago and the Great Conflagration* (New York: C. F. Vent, 1871), 218; Alexander Frear account reprinted in McIlvain, ed., *Reminiscences*, 14, 16; Mrs. Alfred Hebard, account in McIlvain, ed., *Reminiscences*, 38.

37. Sheahan and Upton, *Great Conflagration*, 81, 91, 85.

38. Ibid., 109–114.

39. Andreas, *Chicago*, vol. 3: 684–685; calculation based on "Consumer Price Index (estimate) 1800–2005."

40. Sheahan and Upton, *Great Conflagration*, 127; Angle, "Introduction," 1, 4; Mary Fales to Her Mother, October 10, 1871; Anna E. Higginson to Mrs. Mark Skinner, November 10, 1871, in Angle, ed., *Great Chicago Fire*, 17, 27.

41. Jonas Hutchinson to Betsey Hutchinson, October 9, 1871, and Hutchinson to Hutchinson, October 10, 1871, in Angle, ed., *Great Chicago Fire*, 11, 13.

42. *Evening Journal* extra, October 9, 1871, ibid., 20; Lambert Tree account in McIlvain, ed., *Reminiscences*, 102.

43. Goodspeed, *Great Fires*, 137; Karen Sawislak, *Smoldering City: Chicagoans and the Great Fire, 1871–1874* (Chicago: University of Chicago Press, 1995), 35, 36, 37.

44. Arnold Genthe, "San Francisco, April 18, 1906," photograph reproduced in David Wyatt, *Five Fires: Race, Catastrophe, and the Shaping of California* (New York: Oxford University Press, 1997), 120.

45. Panic studies summarized in O'Nan, *Circus Fire*, 71, and E. L. Quarantelli, "Panic Behavior: Some Empirical Observations," in Donald J. Conway, *Human Response to Tall Buildings* (Stroudsburg, Pa.: Dowden, 1977), 336–350.

46. Proclamation, October 10, 1871, in Angle, ed., *Great Chicago Fire*, 18.

47. Sawislak, *Smoldering City*, 54; Sheridan to "His Honor the Mayor," October 12, 1871, reproduced in Sheahan and Upton, *Great Conflagration*, 186.

48. Ann L. Buttenwieser, *Manhattan Water-Bound: Planning and Developing Manhattan's Waterfront from the Seventeenth Century to the Present* (New York: New York University Press, 1987), 66.

49. William K. Beatty, "When Cholera Scourged Chicago," *Chicago History* 11 (1982): 2–13; Thomas Melville Bonner, *Medicine in Chicago, 1850–1950* (Urbana: University of Illinois Press, 1991); John Duffy, *The Sanitarians: A History of American Public Health* (Urbana: University of Illinois Press, 1990); Sheridan to John M. Palmer, October 11, 1871, Proclamation of the Governor of Illinois, October 10, 1871, reproduced in Sheahan and Upton, *Great Conflagration*, 186, 175.

50. Goodspeed, *Great Fires*, 206, 216, 218, 352; N. S. Emerson, "The Stricken City," quoted in Smith, *Urban Disorder*, 37. On the housing problems of the poor displaced by the fire, Rosen, *Limits of Power*, 102–105.

51. Smith, *Urban Disorder*, 47; William Bross, *History of Chicago, Historical and Commercial Statistics* (Chicago: Jansen, 1876), 100.

52. Joseph Medill, "Inaugural Message, December 4, 1871," reproduced in Sheahan and Upton, *Great Conflagration*, 457, 458.

53. Ross Miller, *American Apocalypse: The Great Fire and the Myth of Chicago* (Chicago: University of Chicago Press, 1990), 90–105; John R. Chapin, "The Rush for Life over Randolph Street Bridge," *Harper's Weekly*, October 28, 1871; Currier and Ives, "The Great Fire at Chicago, Octr 8th 1871" (no. 3917), *Currier and Ives: Printmakers to the American People*, ed. Harry T. Peters (Garden City, N.Y.: Doubleday, 1976), vol. 2: plate 178.

54. On the resilience of cities, particularly post-fire Chicago, Kevin Rosario, "Making Progress: Disaster Narratives and the Art of Optimism in Modern America," in Lawrence J. Vale and Thomas J. Campanella, eds., *The Resilient City: How Modern Cities Recover from Disaster* (New York: Oxford University Press, 2005), 29, 36, 38. Sawislak, *Smoldering City*, passim, is a repository of the other kind of stories.

55. Colbert and Chamberlin, *Chicago and the Great Conflagration*, 319.

56. D. C. Houston letter reproduced in Sheahan and Upton, *Great Conflagration*, 248; Everett Chamberlin, "Five Months After" [1872], reproduced in Angle, ed., *Great Chicago Fire*, 91, 92, 93.

57. For the arguments here and after on race, see N.E.H. Hull and Peter Charles Hoffer, *Roe v. Wade: The Abortion Rights Controversy in American History* (Lawrence: University Press of Kansas, 2001), 38–41.

58. Goodspeed, *Great Fires*, 497, 511, 521; James Milner quoted in Sawislak, *Smoldering City*, 3; Ross Miller, *American Apocalypse*, 60, 64.

59. Rosen, *Limits of Power*, 116–119.

60. This and the following paragraphs rely on the accounts in Robert W. Twyman, *History of Marshall Field & Co. 1852–1906* (Philadelphia: University of Pennsylvania, 1954), 1–82, and Axel Madsen, *The Marshall Fields* (New York: Wiley, 2002), 1–81.

61. Ross Miller, *American Apocalypse*, 77, 83, 84, 85; Andreas, *Chicago*, vol. 3: 63.

62. Donald Hoffman, *The Architecture of John Wellborn Root* (Baltimore: Johns Hopkins University Press, 1973), 6, 10, 12, 14, 19; Thomas S. Hines, *Burnham of Chicago, Architect and Planner* (New York: Oxford University Press, 1974), 24, 25; Charles Moore, *Daniel H. Burnham: Architect, Planner of Cities* (New York: Houghton, 1921), 21, 26, 29.

63. Hoffman, *Root*, 24, 26, 32, 97, 137, 164; Hines, *Burnham*, 48, 53, 64; Deborah Slaton, "Burham and Root and the Rookery," in John S. Garner, ed., *The Midwest in American Architecture* (Urbana: University of Illinois Press, 1991), 79, 80, 84, 88; Hugh Morrison, *Louis Sullivan: Prophet of Modern Architecture* (New York: Norton, 1998), 32, 35.

64. John R. Stilgoe, *Borderland: Origins of the American Suburb, 1820–1939* (New Haven: Yale University Press, 1988), 10, 15, 85, 148; David Hamer, *New Towns in the New World: Images and Perceptions of the Nineteenth-Century Urban Frontier* (New York: Columbia University Press, 1990), 171; Jackson, *Crabgrass Frontier*, 80.

65. Everett Chamberlin, *Chicago and Its Suburbs* (Chicago: Hungerford, 1874), 343, 345, 352.

66. Jackson, *Crabgrass Frontier*, 93; Rosen, *Limits of Power*, 123; Ann Durkin Keating, *Building Chicago: Suburban Developers and the Creation of a Divided Metropolis* (Columbus: Ohio State University Press, 1988), 73.

67. Jackson, *Crabgrass Frontier*, 93; Mayer and Wade, *Chicago*, 83, 84.

68. Jean F. Block, *Hyde Park Homes: An Informal History, 1856–1910* (Chicago: University of Chicago Press, 1978), 2, 3, 9, 10, 11, 19, 20, 22, 23.

69. Keating, *Building Chicago*, 23; Jackson, *Crabgrass Frontier*, 108–109.

70. Donald Miller, *City of the Century*, 266–273; Mayer and Wade, *Chicago*, 139–148.

71. Gladwell, *Tipping Point*, 9–14; Paul Avrich, *The Haymarket Tragedy* (Princeton: Princeton University Press, 1984), 17.

72. Goodspeed, *Great Fires*, 422; Beecher quotation in Sawislak, *Smoldering City*, 70.

73. Account of the relief based on Sawislak, *Smoldering City*, 80–106.

74. Ibid., 97; the other committee was the Committee of Fifty, self-appointed to deal with the San Francisco disaster of 1906. The author of the quotation was Adolphus W. Greely; Fradkin, *Great Earthquake*, 208.

75. Irwin Unger, *The Greenback Era: A Social and Political History of American Finance, 1865–1879* (Princeton: Princeton University Press, 1964), 131–151.

76. Quotations in Sawislak, *Smoldering City*, 142, 146.

77. Tebeau, *Eating Smoke*, 175–185; Harry C. Brearly, *The History of the National Board of Fire Underwriters* (New York: Stokes, 1916), 24.

78. Andreas, *Chicago*, vol. 3: 461–465; Wermiel, *The Fireproof Building*, 173; Henry R. Gall and William George, Jr., *One Hundred Years of Fire Insurance . . . A History of the Aetna Insurance Company* (Hartford, Conn.: Aetna, 1919), 115–116; Sawislak, *Smoldering City*, 77–79; *In Re Republic Insurance Co.*, 20 F. Cas. 544, 545 (1873) (n.d., Illinois); *In Re Merchants Insurance Co.*, 17 F. Cas. 41 (1981) (n.d., Illinois); *In Re Western Insurance Co.*, 29 F. Cas. 763 (1872) (n.d., New York); Rosen, *Limits of Power*, 148.

79. Smith, *Urban Disorder*, 104–105; Avrich, *Haymarket*, 16.

80. Avrich, *Haymarket*, 32, 33; Robert V. Bruce, *1877: Year of Violence* (Indianapolis: Bobbs Merrill, 1959), 41, 63; Smith, *Urban Disorder*, 107.

81. Bruce C. Nelson, *Beyond the Martyrs: A Social History of Chicago's Anarchists, 1870–1900* (New Brunswick, N.J.: Rutgers University Press, 1988), 24.

82. Paul Avrich, *Haymarket*, 97, 197–214; Ray Ginger, *Altgeld's America: The Lincoln Idea Versus Changing Realities* (New York: Funk, 1958), 82, 84, 85, 86.

83. Erik Larson, *The Devil in the White City: Murder, Magic, and Madness at the Fair That Changed America* (New York: Vintage, 2003), 167, 168.

84. Hines, *Burnham*, 73–91.

85. Ibid., 92–124.

86. Donald Miller, *City of the Century*, 488; Cronon, *Nature's Metropolis*, 343.

87. Mr. Dooley in Chicago Sunday *Post*, August 6, 1893, reprinted in Barbara C. Schaaf, *Mr. Dooley's Chciago* (Garden City, N.Y.: Doubleday, 1977), 60; John Coleman Adams, quoted in Donald Miller, *City of the Century*, 492.

88. Theodore Dreiser, *A Book About Myself* (New York: Boni, 1922), 19, 20; Donald Miller, *City of the Century*, 518–527.

89. Ross Miller, *American Apocalypse*, 216; Cronon, *Nature's Metropolis*, 351.

90. Chicago did not forget the Great Fire. On the site where it began, 137 DeKoven, Mayor Richard Daley ordered built the city's fire department academy. Facing the lobby of the academy is a spiral of metal twisting upward–a fire memorial not just to the firefighters and the victims, but to the city itself. To the northeast, where the fire burned out, stands the Chicago Historical Society. Within, the Richard H. Needham Chicago History Galleries documents in words and pictures the terrible course of the conflagration.

BALTIMORE, 1904

1. William Clendenin, "The Fireproof Buildings of Baltimore," *Fireproof* (March 1904): 12 (Burnham quotation).

2. Suzanne Ellery Greene Chapelle, *Baltimore, an Illustrated History* (Sun Valley, Calif.: American Historical Press, 2000), 174; The panorama appears in Harold A. Williams, *Baltimore Afire*, rev. ed. (Baltimore: Schneidereith, 1979), 52–53.

3. "Baltimore Inner Harbor Panorama Photograph, Taken From Federal Hill," http://www.Digitalharbor.info/inner-harbor-panorama.html, accessed March 21, 2005; Ansel Adams, *Ansel Adams, An Autobiography* (Boston: Little, Brown, 1985), 6.

4. Alison Isenberg, *Downtown America: A History of the Place and the People Who Made It* (Chicago: University of Chicago Press, 2004), 16–31; James B. Crooks, *Politics and Progress: The Rise of Urban Progressivism in Baltimore, 1895–1911* (Baton Rouge: Louisiana State University Press, 1968), 137–138; Rosen, *Limits of Power*, 296. On pollution: Martin V. Melosi, "Environmental Crisis in the City: The Relationship Between Industrialization and Urban Pol-

lution," in Melosi, ed., *Pollution and Reform in American Cities, 1879–1930* (Austin: University of Texas Press, 1980), 3–24. I should add that Olmstead's plan for green spaces did take root in a number of Baltimore areas—most notably the Homewood Campus of the Johns Hopkins University.

5. Rosen, *Limits of Power*, 251; Jo Ann E. Argersinger, "The City That Tries to Suit Everybody: Baltimore's Clothing Industry," in Elizabeth Fee, Linda Shopes, and Linda Zeidman, eds., *The Baltimore Book: New Views of Local History* (Philadelphia: Temple University Press, 1991), 81–88.

6. Karen Olsen, "Old West Baltimore: Segregation, African-American Culture, and the Struggle for Equality," in Fee, Shopes, and Zeidman, eds., *Baltimore Book*, 57–67; Harold A. McDougall, *Black Baltimore: A New Theory of Community* (Philadelphia: Temple University Press, 1993), 38–45.

7. Chapelle, *Baltimore*, 1–6.

8. Fire engine: Peter B. Petersen, *The Great Baltimore Fire* (Baltimore: Maryland Historical Society, 2004), 2–3; wide streets: J. Thomas Scharf, *Chronicles of Baltimore*, quoting a 1799 description, reprinted in Robert I. Vexler, ed., *Baltimore: A Chronological and Documentary History, 1632–1970* (Dobbs Ferry, N.Y.: Oceana, 1975), 99.

9. Greenberg, *Cause for Alarm*, 160; Dana, *The Fireman*, 247–248.

10. Harold M. Hyman, *A More Perfect Union: The Impact of the Civil War and Reconstruction on the Constitution* (New York: Knopf, 1973), 81–85; Sylvia Gillett, "Camden Yards and the Strike of 1877," in Fee, Shopes, and Zeidman, eds., *Baltimore Book*, 1–11.

11. J. Scott Howell, "The Founder's Art," in James D. Dilts and Catharine F. Black, eds., *Cast-Iron Buildings and Architectural Ironwork* (Centerville, Md.: Tidewater, 1991), 13–17.

12. On Jackson, I am grateful to Park Ranger David Wymore of the Klondike Gold Rush National Park office, for a tour of the historic park. On the use of cast iron and other construction materials, along with the architectural plans for the commercial blocks after the fire of 1889, see Jeffrey Karl Ochsner and Dennis Alan Andersen, *Distant Corner: Seattle Architects and the Legacy of H. H. Richardson* (Seattle: University of Washington Press, 2003), 57, 142, 150–153, 194–195.

13. Rosen, *Limits of Power*, 254, 255; Phoebe B. Stanton, "Baltimore in the Twentieth Century," in John Dorsey and James D. Dilts, eds., *A Guide to Baltimore Architecture*, 3rd ed. (Centerville, Md.: Tidewaters, 1997), 31–36; Joe Russell and Kate Shelly, *Baltimore in Vintage Postcards* (Charleston, S.C.: Arcadia, 1999), 10, 13 (Baltimore Street before the fire); Sanborn Insurance Company, *Insurance Maps of Baltimore* (New York: Sanborn, 1902), vol. 4, passim, originals in Maryland Historical Society, Baltimore.

14. William Clendinen, "The Fireproof Buildings of Baltimore: Their Condition After the Fire—the Story in Detail," *Fireproof* 4 (March 1904): 12–28.

15. Quotation from *Baltimore Sun* journalist Laura Lippman, *Charm City* (New York: Avon, 1997), 1 (not about 1904, by the way, but Baltimore weather has not changed); 1904 weather: Harold A. Williams, *Baltimore Afire*, rev. ed. (Baltimore: Schneidereth, 1979), 1; city politics: Crooks, *Politics and Progress*, 48–97; the politicians in the newspapers: H. L. Mencken, *Newspaper Days, 1899–1906* [1941] (Baltimore: Johns Hopkins University Press, 1996), 138, 143; on Mencken: Terry Teachout, *The Skeptic: A Life of H. L. Mencken* (New York: HarperCollins, 2002), 53.

16. Marie Van Vorst and Mrs. John Van Vorst, *The Woman Who Toils: Being the Experiences of Two Gentlewomen as Factory Girls* (New York, 1903), 207; J. Anthony Lukas, *Big Trouble: A Murder in a Small Western Town Sets Off a Struggle for the Soul of America* (New York: Simon and Schuster, 1997), 228–229.

17. And this is exactly what happened in the Triangle Shirtwaist Fire of March 25, 1911, destroying the upper three floors of the Asch Building in Washington Square, New York. It could just as easily have been Baltimore. The account above summarizes Leon Stein, *The Triangle Fire* (Ithaca, N.Y.: Cornell, 1962), 11–65, with quotations on 61, 19.

18. Theodore Dreiser, *Sister Carrie, a Novel*, ed. Donald Pizer [1900] (New York: Norton, 1970), 17.

19. *Baltimore American*, February 7, 1904, A16.

20. Sanborn Insurance Company Fire Map of Baltimore, 1902, vol. 1 (Hopkins Place, German, Liberty) and vol. 4 (the rest of the downtown) provide a detailed portrait of building materials, exposures, height and width of buildings, width of streets, and hydrant location. Maryland Historical Society.

21. On the electrical poles and wires, see Rosen, *Limits of Power*, 298–299, 296. The photos of the pre-fire Inner Harbor district in Petersen and Williams amply document the obstructive dangers of the poles and wires. I should note here that just as I was finishing my research, Peter B. Peterson's fine book was published. On the cellar fire: Salka, *First In, Last Out*, 44–45.

22. The cigarette theory is from Petersen, *Great Baltimore Fire*, 15.

23. Daniel Boorstin, *The Americans: The Democratic Experience* (New York: Random House, 1973), 367; Pauline Maier et al., *Inventing America: A History of the United States* (New York: Norton, 2003), vol. 2: 690–693. The Schenectady city museum has a superb display of General Electric's turn-of-the-century technological achievements.

24. Tebeau, *Eating Smoke*, 247, 249, 251.

25. *Baltimore Sun*, February 8, 1904, A1, A2; Petersen, *Great Baltimore Fire*, 16.

26. Description of flip-lid hydrants: "New York City Fire Hydrants," http://www.firehydrant.org/pictures/nyc.html, 2.

27. Much of the psi and gpm information came from the author's teachers

at the Cherry Hill Civilian Fire and Police Academy, May 5–26, 2005. See also "Tales of a Trainee," journal entry number 7, http://www.firefightersreal stories.com/journal7.html.

28. Willis Lamm, Water Supply Officer, Moraga-Orinda (California) Fire District, "Designing Water and Hydrant Systems" (2000), http://www.fire hydrant.org/info/design01.html#2; Rosen, *Limits of Power*, 298–299; *Washington Post*, February 9, 1904, p. 9; *New York Times*, February 9, 1904, A2; *Baltimore Sun*, February 10, 1904, A11.

29. Compare Von Drehle, *Triangle*, 119.

30. This and following details in subsequent paragraphs, where no other citation appears, from *Baltimore Sun*, February 8, 1904, A1–3, and February 9, 1904, A1–2; *Baltimore American*, February 8, 1904, A1, and February 9, 1904, A1–2; *Baltimore Herald*, February 8, 1904, A1, and February 9, 1904, A1–2.

31. *New York Times*, January 24, 2005, A1, B5; "Great Fire of Baltimore," Maryland Historical Society, Maryland Digital Cultural Heritage, http://www.mdhs.org/fire. With captions and photos from the collections of the Maryland Historical Society and photos from the Enoch Pratt Free Library, this Web site is a storehouse of information.

32. Emerson, *Vertical Burn*, 7–8. The book is a novel, but the author is a veteran Seattle fire department officer and the account rings as true as a department post-operational report.

33. Tom Downey, *The Last Men Out*, 179; Curtis Varone, "Not Your Father's Command Post," *Fire Chief* (August 2001): 73; Williams, *Baltimore Afire*, 3; Petersen, *Great Baltimore Fire*, 15. Structural fire: Salka, *First In, Last Out*, 43. Heat: Lynda Turner quoted in "Fire Fighters Use New Strategy in Chicago Highrise Fire," http://www.firetimes.com/subcontent.asp?FragID= 11587. Risk management: U.S. Fire Administration, National Fire Academy Advanced Safety Operations and Management Course, unit 2: "risk management process."

34. *New York Times*, February 9, 1904, A2. Radiant heat in building fires: Dunn, *Command and Control*, 88.

35. *Baltimore Sun*, February 9, 1904, A1.

36. Naoma Welk, *South Orange* (Charleston, S.C.: Acadia, 2002), 37; Petersen, *Great Baltimore Fire*, 193; Tebeau, *Eating Smoke*, 161.

37. Tebeau, *Eating Smoke*, 285–286, 287; Petersen, *Great Baltimore Fire*, 22–23, 25.

38. *Washington Post*, February 8, 1904, A2, 6.

39. Petersen, *Great Baltimore Fire*, 49–50.

40. Ibid., 44; *New York Times*, February 10 1904, A1.

41. Golway, *So Others Might Live*, 157–158.

42. Petersen, *Great Baltimore Fire*, 56.

43. Ibid., 25.

44. Quote and account in ibid., 58.

45. *Baltimore American,* February 9, 1904, A3.

46. Douglas Hickin, story reprinted in Dennis Smith, ed., *Firefighters: Their Lives in Their Own Words* (New York: Doubleday, 1988), 183; Downey, *The Last Men Out,* 116, 181; David Halberstam, *Firehouse* (New York: Hyperion, 2002), 31, 32, 40.

47. Petersen, *Great Baltimore Fire,* 18–19, 180–181; Salka, *First In, Last Out,* 70.

48. The Sanborn fire map of 1902 listed all the shops in the city. It is my bible here.

49. *Baltimore Sun,* February 8, 1904, A1.

50. *Baltimore Sun,* February 10, 1904, A5; *Baltimore American,* February 10, 1904, A3; Charleston report and *Sun* quotation in Ted Steinberg, *Acts of God: The Unnatural History of Natural Disaster in America* (New York: Oxford University Press, 2000), 10.

51. Crooks, *Politics and Progress,* 100; Petersen, *Great Baltimore Fire,* 30–32; *Baltimore American,* February 9, 1904, A2; *Baltimore Sun,* February 8, 1904, A2; February 9, 1904, A1.

52. Petersen, *Great Baltimore Fire,* 144–146.

53. *Baltimore News,* February 8, 1904, A1; *Baltimore American* February 9, 1904, A2.

54. Wermiel, *The Fireproof Building,* 8, 179; *Baltimore Sun,* February 9, 1904, A1.

55. Petersen, *Great Baltimore Fire,* 107–115; Gerald W. Johnson et al., *The Sunpapers of Baltimore* (New York: Knopf, 1937), 249.

56. Mencken, *Newspaper Days,* 276, 277, 278, 279, 280, 281.

57. *Baltimore News,* February 8, 1904, A1.

58. *Washington Post,* February 9, 1904, A1; *New York Times,* February 9, 1904, A1.

59. Dead: Petersen, *Great Baltimore Fire,* 196; injured: *Baltimore Sun,* February 8, 1904, p. 1.

60. Williams, *Baltimore Afire,* 6; *Baltimore American,* February 9, 1904, A3; Petersen, *Great Baltimore Fire,* 23–24.

61. *Official Book of Baltimore Fire* (Baltimore: Crown, 1910), passim; the argument for San Francisco's preeminence is made most recently in Fradkin, *Great Earthquake,* 282: "the first massive photographic documentation of a single event."

62. Petersen, *Great Baltimore Fire,* 26–27; Beaumont Newhall, *The History of Photography from 1839 to the Present* (New York: Museum of Modern Art, 1982), 251–252; George Miller and Dorothy Miller, *Picture Postcards in the United States, 1893–1918* (New York: Crown, 1976), 145; Frank Staff, *The Picture Postcard and Its Origins* (New York: Praeger, 1966), 53–55.

63. F. W. Fitzpatrick, "Lessons of the Baltimore Fire," *Fireproof* 4 (March 1904): 44; images of the gutted Union Trust and the modern Jefferson Building at http://www.mdhs.org/fire/collections/mdbf216/mdbf216.html.

64. http://www.mdhs.org/explore/museum.html (February 7–October 31, 2004); http://www.baltimore.org/visitors/v_events_gbf.html; http://www.memory.loc.gov/ammem/edhtml/edmvhist.htm. The Smithsonian Museum has restored the film image by image, and the Maryland Historical Society displayed thirteen minutes of it in its "Baltimore Ablaze: The Great Fire of 1904" exhibition in 2004.

65. Petersen, *Great Baltimore Fire*, 39, 79.

66. *Baltimore Sun,* February 10, 1904, A11; *New York Times,* February 9, 1904, A1; *Washington Post*, February 11, A2.

67. *Baltimore Sun,* February 10, 1904, p. 11.

68. Tebeau, *Eating Smoke,* 257; *Wall Street Journal,* February 9, 1904, pp. 3, 8; February 10, 1904, p. 1; *Washington Post,* February 9, 1904, A10; February 13, 1904, A3, 14.

69. *Baltimore Sun,* February 10, 1904, A1, 6, 11; February 13, A11; *Baltimore American*, February 10, A1.

70. *Baltimore American,* February 10, 1904, A1; *Baltimore Sun,* February 9, 1904, A7; Rosen, *Limits of Power,* 249; Williams, *Baltimore Afire,* 70.

71. James L. Roark et. al, *The American Promise: A History of the United States* (Boston: Bedford, 1998), 803–809; John W. Johnson, *American Legal Culture, 1908–1940* (Westport, Conn.: Greenwood, 1981), 129; John Spargo, *The Bitter Cry of Our Children* [1906], quoted in Richard Hofstadter, ed., *The Progressive Movement* (Englewood Cliffs, N.J.: Prentice Hall, 1963), 39–40.

72. Petersen, *Great Baltimore Fire*, 133, 134.

73. Ibid., 65, 177.

74. "Progressive Party Platform of 1912," reprinted in Hofstadter, ed., *The Progressive Movement*, 130–131; H. L. Mencken, *A Mencken Chrestomaphy* [1920], reprinted in Arthur Mann, ed., *The Progressive Era* (New York: Holt, 1963), 77, 79; Teachout, *The Skeptic*, 51.

75. John Milton Cooper, Jr., *The Warrior and the Priest: Woodrow Wilson and Theodore Roosevelt* (Cambridge: Harvard University Press, 1983), 218; Arthur S. Link, *Woodrow Wilson and the Progressive Era* (New York: Harper, 1954), 56, 66; Woodrow Wilson, "The Science of Administration," *Political Science Quarterly* 2 (2) (June 1887): 202. For the article's place in the history of political science, *see* Jameson W. Doig, "'If I See a Murderous Fellow Sharpening a Knife Cleverly . . .': The Wilsonian Dichotomy and the Public Authority Tradition," *Public Administration Review* 43 (4) (July–August 1983): 292–304. I am grateful to Williamjames Hoffer for this reference.

76. For the methods the committee adopted, see Rosen, *Limits of Power,* 267. For the larger concept of the characteristically American form of adminis-

tration—collective, ad hoc, political, and nonexpert, see Williamjames Hoffer, "Leviathan Bound," Ph.D. diss. Johns Hopkins University, 2002, passim.

77. Crooks, *Politics and Progress*, 30, 142, 202, 204.

78. Rosen, *Limits of Power*, 254–257.

79. Richard Hofstadter, *The Age of Reform* (New York: Knopf, 1956); Chapelle, *Baltimore*, 174; Isenberg, *Downtown America*, 15–39; Crook, *Politics and Progress*, 137–138.

80. On the transformation from self-governing city corporations to agencies of the state, see Hendrik Hartog, *Public Property and Private Power: The Corporation of the City of New York in American Law, 1730–1870* (Chapel Hill: University of North Carolina Press, 1983).

81. See Ralph E. Boyer, *Survey of the Law of Property*, 3rd ed. (St. Paul, Minn.: West, 1981), 626–628.

82. *Village of Euclid (Ohio) v. Ambler Realty*, 272 U.S. 365 (1926); Daniel R. Mandelker, *Land Use Law*, 5th ed. (Newark: Matthew Bender, 2002), 1.01, 5.71; Alexander Garvin, *The American City: What Works, What Doesn't* (New York: McGraw Hill, 1996), 356–358.

83. Rosen, *Limits of Power*, 259–264.

84. Ibid., 259, 266–268, 273, 275, 276–283.

85. Ibid., 283, 285, 286–287; *Baltimore Sun*, February 13, 2004, A16; February 11, 1904, A1; March 27, A16; April 22, A16. Images of the *Sun* and the *American* buildings on Baltimore and South during the 1880 Baltimore sesquicentennial in Alexander D. Mitchell IV, *Baltimore Then and Now* (San Diego: Thunder Bay, 2001), 72. Both intended to rebuild where they had stood, but in the end did not.

86. Rosen, *Limits of Power*, 288, 290, 294, 295.

87. The author is indebted to Professor N.E.H. Hull for the suggestion that habits entrenched in bachelorhood might not prepare a husband for a society marriage.

88. Petersen, *Great Baltimore Fire*, 136–144, 178.

89. Rosen, *Limits of Power*, 314; *Baltimore American* September 10, 1906, A1; Jim Duffy, "After the Fire," *Baltimore* magazine, February 2004: 87–97.

90. Chapelle, *Baltimore*, 202; On "renewing cities": Boorstin, *The Americans*, 283–285.

91. Nicholas Daben Bloom, *Merchant of Illusion, James Rouse, America's Salesman of the Businessman's Utopia* (Columbus: Ohio State University Press, 2004), 29; Boorstin, *Democratic Experience*, 114–115; Isenberg, *Downtown America*, 175; Garvin, *American City*, 129; Pauline Maier et al., *Inventing America*, vol. 2: 903.

92. Bloom, *Merchant of Illusion*, 39–41.

93. Ibid., 41–43; Chapelle, *Baltimore*, 210; Garvin, *American City*,

129–132; David Harvey, "A View from Federal Hill," in Fee, Shopes, and Zeidman, eds., *The Baltimore Book*, 233.

94. Andres Duany, Elizabeth Plater-Zyberk, and Jeff Speck, *Suburban Nation: The Rise of Sprawl and the Decline of the American Dream* (New York: Farrar, Straus and Giroux, 2000), 153; Joshua Olsen, *Better Places, Better Lives: A Biography of James Rouse* (Washington, D.C.: Urban Land Institute, 2003), 279 (quotation), 280–291; Garvin, *American City*, 114–115; Richard Zoglin, "The Urban Renewer: James W. Rouse: 1914–1996," *Time Magazine*, April 22, 1996, 97; Robert Campbell, "The Man Behind Faneuil Hall," *Boston Globe*, May 5, 1996, A33; Kathy Lally, "Urban Visionary Succumbs at 81," *Baltimore Sun*, April 10, 1996, A1; Paul Goldberger, "James W. Rouse Dies," *New York Times*, April 10, 1996, A1 (includes quotations from Rouse).

95. Thompson quoted in David W. Dunlap, "Benjamin C. Thompson, 84, Architect of Festive Urban Marketplaces, Is Dead," *New York Times*, August 20, 2002, C17, and Edward Gunts, "He Helped Bring Humanity Back to the City," *Baltimore Sun*, August 25, 2002, 5E.

96. David M. Kennedy, *Freedom from Fear: The American People in Depression and War, 1929–1945* (New York: Oxford University Press, 1999), 18; James T. Patterson, *Grand Expectations: The United States, 1945–1974* (New York: Oxford University Press, 1997), 381, 383; McDougall, *Black Baltimore*, 37–57, 66; W. Edward Orser, "Flight to the Suburbs," in Fee, Shopes, and Zeidman, eds., *The Baltimore Book*, 204.

97. Gordana Rabrenovic, *Community Builders: A Tale of Neighborhood Mobilization in Two Cities* (Philadelphia: Temple University Press, 1996), 4–6; Bloom, *Merchant of Illusion*, 2, 175.

98. Michael Stroh, "Unraveling a 9-11 Mystery," *Baltimore Sun*, May 9, 2002, A2; James Glanz, "Wounded Buildings Offer Survival Lessons," *New York Times*, December 4, 2001, F1.

99. Duffy, "After the Fire," 95; "Fire Department Commemorates the 100th Anniversary of the 'Great Baltimore Fire,'" http://www.ci.baltimore.md.us/goverment/fire/pro40212html.

DETROIT, 1967

1. Thomas J. Sugrue, *The Origins of the Urban Crisis: Race and Inequality in Post-War Detroit* (Princeton: Princeton University Press, 1996), 242–244; quotations in and text from Cameron McWhirter, "Life of One Street Mirrors City's Fall," *Detroit News*, June 17, 2001, A1.

2. Raphael S. Ezekiel, *Voices from the Corner: Poverty and Racism in the Inner City* (Philadelphia: Temple University Press, 1984), 7, 5.

3. Cameron McWhirter, "1967 Riot Sent Street into Wrenching Spiral," *Detroit News,* June 18, 2001, A1; Kalema Hasan, in Robert H. Mast, ed., *Detroit Lives* (Philadelphia: Temple University Press, 1994), 75; Gregory Byrd, interview with author, Detroit, June 25, 2005.

4. Reynolds Farley, Sheldon Danziger, and Harry J. Holzer, *Detroit Divided* (New York: Russell Sage, 2000), 24–27; Sugrue, *Urban Crisis*, 18.

5. Phyllis Vine, *One Man's Castle: Clarence Darrow in Defense of the American Dream* (New York: HarperCollins, 2004), 58–69; Robert Conot, *American Odyssey: A Unique History of America Told Through the Life of a Great City* (New York: Morrow, 1974), 231, 232, 235; Kevin Boyle, *Arc of Justice: A Saga of Race, Civil Rights, and Murder in the Jazz Age* (New York: Holt, 2004), 140; Sugrue, *Urban Crisis*, 91–93.

6. Conot, *American Odyssey*, 301–306; Jeffrey Eugenides, *Middlesex* (New York: Farrar, Straus and Giroux, 2002), 141; J. Woodford Howard, *Mr. Justice Murphy: A Political Biography* (Princeton: Princeton University Press, 1968), 59; Farley, Danziger, and Holzer, *Detroit Divided*, 31–33.

7. Sugrue, *Urban Crisis*, 19; Loren D. Estleman, *Jitterbug* (New York: Forge, 1998), 142. Estleman is an adventure story writer but a Detroit native, and his depictions of Detroit are accurate.

8. Dan Georgakas, "Forward," in Mast, ed., *Detroit Lives*, ix.

9. Sugrue, *Urban Crisis*, 63–86.

10. Alfred McClung Lee and Norman D. Humphrey, *Race Riot (Detroit, 1943)* (New York: Octagon, 1968), 20 and after; Farley, Danzinger, and Holzer, *Detroit Divided*, 35, 37; Conot, *American Odyssey*, 362, 400–405.

11. Conot, *American Odyssey*, 404, 405, 414, 415, 448, 449.

12. Frank B. Woodford and Arthur M. Woodford, *All Our Yesterdays: A Brief History of Detroit* (Detroit: Wayne State University Press, 1969), 343–350; Sugrue, *Urban Crisis*, 22–27, 82, 171–172, 174–175.

13. Conot, *American Odyssey*, 449, 459, 483, 488, 492, 499; Hubert G. Locke, *The Detroit Riot of 1967* (Detroit: Wayne State University Press, 1969), 57–58.

14. Roger Robinson, in Mast, ed., *Detroit Lives*, 194, 195.

15. Paul Justman, "Standing in the Shadows of Motown" (2002), documentary.

16. Conot, *American Odyssey*, 505.

17. Mike Hamlin, account in Mast, ed., *Detroit Lives*, 86; Fred Williams quoted in Chafets, *Devil's Night*, 100.

18. *Detroit Free Press*, July 22, 1A (weather), July 23, 1A (weather).

19. Detroit Fire Commission reports, 1967, Jerome Cavanagh Papers, Box 335, Walter P. Reuther Library, Wayne State University, Detroit; Robert A. Mendelsohn, "The Police Interpretation of the Detroit Riot of 1967" [1968], Detroit Public Library typescript, 11–15.

20. Detroit Fire Commission Meeting Notes, June 13, 1967, Cavanagh Papers, Box 335, Walter P. Reuther Library.

21. Detroit Fire Fighters Association to Jerome Cavanagh, May 31, 1967; Cavanagh to DFFA, June 1, 1967; International Association of Firefighters to Cavanagh, June 19, 1967; DFFA "Dear Brothers" letter, July 3, 1967, Cavanagh Papers, Box 335.

22. "As We See It: Newark Is a Case Study in the Cause of Riots," *Detroit Free Press*, July 18, 1967, 6A; Sidney Fine, *Violence in the Model City: The Cavanagh Administration, Race Relations, and the Detroit Riot of 1967* (Ann Arbor: University of Michigan Press, 1989), quoting Cavanagh, 143.

23. Louis Lomax, *Detroit News*, August 6, 1967, A16; Fine, *Violence in the Model City*, 361, quotes other journalists to the effect that Lomax never left the press room to interview anyone. Carmichael quoted in David A. Horowitz, Peter N. Carroll, and David D. Lee, *On the Edge: A New History of 20ᵗʰ-Century America* (St. Paul, Minn.: West, 1990), 474.

24. Brown quoted in Conot, *American Odyssey*, 529; Shakoor recollection in Mast, ed., *Detroit Lives*, 200.

25. Barbara Stanton, "Twelfth Street: A City Within a City," *Detroit Free Press*, July 27, 1967, 1B.

26. Ibid.; "Consumer Exploitation Long Known as Problem," *Michigan Chronicle*, August 5, 1967, A6; Lizabeth Cohen, *A Consumer's Republic: The Politics of Consumption in Postwar America* (New York: Knopf, 2003), 356.

27. Sugrue, *Urban Crisis*, 257, 259; Alex Marshall, *How Cities Work: Suburbs, Sprawl, and the Roads Not Taken* (Austin: University of Texas, 2003), 95; Conot, *American Odyssey*, 530–532; Locke, *Detroit Riot*, 25.

28. Nancy Milio, *9226 Kerchival: The Storefront That Did Not Burn*, rev. ed. (Ann Arbor: University of Michigan Press, 2001), 32, 37, 38, 51, 89.

29. John Hersey, *The Algiers Motel Incident* (New York: Knopf, 1968), 177–191; Van Gordon Sauter and Burleigh Hines, *Nightmare in Detroit: A Rebellion and Its Victims* (Chicago: Regnery, 1968), 161–162.

30. Conot, *American Odyssey*, 523.

31. Ray Girardin, "Statistical Report on the Civil Disorder Occurring in the City of Detroit, July 1967," bound typescript, Detroit Public Library, iv (John F. Nichola memo); "Blind Pig Raid Was Spark," *Detroit Free Press*, July 24, 1967, 1A; Conot, *American Odyssey*, 526–527; Fine, *Violence in the Model City*, 155–217; Locke, *Detroit Riot*, 26–44; Joe R. Feagin and Harlan Hahn, *Ghetto Revolts: The Politics of Violence in American Cities* (New York: Macmillan, 1973), 161.

32. Locke, *Detroit Riot*, 29–30.

33. Fine, *Violence in the Model City*, 179–180.

34. Locke, *Detroit Riot*, 29, 65–66, 73–74.

35. Sauter and Hines, *Nightmare*, vi; Fine, *Violence in the Model City*, 166.

36. Gerald Horne, *Fire This Time: The Watts Uprising and the 1960s* (New York: DaCapo, 1997), 49, map on 48.

37. Quinlan quoted in Fine, *Violence in the Model City*, 535; Harry S. Carter, "Firefighting: Train Hard; Work Hard; Fight Smart," http://www.fire house.com/carter/2002/2/0224.html; on Quinlan, see "Charles J. Quinlan," *The Firefighter* (Detroit) 33 (June 1967): 4.

38. Sauter and Hines, *Nightmare*, 13; Mark Beltaire, "A Night on the Hoses," *Detroit Free Press*, July 25, 1967, 2B; "Weary Fire Fighters Finally Given First Break," *Detroit Free Press*, July 27, 1967, 5B; Gene Goltz, "Vigi-lantee Groups Formed," *Detroit Free Press*, July 25, 1967, 2A; Robbie L. Mc-Coy, "Citizens Patrol a Success in Highland Park," *Michigan Chronicle*, August 5, 1967, A2.

39. Rash: informant quoted in Jimmy Breslin, "Breslin on Riot: Death, Laughter, but No Sanity," *Detroit News*, July 25, 1967, A12; Benjamin D. Singer, "Mass Media and the Communication Processes in the Detroit Riot of 1967," *Public Opinion Quarterly* 34 (1970): 236–245; Cyrus R. Vance, "Final Report, September 12, 1967," Cavanagh Papers, Box 393, Walter P. Reuther Library, 48, 50.

40. "Headquarters Command Post Activity Log, July 23–24, 1967," Gi-rardin Papers, Box 4, Burton Historical Collection, Detroit Public Library.

41. Police "disorder log" July 23, Girardin Papers, Box 4, pp. 1–21, Burton Historical Collection, Detroit Public Library; "Sequence of Events," July 24th copy, Cavanagh Papers, Box 393, Walter P. Reuther Library.

42. Vance, "Final Report," appendix on page 77.

43. Girardin, "Statistical Report on the Civil Disorder," 44; Fine, *Violence in the Model City*, 186.

44. Conot, *American Odyssey*, 537, 538.

45. Fine, *Violence in the Model City*, 200; Smith, *Report from Engine Com-pany 82*, 11; Downey, *Last Men Out*, 70–71, 72; *F.D.N.Y.*, 94; interview with Wally Maloni, New York Fire Museum, June 22, 2005.

46. Charles J. Quinlan, "Civil Disturbance, July 1967, a Partial Report to [U.S.] Senate Subcommittee on Civil Disorder," February 1968, Girardin Pa-pers, Box 5, Burton Historical Collection; Stanton, "Twelfth Street."

47. "Sequence of Events" July 23–24, Cavanagh Papers, Box 393, Walter P. Reuther Library, 1–2.

48. Romney quoted in ibid., p. 4; Fine, *Violence in the Model City*, 186; Romney quotation in Conot, *American Odyssey*, 535.

49. Police "disorder log" July 23–24, pp. 32–80, Girardin Papers, Box 4, Burton Historical Collection, Detroit Public Library.

50. Vance, "Final Report," 9, 15, 17.

51. Quinlan, "Partial Report."

52. James L. Kerwin, "I Saw Fireman Slain," *Detroit News,* July 25, 1967,

A1; Mary Ann Weston, "A Hero Goes to His Grave as Wife and City Mourn," *Detroit Free Press,* July 30, 1967, 1A; Sauter and Hines, *Nightmare,* 52–58 (Ashby); 113–118 (Smith).

53. Girardin, "Statistical Report on the Civil Disorder," 4; Locke, *Detroit Riots,* 33–34; Herbert Weisberg et al., "Arson Investigation and Prosecution: A Study of Four Major American Cities," National Institute of Justice, U.S. Department of Justice, 1984, typescript, University of Pennsylvania Van Pelt Library, xiv, 66–68.

54. James H. Lincoln, *The Anatomy of a Riot: A Detroit Judge's Report* (New York: McGraw Hill, 1968), 3; Josaitis quoted in Mast, ed., *Detroit Lives,* 41; reporters' descriptions in Fine, *Violence in the Model City,* 187.

55. Plofchan photo, *Detroit Free Press,* July 26, 1967, 9A; Rosenberg photo, *Detroit Free Press,* July 24, 1967, 8B. The entire collection of the *Detroit Free Press* negatives is available in the visual reproduction department of the Walter P. Reuther Library. "Go like hell": Eric Frey, Athens Fire Department, communication to the author, June 15, 2005; "come when called": Wally Maloni, FDNY, interview June 22, 2005.

56. Fine, *Violence in the Model City,* 195, 196; Conot, *American Odyssey,* 536–537.

57. Fine, *Violence in the Model City,* 271–290; Hersey, *Algiers Motel,* 189–191.

58. Sauter and Hines, *Nightmare,* 26, 27, 31–32.

59. Detroit Water and Sewage Department, "Water System Brief History," http://www.dwsd.org/history/water_brief.htm.

60. Robert P. Roselle, "Riot Statistics," n.d., Cavanagh Papers, Box 398, Walter P. Reuther Library; City of Detroit, Board of Assessors, Final List, September 1, 1967, Cavanagh Papers, Box 393; Quinlan, "Partial Report."

61. Interview with Wally Malone, New York Fire Museum, June 22, 2005.

62. Robert M. Fogelson, *Violence as Protest: A Study of Riots and Ghettos* (Garden City, N.Y.: Doubleday, 1971), 22, 84. Other studies are summarized in Fine, *Violence in the Model City,* 326–343.

63. Fogelson, *Violence as Protest,* 86; Feagin and Hahn, *Ghetto Revolts,* 176–177; Paul Gilje, quoted in Jonathan J. Bean, "'Burn Baby Burn': Small Business in the Urban Riots of the 1960s," *Independent Review* 5 (Fall 2000): 166; Cohen, *Consumers' Republic,* 372.

64. Fogelson, *Violence as Protest,* 90–94.

65. Roger Simpson and John Riter, "Totaling of Losses Begins," *Detroit Free Press,* July 26, 1967, 6B; Fine, *Violence in the Model City,* 291.

66. "Neighborhoods Burn as Residents Watch," *Detroit Free Press,* July 25, 1967, 3A; Susan Holmes, "Detroit's New Refugees—the Flames Left Little," *Detroit Free Press,* July 25, 1967, 1B. On the carnival and the "rough music" or quasi-political violence that sometimes ensued in the revolutionary era, see

Thomas Humphrey, "Crowd and Court: Rough Music and Popular Justice in Colonial New York," in Dennis, Newman, and Pencak, eds., *Riot and Revelry in Early America*, 107–124, and Alfred F. Young, "English Plebeian Culture and Eighteenth-Century American Radicalism," in Margaret Jacob and James Jacob, eds., *Origins of Anglo-American Radicalism* (London: Allen and Unwin, 1984), 184–212.

67. "Soul Brother," guest editorial, *Detroit Free Press*, July 27, 1967, 6A; McCoy, "Citizen's Patrol."

68. Fine, *Violence in the Model City*, 178; Brent Staples, "A Short History of Class Antagonism in the Black Community," *New York Times*, May 29, 2005, WK9.

69. Arthur F. Curtis, *A Treatise on the Law of Arson* (Buffalo, N.Y.: Dennis, 1936), 6; Weisberg et al., "Arson Investigation," 33; Marc Miller, "Community Based Arson Prevention," Shelterforce Online, March–April 1994, http://www.nhi.org/online/issues/74/arson.html.

70. Evancho, quoted in "Nation's Top Fire Official Labels Arson the Weapon of the 90s," PR Newswire, April 30, 1995; Stampp, *Peculiar Institution*, 127–128; Meranze, *Laboratories of Virtue*, 31; Thomas D. Morris, *Southern Slavery and the Law, 1619–1860* (Chapel Hill: University of North Carolina, 1996), 330–333; Michael Stephen Hindus, *Prison and Plantation: Crimes, Justice, and Authority in Massachusetts and South Carolina, 1767–1878* (Chapel Hill: University of North Carolina, 1980), 144. It should be noted that PR Newswire, cited here and below, is a press-release agency, not a genuine journalism source.

71. Sugrue, *Urban Crisis*, 233; Fine, *Violence in the Model City*, 346; Hazel Erskine, "The Polls: Demonstrations and Riots," *Public Opinion Quarterly* 31 (1967): 662, 671.

72. Breslin, "Breslin on Riot"; Feagin and Hahn, *Ghetto Revolts*, 197; "If It Happened in Detroit, It Can Happen Anywhere," *Michigan Chronicle*, August 5, 1968, A7.

73. Representative figures in Weisberg et al., "Arson Investigation," 27, 55, 56, 59, 295.

74. Horne, *Fire This Time*, 76, 77; *F.D.N.Y.*, 67; Taylor quote in Fine, *Violence in the Model City*, 186; Locke, *Detroit Riot*, 39–40, 41, 43.

75. Milio, *Kercheval*, 136–137, 143; "Young People," *Michigan Chronicle*, August 5, 1967, A7; Conot, *American Odyssey*, 534–535; Sauter and Hines, *Nightmare*, 21–22.

76. Conot, *American Odyssey*, 540, 542; Fine, *Violence in the Model City*, 222–223, 297 (Hoover quote at 213); Vance, "Final Report," 52.

77. Cavanagh to Quinlan, August 1, 1967, Cavanagh Papers, Box 335, Walter P. Reuther Library; Detroit Fire Department, "Plans and Preparations for Future Civil Disorder," February 6, 1968, Cavanagh Papers, Box 403, 2, 3, 4.

78. Quotes in Patterson, *Grand Expectations*, 663, 662; editorial, *Michigan Chronicle*, July 29, 1967, A6; Tom Joyce, "Anatomy of Detroit Rioting," *Detroit News*, July 30, 1967, A1; Lincoln, *Anatomy*, 11–13; Conot, *American Odyssey*, 595; Fine, *Violence in the Model City*, 269; Vance, "Final Report," 43, 44.

79. Rain: *Detroit Free Press*, July 29, 1967, 4B; smoke: Eleanor Josaitis, quoted in Mast, ed., *Detroit Lives*, 41.

80. Data from Feagin and Hahn, *Ghetto Revolts*, 106–108, 289.

81. Wilbur C. Rich, *Coleman Young and Detroit Politics* (Detroit: Wayne State University Press, 1989), 104–105; the promotional information in http://www.detroitrenaissance.com; Dudley Randall, "Detroit Renaissance," quoted in Chafets, *Devil's Night*, 125; David Lee Poremba, *Detroit: A Motor City History* (Charleston, S.C.: Arcadia, 2001), 147–149.

82. Barbara Stanton, *Detroit Free Press*, July 19, 1987, 6A; Farley, Danziger, and Holzer, *Detroit Divided*, 46 (homicide rates and numbers), 49 (racial population figures).

83. Fine, *Violence in the Model City*, 320–322.

84. Charles Butler quoted in Mast, ed., *Detroit Lives*, 192; Maryann Mahaffey quoted in ibid., 172; Maggie DeSantis quoted in ibid., 45; Marilyn Mullane quoted in ibid., 60.

85. Fine, *Violence in the Model City*, 369–370.

86. Ibid., 454–456.

87. Rich, *Young*, 47–48, 62–63, 79–83, 101–106; Isabel Wilderson, "After Four Terms, Us Versus Them Still Plays in Detroit," *New York Times*, September 17, 1989, WR4.

88. Todd C. Shaw and Lester K. Spence, "Race, Politics, and Community Development in U.S. Cities: Race and Representation in Detroit's Community Development Coalitions," *Annals of the American Academy of Political and Social Science* 594 (2004): 125–142; Cameron McWhirter, "Broken Detroit: Progress Blocked," *Detroit News*, October 29, 2001, A1; McWhirter, "Vacant Buildings Haunt City Street," and McWhirter, "Homes Give Way to Urban Prairie," *Detroit News*, June 20, 2001, A1; Errol Henderson interview in Mast, ed., *Detroit Lives*, 97; Chafets, *Devil's Night*, 177.

89. Thomas J. Sugrue, "Expert Report of Thomas J. Sugrue," *Michigan Journal of Race and Law* 5 (1999): 261–309, quotation at 291; Farley, Danziger, and Holzer, *Detroit Divided*, 161–162.

90. Nancy A. Denton, "The Persistence of Segregation: Links Between Residential Segregation and School Segregation," *Minnesota Law Review* 80 (1996): 795–824; Chafets, *Devil's Night*, 68; Farley, Danziger, and Holzer, *Detroit Divided*, 50 (median income), 67 (loss of jobs); Rich, *Young*, 133, 134.

91. Loren D. Estleman, *The Midnight Man* (New York: Pocket, 1982), 50; James Q. Wilson and George L. Kelling, "Broken Windows: The Police and Neighborhood Safety," *Atlantic Monthly* (March 1982), 29; James Risen, "De-

troit Exodus: An Urban Desert in the Motor City," *Los Angeles Times,* October 27, 1988, A1 (Cantor quotation at p. 1); Andy Bull, "Driven to Crime," *Independent,* October 26, 1991, 43.

92. Eric Pope, "Beyond '67: Fallen City Looks to Rise," *Crain's Detroit Business,* June 27, 2001, 17; Judith Cummings, "Once-Proud Store Has Its Last Christmas," *New York Times,* December 31, 1982, A7.

93. James Risen, "Day Bittersweet for Detroit's Aging Parishes," *Los Angeles Times,* December 25, 1988, A1.

94. James and Grace Lee Boggs, in Mast, ed., *Detroit Lives,* 16, 17, 18, 19.

95. Mary Wisniewski, "A Motown Turnaround," *Bond Buyer,* May 3, 2000, 1; Cameron McWhirter, "How to Fix Detroit," *Detroit News,* December 9, 2001, A1; Gordon Trowbridge, "Whites Make Small Gains in Detroit," *Detroit News,* January 28, 2002, B4; Stephanie Simon, "Detroit's Core Is Working on a Comeback," *Los Angeles Times,* July 14, 2003, p. 12; Natalie Y. Moore, "As Tax Cuts End, Detroit Assesses Enterprise Zones," *Detroit News,* December 5, 2004, B1; Brookings Institute, "Living Cities: Detroit in Focus, a Profile from Census 2000, November, 2003," http://www.brookings.edu/es/urban/livingcities/detroit.html; Tom Walsh, "Metro Detroit's Prosperity Grew in the 90s," *Detroit Free Press,* July 6, 2002, 1A; Gordon Trowbridge, "Racial Divide Widest in U.S.: Fewer Detroit Neighborhoods Are Integrated Than 20 Years Ago," *Detroit News,* January 14, 2002, B2; Delores Patterson, "Schools Divided by Race Lines," *Detroit News,* January 20, 2003, B1.

96. Doug Smith, quoted in Mast, ed., *Detroit Lives,* 64; AP, "Warehouse Blaze Kills Three Detroit Firefighters," *Chicago Tribune,* March 13, 1987, C16; Commissioner Watkins quoted in "City of Detroit Declares May 4-10, 1997 Arson Awareness Week," PR Newswire, May 2, 1997; Amy Lane and Robert Ankeny, "Insurance Study Confirms Rates High Because Losses High," *Crain's Detroit Business,* November 25, 1996, p. 3.

97. Patricia Edmonds, "All-Out Offensive," *Detroit Free Press,* October 31, 1985, 1A, 11A; Peter Gavrilovich, "For Fire Fighters, It Was Not Just Another Night's Work," *Detroit Free Press,* 11A; Erik Kinkopf and Jack Kresnak, "Tempers Flare with the Flames for Those Left Homeless," *Detroit Free Press,* 1A.

98. "In Our Opinion: Devil's Night–Suppressing News of It Won't Make It Go Away," *Detroit Free Press,* October 29, 1986, 19A; "City Endures Devil's Night," *Detroit Free Press,* 14A.

99. Brian Flanigan and Patricia Edmonds, "City: Devil's Night Fires Down," *Detroit Free Press,* October 31, 1987, 1A; Chafets, *Devil's Night,* 4, 5; UPI, "Teen Curfew Helps Cut Down on Devil's Night Fires," November 1, 1987; James Risen, "Fire Rampant in Detroit for Devil's Night," *Los Angeles Times,* November 1, 1989, A4; "Mayor Young Says Detroit Will Mobilize Citizens and Organizations to Help Reduce Fires During Halloween Period," PR

Newswire, October 23, 1990; "Detroit Mayor Young Announces Kickoff of Expanded Campaign to Reduce Devil's Night Arson," PR Newswire, September 30, 1991; "Detroit Mayor Comments on 1991 Campaign to Reduce Devil's Night Arson," PR Newswire, October 28, 1991; "Leadership Detroit Brainstorm Will Deter Urban Firestorm," PR Newswire, October 27, 1995; "Detroit Mayor Expresses Thanks to Thousands of Halloween Volunteers," PR Newswire, November 1, 1995.

100. Farley, Danziger, and Holzer, *Detroit Divided*, 83; Eugene Robinson, "Racial Gap in Detroit Narrows Slowly," *Washington Post*, August 31, 1981, A1 (Young quotation).

101. UPI, "Appeals Court Upholds Detroit Hiring Plan for Firefighters," *New York Times*, December 14, 1984, A32 (Jefferson quotation); "Black May Be Named Top Detroit Fire Chief," *Chicago Tribune*, September 5, 1988, M3; "Fire Department Division Chief," *Ebony*, December 1996, p. 10.

102. "City of Detroit Fire Department Dedicates Aerial Ladder Truck," PR Newswire, April 21, 1989; "New Fire Engine Delivered to Detroit Fire Station," PR Newswire, August 2, 1990; "Detroit Fire Department Unveils Fire-Safety Program," PR Newswire, February 15, 1993; "Detroit Fire Department to Use Advanced Fire Fighting Technology at Grand Prix," PR Newswire, June 9, 1995; "Detroit Fire Department Adds New Rigs to Fleet," PR Newswire, August 8, 1995; "Detroit Fire Department Hosts Integrated Emergency Management Course," PR Newswire, June 17, 1996; "Detroit Fire Department Receives 8,000 Smoke Detectors," PR Newswire, October 7, 1996; "Detroit Fire Fighter Ranks Increase," PR Newswire, February 11, 1997.

103. Dunn, *Command and Control*, 32.

104. Charles Hurt and Melvin Claxton, "Faulty Truck's Many Failings Ignored," *Detroit News*, November 5, 2000, A6.

105. Ibid.; Hurt and Claxton, "Faulty Trucks, Mismanagement Lead to Death in Detroit Fires," *Detroit News*, A1.

106. Claxton and Hurt, "Lack of Staff Closes Stations," *Detroit News*, November 6, 2000, A1; Claxton and Hurt, "Bad Decisions, Bad Policies Weaken Fire Protection," *Detroit News*, November 7, 2000, A1.

107. Claxton and Hurt, "Detroit News Report Prompts Overhaul," *Detroit News*, November 6, 2000, A1; Hurt and Claxton, "Questionable Decisions Add to Risks," *Detroit News*, November 7, 2000, A7.

108. Raymond Hanka and Lou Angeli letters in "How Should Detroit Solve Fire Problems?" *Detroit News*, November 27, 2000, A10.

109. Darren A. Nichols, "Fire Boss Won't Take Blame," *Detroit News*, November 28, 2000, D1; Hurt and Claxton, "Firefighters Hit Snags at Fatal Blaze," *Detroit News*, December 3, 2000, A1; Charles Hurt, "Old Hoses Hinder Safety," *Detroit News*, February 9, 2001, A1.

THE EAST BAY: OAKLAND HILLS, 1991

1. Richard C. Paddock (*Los Angeles Times*), "More Than Houses Were Lost," *Oakland Tribune*, October 25, 1991, A12.

2. "Northern California Coast," U.S. Forest Service, Ecological Subregions of the United States, Chapter 32; http://www.fs.fed.us/land/pubs/ecoregions/ch32.html; Wyatt, *Five Fires*, 39–49, 60, 78–106; Theodora Kroeber, *Ishi in Two Worlds: A Biography of the Last Wild Indian in North America* (Berkeley: University of California Press, 1976).

3. Data from http://www.oaklandnet.com/celebrate/historytimeline.htm.

4. Philip S. Foner, "Introduction," in Foner, ed., *The Black Panthers Speak* [1970] (New York: DaCapo, 1995), xxv; Todd Gitlin, *The Sixties: Years of Hope, Days of Rage* (New York: Bantam, 1987), 342; Susan Robinson, "Black Panther Party," http://www.gibbsmagazine.com/Black%20Panther%Pty.htm.

5. The advertisement in Erika Mailman, *Oakland Hills* (Charleston, S.C.: Arcadia, 2004), 2. The History Room of the Oakland Public Library, Oakland history folders, are filled with snapshots of the pre–World War II dwellings.

6. Mailman, *Oakland Hills*, 18; interview with Ashley Dodge, one of the UC–Berkeley undergrads who regularly ran the mountain roads in the early 1970s, April 2, 2005; impressions of the topography are my own.

7. Oakland-Berkeley Recommendations of Task Force, February 22, 1992, p. 8; Oakland Public Library, History Room, Oakland Fire 1991 file. The streets are still too narrow and the residents and visitors still double-park their vehicles.

8. Steinberg, *Acts of God*, 43, 201.

9. Every conversation I struck up with a librarian, archivist, or local historian quickly turned to the disaster-prone nature of the land. Fradkin, *Great Earthquake*, 69–80, attributes the lack of water to the use of explosives. Apparently, they destroyed a number of underground water mains and pipes. U.S. Geological Survey, "The Great 1906 San Francisco Earthquake," quake.wr.usgs.gov/info/1906; Steinberg, *Acts of God*, 44; "Report on the Operations of the San Francisco Fire Department Following the Earthquake and Fire of October 17, 1989," Museum of the City of San Francisco, http://www.sfmuseum.net/quake/report.html; "City of Oakland Loma Prieta Earthquake, After Action Report," Museum of the City of San Francisco, http://www.sfmuseum.not/oakquake/1.a.html. Caldecott Tunnel Fire: Geoffrey Hunter, *Oakland Fire Department* (Charleston, S.C.: Arcadia, 2005), 104.

10. 1991 Oakland Berkeley Firestorm Timeline, "Fire in the Chaparral," http://www.csulb.edu/~djeffrey/hazards/physcial_dynamics.html; Davis, *Ecology of Fear*, 142–143; Childress, "Fire Suppression," *FFH*, 586. "Urban-wildland": Insurance Services Office, *The Urban/Wildland Fire Hazard* (Jersey City, N.J.: ISO, 1997), 10.

11. J. Gordon Routley, *The East Bay Hills Fire, Oakland-Berkeley Califor-*

nia (October 19–22), United States Fire Administration Technical Report Series (Washington, D.C.: FEMA, 1992), 9 [hereafter cited as USFA, "East Bay Hills Fire"].

12. http://www.oaklandnet.com/government/cmo/HistoryofFiresinOakland Hills.html.

13. Linda Fletcher, personal recollection, Oakland Public Library, History Room, Oakland Hills fire, 1991; Deirdre English, recollection in Patricia Adler, ed., *Fire in the Hills, a Collective Remembrance* (Berkeley: privately printed, 1992), 6; Varney quoted in Lance Williams, "She Warned Firefighters of Danger," *San Francisco Examiner,* October 23, 1991, A12.

14. Eric Brazil, "Fire Threatened Oakland Homes," *San Francisco Chronicle,* October 20, 1991, B2; David Dietz, "Oakland Took Few Precautions," *San Francisco Chronicle,* October 23, 1991, A15; Matthews later admitted that he knew about the red flag: "Fire Experts Debate Response to Huge Blaze," *San Francisco Chronicle,* October 30, 1991, A15.

15. Lynn Ludlow and Jane Garrison, "Did Debris Fire Start Inferno?" *San Francisco Examiner,* October 24, 1991, A1.

16. USFA, "East Bay Hills Fire," 22, 23 (quotation).

17. Geoffrey Hunter, *Oakland Fire Department* (Charleston, S.C.: Arcadia, 2005), 92–93.

18. Unger, *Working Fire,* 211.

19. USFA, "East Bay Hills Fire," 9, 13, 19.

20. Hunter, *Oakland Fire Department,* 112; "Engine 13," http://www.oakland13engine.com/aboutus.html.

21. USFA, "East Bay Hills Fire," 22–23.

22. Ibid., 24, 25; Donald R. Parker, "The Oakland-Berkeley Hills Fire: An Overview" (January 1992), http://www.sfmuseum.org/oakfire/overview.html.

23. Unger, *Working Fire,* 210; USFA, "East Bay Hills Fire," 89, 92.

24. Hunter, *Oakland Fire Department,* 31; Yasmin Anwar, "911 Call Dispatchers Rude," *Oakland Tribune,* October 26, 1991, A9; USFA, "East Bay Hills Fire," 20.

25. USFA, "East Bay Hills Fire," 83–84; Steve Geissinger (AP), "Fire Forces Slashed Despite Peril," *Oakland Tribune,* October 26, 1991, A5; Mike Flynn, "History of the Berkeley Fire Department," http://www.ci.berkeley.ca.us/fire/history.html.

26. "What Is the Incident Command System?" http://www.911dispatch.com/ics/ics_describe.html; Emergency Management System, FEMA, "Basic ICS," training.fema.gov/EMI/is/is195.asp (independent study course materials); communications problems: USFA, "East Bay Hills Fire," 75–80.

27. USFA, "East Bay Hills Fire," 26; Blais and Stein personal recollections, 1992, in Oakland Public Library, History Room, Oakland Hills fire, 1991. On wildfire rate of speed, Childress, "Fire Suppression," *FFH,* 561, 562.

28. Bob Roth account in Bill Mann, "Live—the Hillside Inferno," *Oakland Tribune,* October 24, 1991, C1.

29. USFA, "East Bay Hills Fire," 30.

30. Gregory Blais, personal recollection, Oakland Public Library, History Room, Oakland Hills fire, 1991; USFA, "East Bay Hills Fire," selected telephone and radio transmissions log, n.p.

31. USFA, "East Bay Hills Fire," selected telephone and radio transmissions log, n.p.; Diana Walsh, Andrew Ross, and Elizabeth Fernandez, "Fireman Dies 'Exactly the Way He Wanted to Die,'" *San Francisco Examiner,* October 22, 1991, A11; Harry Harris and Janet Byron, "Heroes Lost Their Lives Saving Others," *Oakland Tribune,* October 22, 1991, A8.

32. Harris and Byron, "Heroes Lost Their Lives," A8; April Lynch and Susan Sward, "Days of Heroism, Searches, Shattered Lives," *San Francisco Chronicle*, October 25, 1991, A23.

33. Photographs before the fire show how closely packed the units were and how the hillside and its shrubbery seemed to loom over the complex. Harris and Byron, "Heroes Lost Their Lives," A8; Jim Bainbridge, "First Memorial a Tribute to a Nurse," *Oakland Tribune,* October 26, 1991, A3; Larry Maatz, "Luck Just Ran Out for Cop Hero of Earthquake," *San Francisco Examiner,* October 23, 1991, A10; USFA, "East Bay Hills Fire," selected telephone and radio transmissions log, n.p.

34. USFA, "East Bay Hills Fire," selected telephone and radio transmissions log, n.p., 34; Harriet Chiang, "Parkwoods Complex Destroyed by Fire," *San Francisco Chronicle*, October 22, 1991, A20.

35. Jonathan Marshall, Rick Delvecchio, and Elaine Herscher, "How a Planned Community Was Ravaged in Minutes," *San Francisco Chronicle,* October 23, 1991, A18; ISO, *Urban/Wildland Fire,* 34; Janet Byron, "UC-Berkeley Sophomore Dies in Fire," *Oakland Tribune*, October 25, 1991, A8.

36. Robert C. Maynard, "An Eyewitness Account," *Oakland Tribune,* October 21, 1991, A1; USFA, "East Bay Hills Fire," 34; Lori Olazewski and Michael Taylor, "Unsung Heroes of the East Bay," *San Francisco Chronicle*, October 22, 1991, A19; English, in Adler, ed., *Collective Remembrance,* 7.

37. USFA, "East Bay Hills Fire," 29.

38. Ibid., 33. The conclusions are mine, however.

39. Elliot Diringer, "Swimming Pool Saved Woman, 2 Firemen," *San Francisco Chronicle*, October 28, 1991, A16.

40. Harris and Byron, "Heroes Lost Their Lives," A8; Michael Taylor, "Some Fire Victims Died While Doing the Job They Loved," *San Francisco Chronicle*, October 22, 1991, A28.

41. USFA, "East Bay Hills Fire," 39–40; Charles Petit, "Fire Created Its Own Wind System," *San Francisco Chronicle*, October 22, 1991, A25.

42. "San Francisco Fire Department, Central Fire Alarm Station," Mu-

seum of the City of San Francisco, 1991 Oakland Firestorm, http://www.sf museum.org/oakfire/cfas.html; "San Francisco Communications Center," http://www.sfmuseum.org/oakfire/comm.html; Teresa Moore, "Roiling Cloud Darkens a Brief Indian Summer," *San Francisco Chronicle*, October 21, 1991, A20.

43. Gerry Trainor and Leonard DeStefano, personal accounts, http://www.sfmuseum.org/oakfire/lt.trainor.htm and http://www.destefano. html.

44. "Central Fire Alarm Station," http://www.sfmuseum.org/oakfire/cfas. html.

45. "San Francisco Mutual Aid Response" and "Strike Team One Operations," http://www.sfmuseum.or/oakfire/response.html; and http://www.st1. html.

46. "Strike Team 2," http://www.sfmuseum.org/oakfire/st2.html; USFA, "East Bay Hills Fire," 41–44; "San Francisco Communications Center," http://www.sfmuseum.org/oakfire/comm.html.

47. "San Francisco Communications Center," http://www.sfmuseum.org/ oakfire/comm.html; USFA, "East Bay Hills Fire," 48–49.

48. "SFFD Alvarado Road Fire Operations," http://www.sfmuseum.org/ oakfire/alvarado_pt.1.html.

49. Paul Grabowicz and William Brand, "Berkeley Rallies to Firelines," *Oakland Tribune*, October 21, 1991, A6.

50. "Residents Volunteered to Help Direct Water Hoses," *San Francisco Chronicle* October 21, 1991, A17; Martin Snapp, "Hillside Inferno: The Stories," *Oakland Tribune*, October 22, 1991, D1. National Institute of Standards and Technology, U.S. Department of Commerce, "Major U.S. Cities Using National Standard Fire Hydrants, One Century After the Great Baltimore Fire," NISTIR 7158, http://www.fire.gov/newsletter/fall2004/hydrants_NISTIR7158. pdf, (blowup of hydrant at Baltimore 1904 fire scene at p. 3).

51. USFA, "East Bay Hills Fire," 49–50; "Chief's Aide Leonard DeStefano," http://www.sfmuseum.org/oakfire/destefano.html.

52. USFA, "East Bay Hills Fire," 50; "Alvarado Road Operations, Continued," http://www.sfmuseum.org/oakfire/alvarado_pt.11.html.

53. USFA, "East Bay Hills Fire," 49–50; John Wildermuth, "Why Hydrants Went Dry at Critical Time," *San Francisco Chronicle*, October 21, 1991, A15.

54. "Strike Team No. 1 Operations, Reata Place and Chabot Road," http://www.sfmuseum.org/oakfire/e3and36.html.

55. "Broadway and Ocean View Operations," http://www.sfmuseum.org/ oakfire/broadwayops.html.

56. William Brand, "'The Man Who Saved Montclair,'" *Oakland Tribune*, October 24, 1991, A3.

57. A simple calculation: Water weighs a little over eight pounds per gallon.

A one-foot length of 1-3/4 inch hose holds about a gallon of water. The hoses the firefighters were hauling were 50 or 75 foot lengths, the former about 25 pounds, the latter about 30 pounds. You do the math.

58. John Harrenhill, personal recollection, Oakland Public Library, History Room, Oakland Hills fire, 1991; Brett Mahoney, "Indoors Best Shelter from Debris," *Oakland Tribune*, October 21, 1991, A3; Candy J. Cooper, "Surviving Homes Present a Puzzle," *San Francisco Examiner*, October 24, 1991, A19.

59. USFA, "East Bay Hills Fire," 37–38.

60. Daniel B. Levine, "Volunteers Come Forth with Cookies and Cots," *Oakland Tribune*, October 21, 1991, A3; Rick Delvecchio, "Firefighters Make Desperate Stand," *San Francisco Chronicle*, October 21, 1991, A19.

61. USFA, "East Bay Hills Fire," 52–53, 55, 56, 60, 61, 89.

62. Peter Lloyd, *San Francisco Houses* (London: Ellipsis, 1997), 10; Alice Kahn, "Priceless Art, Architectural Gems Destroyed in Fire," *San Francisco Chronicle*, October 22, 1991; Lynn Ludlow, "Diary of Destruction," *San Francisco Examiner*, October 22, 1991, A11.

63. Carl Noltz, "One Man Who Stayed and Fought," *San Francisco Chronicle*, October 23, 1991, A15; Kevin Fagan, "Hill Residents Watch Dance of Destruction," *Oakland Tribune*, October 21, 1991, A1; Sarah Thalling, "Fire Destroyed Architectural Gems of Area," *Oakland Tribune*, October 21, 1991, A9; Brett Mahoney, "Estimated 2,000 Cars Reduced to Scrap," *Oakland Tribune*, October 25, 1991, A3.

64. Larner and Rome in Adler, ed., *Collective Remembrance*, 32, 38; USFA, "East Bay Hills Fire," 52–53; "Horrified Residents Watch Destruction," *Oakland Tribune*, October 21, 1991, A6; "Evacuees Describe Their Flight," *San Francisco Chronicle*, October 21, 1991, A18.

65. Ledesman, Lee, and Russomanno recollections in Bill Mann, "Live— Hillside Inferno," *Oakland Tribune*, October 24, 1991, C1.

66. USFA, "East Bay Hills Fire," 62, 95; Lloyd Calder to the author, April 11, 2005.

67. Nanette Asimov, "Fire, Fate, Played No Favorites," *San Francisco Chronicle*, October 22, 1991, A20.

68. Brenda Payton, "Burned by the Winds of Satan," *Oakland Tribune*, October 22, 1991, B5.

69. Feinberg quoted in Lisa M. Krieger, "Victims Numb; Feelings of Loss Come Days Later," *San Francisco Examiner*, October 22, 1991, A10; William Wong, "An Unbelievable Tragedy," *Oakland Tribune*, October 23, 1991, C3.

70. Oliveres and Simpson personal recollections in Oakland Public Library, History Room, Oakland Hills fire, 1991; Larner in Adler, ed., *Collective Remembrance*, 31; Paul Grabowicz and Bill Snyder, "Spectators Take a Walk Through Hell," *Oakland Tribune*, October 22, 1991, A3.

71. Janet Silver Ghent, "Trying to Get On With Life," *Oakland Tribune*,

NOTES TO PAGES 291–296

October 23, 1991, D3; Jacqueline Cutler, "Hill Residents Take a Grim Pilgrimage," *Oakland Tribune,* October 23, 1991, A8.

72. Shorb and Levil poems in Oakland Public Library, History Room, Oakland Hills fire, 1991.

73. Two collections of student papers are preserved in the Oakland Public Library, History Room, Oakland Hills fire, 1991.

74. Keay Davidson, "Owners, Lost Pets Reunited After Fire," *San Francisco Examiner,* October 27, 1991, B9.

75. Kelly Guest, "Survivors' Lament," *Oakland Tribune,* October 25, 1991, A3; Janet Byron and Paul Grabowicz, "Precious Few Pockets Unscarred by Firestorm," *Oakland Tribune,* October 23, 1991, A18; Susan Ito, in Adler, ed., *Collective Remembrance,* 24–25; William Brand, "Tales of Heroism Emerge from Disaster," *Oakland Tribune,* October 23, 1991, A14; Candy J. Cooper, "Surviving Homes Present a Puzzle," *San Francisco Examiner,* October 24, 1991, A19.

76. Elliot Diringer, "Experts Fear That Wind-Driven Smoke Will Spur Health Woes," *San Francisco Chronicle,* October 21, 1991, A16; Charles Petit, "Officials Say Fire Retardant Isn't Dangerous," *San Francisco Chronicle,* October 25, 1991, A24; Leslie Guttman, "Fearful Views from Downhill," *San Francisco Chronicle,* October 25, 1991, A24; Carl Nolte, "Burned Areas Face Threat of Mudslides," *San Francisco Chronicle,* October 23, 1991, A15; Lynn Ludlow and Eric Brazil, "New Fear: Mudslides," *San Francisco Examiner,* October 23, 1991, A1; Margaret Sullivan, *Firestorm! The Story of the East Bay Fire in Berkeley* (Berkeley: City of Berkeley, 1993), 135–136.

77. Robert J. Lopez, "Fire Department Challenged," *Oakland Tribune,* October 22, 1991, A1, A18; Will Jones, "Firefighters Claim Legal Immunity," *Oakland Tribune,* October 23, 1991, A10; Lance Williams and Scott Winokur, "How Missteps May Have Led to Blaze," *San Francisco Examiner,* October 22, 1991, A1, A12.

78. David Dietz, "Oakland Took Few Precautions," *San Francisco Chronicle,* October 23, 1991, A15; Judy Miller and David Dietz, "Calls for Air Support Came Too late, Some Say," *San Francisco Chronicle,* October 25, 1991, A17.

79. City of San Diego, City Manager's Office, Executive Team [bio of Ewell], http://www.sandiego.gov/city-manager/Ewell.shtml.

80. Dunn, *Command and Control,* 3; Lopez, "Fire Department Challenged," *Oakland Tribune,* October 22, 1991, A12; Elliot Diringer and Pearl Stewart, "Oakland Fire Chief Hints East Bay Blaze Was Set," *San Francisco Chronicle,* October 24, 1991, A1.

81. John Flinn and Scott Winokur, "Angry Fire Crews Disgusted with Post-Fire Critics," *San Francisco Examiner,* October 27, 1991, B3; P. Lamont Ewell, "Lessons of the Firestorm," Oakland City Employee *News,* January 1992.

82. USFA, "East Bay Hills Fire," 65, 73–84, 86, 91.

83. Pyne, *Fire*, 36, 179, 180.

84. Diringer and Stewart, "Oakland Fire Chief," A24.

85. Brian Johns, "City Officials Pledge to Cut Through Red Tape," *Oakland Tribune*, October 22, 1991, A13; Erik Ingraham, "Officials Vow to Help Speed Rebuilding Process," *San Francisco Chronicle*, October 22, 1991, A20; Brian Johns, "Mayor Warns Landlords on Gouging Burned-Out Renters," *Oakland Tribune*, October 26, 1991, A16; Pearl Stewart, "Oakland Passes Rent Moratorium," *San Francisco Chronicle*, October 30, 1991, A15; Daniel S. Levine, "Scramble for Interim Housing," *Oakland Tribune*, October 23, 1991, C1.

86. Jacqueline Cutler, "Fire Victims Prepared to Rebuild," *Oakland Tribune*, October 22, 1991, A13; Carla Lazzarecchi, "Building a Dream House," *Oakland Tribune*, October 26, 1991, C9, 10; Carolyn Marshall, "Starting Over," *Oakland Tribune*, October 26, 1991, C1; David Tong, "Homeowners Lose, Builders Win in Fire Devastation," *Oakland Tribune*, October 22, 1991, A12.

87. John Evan Frook, "What to Look for When Insuring Property Against Loss from Fire," *Oakland Tribune*, October 24, 1991, B1; Sabin Russell, "Insurance Companies Prepare for Flood of Claims," *San Francisco Chronicle*, October 21, 1991, A19; Sabin Russell, "Insurance Matters, a First Hurdle," *San Francisco Chronicle*, October 22, 1991, A21; Sabin Russell, "Assessing Insurance Coverage," *San Francisco Chronicle*, October 23, 1991, A17; Tupper Hull and Steven A. Cappa, "Insurance May Be Easy This Time," *Oakland Tribune*, Ocotber 22, 1991, A14.

88. Advertisements: *San Francisco Chronicle*, October 23, 1991, A6; October 25, 1991, A24, A29.

89. David Tong, "Claims Deluge Expected," *Oakland Tribune*, October 21, 1991, A9; U.S. Department of Labor, Bureau of Labor Statistics, Occupational Outlook Handbook, "Claims Adjusters," http://www.bis.gov/oco/ocos125.htm.

90. Tong, "Claims Deluge Expected," A9; Personal Insurance Federation of California, "2001 Insurance Reference Manual," http://www.pifc.org/insurance/prop103.html.

91. E. Scott Rockard, "'91 Insurers 2nd-Worst Year," *San Francisco Examiner*, October 23, 1991, B1; Greg Lucas, "First Big Insurer Grants Rebates Under Prop. 103," *San Francisco Chronicle*, October 24, 1991, A25.

92. Michael Calder interview with author, January 3, 2005.

93. John Garamendi, *Statement to Senate Committee on Insurance, Hearing on Oakland Hills Firestorm, October 14, 1993* (Sacramento, Calif: Senate Publications, 1994), 2, 3,4, 5, 7.

94. Dempsey, Serais, and Bruce statements in ibid., 56, 14, 19, 21, 23.

95. Holland statement in ibid., 64, 66.

96. Ibid., 66–70; "Senator Art Torres, Candidate for Insurance Commissioner," 1994, http://www.calvoter.org/archive/94general/cand/ins/torr/bio.html.

97. Jonathan Marshall, "$5 Billion Fire Damage Estimate May Be Too High," *San Francisco Chronicle*, October 25, 1991, A19; Henry L. Gardner, Oakland City Manager, "Oakland Hills Update," November 5, 1991; "Report," November 12, 1991; "Policy Specifications for the Rebuilding of the Fire-Damaged Oakland Hills," November 26, 1991; Oakland Public Library, History Room, Oakland Hills fire, 1991, city reports file; Jonathan Broder, "U.S. Funds Scarce for Disaster Relief," *San Francisco Examiner,* October 22, 1991, A6; "President Declares Eastbay a Disaster Area," *Oakland Tribune*, October 23, 1991, A11.

98. David Brower, "A Tale of Two Fires and One to Come," *San Francisco Examiner*, October 27, 1991, A17.

99. Louis Freedberg, "Schools Stand as Islands in East Bay Destruction," *San Francisco Chronicle*, October 23, 1991, A18.

100. Tupper Hull, "Will Inertia, Lobbyists Help Fan Next Fire?" *San Francisco Examiner*, October 27, 1991, B6; Charles Petit, "Some in Berkeley Want to Rid Hills of Eucalyptus, Monterey Pine," *San Francisco Chronicle*, October 23, 1991, A19; Susan Sward, "Industry Supports Fireproof Shakes," *San Francisco Chronicle*, October 25, 1991, A19; Chris Bowman, "Beloved Eucalyptus No Friend," *Oakland Tribune*, October 24, 1991, A22.

101. Office of the City Manager to City Council, "Amendments to Emergency Order," January 14, 1992, Oakland Public Library, History Room, Oakland Hills fire, 1991, city reports file, 2, 3, 4, 6, 7–8.

102. "Task Force on Emergency Preparedness and Community Restoration Report," February 22, 1992, Oakland Public Library, History Room, Oakland Hills fire, 1991, city reports file, 21, 7, 9, 20, 25, 26, 27; Donald R. Parker, "The Oakland-Berkeley Hills Fire: An Overview," http://www.sfmuseum.org/oakfire/overview.html.

103. City of Oakland, Municipal Services Center, April 11, 1994, letter and memo in Oakland Public Library, History Room, Oakland Hills fire, 1991, city reports file; North Hills Phoenix Association, "Mission Statement" and "Neighborhood News," July 11, 2004, http://www.nhphoenix.org.

104. North Hills Phoenix Association Newsletter, March 2005, http://www.nhphoenix.org/newsletter/pdfFiles/x05March.pdf. "For the real estate listings, see, e.g., http://www.findhome.com listings for Oakland, accessed April 15, 2005.

LOWER MANHATTAN, 2001

1. Paul Goldberger, *Up from Zero: Politics, Architecture, and the Rebuilding of New York* (New York: Random House, 2004), 32.

2. Mumford and Jacobs quoted in Leonard I. Ruchelman, *The World Trade*

Center: Politics and Policies of Skyscraper Development (Syracuse: Syracuse University Press, 1977), 50; Goldberger, *Up from Zero*, 29; Marshall Berman, "When Bad Buildings Happen to Good People," in Michael Sorkin and Sharon Zukin, eds., *After the World Trade Center: Rethinking New York City* (New York: Routledge, 2002), 7; Angus Kress Gillespie, *Twin Towers: The Life of New York City's World Trade Center* (New Brunswick, N.J.: Rutgers University Press, 1999), 4, 9, 47; Jim Dwyer et al., *Two Seconds Under the World: Terror Comes to America–The Conspiracy Behind the World Trade Center Bombing* (New York: Crown, 1994), 9; Dwyer and Flynn, *102 Minutes*, 3.

3. F. Scott Fitzgerald, "My Lost City," in *The Crack-Up,* ed. Edmund Wilson (New York: Scribners, 1931), 26; Edwin G. Burrows and Mike Wallace, *Gotham: A History of New York City to 1898* (New York: Oxford University Press, 1999), 42–43.

4. John Kuo Wei Tchen, "Whose Downtown?" in Sorkin and Zukin, eds., *After the World Trade Center*, 33.

5. Burrows and Wallace, *Gotham*, 129; Andrew Ross, "The Odor of Publicity," in Sorkin and Zukin, eds., *After the World Trade Center*, 121; "Slavery's Buried Past," PBS, December 18, 1996.

6. Ruchelman, *World Trade Center*, 39; James Glanz and Eric Lipton, *City in the Sky: The Rise and Fall of the World Trade Center* (New York: Times Books, 2003), 145–154.

7. Beverly Gage, "The First Wall Street Bomb," in Sorkin and Zukin, eds., *After the World Trade Center*, 46.

8. Rebecca Read Shanor, *The City That Never Was: Two Hundred Years of Fantastic and Fascinating Plans That Might Have Changed the Face of New York City* (New York: Viking, 1988), 6, 18, 22, 23, 24; 151, quotations at 6 and 23.

9. Burrows and Wallace, *Gotham*, 241, 250; quotations in Schecter, *The Battle for New York*, 205, 207.

10. "Burning of the Merchants' Exchange" (1835), Museum of the City of New York, http://www.mcny.org/collections/paint/Painting/pttcat11.htm; Burrows and Wallace, *Gotham*, 596–597; Dana, *The Fireman*, 40–44 (quotation on 42), 44–58.

11. Burrows and Wallace, *Gotham*, 688; Donald Martin Reynolds, *The Architecture of New York City: Histories and Views of Important Structures, Sites, and Symbols* (New York: Macmillan, 1984), 128; "New York, 1853," http://www.lib.umd.edu/ARCH/honr219f/1853nyci.html.

12. O'Donnell, *Ship Ablaze*, 132 (quote from the newspaper), 97 (origin of fire); Keith D. Revell, *Building Gotham: Civic Culture and Public Policy in New York City, 1898–1938* (Baltimore: Johns Hopkins University Press, 2003), 101, 102; Von Drehle, *Triangle*, 164.

13. Jeff Kisseloff, *You Must Remember This: An Oral History of Manhattan*

from the 1890s to World War II (San Diego: Harcourt, 1989), 8; Golway, *So Others Might Live,* 112–113, 247.

14. Buttenwieser, *Manhattan Water-Bound,* 11, 12, 13, (quotation at 22, landfill data at 30), 37, 38, 46, 47, 58, 63; Revell, *Building Gotham,* 259–260.

15. Burrows and Wallace, *Gotham,* 419–420; Carol Willis, "Introduction," in Willis, ed., *The Lower Manhattan Plan: The 1966 Vision for Downtown New York* (New York: Princeton Architectural Press, 2002), 11.

16. Pete Hamill, *Downtown: My Manhattan* (New York: Little, Brown, 2004), 3, 17; Ruchelman, *World Trade Center,* 19–20; Gillespie, *Twin Towers,* 20, 33, 38.

17. Eric Darnton, *Divided We Stand: A Biography of New York's World Trade Center* (New York: Basic, 1999), 62, 74, 91, quotation at 91; Ross, "Odor of Publicity," 122–123; Herbert Asbury, *The Gangs of New York: An Informal History of the Underworld* (1928; New York: Thunder's Mouth Press, 1998), 80; Charles Lockwood, *Manhattan Moves Uptown: An Illustrated History*(Boston: Houghton, 1976), 92.

18. Karl Koch III, with Richard Firstman, *Men of Steel: The Story of the Family That Built the World Trade Center* (New York: Crown, 2002), 244.

19. Nadel quoted in Darnton, *Divided We Stand,* 92.

20. Ibid., 72, 95; "National Goals," in Willis, ed., *Lower Manhattan Plan,* 56; Gillespie, *Twin Towers,* 43, 49, 44.

21. David M. Dornbush and Pat M. Gelb, "High-Rise Visual Impact," in Donald J. Conway, ed., *Human Response to Tall Buildings* (Stroudsburg, Pa.: Dowden, 1977), 103; Ruchelman, *World Trade Center,* 30–32.

22. Ruchelman, *World Trade Center,* 39–42; Gillespie, *Twin Towers,* 59.

23. Koch, *Men of Steel,* 366. The flight was American Airlines 11, scheduled to fly from Boston to Los Angeles. The plane was hijacked at 8:14 and the collision took place at 8:46.40. *The 9/11 Commission Report: Final Report of the National Commission on Terrorist Attacks upon the United States* (New York: Norton, 2003), 32. There are thousands of stories surrounding the events that day at the WTC. Many have been collected by the Oral History and Memory Project, at the Library of Congress. There is a file with the PA tapes at http://www.thememoryhole.org that includes a transcription of the towers' fire control center communications with the FDNY and the EMS radio communications. The *New York Times* has archived all the oral histories taken by the FDNY in 2001 and 2002 and released in typescript on August 8, 2005. They can be found at http://www.nytimes.com/sept11. Other accounts appear in published compilations. Some of those are reported here. But a word of apology or explanation is in order—without meaning in any way to slight the suffering or the sacrifice of the civilians caught in and around the towers that day, I have focused on the fires, the firefighting efforts, and the firefighters' accounts in this chapter.

24. Obenhaus quoted in Newseum, with Cathy Trost and Alicia C. Shepard, comps., *Running Toward Danger: Stories Behind the Breaking News of 9/11* (Lanham, Md.: Rowman, 2002), 31.

25. Joanne Lipman, in ibid., 22, 23; Maisel, in ibid., 47.

26. Nancy Cass, story in Damon DiMarco, comp., *Tower Stories: The Autobiography of September 11th* (New York: Revolution, 2004), 25; Dwyer and Flynn, *102 Minutes*, 37–41.

27. Gillespie, *Twin Towers*, 168; Darton, *Divided We Stand*, 147; Dwyer and Flynn, *102 Minutes*, 2–3.

28. Mark Wigley, "Insecurity by Design," in Sorkin and Zukin, eds., *After the World Trade Center*, 78; Gillespie, *Twin Towers*, 211, 212, 213; Gabriel Torres, quoted in DiMarco, comp., *Tower Stories*, 56.

29. Fiske Kimball, quoted in Revell, *Building Gotham*, 29; Ernst Schumacher, *Small Is Beautiful: Economics As If People Mattered* (London: Blond, 1973), 61; Tozzoli quoted in Gillespie, *Twin Towers*, 46.

30. Yamasaki quoted in Ruchelman, *World Trade Center*, 47–48.

31. James Glanz and Eric Lipton, "The Height of Ambition," *New York Times,* September 8, 2002, sect. 6, p. 32; "World Trade Center: Anatomy of the Collapse," DVD, Darlow Smith Film for The Learning Center, release 2002; "Why the Towers Fell," DVD, Garfield Kennedy and Larry Klein for NOVA, released 2002.

32. Goldberger, *Up from Zero*, 26; Koch, *Men of Steel*, 214, 226–243.

33. Koch, *Men of Steel*, 259, 261, 263, 273, 282–283; Glanz and Lipton, "Height of Ambition," 48.

34. Description from FEMA, "World Trade Center Building Performance Study: Data Collection, Preliminary Observations, and Recommendations," Washington, D.C., May 2002, 1–17; Ruchelman, *World Trade Center*, 86–112; Gillespie, *Twin Towers*, 56–85, 108, 133, quotations at 79 and 81.

35. Jim Dwyer and Eric Lipton, "3-Year Federal Study of 9/11 Urges Safer Skyscraper Rules," *New York Times,* June 22, 2005, A1; Smith, *Report from Ground Zero*, 210.

36. FEMA, "World Trade Center," 1–17–18; NIST, "WTC Investigation," 19–20; Dwyer and Flynn, *102 Minutes*, 25–26.

37. FEMA, "World Trade Center," 2–23 (oxygen supply); Dwyer and Flynn, *102 Minutes*, 253.

38. On fire precautions and problems: Ruchelman, *World Trade Center*, 103–109.

39. Dwyer et al., *Two Seconds*, 176–240; Richard Bernstein, *Out of the Blue: The Story of September 11, 2001, from Jihad to Ground Zero* (New York: Times Books, 2002), 57.

40. Dwyer et al., *Two Seconds*; Bernstein, *Out of the Blue*, 9–33.

41. Dwyer, et al., *Two Seconds*, 33–63, quotation at 39; information on

smoke deaths from Captain James Bannar, public information officer, Cherry Hill (N.J.) Fire Department, May 12, 2005. On the terrorists' plans, Bernstein, *Out of the Blue*, 120–121.

42. Dwyer and Flynn, *102 Minutes*, 3–4; *9/11 Commission Report*, 281; Goldberger, *Up from Zero*, 38.

43. Glanz and Lipton, "Height of Ambition," 34.

44. Potter in Smith, *Report from Ground Zero*, 46; statistical and anecdotal evidence for the following paragraphs from Fire Department City of New York Statistics, 1993–2001; New York City Fire Museum, "Education and Fire Safety: History of the FDNY," http://www/nycfiremuseum.org/education/history; Golway, *So Others Might Live*, 217–300; Von Essen, *Strong of Heart*, 63–122; Downey, *Last Men Out*, 67–165; *F.D.N.Y.*, 88–117.

45. CHFD Captain Kevin Kenniff to the author, May 5, 2005; Galione in Downey, *Last Men Out*, 10–11; Weiss speaking in Episode 1 of "The Bravest," DVD edition, with additional footage commemorating 9/11, March 19, 2002.

46. Lake in "The Bravest."

47. "9/11: The filmmakers' Commemorative Edition," released September 12, 2002; Dwyer and Flynn, *102 Minutes*, 49–50; Joseph Natale Schneiderman, *The Firefighting Buff's Guide to New York City* (San Jose, Calif.: Writers Club, 2002), 66–67; Joseph Pfeifer interview, *Firehouse Magazine*, September 9, 2002, http://www.firehouse.com/terrorist/911/magazine/gz/pfeifer.html.

48. Smith, *Report from Ground Zero*, 5.

49. Dominick Maggiore, interview no. 9110120, October 19, 2001, and Mark Harris, interview no. 9110057, October 11, 2001, oral histories, http://www.nytimes.com/sept11.

50. Todd Maisel, in Trost and Shepard, comps., *Running Toward Danger*, 47; Richard Erdey, interview no. 911025, October 10, 2001, oral histories, http://www.nytimes.com/sept11; Bolívar Arellano, in Trost and Shepard, comps., *Running Toward Danger*, 55; *9/11 Commission Report*, 300 (first firefighter killed); Mark Harris, interview no. 9110057, October 11, 2001.

51. Dwyer and Flynn, *102 Minutes*, 188–190, 198, 204–206, 208–209.

52. Joseph Callan, interviewed November 2, 2001, file no. 9110195, oral history, http://www.nytimes.com/sept11; McKinsey Report, "FDNY Performance in 9/11," 6, http://www.nyc.gov/html/fdny/html/mck_report/toc.html; Dwyer and Flynn, *102 Minutes*, 50, 53. Hayden quoted in Smith, *Report from Ground Zero*, 39.

53. Childress, "Rescue," *FFH*, 580; Dunn, *Command and Control*, 2 (reconnaisance), 101 (life safety).

54. *9/11 Commission Report*, 306; Dunn, *Command and Control*, 167–168; Robert F. Hancock, "Rescue Procedures," *FFH*, 433–446.

55. On defensive tactics in a high-rise, see Dunn, *Command and Control*, 99, 161, 48 (trusses).

56. Nigro, in Smith, *Report from Ground Zero*, 19; Nevins, in ibid., 94; Tardio account in ibid., 17. The faces of all 343 firefighters and officers adorn a display at the New York Fire Museum. Short bios of all the men can be found at http://www.bravestmemorial.com.

57. McKinsey Report, 7.

58. Excerpts from Firefighters WTC tape, 9/11, 9:25 AM to 9:58 AM (South Tower), http://www.thememoryhole.org/911/firefighter-tape-excerpts.htm.

59. *9/11 Commission Report*, 306; Dunn, *Command and Control*, 261, 262; Kevin Flynn and Jim Dwyer, "Fire Department Tape Reveals No Awareness of Imminent Doom," *New York Times*, November 9, 2002, B2. Callan transmission identified in Dwyer and Flynn, *102 Minutes*, 63, and in Dirck Halstead, "Missed Communications," February 2005, http://www.dirckhalstead.org/issue0502/halstead.html. Halstead's source was retired Chief Vincent Dunn. The same order, from an unidentified command transmission, appeared three years earlier, in Smith, *Report from Ground Zero*, 38–39. Callan recalled why he gave the order in his November 2, 2001, interview.

60. McKinsey Report, 7, 8; Peter Hayden interview with *Firehouse Magazine*, September 9, 2002, http://www.firehouse.com/terrorist/911/magazine/gz/hayden.htm; Picciotto, *Last Man Down*, 63; Pfeifer account in Smith, *Up from Ground Zero*, 38, 41.

61. Gregg Hansson interview with *Firehouse Magazine*, September 9, 2002, http://www.firehouse.com/terrorist/911/magazine/gz/hansson.html.

62. *9/11 Commission Report*, 307; Picciotto, *Last Man Down*, 79, 64, 65, 93, 103–108; Jonas, in Smith, *Report from Ground Zero*, 95, 97–98; Mike Cancel, interview with *Firehouse Magazine*, September 9, 2002, http://www.firehouse.com/terrorist/911/magazine/gz/cancel.html; William Walsh, interview no. 9110442, January 11, 2002, oral history, http://www.nytimes.com/sept11; Steve Modica, interview with *Firehouse Magazine*, September 9, 2002, http://www.firehouse.com/terrorist/911/magazine/gz/modica.html.

63. Michael Smith in Michelle Garcia, "Project Preserves Stories from 9/11," *Washington Post*, July 16, 2005, A3. Jules Naudet, in CBS News, *What We Saw* (New York: Simon and Schuster, 2002), 22–25. The climax of the Naudet story—the remarkable return of every Ladder 1 and Engine 7 member to the Duane Street firehouse—is recorded in his video.

64. Trost and Shepard, "Introduction," in Trost and Shepard, comps., *Running Toward Danger*, x.

65. Dreher, in ibid., 33; Guy D. Massaro, Jr., quoted in "Readers Respond: Where Were You on September 11?" New Orleans *Times-Picayune*, September 8, 2002, A18.

66. Mika Brzezinski, in Judith Sylvester and Suzanne Huffman, *Women Journalists at Ground Zero–Covering Crisis* (Lanham, Md.: Rowman, 2002),

109–110; Arellano, in Trost and Shepard, comps., *Running Toward Danger*, 67; Wendy Doremus (Biggart's wife), in ibid., 24.

67. Susan Watts, in Trost and Shepard, comps., *Running Toward Danger*, 87; Handschuh, in ibid., 31. On the rescue squads, Downey, *Last Men Out*, 67–97.

68. Handschuh, in Trost and Shepard, comps., *Running Toward Danger*, 100.

69. Maisel, in ibid., 101; Ryan and Donovan quoted in Kevin Flynn and Jim Dwyer, "9/11 In Firefighters' Words," *New York Times*, January 31, 2002, B1; on Shea, see Halberstam, *Firehouse*, 109–113.

70. John Bussey, in Trost and Shepard, comps., *Running Toward Danger*, 87; Carol Marin, in ibid., 119; Mark Harris, interview no. 9110057, October 11, 2001, oral history, http://www.nytimes.com/sept11.

71. Ruth Fremson, in Trost and Shepard, comps., *Running Toward Danger*, 90.

72. On Feehan: Von Essen, *Strong of Heart*, 129–133; Elizabeth Kolbert, "William Feehan's Last Fire, After Four Decades on the Job," *New Yorker*, October 8, 2001, 42; on Downey: Downey, *Last Men Out*, 140, 143, 145, 147; on Ganci: Smith, *Report from Ground Zero*, 112–113; Bernstein, *Out of the Blue*, quotations at 150, 151, 152.

73. *Firehouse Magazine* interviews with Bill Wall, Ray Brown, and John Breen, September 9, 2002, http://www.firehouse.com/terrorist/911/magazine/gz/wall.html, brown.html, and breen.html.

74. Smyth quotations in DiMarco, comp., *Tower Stories*, 178, 179, 184; Arthur Myers, interview October 11, 2001, no. 9110052, http://www.nytimes.com/sept11.

75. Robert Browne, interview October 24, 2001, no. 9110155, http://www.nytimes.com/sept11; Gerstle account in DiMarco, comp., *Tower Stories*, 67–68.

76. *9/11 Commission Report*, 309, 311, 314, 318. A fourth hijacked plane went down in rural Pennsylvania. Evidence indicates that the passengers had attempted to recover control of the plane from the hijackers. For the larger aspects of the story, including the identification of the terrorist cell that hijacked the aircraft, see *9/11 Commission Report*, 215–253, 325–338; Steven Brill, *After: How America Confronted the September 12 Era* (New York: Simon and Schuster, 2003); and Bernstein, *Out of the Blue*, 78–148.

77. The NYPD photographs are collected in Christopher Sweet, ed., *Above Hallowed Ground: A Photographic Record of September 11, 2001, by Photographers of the New York City Police Department* (New York: Penguin Putnam, 2002).

78. Picture in Smith, *Report from Ground Zero*, after 210; Ray Murphy, http://www.bravestmemorial.com/html/members/murphy_raymond_lt_l016.

html. Paul Oyler, "Brothers," written by a Los Angeles Fire Department Captain as he left the debris pile to return to his own service, October 2001; http://www.firefightersrealstories.com/brothers.html.

79. The information on the photograph and on FF Higgins is from Dennis Smith to the author, July 28, 2005.

80. Caryn Jones, in CBS News, *What We Saw*, 83–85.

81. Smith, *Report from Ground Zero*, 276, 355; Halberstam, *Firehouse*, 127; Picciotto, *Last Man Down*, 168 and after; pancake collapse: Robert F. Hancock, "Rescue Procedures," *FFH*, 458.

82. John Norman interview in *Firehouse Magazine*, September 9, 2002, http://www.firehouse.com/terrorist/911/magazine/gz/norman.html; Smith, *Report from Ground Zero*, 107; Glanz and Lipton, *City in the Sky*, 287.

83. Smith, *Report from Ground Zero*, 98–103, 236, 240, 251, quotes on 234, 242, and 248; Salvatore S. Torcivia, in DiMarco, comp., *Tower Stories*, 189; Glanz and Lipton, *City in the Sky*, 316.

84. "Brothers on Holy Ground," released January 2004.

85. Von Essen, *Strong of Heart*, 264–265; Dan Barry and Kevin Flynn, "Firefighters in Angry Scuffle with Police at Trade Center," *New York Times*, November 3, 2001, A1; Eric Westervelt, "Protest by New York City Firefighters," on NPR, *All Things Considered*, November 2, 2001.

86. Dennis Smith, "Testimony, June 19, 2004," United States Commission on Terrorism, http://www.9-11commission.gov/hearings/hearing11/Smith-statement.pdf. On the other issues dividing the two services, see Golway, *So Others Might Live*, 265; Dorothy Gaiter, "Audit Criticizes Fire Department's Overtime Costs," *New York Times*, December 21, 1980, 40; William Murphy, "Firefighters Burned in City Pact," *Newsday*, March 13, 1993, 3.

87. Mike McIntire and Michelle O'Donnell, "Disaster Plan Deeply Flawed, Council Is Told," *New York Times*, May 10, 2005, B1, B6; Mike McIntire, "Bloomberg Says Fire Chief Must Support Emergency Plan or Leave," *New York Times*, May 11, 2005, B1.

88. Berman, "Bad Buildings," 3.

89. Bruce H. Young, Julian D. Ford, and Patricia J. Watson, "Survivors of Human-Caused and Natural Disasters," National Center for Post Traumatic Stress Disorder, U.S. Department of Veterans Affairs, http://www.ncptsd.va.gov/facts/disasters/fs_survivors_disaster.html.

90. Kenneth R. Feinberg, *What Is Life Worth? The Unprecedented Effort to Compensate the Victims of 9/11* (New York: PublicAffairs, 2005), 42.

91. Halberstam, *Firehouse*, 177–178; Tina Kelley, "Kevin Shea: A Firefighter Asks Why He Remembers So Little," *New York Times*, September 11, 2002, G15; Downey, *Last Men Out*, 286; Robin Finn, "Binding Firefighters' Psychological Wounds," *New York Times*, October 14, 2004, B4.

92. Al Baker, "City's Fire Department Facing an Exodus of Its Supervi-

sors," *New York Times*, August 7, 2002, A1; Alan Feuer and Michael Wilson, "Its Ranks Depleted, a Weary Fire Department Is Trying to Regroup," *New York Times*, September 11, 2002, A1; Feinberg, *What Is Life Worth?* 71–72.

93. Von Essen, *Strong of Heart*, 208.

94. Salka, *First In, Last Out*, 11.

95. Wutz, "Fire Department Organization," *FFH* 34 (SOP), 36–37 (ICS), 39 (staging and planning); Dunn, *Command and Control*, 64. Bear in mind that these basic concepts are part of manuals published in 2000 and 1999, respectively. The principles should have been well established by 2001.

96. Brian Becker, interview no. 9110019, October 9, 2001, oral history, http://www.nytimes.com/sept11.

97. Ibid.; Bernstein, *Out of the Blue*, 152–153; Modica interview in *Firehouse Magazine*, September 9, 2002; McKinsey Report, 10–14.

98. Jim Dwyer and Kevin Flynn, "9/11 in Firefighters' Words: Surreal Chaos and Hazy Heroics," *New York Times*, January 31, 2002, B1; Dwyer and Flynn, *102 Minutes*, 251–252; Kevin Flynn, "Fire Unions Call for Inquiry on Failure of Radios," *New York Times*, September 20, 2002, B4. The results of the effort—the FDNY's comprehensive interview of all personnel on the scene—can be found at http://www.nytimes.com/sept11, all 12,000 pages of it. I have read the interviews with a growing admiration for the courage and inventiveness of the men and women, and mounting frustration at the lack of incident command preparedness.

99. Kevin Flynn, "Fire Officials Begin a Search for Feedback on Sept. 11," *New York Times*, May 10, 2002, B6.

100. http://www.mckinsey.com/aboutus/whatwebelive/index.asp; McKinsey Report, 3–4. On McKinsey reputation, Williamjames Hoffer, communication to author, April 1, 2005.

101. McKinsey Report, 13; WTC Channel 18, Fire Command, Two WTC, p. 1, http://www.thememoryhole.org/911.

102. McKinsey Report, 7, 8, 9, 10, 11, 13; Von Essen, *Strong of Heart*, 181–182.

103. McKinsey Report, 13.

104. Dunn, *Command and Control*, 64; McKinsey Report, 13, 14, 15, 18, 19.

105. I want to reiterate here that nothing in the following paragraphs should be taken to suggest that McKinsey did a less than superb job.

106. Accident chain: David W. Dodson, "Firefighter Safety," *FFH*, 106.

107. U.S. Fire Administration, National Fire Academy Advanced Safety Operations and Management Course, unit 2: "risk management process" R154 (June 22, 2005), http://www.usfa.fema.gov/training/nfa/pre-course; Dunn, *Command and Control*, 260, 261 (quotation).

108. Mickey Kross, journal, in http://www.mrbellersneighborhood.com/story.php?storyid=177.

109. Dunn, *Command and Control*, 175, 180; Robert P. Smith, "The Island's Burning," *Housewatch* (Summer 2005): 1, 2, 4.

110. The maps in Dwyer and Flynn, *102 Minutes*, facing 1, 19, and 93 were especially useful in my virtual return to the site. On the long climb, see ibid., 174–176. On the equipment, see the photos of basic gear and additional tools in James Bronzan, "The Burden of Saving Lives," *New York Times*, June 12, 2002, N41. The calculations are my own.

111. Smith, *Report from Ground Zero*, opposite 210.

112. Nicholas Scoppetta, "Testimony Before the National Commission on Terrorist Attacks, May 18, 2004," http://www.9-11commission.gov/hearings/hearing11/scoppetta-statement.pdf, 7.

113. Mickey Kross, interview in Smith, *Report from Ground Zero*, 71.

114. Alice McQuillian, "Fallen Fire Rookies Hailed," New York *Daily News*, June 28, 2002, p. 10; New York City Fire Museum has a room dedicated to 9/11 and wall of honor with the department photos of the men lost on 9/11.

115. Von Essen, *Strong of Heart*, 221, 229; Halberstam, on Michael Otten, in *Firehouse*, 189; Salka, *First In, Last Out*, 209; Von Essen at Weiss funeral, http://www.bravestmemorial.com/html/members_individual/weiss_david/weiss_firehouse_article.html.

116. Scoppetta, "Testimony," p. 3; Golway, *So Others Might Live*, 338–339; Patrice O'Shaughnessy, "Rescue 3: Back from the Abyss," New York *Daily News*, February 17, 2002, p. 6.

117. Downey, *Last Men Out*, 291.

118. Michelle O'Donnell and Janon Fisher, "As 4 Jumped, 2 Firefighters Survived by a Bit of Rope," *New York Times*, January 27, 2005, B1; Alan Feuer, "For Recovering Firefighter, Bells and Whistles Ring Out," *New York Times*, February 19, 2005; Kareem Fahim, "A Day Filled with Sadness and Hope for Firefighters," *New York Times*, May 11, 2005, B6.

119. Scoppetta, "Testimony," 5–6; Michelle O'Donnell, "Wanting a Safer Escape System, City Firefighters Build Their Own," *New York Times*, June 6, 2005, A1; Downey, *Last Men Out*, 295; Golway, *So Others Might Live*, 339, 341.

120. Tebeau, *Eating Smoke*, 321; Scoppetta, "Testimony," 7, 18.

121. Dwyer and Flynn, "Height of Ambition," 36–37; James Glanz, "A Nation Challenged: The Buildings, in Collapsing Towers, a Cascade of Failures," *New York Times*, November 11, 2001, B1. The photo of the Singer Building appears in Annette Witheridge, *New York: Then and Now* (San Diego: Thunder Bay, 2001), 24.

122. Dwyer and Flynn, *102 Minutes*, 66–69, 207; FEMA, "WTC," 2–15, 21, 25.

123. Koch, *Men of Steel*, 369, 370.

124. James Glanz, "U.S. Announces New, Tougher Look into Why the Towers Collapsed," *New York Times*, August 22, 2002, B1; Eric Lipton, "Study Suggests Design Flaws Didn't Doom Towers," *New York Times*, October 20, 2004, A1, B8; Michael E. Newman, NIST, "WTC Investigation," April 5, 2005, "Latest Findings," http://www.nist.gov/public_affairs/releases/wtc_briefing_april0505.html.

125. Grant McCool, "New York: An End to Innocence," in Reuters, *After September 11: New York and the World* (Saddle Brook, N.J.: Prentice Hall, 2003), 50–75; Frank Rich, "Ground Zero Is So Over," *New York Times*, May 29, 2005, WK10. The author returned to the site himself a number of times after 9/11 to watch the hole become a shrine.

126. Goldberger, *Up from Zero*, xiii–xiv.

127. Dwyer and Lipton, "3-Year Federal Study." Submissions described in Goldberger, *Up from Zero*, passim.

128. Goldberger, *Up From Zero*, x; Page, "Creatively Destroying New York," in Joan Ockman, *Out of Ground Zero*, 179. Robert Browne, interview October 24, 2001, no. 9110155, http://www.nytimes.com/sept11.

CONCLUSION

1. Arthur M. Schlesinger, *Paths to the Present* (New York: Macmillan, 1949), 225.

2. Michael Kammen, *People of Paradox: An Inquiry Concerning the Origins of American Civilization* (New York: Knopf, 1972), 292, suggests that such self-contained "paradoxes, tensions, and biformities" are themselves a fundamental part of American experience.

3. San Francisco Real Estate Circular, October 1868, "The Earthquake and Real Estate," http://www.sfmuseum.org/hist1/1868.html; *East Bay Quarterly*, Economic Development Alliance for Business, "Oakland, San Francisco Housing Prices," table 4, http://www.edab.org/newsletter/Quarterly/q7-04_files/real_estate.html.

4. Buttenwieser, *Manhattan Water-Bound*, 11, 41.

5. Eric Lipton and Jim Dwyer, "Time for Drastic Changes in Tall Buildings? Experts Disagree," *New York Times*, June 24, 2005, B1, B7.

6. Winnie Hu, "'04 Fire Deaths May Be Fewest in 80 Years," *New York Times*, December 24, 2004, B3; Stephen J. Pyne, *Year of the Fires: The Story of the Great Fires of 1910* (New York: Viking, 2001), 226, 243; ISO, *Urban/Wildland Fire,* 39; National Fire Protection Association, *Fire Protection Handbook,* 19th ed. (Quincy, Mass.: National Fire Protection Association, 2003). The first edition came out in 1935.

INDEX

Fire safety/prevention (*continued*)
  national lessons on, 373–377
  Pittsburgh fire of 1845 and, 71–72,
    85, 97
  post-fire East Bay, 303–305, 306
  sprinkler systems and, 175
  World Trade Center and, 325–327
Fire triangle, 5–6
Fireboxes
  Chicago fire of 1871 and, 118, 120
  early Chicago and, 114–115
Firefighters. *See also* FDNY (New
    York City Fire Department);
    Volunteer firefighters
  average age of, 15
  Baltimore fire of 1904 and, 165,
    169
  and control of fire, 120
  D.C. Fire Department and,
    169–170
  deaths in "Great Fire of London,"
    14
  deaths in New York City
    (1980–2001), 14
  Detroit fire of 1967 and, 220–221,
    226–228
  East Bay: Oakland Hills fire 1991
    and, 265–267, 283–285
  "fireman's carry" of, 334
  first Boston (1678), 36
  funding cuts to Detroit, 256
  heroism on 9-11, 336
  historical aspects and, 10–12
  injuries of, 179
  lumberyard fire in Chicago 1871
    and, 112–113
  physical demands of, 15–16
  Pittsburgh fire of 1845 and, 74–77,
    78–79
  retirement after 9-11, 353
  role of, in modern society, 11

  salaries of early Chicago
    firefighters, 115
  September 11, 2001 and, 329
  and SOP safety of, 354
  "survivor syndrome" and, 292–293,
    352–353
  techniques of, 10
  training and, 268
  wildfires vs. structural fires and,
    359–360, 362
Firefighting Resources of California
    Organized for Potential
    Emergencies (FIRESCOPE),
    269
Firehouses, collective activity of
    firefighting and, 12
Fireman's insurance
  Pittsburgh fire of 1845 and, 92
"Fire-proof" structures, 138–139
First Church (Boston), 31–32
Fish Ranch Road Fire of 1970 (East
    Bay Hills), 266
Fishbourn's Wharf, 36
Fisheries Hall, 149
Flashover, 7, 15
Fletcher, Linda, 264
"Footprints of the Fire" (Baltimore),
    199
Ford Motor Company (Detroit),
    207–208, 242
Forest Service smoke jumpers, 4
Fort Pitt, 64
Foster, J. Heron, 90, 94
Foster, John, 22
Fowle, Rebecca, 26
Frank, Gerald, 291
Franklin, Benjamin, 36–37
Frear, Alexander, 125
Freeland, Eleanor, 102
Fremont Fire Department, 282
Fremson, Ruth, 343

PublicAffairs is a publishing house founded in 1997. It is a tribute to the standards, values, and flair of three persons who have served as mentors to countless reporters, writers, editors, and book people of all kinds, including me.

I. F. Stone, proprietor of *I. F. Stone's Weekly,* combined a commitment to the First Amendment with entrepreneurial zeal and reporting skill and became one of the great independent journalists in American history. At the age of eighty, Izzy published *The Trial of Socrates,* which was a national bestseller. He wrote the book after he taught himself ancient Greek.

Benjamin C. Bradlee was for nearly thirty years the charismatic editorial leader of *The Washington Post.* It was Ben who gave the *Post* the range and courage to pursue such historic issues as Watergate. He supported his reporters with a tenacity that made them fearless, and it is no accident that so many became authors of influential, best-selling books.

Robert L. Bernstein, the chief executive of Random House for more than a quarter century, guided one of the nation's premier publishing houses. Bob was personally responsible for many books of political dissent and argument that challenged tyranny around the globe. He is also the founder and was the longtime chair of Human Rights Watch, one of the most respected human rights organizations in the world.

·   ·   ·

For fifty years, the banner of Public Affairs Press was carried by its owner, Morris B. Schnapper, who published Gandhi, Nasser, Toynbee, Truman, and about 1,500 other authors. In 1983 Schnapper was described by *The Washington Post* as "a redoubtable gadfly." His legacy will endure in the books to come.

Peter Osnos, *Founder and Editor-at-Large*

ELKHART PUBLIC LIBRARY

3 3080 01201 9322

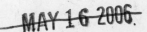

WITHDRAWN

ELKHART PUBLIC
LIBRARY
Elkhart, Indiana

DEMCO